Anthony Trollope

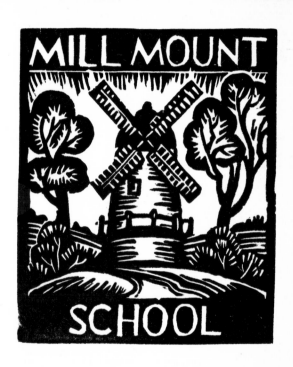

MILL MOUNT SCHOOL

Panther

Granada Publishing Limited
Published in 1973 by Panther Books Ltd
Frogmore, St Albans, Herts AL2 2NF

First published in Great Britain by
Jonathan Cape Ltd 1971
Copyright © James Pope Hennessy 1971
Made and printed in Great Britain by
Richard Clay (The Chaucer Press) Ltd
Bungay, Suffolk
Set in Linotype Plantin

For
Cristina Cholmondeley
XXXX

Contents

ILLUSTRATIONS

Preface

As in the cases of W. M. Thackeray, of George Eliot, of Algernon Swinburne and of several other Victorian writers of major importance, our knowledge of Anthony Trollope's life and work has been enormously enhanced by the meticulous researches of American scholars. Most notable of all these was the late Professor Bradford A. Booth, Associate Professor of English at the University of California, Los Angeles. His sudden death in the winter of 1968 must be deeply regretted by all lovers of Anthony Trollope's novels. It was Professor Booth who edited the comprehensive volume of Trollope's letters, issued in this country by the Oxford University Press in 1951. Professor Booth was also founder-editor of *The Trollopian* in the summer of 1945. This periodical was originally planned to appear twice a year; it has since then become a quarterly with a change of title which allows for articles on other great Victorian novelists as well. Further important American contributions to our knowledge of Trollope consist of *A Guide to Trollope* by W. G. Gerould and J. T. Gerould (Princeton University Press, 1948), Professor Donald Smalley's bulky anthology of contemporary reviews of Trollope's novels in the *Critical Heritage* series (Routledge and Kegan Paul, 1969) and the recent important study *The Changing World of Anthony Trollope* by Professor Robert Polhemus of California University (University of California Press, 1968). The greatest collection of Anthony Trollope's letters and papers, assembled by the late Morris L. Parrish, is now at Princeton University; through the kindness of Mr Alexander Wainwright, Librarian of the Firestone Library at Princeton, I have been able to obtain copies of Trollope letters discovered subsequent to the publication of Professor Booth's *Collected Letters of Anthony Trollope*. I wish also to thank the Librarians of the Widener and of the Houghton Libraries at Harvard, in both of which I was allowed to research.

On a more personal basis I wish to thank Mrs Gordon Waterfield for her invaluable advice and for her pertinent comments on the text of this book; Miss Diana Crawfurd for encouragement; Sir Basil Bartlett for his hospitality while I was completing my work; and Mr Jack Edwards of the Cheshunt Public Library, who supplied me with photographs of the now demolished house at Waltham Cross in which Trollope lived for eleven years. Mr Edgar Buckley has done research for me amongst Anthony Trollope's business papers in the Bodleian Library, Oxford. Of my Irish friends and compatriots I particularly wish to thank Mrs Thomas Corcoran of the Shannon Hotel, Banagher, where I wrote this book, and her son and daughter-in-law, Mr and Mrs Desmond Corcoran, for showing me towns such as Clonmel and Mallow in which Anthony Trollope lived during his eighteen years as a postal official in Ireland.

Finally, I wish as always to record my thanks to Mr Len Adams for all the trouble he has taken during the two and a half years I have spent on the construction of this book.

Banagher and London

J.P.H.

One evening of early November 1882, Anthony Trollope suffered a paralytic stroke while seated in the friendly first-floor drawing-room of a house in Pimlico. It was in this mournful region of Victorian London that he had, in his day, domiciled several of the less fashionable minor characters that throng his forty-five novels. 'For heaven's sake, my dear, don't let him take you anywhere beyond Eccleston Square!' a kind married friend counsels Lady Alexandrina de Courcy, whose future husband, Crosbie, had been trying to persuade her that 'the new Pimlico Squares down near Vauxhall Bridge and the river' were quite delightful. We find this passage in *The Small House at Allington*. In another novel, *He Knew He Was Right*, Trollope had whimsically dismissed Pimlico as 'ever so far away'. Far away indeed it was in an era still dominated by the horse—far from Mayfair and its denizens, and quite far enough, too, from Garlant's Hotel in Suffolk Street where Mr and Mrs Anthony Trollope had taken winter lodgings so as to have the best doctors within call. Consulted for the old novelist's asthma, these doctors had recently diagnosed *angina pectoris*, a verdict which Anthony Trollope found ridiculous, but which made his elegant little wife, Rose Trollope, quail.

On the night that he was stricken, the Anthony Trollopes had set off from the hotel to dine in St George's Square, driving in a hansom along Pall Mall and round by Buckingham Palace stables, the gas-lamps making blurred and greenish haloes in the fog. His host in the Square was Sir John Tilley, K.C.B., manager of the Metropolitan Asylums Board and also of the West London schools. Tilley had been thrice widowed. His first wife, Cecilia Trollope, Anthony's sister, had died of the family scourge, consumption, in 1849. His second wife was Anthony Trollope's first cousin, Miss Mary Anne Partington; after her demise he had married a Miss Montgomerie from Ayrshire, whom he had buried in 1880. But between John Tilley and Anthony Trollope there were other, stronger ties than formal kinship. Lifelong friends, they had both been young and carefree clerks in the General Post Office in the distant reign of the Queen's uncle, William IV. Tilley had been consistently promoted and had succeeded Sir Rowland Hill as Secretary at the Post Office in 1864; Trollope, on the other hand, had been disappointed in his expectations of promotion and had resigned from the Post Office in 1867, in a mood of pique. He had thenceforth depended entirely upon literary endeavour to keep himself, his wife and his hunters, and to help their two sons.

Anthony Trollope's relatives attributed his final seizure that November night to a couple of immediate causes. Both of these were highly characteristic, and comprised firstly a bout of fury and secondly an attack of what the French so untranslatably call *fou rire*. During the afternoon before the fatal dinner-party, Trollope had been exacerbated by the noise of an itinerant German band, which seemed to him to have stationed itself deliberately beneath his windows at Garlant's Hotel. On the whole a genial man, Anthony Trollope was notorious for his sudden bursts of anger, and on this occasion he had told the bandmaster—presumably in English, since Trollope was no linguist—exactly what he thought of him. He was still bubbling with rage when he arrived to dine with Sir John Tilley and his daughter; hindsight afterwards reminded them how overexcited the old novelist had been at the dinner-table. The meal over, the ladies mounted the narrow staircase to the drawing-room to be later joined by the men. They all decided to take it in turns to read aloud from the season's best-seller, Anstey's *Vice Versa*. This artless book aroused their mirth, and they were all laughing so freely that it was some minutes before Sir John realized that 'the loudest laugh of all had failed to sound'. The old man, who in his prime had been one of the three most popular novelists in England, lay crookedly slumped in his armchair, speechless and paralysed down the right side. The ruddy countenance which had once seemed to a young American acquaintance on a transatlantic liner 'gross and repulsive' was now contused by what *The Times* report next day vaguely described as 'blood to the head'. The sharp observant blue eyes stared sightlessly behind the gold-rimmed spectacles. The impressive, taurine head, bald and shaped 'like a lemon cut transversely in two', was lolling back on the upholstery, the thick white beard jutting up into the air. A doctor was hurriedly summoned, and the famous novelist was taken in a carriage to a nursing home north of the Park.

As befitted his past renown, *The Times* during the next five weeks kept its readers intermittently informed of Anthony Trollope's progress. 'He is now able to walk and also to use his right arm a little ... he sleeps well and his nights are quiet', was one reassuring bulletin signed by the Queen's Physician-in-Ordinary, Sir William Jenner. 'Progress on the whole satisfactory', and 'slow but sure progress towards recovery', were the gist of further optimistic bulletins, for like many physically robust persons Trollope lingered with deceptive reluctance upon the brink of the grave. In the first week of December the doctors began to admit that their patient was losing strength and was altogether 'in a less satisfactory condition', and finally they announced a lapse into unconsciousness followed by death. In health a blustering, boisterous man, Anthony Trollope did not recover his power of speech before he died. Silent for ever was that well-known voice, 'the ordinary tones [of which] had the penetrative capacity of two people quarrelling', and which 'would ring through and through you, and shake the windows in their frames'.

Anthony Trollope died in what he surely would himself have termed 'harness', with an unfinished novel about Ireland on his hands, two completed manuscript novels packaged in his desk, and his iconoclastic *Autobiography* prepared for posthumous publication by his elder son. A lengthy obituary notice in *The Times* recalled that Trollope had been 'born in the famous Waterloo year', and, in an odd use of the verb 'to remove', the anonymous memorialist reflected that Anthony Trollope had been 'removed in a lusty majority, and before decay had begun to cripple his indefatigable industry or dull the brightness of his versatile fancy'. He had, in fact, died at the age of sixty-seven. Two days after his death in the nursing home in Welbeck Street, a hearse, followed by slowly moving carriages filled with his friends, carried Anthony Trollope's corpse to the densely peopled, shadowy cemetery at Kensal Green, where his literary hero William Makepeace Thackeray already lay beneath a stone slab hemmed in by a low railing of wrought iron.

(ii)

Reading a novel aloud in the evenings was by no means a habit confined to the Tilley and Trollope families. It became popular in the 1840s when novels first began to be published in monthly parts, a method which kept the literate public on tenterhooks. Each successive instalment was 'anticipated with more anxiety than the Indian Mail, and ... a great deal more talked about'. The excitement was, of course, higher pitched in isolated country houses and in trim vicarages than in the capital—but in London, too, there were many long evenings to fill between the five or six o'clock dinner and bedtime. Prosperous dwellers in the outskirts who did not frequent theatres and concert halls would while away the time with family readings. In the early 1860s these part-issues of novels were being superseded by serialization in such new magazines as *Macmillan's* and the *Cornhill* which sold for one shilling and ran serial novels as an attraction additional to informed topical articles and book reviews. Through the shilling magazine, works of fiction now reached a still wider public. Some novelists, notably Charles Dickens, would send one section of a book to press before they had embarked upon the next. This hand-to-mouth system did not appeal to Anthony Trollope. With the two exceptions of *Framley Parsonage* and *The Landleaguers*, he invariably completed a manuscript before handing it to the magazines, a system typical of his methodical attitude to his profession. When he first began to write, people of middle age could easily recall the days when novels were not considered suitable for reading aloud in the presence of younger members of the family. Queen Victoria, whose name has been so misleadingly allotted to a lengthy span of English literary history in reality containing at least three well-defined literary epochs, was allowed in her girlhood to read nothing more thrilling than the tales of Hannah More. *The Bride of Lammermoor* was her first true novel, for it was Walter Scott who initially had made the novel-form respectable—and, in the words of a modern scholar, Kathleen Tillotson, 'through the breach he had made rushed Dickens'. After Dickens, whom he could never bring himself to admire, lumbered Anthony Trollope, 'seated', as Henry James once wrote, 'upon the back of heavy-footed prose'.

This new habit of young persons themselves reading works of fiction, or of hearing them read aloud, imposed upon the author that reticence in sexual matters which makes the English novel of the nineteenth century so astoundingly unlike the contemporary novel in France. For a variety of reasons the 1860s in England were marked by a form of humbug loosely referred to as 'Podsnappery' after the famous character in *Our Mutual Friend*. Anthony Trollope took pains to make his books conform to the new prudishness. The first novel he ever wrote, *The Macdermots of Ballycloran*, begun in 1843 and published four years later, had been enlivened by a seduction, a revenge murder, the still-birth of a bastard child, the mother's sudden death in the court-house and the public hanging of the murderer. By the next decade Trollope had moved on into the halcyon meadow-lands of Barsetshire where such happenings were unheard of and where the only hint of licentiousness lay in the mystery surrounding Mary Thorne's origins—a rather special case whereby Miss Thorne suddenly inherits a fortune for the sole reason that she *is* illegitimate. By 1871, when he was writing *The Vicar of Bullhampton* with its secondary theme of a miller's daughter made into a London 'castaway' by a criminal lover, Trollope broke his own rule of never writing a preface, and apologized in one for having drawn attention to Carry Brattle at all:

'There arises of course the question of whether a novelist who professes to write for the amusement of the young of both sexes, should allow himself to bring upon his stage such a character as that of Carry Brattle? It is not long since—indeed it is well within the memory of the author,—that the very existence of such a condition of life, as was hers, was supposed to be unknown to our sisters and daughters and was, in truth, unknown to many of them. Whether that ignorance was good may be questioned; but that it exists no longer is beyond question.'

He ends this foreword with a plea for sympathy with Carry Brattle—for that general sympathy of which he himself was a shining example. 'It may also be felt,' he concludes, 'that this misery is worthy of alleviation, as is every misery to which humanity is subject.' None the less, he thought it would be wrong to suggest that the repentant Carry Brattle had a happy future before her, or indeed any future worthy of the name at all.

Trollope made no bones about his own moralistic aims: 'The object of a novel should be to instruct in morals while it amuses.' The novelist's influence upon young women was particularly on his mind. He believed it to be stronger than that of parents or of schoolteachers: '... the novelist creeps in closer than the schoolmaster, closer than the father, closer almost than the mother. He is the chosen guide, the tutor whom the young pupil chooses for herself.' With this in mind he always strove to make the punishment fit the crime; in the short, melodramatic tale of Irish life, *An Eye for an Eye*, the feckless young philanderer Fred Neville is pushed over the cliffs of Mohir because his behaviour had been that of 'a self-indulgent spoiled young man who had realized to himself no sense of duty'. But such is Trollope's skill that he cannot help making his bad characters as attractive as, and frequently more interesting than, his heroes and his heroines. Idle Fred Neville is a more appealing character than his virtuous brother Jack; Lady Eustace is more beguiling than Lucy Morris, Lady Ongar than Florence Burton.

When the moralizing mood was on him Anthony Trollope would castigate not merely cunning and calculation, but obstinacy and disobedience as well. Emily Wharton, the stubborn heroine of *The Prime Minister* who marries out of obstinacy and against her father's wishes, has a truly horrible life until her husband kills himself under a train. Yet Emily's ultimate fate is not nearly so bleak as that of Lily Dale in *The Small House at Allington*, condemned to spinsterhood because she had fallen in love with the wrong man and could not bring herself to love the right one. The fate of Lily Dale was much criticized, for publishing novels in serial form had brought with it a disquieting new phenomenon—that of attempted participation, or more properly interference, by enthusiastic members of the public. Dickens and Thackeray suffered from this, and so did Trollope also. Writing in May 1864, to some young sisters, the Misses Rowe, who had evidently begged him to allow Lily Dale to marry Johnnie Eames, he explained:

'My dear girls ... I do not know that I can tell you anything about Lily Dale and her fortunes that will be satisfactory to you. You are angry with me because I did not make my pet happy with a husband, but you would have been more angry if I had made it all smooth ... Indeed the object of the story was to show that a girl under such circumstances should bear the effects of her own imprudence, & not rid herself of her sorrow too easily. I hope none of you will ever come to such a misfortune as hers;—but should such a fate be yours do not teach yourself to believe that any other man will do as well.'

On occasions—and the case of the worldly Julia Ongar in *The Claverings* is a case in point—Trollope would try, in a desperate bout of topiary work, to snip and prune a bold, ignoble character into acceptably virtuous shape. These frenetic efforts usually come towards the end of a book and form his awkward tribute to Establishment morality. But art and morality are ever poles apart, and his description of Lady Ongar's schemes for undermining Harry Clavering's engagement to Florence Burton is far more convincing than her belated and improbable repentance. We may fancy that the innocent girl reader, the young pupil towards whom the author creeps in so very close, must have learned a good deal from Lady Ongar's thoughtful campaign. Lizzie Eustace, also, could provide helpful lessons in how to be at once venal and seductive, while *Orley Farm*, in the person of Lady Mason, invests forgery and lying with a specially impressive stoic grandeur. To condemn Lady

18

Ongar to perpetual widowhood, to marry Lady Eustace off to dreadful Mr Emilius and to banish Lady Mason to a round of continental spas might satisfy English middle-class morality but would it assuage the curiosity of Trollope's favourite readers in the schoolroom?

Poor bright-eyed Lily Dale, her life for ever wrecked by an innocent and romantic misjudgment, has, however, a fate rare amongst Trollope's heroines, for the majority of these gracefully surmount the perils of the non-event. Thus Lady Glencora Palliser does not run away with Burgo Fitzgerald—though we may agree with Henry James that, given her impulsive nature, she would have done so in real life. Eleanor Bold does not marry Bertie Stanhope or Mr Slope. Florence Burton is not defeated by Julia Ongar. Women who have loved and lost are infrequent in the world of Anthony Trollope but when they do cross our path they are basically unlovable, like Lady Laura Kennedy or Lady Mabel Grex. In the sole instance of Lily Dale one is tempted to think that Trollope could not bring himself to marry her to faithful Johnnie Eames because he was in love with her himself.

(iii)
Save for an avowed preference for 'little brown girls'—by which he may be presumed to mean brunettes of English birth rather than African or Asiatic houris—we know next to nothing of Trollope's emotional life, or whether or how often he fell in love. The *Autobiography*, that masterpiece of self-deprecation, is mute upon this subject, as might have been expected. His happy marriage is recorded as 'like the marriage of other people and of no special interest to any one except my wife and me'; in which it most emphatically differed from the marriages explored in his novels, with all their intricate tensions and doubts and miseries, marriages which are often little more than lessons in incompatibility and collisions of self-will. He never kept letters, and he destroyed his few youthful journals. There is evidence that in middle age he fell in love with the Boston blue-stocking Kate Field, but his letters to her display a fatherly affection which can have caused his wife no justifiable anxiety. It seems probable that, noisy, heavy and unattractive, he confined his passions to the creation of his own fictional heroines, those heroines whom Henry James declared to be 'so affectionate' and to 'have a kind of clinging tenderness, a passive sweetness, which is quite in the old English tradition. Trollope's genius is not the

genius of Shakespeare, but his heroines have something of the fragrance of Imogen and Desdemona.'

As a young man of twenty-two, Henry James had ridiculed three successive novels of Anthony Trollope's in the New York *Nation*. He had there declared the characters in *Miss Mackenzie* to be 'a company of imbeciles', and *The Belton Estate* to be seemingly 'a work written for children; a work prepared for minds unable to think'. Of *Can You Forgive Her?* and its heroine, the vacillating Alice Vavasor, he had remarked: 'Can we forgive Miss Vavasor? Of course we can, and forget her too, for that matter.' At the time Henry James was steeped in the novels of Balzac and of Merimée; the only contemporary English novelist of whom he approved was George Eliot. Also in the pages of the *Nation* (then a very new publication) he had recently called *Bleak House* 'forced', *Little Dorrit* 'laboured', and *Our Mutural Friend* 'dug out as with spade and pickaxe'. It was at this period, too, and again for the *Nation* that he had labelled *Drum Taps* 'a melancholy task to read' and had suggested that Walt Whitman could only offer 'flashy imitations of ideas'. In so far as Anthony Trollope was concerned, James revised these brash judgments, for in 1883, the year after Trollope's death, he wrote for the *Century* magazine a long valedictory article on his work, later published with some amendments in his volume, *Partial Portraits*. In this species of obituary he frankly used the word 'genius' to describe Trollope's gifts, remarking that 'his first, his inestimable merit was a complete appreciation of the usual'. He explained that Trollope:

'did not write for posterity; he wrote for the day, the moment; but these are just the writers whom posterity is apt to put into its pocket. So much of the life of his time is reflected in his novels that we must believe a part of the record will be saved ... Trollope will remain one of the most trustworthy, though not one of the most eloquent of the writers who have helped the heart of man to know itself.'

James regretted, as most readers of Trollope must regret, that the corpus of the novels was so vast:

'... Trollope's fecundity is gross, importunate ... Not only did his novels follow each other without visible intermission, overlapping and treading on each other's heels, but most of these works are of extraordinary length ... There is sadness in the thought that this enormous mass does not present itself in a very portable form to posterity.'

It would seem probable that Henry James grew to like Trollope's work more and more as he himself knew and liked England better and better. 'It needs an English residence to make them thoroughly comprehensible', Nathaniel Hawthorne had once written to an actor friend in St Louis, urging him to try Trollope's novels:

'They precisely suit my taste, solid and substantial, written on the strength of beef and through the inspiration of ale, and just as real as if some giant had hewn a great lump out of the earth, and put it under a glass case, with all its inhabitants going about their daily business, and not suspecting that they were being made a show of.'

That the author of such esoteric tales as *The Scarlet Letter* should have admired Anthony Trollope is unexpected; that Henry James in his maturity should have done so is not.

(iv)

James attributed Trollope's immense popularity amongst his Anglo-Saxon readers to the sense of security which his work inspired: 'With Trollope we were always safe; there were sure to be no new experiments.' But at the same time James drew attention to the disenchanted mood of many of the later novels, the bitterness which permeates a book like *The Way We Live Now*—'a more copious record of disagreeable matters could scarcely be imagined'. What James admired most in Trollope was his infinite knowledge of character, and, in particular, of the character of that strictly insular product, the English girl:

'Trollope settled down steadily to the English girl; he took possession of her, and turned her inside out ... he bestowed upon her the most serious, the most patient, the most tender, the most copious consideration. He is evidently always more or less in love with her ... But, if he was a lover, he was a paternal lover, as competent as a father who has had fifty daughters. He had presented the English maiden under innumerable names, in every station and in every emergency in life ... A gentleman who had sojourned in many lands was once asked by a lady (neither of these persons was English), in what country he had found the women most to his taste. "Well, in England" he replied. "In England?" the lady repeated. "Oh yes" said her interlocutor, "they are so affectionate!" The remark was fatuous, but it has the merit of describing Trollope's heroines.'

Much more could profitably be quoted from Henry James's essay in *Partial Portraits*—of Trollope's 'love of reality', of his 'happy, instinctive perception of human varieties', of how he 'struck the right note because he had, as it were, a good ear'. But it seems to me that here we should concentrate upon a single one of James's comments which I have already quoted—that in which he praises Trollope's 'first' and 'inestimable' gift for 'a complete appreciation of the usual'. This statement is at once interesting and provocative, for the simple reason that it no longer holds good for the reader of Anthony Trollope today.

The Trollope revival during the Second World War, when his books were as avidly read in urban air-raid shelters as in the paddy-fields along the Chindwin River, was precisely due to the fact that they had come to seem epitomes of the non-usual, depicting a world so much at variance with present actualities that it inspired nostalgia. In less than six decades the sturdy realist of mid-Victorian England had achieved a fresh fame as a leading writer of escapist literature. In an essay on that wonderful but forgotten satirist of *la Belle Epoque*, Octave Mirbeau, the critic Edmund Wilson has suggested that Mirbeau's eclipse was due to the fact that the horrors of the First World War far surpassed those of Mirbeau's own twisted imagination. Wilson thinks that Hemingway similarly ceased to seem brutal and so went out of fashion with a generation acclimatized to crimes on such a world scale as those of Belsen, Dresden or Hiroshima. We may surely invert his argument and apply it to the vogue for Trollope's novels in the Second World War; but that war has been over for a quarter of a century, and Trollope's popularity shows no signs of waning. Why?

Leaving aside his powers of observation and of drawing character, and also his skill in manipulating his usually uncomplicated plots, I believe Trollope's attraction for us today lies somewhere in that vague, neglected area of the commonplace. He created a world as complete, and almost as remote from ourselves, as that of *The Tale of Genji*. Like Murasaki he recorded exactly what he and his contemporaries saw, and, like her, he included a mass of data which these last did not consciously see, because they took it for granted, and because what is taken for granted becomes in a sense invisible. Thomas Carlyle, in other ways so pernicious, was unique amongst Victorian writers in being fully aware of this fact, and of the way in which an incredulous posterity will view the immediate past. 'Consider, brethren,' he declaimed in the *London and Westminster Review* for 1838, 'shall we not too one day be antiques, and grow to have as quaint a costume as the rest? The stuffed Dandy, only give him *time*, will become one of the wonderfullest of mummies.' It is in this light that we should recognize our gratitude to Anthony Trollope. By it we may even be grateful for that literary fecundity of which, in his lifetime, his contemporaries gradually grew weary. In his *Autobiography* he tells us that he wrote merely to make money, though he does admit that he would have written novels in any case. Like Balzac, Trollope hastened to record every aspect of contemporary life, but his was not the breathless haste that killed Balzac off in middle age. Nor did he ever believe in his own artistic vocation. Moreover he was forced to consider the proprieties in a way which Balzac never found it necessary to do. Trollope's life was even and conventional, yet his scope as a novelist was deep and wide. His characters move purposefully, bothered seldom by the past and never by the remoter future, unaware that they are being watched, reported on and judged by onlookers outside Hawthorne's dome of glass.

For his biographer, a dead man who has judiciously left behind him his own self-portrait poses a number of problems. What, for example, were his motives? How far can we trust his memory? What has he omitted, and why? Where are the limits of his sedulous objectivity? Where does discretion end and deception begin? Should his reticences be respected? Does he deserve to be left in peace?

Anthony Trollope's *Autobiography*, written in 1876 and bequeathed to his elder son who published it in 1883, created immediate consternation by the frankness with which he dealt, not with his private life, but with his successful writing career. He described in what then seemed offensive detail the exact sums of money he had accumulated during a lifetime of novel-writing, and, in one notorious passage, he compared the novelist with the shoemaker. Writing a novel, he explained, was exactly like making a pair of shoes. The novelist had simply to stick to his desk with the same diligence and application as the cobbler to his last. Complacent over his financial gains, he set out deliberately to disparage fiction-writing as an art, and he did his level best to make his profession appear not merely unromantic but mundane. To the aesthetes of the 1880s the old man's confessions were shocking but willingly believed. He has been taken at his word ever since. Yet, while he always fought shy of any claim to be an artist, Trollope knew perfectly well that writing fiction as he wrote it was a great deal more than an artisan craft.

In the short life of Thackeray, which he compiled for the *English Men of Letters* series in 1879, Anthony Trollope stated that to write a good novel an author must not only invent a plot, co-ordinate his characters and work regular hours, but be obsessional as well. He must think about his characters when he is lying in bed, when he is walking about, or when he is just sitting over the fire. The easiest part of writing (he rather unfortunately believed) was the mere arrangement of words which he likened to 'walking simply along a road'. The actual development of the story was like carrying a sack of flour as you walked: 'Fielding had carried his sack of flour before he wrote *Tom Jones* and Scott his before he produced *Ivanhoe*.' In another similarly unhappy analogy he called forethought 'the elbow-grease which a novelist—or poet, or dramatist—requires'. To his American friend Kate Field he once explained that no novelist could be any good who did not live with and by his characters all of the time, no matter what his other occupations might be. There is little of the shoemaker–novelist here.

In the considerable section of the *Autobiography* devoted to the unhappiness of his childhood and schooldays, Trollope tells us that, through neglect and loneliness, he had taken to living in a world of his imagination—'in a world altogether outside the world of my material life'. But his was not the fantasy world of the children of Haworth Parsonage, for it was shared with no one else and its incidents were not written down in tiny illustrated books. He kept all the scenes and happenings within his head: 'I was always going about with some castle in the air built within my mind. Nor were these efforts in architecture spasmodic or subject to constant change from day to day. For weeks, for months, if I remember rightly, from year to year, I would carry on the same tale.' He was careful to keep strictly to certain proportions, 'properties' and 'unities': 'Nothing impossible was ever introduced ... I learned in this way to maintain an interest in a fictitious story.' This fruitful double life, this sustained exercise of the imagination, Trollope for no very apparent reason condemns as though it were a form of masturbation: 'There can hardly be a more dangerous mental practice.' Yet he admits that without this practice he would probably never have written a novel at all. This imaginary world, peopled by imaginary people, with himself as the hero beloved of 'beautiful young women' continued to prove a refuge for him long after adolescence. As a gawky, shy young Post Office clerk living in dingy London lodgings, he withdrew into it still. Then, at the age of twenty-seven, he was dispatched as Surveyor's clerk to settle in the little town of Banagher on the placid River Shannon. In the kindly, easy-going atmosphere of the west of Ireland in those last years before the Great Hunger, Trollope began, with much hesitation, to sketch out his first novel. In this melancholy but gripping tale of Irish country life he kept to the proportions, the proprieties and the unities that had for so long regulated and made credible the happenings of his imaginary world. Despite its violence, the story of the Macdermots of Ballycloran likewise contains no impossible event. It was inspired by the sight of a ruined house outside Drumsna in the unfertile county of Leitrim.

Throughout his novels, both good and bad, Anthony Trollope excelled at evoking the spirit as well as the appearance of any place he found it necessary to his story to describe, whether it was Ullathorne which he created with Montacute in mind, or Barchester, a combination of the cathedral closes of Salisbury and Winchester. Places had an immediate effect upon his imagination, a process as clearly revealed in his four travel books as in his fiction. The plot and characters of *The Warden*, the opening novel of the great Barsetshire series, surfaced in his mind as he was strolling one summer's evening about Salisbury close. In the same way his first novel formed itself in his mind while he was walking with one of his few close English friends, John Merivale, in the barren countryside of County Leitrim.

It was a countryside which they both found 'most uninteresting' until they 'turned up through a deserted gateway, along a weedy grass-grown avenue' which led to 'the modern ruins of a country house':

'It was one of the most melancholy spots I ever visited. I will not describe it here because I have done so in the first chapter of my first novel. We wandered about the place, suggesting to each other causes for the misery we saw there, and while I was still among the ruined walls and decayed beams I fabricated the plot of *The Macdermots of Ballycloran*.'

He goes on to say that he did not know that he had ever again made a plot so good, although he was aware that he had 'broken down in the telling, not having yet studied the art'. When Merivale returned to England, Trollope began trying to write the first few chapters, but the book, he says, 'hung fire', and he could only now and then find 'either time or energy for a few pages'. But, however slowly, he had at last found his true vocation, and a proper use for his imaginary world: 'Up to this time I had continued the practice of castle-building ... but now the castle I built was among the ruins of that old house.' Although men who knew Ireland thoroughly, Sir William Gregory of Coole for instance, or Sir Patrick O'Brien, the perennial member for King's County, called the book 'the best Irish story that had appeared for something like half a century', *The Macdermots* did not sell. The London publisher, Newby of Mortimer Street, who produced the book at his own expense, promising Trollope half the profits, thought it 'very cleverly written' but added that 'Irish stories are very unpopular'. *The Macdermots* came out in the year 1847, which was also the second year of the Irish famine; English readers, who had been amused by the novels of Charles Lever, and so expected all novels with an Irish setting to be hilarious in tone, fought shy of a book that dealt realistically with Irish poverty and despair. In a guilty way they did not want that maltreated country brought seriously to their attention, nor a tale of Irish wrongs introduced into their own homes. The Great Hunger had lasted too long for the English public to feel anything now but apathy and indifference. Anthony Trollope himself felt insecure about this first novel, and pessimistic of its possible success: 'I can with truth declare that I expected nothing. And I got nothing. Nor did I expect fame or even acknowledgment.' In fact *The Macdermots* was reviewed in seven English journals, and in most of them favourably.

Trollope's second novel, *The Kellys and the O'Kellys,* also on an Irish theme, followed *The Macdermots* in 1848, and this, too, fell flat:

'I changed my publisher but I did not change my fortune ... Any success would, I think, have carried me off my legs, but I was altogether prepared for failure. Though I thoroughly enjoyed the writing of these books, I did not imagine, when the time came for publishing them, that any one would condescend to read them.'

His third novel, *La Vendée,* a dull historical tale in the manner of Alexandre Dumas, was also a failure. It was not until some months after the publication in 1855 of *The Warden,* a short and brilliant book (which Henry James declared to be 'a signal instance of Trollope's habit of offering us the spectacle of a character'), that it began to dawn upon critics and readers alike that here was a new English novelist of exceptional gifts.

Despite the cool reception of his first three novels, Trollope had discovered that he enjoyed writing. His imaginary world now ceased to be private, and soon became the public domain of anyone who subscribed to magazines, bought books or took out a subscription to the new lending libraries. His imaginary world still remained altogether outside the world of his post-office duties and of his material life; but it soon began to nurture and later indeed to support that life by means of fame and money. He was perfectly aware of the benefits of both of these, but even they could never exorcize the embittering memory of a penniless childhood and a friendless youth. For the first of these he was correct in believing that his barrister father was wholly to blame.

The enduring effects of a happy or of an unhappy childhood upon later life are now so widely recognized that by most people they are taken for granted. But thoughtful persons—let alone psycho-analysts—also know that these effects often have less to do with childhood facts than with childhood fears and fancies, and that in this context what actually happened may be of less consequence for adult life than what to the child seemed to be happening at the time. Those who have read Anthony Trollope's *Autobiography* can never, I think, forget his account of an atrocious childhood and adolescence, so atrocious indeed that some of his contemporaries could not believe it to be altogether true. Thomas Sweet Escott, the intimate friend and first biographer of the novelist, attributed what he termed Trollope's morbid sensitivity to these childhood memories. Even as far on as 1882, the very year of his death, Anthony Trollope would still speak of them:

'My mother [he told Escott at that time] was much from home or too busy to be bothered. My father was not exactly the man to invite confidence. I tried to relieve myself by confiding my boyish sorrows to a diary that I have kept since the age of twelve, which I have just destroyed, and which, on referring to it for my autobiography some time since, I found full of a heartsick friendless little chap's exaggeration of his woes.'

Exaggeration there may perhaps have been in these vanished diaries, but two other reliable sources corroborate what Anthony wrote of the little Trollopes' truly gruesome childhood. These sources are, firstly the three-volume memoirs of his eldest brother, Thomas Adolphus Trollope, entitled *What I Remember* and published in 1887, and, secondly, the *Life* of their mother, Fanny Trollope, composed by the second wife and widow of Thomas Adolphus and published in 1895. The latter book is based on letters and journals which would seem to have been subsequently destroyed, and on the authoress's conversations with her husband.

Thomas Adolphus Trollope, commonly called Tom Trollope, had the supreme advantage of being his mother's favourite. He travelled everywhere with her, and they finally set up house together in Florence, a situation which even survived Tom's marriage in middle age. Tom Trollope also became well known, but as an historian, a collector and an authority on Italian politics. Although, as we shall presently see, Tom disagreed with his brother's public assessment of their mother's character, he was much bolder or less scrupulous than Anthony in portraying that of their father, whom he described as a 'highly respected but not popular man'. 'Worst of all, alas!' Tom continues, 'he was not popular in his own home. No one of all the family circle was happy in his presence.' The children, according to Tom, tried at all costs to avoid their father's company and came

'to consider as hours of enjoyment only those that could be passed away from it ... I do not think it would be an exaggeration to say that for many years no person came into my father's presence who did not forthwith desire to escape from it ... Happiness, mirth, contentment, pleasant conversation seemed to fly before him as if a malevolent spirit emanated from him.'

Even their father's habit of reading aloud to the family failed to win their sympathy: 'there was not one individual of those who heard him who would not have escaped from doing so, at almost any cost'. We had now better glance at the case history of this deplorable and detested parent.

(iii)

Thomas Anthony Trollope was born in 1774, in the reign of George III. His father was a country vicar, and his grandfather was Sir Thomas Trollope, the fourth baronet. The family apparently originated in Hampshire, and then moved to Lincolnshire. The baronetcy dated from 1641, but the first Trollope of note was Sir Andrew Trollope, who had been knighted during the Wars of the Roses. There lingered in the family, who were proud of their descent, a mythical story that the first Trollope had come over with William the Conqueror, had originally been named Tallyhosier, but on killing three wolves while hunting with the king in the New Forest had been ordered by his royal master to change his name to 'Troisloups'. This tale, in an unwise moment, was recounted to his sceptical schoolfellows at Harrow by the future novelist Anthony Trollope. These boys never allowed him to forget it, and decades later it used to be repeated as a joke by Sydney Herbert, who had at the time been the Harrow head boy. What might have been more useful in those days of patronage was that Thomas Anthony Trollope's cousin, Sir John Trollope, seventh baronet, represented the southern division of Lincolnshire. Sir John was a follower of Lord George Bentinck and an ardent Protectionist. He sat in the House of Commons for close on a quarter of a century before accepting a peerage as Lord Kesteven in 1868. Sir John and Lady Trollope remained on amiable, cousinly terms with

Anthony Trollope's parents, to whom it gave self-confidence in the midst of their crass financial disasters to remember that there was at least a baronet in the family. It may also have been this connection, much stressed in his boyhood, which gave Anthony Trollope the rather exaggerated respect for rank which the characters in his novels too frequently betray.

In 1809 Thomas Anthony Trollope, whom for clarity we had best call Mr Trollope, had married a friend's sister, Fanny Milton, whose father was, like his own, a country rector. Young Mr Trollope was then twenty-five years old and had already begun to make his name at the Chancery Bar. He was an austere product of Winchester and of New College, where he held the Venerian Fellowship, and he thought more highly of his famous and ancient school, and of his Oxford college than of anything else in the world. Letters no longer in existence showed his sons that, in his youth, he had been much esteemed by his friends at college, by the fellows and by many of his intelligent contemporaries. Neither he nor Miss Milton had much money, but they settled comfortably into a small house in Keppel Street, Russell Square, a region of London then chiefly inhabited by professional men, most of them lawyers. In the squares of Bloomsbury—Bedford Square, Russell Square, Red Lion Square and Bloomsbury Square—many of the large and dignified eighteenth-century houses were still owned by the richer lawyers and more eminent judges, although the tendency to move westward into more modern parts of London had already begun. The scale on which the Trollopes lived was a modest one. In the evening their dining-room and drawing-room were illuminated solely by two tallow candles, which had to be constantly snuffed with snuffers placed on the table in a little plated tray. Wax candles costing half-a-crown a pound they could not afford, and one of their sons remembered that the tallow only 'partially illumined' the mahogany table. All the same, port and sherry were placed on the dining-table when the cloth had been removed at the end of the five o'clock dinner; and for seven o'clock breakfast—laid in the back drawing-room to avoid lighting the downstairs fire—a silver tea-urn was brought up by the footman. This footman, who wore the family livery, was regarded by the young couple as indispensable—writing of his father in these days Tom Trollope remarks that 'it would never have occurred to him or to my mother that they could get on without a man-servant in livery'. In these first years of married life limited means did not seem of any consequence to Mr and

Mrs Trollope, for he was through his mother the recognized and accepted heir to the estate of his uncle, a rich old squire called Adolphus Meetkerke, who lived with his childless wife at Julians, a sixteenth-century house in Hertfordshire. Although disappointingly robust, Mr Meetkerke could not live for ever.

For Frances Milton, whose father could give her but a nominal jointure, it was deemed a very good marriage in every way. Her mother, who had died young, had been born a Gresley, that is to say a member of an old Derbyshire family, and as a girl Frances would jest with her brother Henry about the 'illustrious Norman blood that flows in our veins'. On her father's side, on the other hand, there flowed blood which it was best to keep quiet about, for he was the son of a Bristol saddler and his heritage therefore brought with it the contamination of trade. It was perhaps this good middle-class strain that made Mrs Trollope so mentally indestructible in later years, when she had to support by her pen her mad husband, two moribund children, Henry and Emily, a daughter and two growing boys; but it may also have been this strain which made some of her more genteel contemporaries consider her as pushing, and indelicate in her ways. Her father, who had been, like her husband, a Fellow of New College, was a markedly charming, suave and liberal-minded old gentleman, and, according to his grandson Tom Trollope, was 'clever unquestionably in a queer, crotchety sort of way'. He spent a minimum of his time on parish duties, but had for many years devoted most of it to the construction of models of patent stage-coaches designed not to capsize. His coach-house was full of such miniature contraptions, and full-scale machines with enormous wheels encumbered the pretty evergreen-bordered lawn at Heckfield Rectory. One of his most startling eccentricities was a horror of the squeak of a knife's edge on earthenware or porcelain. To save himself from this he had dinner-plates made 'with a little circular depression some two inches in diameter and about as deep as a crown piece in the centre and had some round pieces of silver to fit into these receptacles, on which he cut his meat'.

Mr Milton's daughter Frances had not inherited his eccentricities, but she had certainly inherited his charm. She was by nature gay and vivacious, with an irrepressible sense of humour and gift for happiness. 'She was the happiest natured person I ever knew,' her son Tom wrote after her death, '—happy in the intense power of enjoyment, happier still in the conscious power of making others happy.' Her younger son, Anthony, who felt that she had neglected him in his childhood, has described her as an

'unselfish, affectionate and most industrious woman, with great capacity for enjoyment and high physical gifts ... But she was neither clear-headed nor accurate; and ... was unable to avoid the pitfalls of exaggeration ... She loved society, affecting a somewhat Liberal *rôle*, and professing an emotional dislike to tyrants ... An Italian marquis who had escaped with only a second shirt from the clutches of some archduke whom he had wished to exterminate ... [was] always welcome to the modest hospitality of her house. In after years, when marquises of another caste had been gracious to her, she became a strong Tory, and thought that archduchesses were sweet. But with her, politics were always an affair of the heart, as indeed were all her convictions. Of reasoning from causes I think that she knew nothing.'

When this verdict on their mother appeared in Anthony's posthumous autobiography, it exasperated her favourite son, Tom:

'Now there is hardly a word of this in which Anthony is not more or less mistaken; and that simply because he had not adequate opportunities for close observation ... From the time that he became a clerk in the Post Office to her death, he and my mother were never together but as visitors during the limited period of a visit ... I think that I knew her, as few sons know their mothers.'

Physically, Mrs Trollope was a small woman who 'held herself very upright and walked with a firm step'. Her eyes were bluish-grey and set far apart; when speaking to you she looked up into your face. Her full lips were always smiling, her hands and feet were small, and in her youth she had been much admired for the beauty of her arms. Fortunately for herself and for her family, she was possessed of an optimism which bordered on the supernatural. Such was her resilience that she could never stay sad for long. 'Her mind', wrote her elder son Tom, 'refused to remain crushed any more than the grass is permanently crushed by the storm wind that blows over.' When in 1832 the publication of her first book, *Domestic Manners of the Americans*, made her a literary celebrity overnight, she accepted the fame and the money gratefully but her head was never turned. Fêted in the society of London, of Paris and of Vienna, she remained the same bustling, laughing little person, and was alone amongst the female authoresses of the 'thirties and 'forties to give herself no airs. The acid Mrs Lynn Lynton has remarked on this in her memoirs, when describing the handful of successful and conceited women writers of her London youth:

'All the women I remember in my early days were thus conscious of themselves and of their achievements—all save Mrs Trollope who was in no sense a poseuse, but just a vulgar, brisk and good-natured kind of well-bred hen-wife, fond of a joke and not troubled with squeamishness.'

None the less Mrs Trollope had critics as well as admirers— to Madame Récamier she was a woman of 'straightforward, unflinching, courageous integrity', but to Robert Browning she seemed vulgar and coarse; 'I do hope, Ba, that you won't receive that vulgar pushing woman, who is not fit to speak to you,' he wrote to his wife when, in 1843, Mrs Trollope and her eldest son first descended upon Florence. No blue-stocking, Fanny Trollope was happiest arranging little dances, charades, picnics and private theatricals centring round 'a knot of nice girls'. 'The domestic side of her nature,' her daughter-in-law and biographer observes, 'was intense.' She was a great walker but hated to walk alone, and she was so nervous of the elements that a mild squall on the way back to Venice from Murano rendered her panic-stricken. The only aspect of her character which sometimes made living with her difficult was her habit of continuously changing her mind. She was a restless rather than a restful mother, as Anthony Trollope knew to his cost.

A more disparate couple than Mr and Mrs Trollope it would have been hard to find. While she was warm-hearted, illogical and impetuous he was chilling and rational, cold and phlegmatic. She had evidently realized this during their engagement, for she wrote to him only three weeks before their wedding to complain that his letters to herself lacked feeling. He replied that he ran his life on reason and observation, and he always distrusted persons who were 'vehement' in their expressions. He admitted that he himself often seemed 'to be too cautious of making use of what might be considered a natural and becoming warmth in my declarations'. His only unrestrained emotion was that of anger. It was this that was destined to ruin himself and his family, and to pulverize a promising legal career.

While they were living in Keppel Street, five children were born to the Trollope couple. Thomas Adolphus ('Tom') was the eldest and was born in 1810. Their second child, Henry, was born in 1811 and died of consumption while still a young man. Arthur, the third son, was born in 1812 and died of consumption when he was eleven years old. Their first daughter, Emily, was born in December 1813; she was christened and died on the day of her birth. The fourth son, Anthony, the subject of this book, was born on April 24th, 1815, and, as we have already noted, was 'a Waterloo baby'. The year after Anthony's birth his sister Cecilia was born. She it was who married Anthony's crony John Tilley; she died of consumption when she was thirty-two. In 1818 the last child appeared, another daughter. With a curious lack of superstition on her parents' part, she was given the unlucky name of Emily, and died of consumption in her seventeenth year. All but the last two children were born in Keppel Street, where an Anabaptist nurse, Mrs Farmer, presided over the brimming nursery. Although it does not seem to have strengthened their constitutions, Cecilia and the second Emily were country-born, for by then the Trollopes not only occupied their Keppel Street abode but were also living in a large villa which Mr Trollope had designed himself and had had built on farm-land at Harrow-on-the-Hill. This villa was the outward symbol of Mrs Trollope's optimism and of her husband's apparent success at the Chancery Bar.

The land at Harrow constituted a big property, and did not belong to Mr Trollope but was only leased from Lord Northwick on exorbitant terms. 'I well remember', Anthony Trollope tells us, 'that we all regarded the then Lord Northwick as a cormorant who was eating us up.' It was an audacious step to build a house and lay out gardens, a park and policies on somebody else's land; it was a foolhardy one for a Chancery barrister to embark on large-scale farming for which he had neither aptitude nor training. 'That farm was the grave of all my father's hopes, ambition and prosperity,' Anthony explains, 'the cause of my mother's sufferings and of those of her children, and perhaps the director of her destiny and of ours.'

The Trollopes had selected Harrow-on-the-Hill as a residence because it was within fairly easy reach of Lincoln's Inn, where

Mr Trollope kept chambers, and because they had discovered that Harrow School 'offered an education almost gratuitous to children living in the parish'. The three surviving Trollope boys were sent in succession to Harrow School so soon as they were seven years old. Here they found themselves ridiculed by the wealthier and more aristocratic boarders. Their schooldays were, moreover, disrupted by their father's unorthodox intention of leaving them at Harrow for only four or five years, and then sending them on to his own school, Winchester. Harrow had never before, nor has it ever since, been treated as a mere prep-school for Winchester. Although the Trollopes were on visiting terms with some of the Harrow masters and their families, these must surely have resented so cavalier an attitude towards their famous and selective school.

Just as the expensive country house was completed, the clients of Mr Trollope began to bring him fewer and fewer briefs. His temper had by now become notorious, and brilliant though he was, and wonderfully well-versed in Chancery law, his practice dwindled rapidly and finally came to an end. He was an extremely disputatious man, and when he disagreed with his attorney-clients on a point of law he would berate them violently, often treating them as though they were opposing counsel on the other side. He was entirely impartial in these scourgings and, as Escott pointed out,

'would demonstrate the folly of a rich client, as eagerly as he would scold a poor one. Verbal nonsense was to him as a rat to a terrier, and he set upon it and worried it whenever and wherever it showed itself. Once having discovered that they could get their work done practically as well elsewhere by counsel not superior to the common courtesies of life, the long-enduring solicitors brought their papers to Trollope no more. Every week, ruin, crushing and complete, drew visibly nearer. At last there was decided on a move of the whole family from Keppel Street to Julians.'

The house at Harrow had been named Julians after the very large property in Hertfordshire, of which we may remember that Mr Trollope was sole heir. The entail (a subject round which so many of Anthony Trollope's own novels intricately revolve) was perfectly clear and defined. Mr and Mrs Trollope would go to stay with their old uncle, sometimes taking little Tom Trollope with them so that the local cottage-folk should grow accustomed to the sight of the child who would one day be their landlord. Mr Adolphus Meetkerke, who was the brother of Mr Trollope's mother, was an early nineteenth-century Squire Weston, strident, rustic, hard-drinking and a convinced Tory. During these visits Mr Trollope, who was a Whig, would bitterly taunt his uncle, contradicting his Tory views with all a London barrister's skill, until in the end the visits of his nephew and heir became to Mr Meetkerke nothing but a nuisance and an affront. The squire's wife and his old maiden sister formed the family household at Julians. The apple-cheeked old sister did all the housekeeping and would trip about the house with a basket containing the keys, and a single volume of *Pride and Prejudice*, 'which she always recommenced as soon as she had worked her way to the end of it'. Old Mrs Meetkerke came down to breakfast in the morning 'clad in a green riding-habit, and passed most of her life on horseback'. Julians was an old-fashioned, self-sufficient, peaceful little kingdom of its own—peaceful, that is to say, when the heir was not holding up his uncle's political views to ridicule before his face. This tactlessness turned out to be very costly, for when old Mrs Meetkerke died without any warning, the squire married a young wife who produced six healthy children. Mr Trollope, who had long ceased to be *persona grata* in his uncle's house, now automatically ceased to be the heir to Julians, or indeed heir to anyone or anything at all.

Having destroyed his own legal practice (although he would continue to go up in the trap to his gloomy chambers in Old Square, Lincoln's Inn—chambers made eerie to his children by the fact that a pupil of his had committed suicide there), Mr Trollope had helped to wreck his own prospects at Julians. It was thought by some of his family that had he shown more affection and tact to Mr Meetkerke the lonely old man might never have remarried and thus cut his nephew out of the entail. After the letting of 16 Keppel Street, there came the letting of the new Harrow house. The family moved literally downhill to an old farm at Harrow Weald. From now on they were pursued as though by furies. Their third son, Arthur, sickened and died at the age of eleven. They mislaid the title-deeds of some London properties. It was at this late stage discovered that the deed embodying Mrs Trollope's small but solid marriage portion had been neither registered nor witnessed and was hence invalid. By this stage of their misfortunes her husband's mental and bodily health were noticeably beginning to give way.

In after years Mr Trollope's surviving children agreed amongst themselves that their father's brain and physique had become deranged through excessive use of calomel, which causes severe mercury poisoning. All his life he had been subject to violent migraines, for which calomel in appropriate doses was then believed to bring relief. But instead of small, regular doses, Mr Trollope took to calomel with the blind zeal of a modern heroin-addict. He became more and more excitable, making scenes with his sons about money; and to everyone who came his way he would behave as unpleasantly as only he knew how to do. As prime victim for his rage he would especially pick upon his second son, Henry, who was indolent and apathetic but who was probably already riddled by consumption. During such scenes Henry would appeal to his mother for help. After them Mrs Trollope, like many of her contemporaries, would take laudanum in order to sleep.

Even before his financial collapse, Mr Trollope had been an unnerving parent to his sons. He was determined that they should all three get scholarships to Winchester and then to New College, as he himself had done in his days of unimpaired youth. He had started them off on Latin grammar at six years old, and soon after that they were set to learning and construing the Latin poets. He never beat them, but if they used a false quantity he would tweak their hair. In the Keppel Street days the two elder little boys would trudge to his chambers at half-past four, repeating their morning's task as they returned homewards with their father. Any form of rest or recreation was denounced by him as 'idling', so that once a day's task was accomplished he set them another one at once; 'this', writes Tom Trollope, 'we considered to be unjust and unfair'.

Mr Trollope himself worked very hard—first at his briefs when briefs there were, and later at farming in Harrow, which he did not understand. He ultimately found for himself a ceaseless form of personal labour—the compilation of an universal dictionary of ecclesiastical terms, at which he would work, shut away in his bookroom, till far into the night. 'He had quite sufficient learning and sufficient industry to have produced a useful book on the subject,' his eldest son tells us, 'if he had only had the possibility of consulting the, of course, innumerable necessary authorities.' The book was issued in quarto volumes to unwilling subscribers. 'I do not suppose', Tom adds, 'that any human being purchased the book because they wished to possess it.' It is probable that Mr Crawley, the austere and penniless clergymen in *Framley Parsonage*, who suffers from pride and melancholia and who is for ever drilling Latin into his children, may have been suggested to Anthony Trollope by his father's stern character and gloomy pursuits.

(ii)

When Anthony Trollope was ten years old, and was still fairly unaware of his family's dire circumstances, he was taken away from Harrow (where he had achieved the reputation of being the dirtiest and most slovenly boy in the school), sent for two years to a private school at Sunbury, and then admitted to Winchester. So far Mr Trollope's novel educational scheme had more or less worked out, for his two elder sons had already been taken as scholars at Winchester, and Tom was in fact still there in April 1827 when Anthony, ill-dressed and very frightened, arrived in the college. Their mother had penned a letter to Tom to remind him that he was now responsible for Anthony:

'Your father must certainly consider himself as very fortunate in getting three boys into College, and yet it will not do us much good, unless we get some dispers [sic] of the New College loaves and fishes. As far as Anthony is concerned this must very much depend on you. I dare say you will often find him idle and plaguing enough. But remember, dear Tom, that, in a family like ours *everything* gained by one is felt personally and individually by all. He is a good-hearted fellow, and clings so to the idea of being Tom's pupil, and sleeping in Tom's chamber, that I think you will find advice and remonstrance better taken by him than by poor Henry. Greatly comforted am I to know that Tony has a praefect brother. I well remember what I used to suffer at the idea of what my "little Tom" was enduring.'

When he reached Winchester, and bedded down in his brother's room, 'Tony' soon found that having a prefect brother was without any question the worst fate that could have been devised for him. At that time there flourished at Winchester College a system by which the smaller boys were allotted as pupils to the prefects, who thus became answerable for much of their education. 'Few brothers have had more of brotherhood,' Anthony writes of Tom and himself in his *Autobiography*:

'But in those school-days he was, of all my foes, the worst ... he was my tutor; and in his capacity of teacher and ruler, he had studied the theories of Draco. I remember well how he used to exact obedience after the manner of that lawgiver. Hang a little boy for stealing apples, he used to say, and other little boys will not steal apples. The doctrine was already exploded elsewhere, but he stuck to it with conservative energy. The result was that, as a part of his daily exercise, he thrashed me with a big stick. That such thrashings should have been possible at a school as a continual part of one's daily life, seems to me to argue a very ill condition of school discipline.'

Yet when Tom Trollope left Winchester, Anthony found himself alone and without any friends at the College:

'I was big and awkward, and ugly, and, I have no doubt, skulked about in a most unattractive manner. Of course I was ill-dressed and dirty. But ah! how well I remember all the agonies of my young heart; how I considered whether I should always be alone; whether I could not find my way to the top of that college tower, and from thence put an end to everything?'

Just at this time his miseries were increased by the fact that as his bills had not been paid, the Winchester tradesmen who sold the boys boots, waistcoats, handkerchiefs and other articles of apparel were told not to give young Trollope any more credit. His pocket-money was next stopped, and all the boys in the school knew of it. Yet his holidays rendered him equally abject, because there was now no home for him to go to. One midsummer holidays he spent living at his father's chambers in Lincoln's Inn, 'wandering about among those old deserted buildings' and reading Shakespeare in a bi-columned edition: 'It was not that I had chosen Shakespeare but that there was nothing else to read.'

The cause of Anthony's waif-like state is in itself an interesting one. His school bills had not been paid and he had no home to go to because his father and his brother Tom had taken steerage passages to New York, whence they travelled overland to Cincinnati, Ohio, where Mrs Trollope, Henry, Cecilia and Emily were currently marooned. The story of Fanny Trollope's American adventure, which produced the book that made her famous, would seem, if we were dealing with any other woman or any other family, too improbable to be true.

(iii)

In spite of their recurrent financial crises, Mr and Mrs Trollope still liked to have friends to stay. Prominent amongst their guests was Miss Frances—or 'Fanny'—Wright, an emancipated girl who had rejected revealed religion and the ties of marriage at the age of eighteen. Fanny Wright and her sister Camilla, the orphaned daughters of a rich intellectual Dundee merchant, had been brought up as wards in Chancery. Fanny, who liked declaring that she was a follower of Epicurus, held more advanced views than did Camilla, and was quite ready to discuss birth control or the liberation of slaves with anyone she met. She was tall and slender, with curling auburn hair, and she wore trousers and a tunic with a sash; she eschewed the conventional bonnet, and habitually appeared with a broad-brimmed cartwheel hat upon her head. She was an enthusiast with little sense of reality but with enough money to launch lost causes and satisfy her own whims. Having read Botta's book on the American War of Independence, she hurriedly set off for the United States, returned to England in May 1820, and published a panegyric volume on her experiences on the other side of the Atlantic. The book was read by Lafayette, who wrote the authoress a pleasing letter of congratulation; he was then in his middle sixties but, by wearing a brown wig, he managed to make himself look younger. On receipt of the old general's letter, the Wright sisters scampered over to Paris and were soon treated by Lafayette as though they were his daughters. But they were not his daughters, and when his family found out that the Wright girls had been imploring Lafayette to adopt them legally, steps were taken to prevent his doing so. All the same, they were often with him in Paris and staying, too, at his country house, La Grange. In the late summer of 1823 Mr and Mrs Trollope were staying with English friends of theirs who lived in Paris. They met Lafayette at a dinner-party: 'Never,' wrote Mrs Trollope, 'did I meet a being so perfect in every way.' It was from Lafayette that evening that Fanny Trollope first heard tell of the Nashoba Settlement.

The Nashoba Settlement was the brain-child of Miss Frances Wright and consisted of an estate in the virgin forests near Memphis, Tennessee. The worthy object of this establishment was to enable Negroes to work the estate for a regular wage so that, when they had earned their freedom, they could be shipped to Haiti as free men and women. Nashoba had already been bought, and was described by the Wright sisters as having an apple orchard of five acres, fifteen acres of corn and a nice potato patch; the accommodation, they said, was excellent, with log-cabins for the white owners, shacks for the Negroes and a model school for Negro children. The whole project intrigued Mrs Trollope—and since Lafayette himself had praised it, surely there could be nothing wrong with it? Soon the elder Miss Wright was staying with the Trollopes at Harrow, and while there she suggested that the whole family should emigrate.

They could spend as long as they liked in Nashoba and, later, go to live in Cincinnati and set up what would now be called a boutique, to sell gewgaws, bric-à-brac and imitation jewellery to the benighted inhabitants of Cincinnati—where, in actual fact, there already were shops selling exactly the same kind of slave-traders' goods. Moreover the Trollopes' close friend, a French painter named Auguste Hervieu, could travel over with them to teach picaninnies to draw and paint in oils at the Nashoba school. The more Mrs Trollope thought it over the more flawless did this crazy plan seem. It was arranged that Mrs Trollope, Henry (who could allegedly complete his schooling at the Robert Owen settlement at New Harmony), Cecilia and Emily should go out as the family vanguard, with Mr Trollope and Tom following them some months later; before he left England Mr Trollope was to raise money to buy stock for the Cincinnati bazaar. Anthony had no role to play in this migration. He was simply to be left in England on his own. He did not see his mother and sisters again for three and a half years.

Like many of her contemporaries Mrs Trollope then viewed America as a freer and unshackled England; Fanny Wright's ecstatic praise of all things American also impressed her deeply. On Christmas Day, 1827, the British sailing ship *Edward* glided towards the mouth of the Mississippi; on board, were Mrs Trollope and Henry and his sisters, Auguste Hervieu, Miss Fanny Wright and the Trollopes' footman, William. The voyage had taken seven weeks. During it Fanny Wright had harangued her companions about the beauties of the Nashoba Settlement, and the glorious equality that ruled in the United States.

Mrs Trollope quickly found that there was indeed social equality in the United States, but it was not of a nature that she liked. People jostled her in the streets and addressed her as 'old woman'. In a milliner's shop in New Orleans she was told to shake hands with the girl behind the counter. The Grand Hotel at Memphis was an unexpected revelation of horror: it smelled of damp and of fresh plaster, and the manager refused to let her have tea up in her room unless she could prove that she was really ill. On repairing to the ground-floor dining-room she was forced to sit at the same table as her footman. She began to judge that American life was definitely crude, and she was riled by the constant use—in hotel, restaurant or paddle-boat—of the spittoon. People would never thank you for some favour or modest tip because they thought they might be being patronized. Worse, however, was to come.

From Memphis the next morning they set off in a wagonette for the Nashoba Settlement. The bumpy road dwindled to a bumpy track through the grey and ominous Tennessee forests. They finally reached a clearing where a few shacks stood: this, they were given to understand, was Nashoba. Mrs Trollope summed the whole place up as 'vividly dreadful'. Not only was there no school for M. Hervieu to teach in, but even the log-cabins for the Europeans only existed in Miss Wright's mind's eye. Orchard there was none; the potato patch did not exist. There was a rudimentary fence round the settlement, and beyond this brooded the eerie forest. It rained unceasingly and none of the shacks was properly roofed; they had fireplaces of a sort but these were made of mud and wood, and caught fire 'a dozen times a day'. There was nothing but rain water to drink and wheaten bread and Indian corn bread to eat. There were no vegetables, no meat, no butter and no cheese. Camilla Wright greeted them and spent the next two or three days bemoaning her fate to Mrs Trollope. The burden of her theme was that the Negroes did not understand being expected to work without the salutary threat of the lash. Owing to Fanny Wright's idealism, none of the Negroes' shacks had locks on the door, and, in consequence of this, the male Negroes would blunder into the women's quarters and attempt rape.

Mrs Trollope and Hervieu and the children stuck it out for less than a month, and then, to Fanny Wright's astonishment, declared that they could stand the Nashoba Settlement no longer. They returned to the muddy yellow Mississippi and arrived in Cincinnati. Since this book purports to be a biography of Anthony Trollope rather than of his mother, we do not have to follow the half-family to Ohio. All that we need to know is that the oriental-looking shop, bar and concert-hall built to Mrs Trollope's specification in that city turned out to be a monumental failure. Mr Trollope and Tom came out to Cincinnati, but soon returned to England. The knick-knacks the bazaar was supposed to sell were sequestered by the builders, to whom Mrs Trollope owed several thousand dollars. She and her children subsequently travelled about the eastern States, living chiefly on what M. Hervieu could gain by painting portraits. They reached England in August 1831, and, there at Harrow, Mrs Trollope began to write the book which brought her international acclaim. Its biggest circulation was, naturally enough, in the United States. Travellers coming back from the United States reported that the one question on steamboat, stage or in hotel was 'Have you read Mrs Trollope?' The more the work was abused the larger became its sale.

(iv)

When Mr Trollope and his son Tom finally returned from the United States in 1830, Anthony was lofted out of Winchester and, from motives of economy, once more deposited at Harrow School as a day pupil. Now an inhibited hobbledehoy of fifteen he was as unable as ever to make a single friend at school: 'I had not only no friends, but was despised by all my companions.' A handsome and clever Irish boy, William Gregory of Coole, in adult life a gay, hard-riding companion of Anthony's in the hunting fields of Galway, has explained in his memoirs how he came to know, and to ignore Anthony Trollope at Harrow. Sent down to the bottom of his 'remove' for a variety of misdemeanours, Gregory found himself seated next to young Trollope, the school dunce. Trollope was a heavily built boy, older than the rest and filthy to look at.

'He was not only slovenly in person and dress, but his work was equally dirty. His exercises were a mass of blots and smudges. These peculiarities created a great prejudice against him, and the poor fellow was generally avoided ... I had plenty of opportunities of judging Anthony, and I am bound to say ... that I did not dislike him. I avoided him because he was rude and uncouth, but I thought him an honest, brave fellow. He was no sneak. His faults were external ... but the faults were of that character for which schoolboys will never make allowances, and so poor Trollope was tabooed ... He gave no sign of promise whatsoever, was always in the lowest part of the form, and was regarded by masters and boys as an incorrigible dunce.'

Tom Trollope had meanwhile been sent up to Oxford, which meant that Anthony was living alone with his father in the dingy farmhouse at Harrow Weald, which he describes as 'not only no more than a farmhouse but ... one of those farmhouses which seem always to be in danger of falling into the neighbouring horsepond'. Mr Trollope's main source of income was the farm, the rent to Lord Northwick was always in arrears, and the local tradesmen were constantly owed money. The furniture of the farmhouse was 'mean and scanty', the food the poorest possible. The wild, seedy kitchen garden contributed little to the table because there was no gardener, and because Anthony refused to obey his father's orders to dig or plant in it. The father lived mainly in the farmhouse parlour 'shut up among big books' and Anthony's only happy hours were spent in the kitchen, 'making innocent love to the bailiff's daughter'. Even these relaxing evenings only served to emphasize the horrors and the loneliness of next day at school, to and from which he would tramp in all weathers and in worn-out shoes. Mr Trollope had a pronounced distaste for spending money on his family's clothes. He used to write to the boys at Winchester telling them to have their clothes patched and shoes mended rather than to buy anything new. One springtime Mrs Trollope, aided by the old nurse Farmer, had been driven to make the boys' cricketing flannels and other school garments herself. She wrote to them at Winchester that she was sure these homespun products would 'turn out something worthy of a very good tailor'.

In August 1831 Mrs Trollope, with Cecilia and Emily in her wake, reached England again after her transatlantic fiasco. Henry, who was ill, had returned the previous year. She cheerfully settled down to write up her acidulated notes on the American way of life, and this, her first book, became a bestseller and its authoress a household word in Great Britain and in the United States as well. In these latter, in fact, her name literally became a household verb, for her complaints of the American male's use of the spittoon caused so much offence that 'to spit' became 'to trollope'. Though the American editions of *Domestic Manners* were, of course, pirated, that produced by her London publisher brought in substantial sums of money. She found herself suddenly able to pay for everything. Lord Northwick's agent received a full half-year's rent in advance, taxes were paid on the nail, a new bed, sofa and chest of drawers were bought, as well as bolsters and pillows. She had found that the farmhouse had been totally neglected during her absence: 'You know', she wrote to her husband, 'that not one of our five children has a pillow for his head,' and in another letter she refers to Tom (who had inherited his father's headaches) as 'lying in a comfortless garret, without a pillow under his poor aching head'. Anthony felt that, after his mother's return and her book's success, the sombre farmhouse 'resembled the transformation scene in a pantomime that takes place at the advent of the good fairy'. For the first time in his adolescent life he was comparatively happy, although his resentment at what had seemed to be his mother's long desertion smouldered on.

Buoyed up by money and celebrity, Mrs Trollope, in September 1832, moved the whole family out of the old farmhouse in Harrow Weald, and into another one which Mr Trollope had converted some years previously. This Anthony considered to be 'a very good house ... a very comfortable residence'. The new house was once again somewhat perversely called Julians, but to differentiate it from their original grand villa at Harrow it was known as Julians Hill. Thirty years later, in 1862, a drawing of Julians Hill by John Millais formed the frontispiece of Anthony's novel *Orley Farm*. In this well-known book Julians Hill becomes Orley Farm, the house and small property for which Lady Mason forges, then lies and commits perjury in open court. Is it far-fetched to suggest that the value attached to Orley Farm by the protagonists in this novel reflects Anthony's grateful memories of the first house in which, as an adolescent, he had ceased to feel an outcast?

When the family established themselves at Julians Hill, Anthony Trollope was seventeen. He already knew more about loneliness and penury than most boys of his age. 'My boyhood,' he writes early on in his *Autobiography*,

'was, I think, as unhappy as that of a young gentleman could well be, my misfortunes arising from a mixture of poverty and gentle standing on the part of my father, and from an utter want on my own part of that juvenile manhood which enables some boys to hold up their heads even among the distresses which such a position is sure to produce.'

Looking back on the year 1832 it must certainly have seemed to him that the wand of some benignant fairy had transformed all their lives. This transformation was, however, illusory. The Trollope family may have been out of the wood, but they were now doomed to enter the forest—a forest of thwarted hopes, of bankruptcy, foreign exile, illness, death and near-despair.

At the close of the auspicious year 1832, Mrs Trollope discovered that the nine hundred pounds earned by her first book was, as she put it, 'oozing fast'.

4: In Bruges Town

By 1833, the year following the family *annus mirabilis*, the proceeds of *Domestic Manners* had entirely oozed away. There was also a bad harvest, but even with a good one any profit the Harrow farmland might make would be swallowed up by Lord Northwick, who never again got a half-year's rent from the Trollopes in advance. Mr Trollope, enmeshed in his intricate dictionary of ecclesiastical terms, had more or less opted out of his position as head of the family, and it was henceforth on Mrs Trollope and her earning capacity as an author that their actual survival depended. Her husband was now forever adrift in a private world of calomel and anger. He had prematurely aged— one French doctor whom he consulted took him to be eighty-two, and was astonished to learn that he was in fact just twenty years younger. He was obsessed by the knowledge of his own failure and aggrieved that all his ambitious plans to turn his sons into brilliant university men had come to dust. But even in this lamentable state, he was not exactly a cypher, for he continued to make savage scenes with Henry and his brothers over money. His daughter-in-law, in her *Life* of Mrs Trollope, tells us that he was now 'absolutely a prey to a sort of monomania on the subject of allowing his sons any money'.

His second son Henry had managed to squeeze into Caius College, Cambridge, but he was withdrawn after a few months because his parents could not afford to keep him there. He was sent to read law with a Mr Lovat in London chambers, but as his father would not give him an allowance 'deemed sufficient to supply [him] with the bare necessities of life', this experiment did not last long either. He next took a job as a private tutor, but on his coming home one day to Harrow he looked so desperately ill that his mother sent for a local doctor, who pronounced that Henry 'required the most extreme care' and '*hoped* that his lungs were not yet touched'. Like his brothers Henry was a powerfully built, muscular young man. A few months later, when it was accepted that Henry did indeed have consumption, Tom Trollope noted in his diary that 'owing to his youth and strength Henry's struggle with the dread disease may be long and painful'. This dismal prophecy proved right.

As the gulf of their financial crisis yawned and widened, Mrs Trollope's friends, especially their next-door neighbours Colonel

Grant and his family, tried their best to help. Old Lady Milman would ask one or both of the Trollope girls to stay at her house in Pinner for as long as they liked. An intimate friend, Lady Dyer, lent Mrs Trollope money and refused to take back her loan when it was offered to her. John Murray the publisher paid royalties promptly, although he would never give his popular authoress an advance. Particularly active on their behalf was Fanny Trollope's brother Henry Milton, who may perhaps have felt a vicarious responsibility for his sister's troubles since it was he who had first introduced her to her husband. Mr Milton employed his own solicitor to try to disentangle the title deeds to 16 Keppel Street and other London properties which, we may recall, had been so mysteriously lost. It transpired that these deeds were not in any accepted sense 'lost' but had been handed over by Mr Trollope as security on money received from various persons from whom he had never bothered to demand a receipt. These creditors were most unwilling to hand back the title deeds—we may presume that Mr Milton was ready to pay them off—and some of the deeds, and thus the properties, were, in consequence, irredeemably alienated. The net result of these researches by Mr Milton's solicitor was sufficient to allot to Mrs Trollope a very small annual sum over which she was given personal control. Even this, however, proved a dubious blessing, as tenants of the redeemed properties would fail to pay up on rent-day, and the houses themselves had frequently to be repaired at Mrs Trollope's own expense. The solicitor, who had taken very great pains on her behalf, would not permit any member of the family to pay him, and courteously insisted that all he required as fee was an autographed copy of *Domestic Manners of the Americans*.

Throughout these trials Mrs Trollope somehow retained her native buoyancy of spirit. She was always saying that good times were just around the corner, but even she soon realized that this corner was more likely to be turned on the other side of the English Channel than on this one. She determined, in fact, that her family should follow the immemorial custom of Britons in financial difficulties, and go to live cheaply on the Continent:

'We are in truth [she wrote to Tom] at the *corner* I have so often talked about, and if we can turn it things must be better with us than we have seen them for years. £250 in a cheap country, with my own management, and the hope of gaining more by my own means, yours and Henry's, cannot be called a dreary prospect.'

As in many of their mother's letters to Tom Trollope no mention is here made of Anthony. A pariah at school, he would seem to have been considered a negligible quantity by his mother —a clumsy youth of eighteen who would never be able to contribute to his family's earning power, and who was, in consequence, excluded from their counsels. Mrs Trollope's special relationship with her eldest son Tom had always existed, but with the décay of her husband's faculties it was now becoming closer than ever. His mother was, in a sense, already grooming Tom for the role of substitute husband which he willingly played for the rest of her long life. It was a relationship of interdependence which kept Tom a bachelor for many, many years. As we have noticed, it was not even threatened when, in middle life, he married.

The place abroad which Fanny Trollope selected as their future home was the silent, sleepy little medieval city of Bruges, of which Wordsworth had once written:

> 'In Bruges town is many a street
> Whence busy life hath fled,
> Where, without hurry, noiseless feet
> The grass-grown pavement tread.'

Mrs Trollope had Belgian friends in Bruges, a M. and Mme Fauche, whom she had met during a rather scurried tour of their country for a piece of literary hack-work, *Belgium and Western Germany in 1833*, which her new publisher John Murray was producing in the hope that the success of *Domestic Manners* might be repeated—or if not repeated that at least it might tempt the authoress's admirers to read what she had to say about scenery and domestic manners in a part of the Old World. The Fauches had assured her that life in Bruges was inexpensive; the town was also selected because it offered 'easiness of access to London' by the Ostend packet. In the spring of 1834 Fanny Trollope's migratory plans were completed, but, as she did not wish to choose a house which her husband and children might dislike, it was arranged that when the whole family and Mrs Cox the maid should first sweep down on Bruges they would begin by boarding with the Fauches while house-hunting for themselves. It was a modest, practical plan, and would have been completely foolproof had it been activated with secrecy and speed. As it turned out, they got their timing wrong.

In recounting the circumstances of the flight to Flanders, Fanny Trollope's daughter-in-law and biographer loyally states that this was planned in two stages—Mr Trollope was to leave first, on April 18th, 1834, and his wife, with Henry, Anthony and the two daughters, was to follow in a week's time. What in fact happened was that Mr Trollope had to be spirited urgently away that April morning, to avoid arrest for debt and, presumably, incarceration in the Marshalsea. Anthony relates how he was summoned very early in the morning of that April day and told to drive his father to London in the gig:

'He had been ill, and must still have been very ill indeed when he submitted to be driven by anyone. It was not till we started that he told me that I was to put him on board the Ostend boat. This I did, driving through the city down to the docks. It was not within his nature to be communicative, and to the last he never told me why he was going to Ostend. Something of a general flitting abroad I had heard before, but why he should have flown the first, and flown so suddenly, I did not in the least know till I returned.'

Five hours after Mr Trollope's hasty departure, Julians Hill was invaded by bailiffs who, his mother wrote to Tom at Oxford, 'seized on everything it contained at the suit of Lord Northwick'. The destitute family were turned out on to the road, and sought shelter with their kindly next-door neighbours, the Grants. Later that day young Anthony, after a long drive home on his own in the gig (doubtless occupied with fabricating some portion of his imaginary world) was stopped on the road to Julians Hill by a former gardener, who quietly informed him of the seizure, and urged him not to allow the horse, the gig and the harness to fall into the bailiff's hands. He therefore drove the gig into the village and sold horse and equipage to the iron-monger for seventeen pounds, the exact sum, as it happened, of the bill which his impecunious family owed in that particular shop. He then walked up to his former home where he found an animated outdoor scene in progress. Perhaps at the instigation of their mother, perhaps on their own initiative, Henry and his sisters had converted the preparations of the forced sale into a merry game of smugglers. Aided by the Grant children, they were scampering about the house, surreptitiously snatching up choice *bibelots* and favourite books to pass through the hedge to their next-door neighbours. Anthony joined in. In the following days Mrs Trollope was allowed to buy back with her own money 'many indispensable articles of household furniture at the appraiser's valuation'. Although, in his later youth in London, Anthony was often tormented by duns, the execution at Julians Hill in 1834 was his only direct or personal experience of a house being taken over lock, stock and barrel by the bailiffs. He surely drew on his memories of this scene when writing, nearly thirty years later, the distressing passage about the bailiffs at Framley Parsonage.

In any case, the newly found sense of security and almost of happiness which had seemed to him to have bloomed with his mother's return from America had suffered a withering blow. Julians Hill now painfully resembled a pantomime transformation scene organized by a bad fairy. Cinderella's coach had become a pumpkin once more.

The departure of his father for Ostend was not Anthony's only sight of the London docks that April. Mrs Trollope had packed, and her corded trunks were already on board the Channel ferry, when the Harrow doctor peremptorily announced that the coast of Ostend, or even its neighbourhood, 'would be *fatal* for Henry,' 'I will not say a word of the agony this occasioned,' his mother wrote to Tom Trollope. She sent Anthony and the ever-useful Hervieu, the painter of Cincinnati days, back to the docks to take all the luggage off the boat again, while she herself conducted Henry down to Dawlish in Devonshire—'I did this at great expense, for he was obliged to sleep on the road.' In Dawlish there lived Mrs Trollope's spinster cousin, old Fanny Bent, whose forthright character and kind heart were said to have inspired Anthony's portrait of Miss Stanbury of Exeter in *He Knew He Was Right*. At long last, Mrs Trollope set off for Bruges, taking with her only one child, Emily. She was in, for her, a most despondent mood. 'I *must* send Fanny Bent some money to pay Henry's expenses at Dawlish,' she wrote to Tom. 'And whether we shall have enough to find us bread till the June rents come in, I am very doubtful.'

At Bruges the Trollopes leased an 'uncompromisingly ugly', but solid and comfortable house, the Château d'Hondt, out beyond the Smeeden Poort. Revisiting Bruges with his second wife in 1867, Tom Trollope went to look at the Château d'Hondt, which he found 'as defiant of the pretty or the picturesque as ever'. On this pilgrimage Tom Trollope, who was nearing sixty, was disappointed to find the Château d'Hondt looking so unconcerned: 'It seemed strange that it should look so much as if it had nothing to say to me! Was it,—could it be absolutely I, who within those very walls had done so many things, thought so many thoughts, felt so much love, laughed so many laughs, and shed so many tears?'

(ii)

That Tom Trollope, who was, in 1834, working in England as a private tutor, and whose first visit to Bruges was immediately after his brother Henry's death there in December 1834, should have laughed so many laughs in the Château d'Hondt seems to argue a curious insensitivity. For his mother, certainly, there was little that was overtly humorous in life within those solid Flemish walls. Three months after the eviction from Julians Hill and his journey to Dawlish, Henry Trollope insisted that he was well enough to join his parents in Bruges. Put on board the channel boat by his brother Tom, who thought him looking ghastly, Henry arrived at the Château d'Hondt in mid-July, bringing with him, at his mother's request, domestic supplies, including Old Brown Windsor soap and six pounds of 'wax ends'—that is to say the stumps of good wax candles which were collected from affluent London houses and from the clubs by chandlers for bulk resale. For the next seven months Mrs Trollope's life became a purgatory. Henry, who was not supposed to know that he was dying, developed, under the strain of his disease, a character as difficult as that of his father. He was fearfully exacting and his bursts of temper became unendurable. He wanted his mother to sit and talk to him, or to read aloud to him, 'almost all her waking hours'. Her writing time thus reduced, she would then sit up into the small hours, drinking strong coffee, and feverishly working at a new novel, *Tremordyn Cliff*. It was only by producing books at high speed that she could keep the family going, and could afford the medical attention which Henry required—yet Henry's incessant demands prevented her from producing her books at sufficient speed. It was clear also that her husband had not himself very much longer to live. Emily was delicate and 'drooping more and more'; and there was the additional problem of contriving to keep Emily out of her consumptive brother's way without its becoming apparent that this was being done. On top of everything, Mrs Trollope was wracked with rheumatism: 'My shoulders are in such very severe pain that I can hardly guide my pen,' she wrote to Tom.

It seems peculiar that, in an age when consumption was so widespread, so little was yet known either of the origins of the disease, or of its cure. Mrs Trollope was always seeking fresh medical advice. Someone convinced her that a voyage to Jamaica would cure Henry, someone else that Madeira would prove beneficial. The cost of either journey was beyond their means, and Mrs Trollope fell back on an idea, suggested by yet another expert, that 'sailing about from port to port in the Mediterranean, and passing the winter months on its shores, would be better for Henry than the West Indies'. None of these pathetic projects was carried out. Instead, in September 1834, when the old friend of Mrs Trollope's already mentioned refused to accept the return of a loan, Henry pleaded that this unexpected windfall should be spent on a trip to London to consult another specialist. There two leading physicians told his mother that Henry was doomed, and that Emily was already in a precarious state. On hearing their opinion on Henry, Mrs Trollope, who had been clinging to hopeful symptoms such as the days on which her son coughed less than usual, now had to face the harsh fact that he was very slowly dying. On the afternoon following the doctor's morning visit to her Marylebone lodgings, Mrs Trollope made Tom take her for a long walk round the Regent's Park, during which she told him that his brother could not live. She went back with Henry to Bruges, where, in a last defiant bid to clutch hold of life, he took up carpentry: 'It is astonishing to see the steadiness and firmness with which he hammers,' wrote his mother to Tom. His struggle was of no avail; after great suffering, he died on the snowy morning of December 23rd, 1834, and lies buried in the Protestant cemetery at Bruges. His mother sent urgently for Tom and Cecilia: 'After all I have suffered—and it has been *very much*—I need the comfort of your presence ... Give our affectionate love to dear, dear Anthony. Tell him I will write to him in a day or two, but *cannot* do it now.' Anthony, we may notice, was not summoned to Bruges either to console his mother or to attend his brother's funeral.

In the autumn of the next year, 1835, Mrs Trollope's husband—for such had for long been his only sad claim to attention—died at the Château d'Hondt and was laid in a grave next to that of his son Henry. His death was not unexpected nor can it have been altogether unwelcome. Leaving Tom and Cecilia to wind up the household at Bruges, Mrs Trollope once more took London lodgings. She was busy over her late husband's will and trying to write novels at the same time; but all her true energies were at the moment concentrated on the health of her favourite daughter, Emily, who was sixteen and fading fast. 'She is very weak, and hardly eats anything. I am *miserably* anxious, but struggle to keep up my spirits, as I must set to work again directly,' she wrote to Tom. 'My fears are all directed to one point,—the health of my dear Emily,' she told him in another letter. 'If she is *very* ill, I much misdoubt my powers of writing. Yet in any case I shall remember, dear Tom, that you have claims on me as well as my dear girl in her sick chamber; and I will earnestly try to do my duty to both.' Her duty to her only other surviving son, Anthony, went unmentioned, and, as he would have assumed, unrecognized.

At the time of his sister Emily's fatal illness, Anthony Trollope was living in a dingy boarding-house bedroom in Marylebone, the windows of which looked out on to the back door of the borough workhouse. Through influential friends his mother had obtained for him a clerkship at the General Post Office with the annual stipend of ninety pounds a year, from which he was expected to pay for his lodgings, his food, his clothes, his laundry bills and his omnibus fares to and from St Martins-le-Grand. On this meagre salary he was also expected to keep up his 'character as a gentleman, and be happy'. For the next seven dreary years, which we will be considering in the following chapter, he was half-starved, always in debt and more thoroughly miserable than he had even been at Harrow or at Winchester. While he was living at Bruges with his family a sharp element of incongruity had thrust itself into his life for a short time, for he was offered a commission in an Austrian cavalry regiment. We do not know who made the offer, nor why it was made, although we may pretty safely suppose that this baroque project can only have emanated from his mother's fertile and fanciful brain. In order to equip himself for service under the Emperor Ferdinand I, he was obliged to learn French and German, for of both these languages he was ignorant. It was rather strangely decided that the best way of achieving this would be to work as usher at a Brussels school for English boys run by a former Harrow master, Mr Drury. This ushering interlude only lasted six weeks, for while at Mr Drury's establishment he received an official letter instructing him to go to London for an interview at the General Post Office. Before taking the Ostend boat he had passed through Bruges, where he saw his father and his brother Henry for the last time. 'A sadder household never was held together,' he writes in his autobiography:

'They were all dying; except my mother who would sit up

night after night nursing the dying ones and writing novels the while ... It is now more than forty years ago and looking back over so long a lapse of time I can tell the story, though it be the story of my own father, of my own brother and sister, almost as coldly as I have often done some scene of intended pathos in fiction ... I was then becoming alive to the blighted ambition of my father's life, and becoming alive also to the violence of the strain which my mother was enduring. But I could do nothing but go and leave them.'

In January 1836, Mrs Trollope moved out of her London lodgings and took and furnished a house on the pretty, peaceful village green of Hadley, near Barnet and on the edge of Enfield Chase. Here, a month later, Emily died; unlike her brother Henry or their father, she had been a sweet-tempered, un-demanding patient. Her death was tranquil and seemed to Anthony hallowed by a kind of beauty. 'It is all over!' he wrote to Tom at Bruges:

'Poor Emily breathed her last this morning. She died without any pain, and without a struggle. Her little strength had been gradually declining, and her breath left her without the slightest convulsion, or making any change in her features or face. Were it not for the ashy colour, I should think she was sleeping. I never saw anything more beautifully placid and composed ... It is much that it is now, than that her life should have been prolonged only to undergo the agonies which Henry suffered.'

Nearly a quarter of a century later Anthony Trollope chose as a setting for *The Bertrams* the large old countrified house which still stands close to Hadley churchyard. He called up his memories of Emily's funeral to describe that of the rich old miser, Mr George Bertram:

'The bells rang out a dirge, but they did it hardly above their breath ... And then there was a scuffling heard on the stairs—a subdued, decent undertaker's scuffling—as some hour or two before had been heard the muffled click of the hammer. Feet scuffled down the stairs, and along the passage.'

The undertaker hands out black gloves to the mourners; the local doctor does not put his gloves on, because he has an understanding with the undertaker that he can exchange them for ordinary, light-coloured gloves after the burial is completed: 'What could a country doctor do with twenty or thirty pairs of black gloves a year?' The inauspicious marriage of old George Bertram's granddaughter, Caroline Waddington, to Sir Henry Harcourt takes place in Hadley Church; yet even so

Trollope can only connect Hadley with death:

'And then the bells were rung, the merry marriage bells. I know full well the tone in which they toll when the soul is ushered to its last long rest. I have stood in that green churchyard when earth has been laid to earth, ashes to ashes, dust to dust—the ashes and the dust that were loved so well.'

Mrs Trollope and her son chose a site for Emily's grave up against the east end of the church. The headstone, with its simple, sorry facts, can be seen there, still in excellent condition, to this day.

Memories of Emily's illness and death, as well as those of her burial, remained with Anthony; they ultimately inspired the little-known, rather grim novel *Marion Fay* which was serialized in *The Graphic* in 1882, the year in which he died himself. This book, with its improbable theme of a poor Quaker girl who is sought in marriage by young Lord Hampstead, heir to the Marquess of Kingsbury, depends for its interest upon the fact that Marion, last survivor of a large consumptive family, will not marry the youth she loves because she knows that she is dying also; and die she does, of consumption, at Pegwell Bay. Marion's symptoms—the hectic cheek, the languid manner—were described by the old novelist from his own vivid recollections of his sister's death almost fifty years before.

The tenure of the house at Hadley proved as temporary as most of Mrs Trollope's varied homes—Anthony once reckoned that she had 'established and re-established herself six times in ten years'. Cecilia lived with her there, and Tom, who briefly held a job at the Birmingham Grammar School, came home for the holidays. Anthony would visit his mother whenever he could get away from London, and recalled 'how gay she made the place with little dinners, little dances and little picnics, while she herself was at work every morning long before the others left their beds'. This was the last period of his life in which Anthony saw his mother with any regularity, and even these meetings were intermittent, for in the spring of Emily's death the famous authoress was off to Vienna, to hobnob with the Austrian nobility, make bosom friends with Princess Metternich and take notes for yet another book on foreign manners, *Vienna and the Austrians*, published by Bentley in 1838, and another novel, *A Romance of Vienna*, which appeared in the same year. After little more than a year at Hadley, Mrs Trollope was back in London, furnishing a new house so that her remaining daughter Cecilia could be married from it. Cecilia had become engaged to Anthony's Post Office colleague and friend, John Tilley, who had courted her amid the June roses of the Hadley garden. When, a few years later, Cecilia herself died a long-drawn-out consumptive death, Anthony wrote to the widower, in April 1849, from Mallow: 'God bless you, my dear John—I sometimes feel that I led you into more sorrow than happiness in taking you to Hadley.'

After their marriage, Tilley was transferred on postal duties to Cumberland, where Mrs Trollope and the faithful Tom soon caught up with them. Here Fanny Trollope, unconsciously following her dead husband's example, bought land and built a large house, leaving Tom to lay out the gardens and to plant trees; but the house-warming was scarcely over before Mrs Trollope grew tired of Cumberland, sold the house and took Tom to Florence for a holiday in 1844. There at long last she settled, and there, as a very old lady, she died in 1863. Anthony Trollope and his wife went to stay at the Villino Trollope three times, and Mrs Trollope made one somewhat inauspicious visit to the Anthonys in Ireland. Otherwise Anthony Trollope's future relations with the mother he admired but had had little opportunity to love were maintained by correspondence only. Until his own marriage in 1844, at the age of twenty-nine, he faced the world unwanted and alone.

The conviction of being unwanted, which had distorted Anthony Trollope's childhood and adolescence, was not minimized by his new, independent London life. He tells us that in those days he would often curse the hour in which he was born:

'There had clung to me a feeling that I had been looked upon always as an evil, an encumbrance, a useless thing—as a creature of whom those connected with him had to be ashamed. And I feel certain now that in my young days I was so regarded. Even my few friends ... were half afraid of me. I acknowledge the weakness of a great desire to be loved,—of a strong wish to be popular with my associates. No child, no boy, no lad, no young man, had ever been less so. And I had been so poor; and so little able to bear poverty.'

He found it perfectly impossible to live in London on ninety pounds a year. His rent at the boarding-house in Northumberland Street, Marylebone, was constantly in arrear. His landlady, a good-natured but perforce practical woman, would from time to time refuse to give him any more breakfasts on credit; frequently he could not afford to buy an evening meal. He began running up small debts, and borrowing from an extortionate old money-lender who lived in an alley behind Mecklenburgh Square. So long as his mother was within reach—first at Hadley, and later in her London house—she would help to pay his debts, or rather those debts which he acknowledged to her that he owed, for naturally enough he could never bring himself to make a clean breast of all his financial transactions. But once Mrs Trollope had begun house-building in Cumberland, Anthony had no one in London to whom he could turn for sympathy or help. His uncle Henry Milton did live in the metropolis, but four miles away up the Fulham Road, so that Anthony, who had to save on omnibus fares, saw him seldom. At the General Post Office he was both idle and unpopular: 'I hated the office. I hated my work. More than all I hated my idleness.' Hinting at questionable leisure-time activities he declares that at this period of his life he was 'entirely without control,—without the influence of any decent household around me'.

Mrs Trollope, who had got Anthony his job by a piece of cursory, almost absent-minded wire-pulling, was, however, perfectly satisfied with her younger son's position and future prospects—these last being limited to a rise of twenty pounds per annum when he should have completed three years of drudgery. Writing to Tom at his Birmingham school in 1837, the year in which the late King's little niece, Princess Victoria of Kent, mounted the throne, she told him how lucky he and Anthony were to have got employment at all: 'I can give you no idea of the *multitude* of young men—gentlemen in every sense—who are pining and starving for lack of employment. It seems, sometimes, as if the knowledge of such cases reached me on purpose to make me feel grateful that my two dear sons possess the means of existence without setting off for New Holland.' She was using the term 'means of existence' in a very broad sense indeed.

Amongst Mrs Trollope's many friends and admirers was Mrs Clayton Freeling, whose father-in-law, Sir Francis Freeling, was Secretary to the Post Office in its new headquarters at St Martins-le-Grand. Much impressed by Fanny Trollope's now legendary sorrows, Mrs Freeling appealed to her father-in-law for a place in the Post Office for Anthony; the official letter summoning him from Brussels to London was the result. At this moment the Freelings worked within the Civil Service as a potent family combine. Clayton Freeling, who was Secretary at the Stamp Office, personally conducted Anthony to St Martins-le-Grand for his interview. As a candidate for a very junior clerkship, Anthony did not, of course, see Sir Francis Freeling himself, but he was interviewed by Sir Francis's elder son, Henry, who held the position of Assistant Secretary, or second-in-command to his father. There were then no competitive examinations for the Civil Service, and places were allotted by patronage—a system which Anthony Trollope always extolled, for he firmly believed that it ensured the staffing of the Post Office by gentlemen:

'As what I now write will certainly never be read till I am dead, I may dare to say what no one now does dare to say in print—though some of us whisper it occasionally into our friends' ears. There are places in life which can hardly be well filled except by 'Gentlemen'. The word is one the use of which almost subjects one to ignominy ... A man in public life could not do himself a greater injury than by saying in public that commissions in the army or navy, or berths in the Civil Service, should be given exclusively to gentlemen ... The gates of one class should be open to the other; but neither to the one class nor to the other can good be done by declaring that there are no gates, no barrier, no difference. The system of competitive examination is, I think, based on a supposition that there is no difference.'

In spite of the lack of any actual examination for his Post Office job, Anthony Trollope was asked whether he knew mathematics (he did not) and what his handwriting was like. In that lively novel *The Three Clerks*, which was published in 1857 and immensely admired by such disparate critics as Thackeray and Elizabeth Barrett Browning, we find, in Charley Tudor's means of admission to the Internal Navigation Office, an accurate account of Trollope's own entry into Post Office administration. Anthony's interview with Mr Henry Freeling seemed to himself to have been a fiasco, since, asked to display his penmanship by copying out a paragraph from *The Times* with an old quill pen, he 'at once made a series of blots and false spellings'. 'That won't do, you know,' said the elder Freeling to his brother Clayton. Pleading that young Trollope was nervous, Clayton Freeling suggested that the fair-copying might be more profitably done at home. Aided by his brother Tom, who was then in London, Anthony prepared five pages of Gibbon in his best hand, but when he took this calligraphic marvel to St Martins-le-Grand next morning he was pained to find that nobody wanted to see it, or mentioned handwriting at all. Instead he was sat down at a desk in a room containing six or seven junior clerks, and so began his Post Office career.

(ii)

Nothing in Anthony Trollope's upbringing had prepared him for the discipline and the tedium of office life and office hours. The work—that of drafting letters in reply to the public's complaints or, worse still, of copying out into folio letter-books those for dispatch—bored him intensely. From the outset of this new career he gave his superiors no satisfaction at all. He would arrive ten minutes late each morning, and muddle through his tasks in a slovenly, higgledy-piggledy way. Threats of dismissal from the Service had no effect on him whatsoever; in one instance he was sent for by Mrs Clayton Freeling herself, who begged him, with tears in her eyes, to think of his mother. Anthony did in fact think very often of his mother, but it was hardly in an inspirational way, for he would brood upon the wrongs of his childhood and become 'wretched—sometimes almost unto death'. All the same, old Sir Francis Freeling remained tolerant, and even showed him 'signs of almost affectionate kindness'. But just a year after Anthony Trollope joined the office, Sir Francis Freeling died. To his successor, Colonel Maberley, young Trollope became at once anathema. The mutual hatred between 'the Colonel-Secretary' and the junior clerk led, in the fullness of time, to Anthony Trollope's banishment to a surveyor's clerkship in a remote town upon the Shannon. It was this exile that changed his whole attitude to life, made him happy and made him a novelist.

Colonel Maberley was a large elderly gentleman who would call a junior clerk 'my good fellow', swore frequently and had many things apart from the Post Office on his mind. He was an absentee Irish landlord, and would worry about his rents; his wife was a fashionable lady novelist, a beautiful and extravagant person who was one of the very few women in London society who chose to go to see Lady Blessington and Count d'Orsay at Gore House. The Colonel would reach his office at St Martins-le-Grand at eleven o'clock and would 'announce his arrival by tearing at the bell for his breakfast'. He soon annexed the distinguished-looking old head messenger, Francis, as a species of private valet, making him pull off riding boots and bring in breakfast. His handwriting was so illegible that the only trace of his holograph amongst the official records was his signature to fair-copies made from his scrawls. Breakfast over, Anthony Trollope or one of the other clerks would perform a ceremony called 'taking in papers to the Colonel'. The duty clerk would find Colonel Maberley seated in a big easy-chair, with a handkerchief over his knees and his own private correspondence piled on top of it. It was the clerk's duty to read aloud to the Colonel any important papers or letters which had come in that morning. 'Well, my good fellow, what have you got there—very important papers, eh?' was the Colonel-Secretary's invariable greeting. 'I don't know, sir; some of them are, perhaps,' the clerk would murmur. 'Yes, yes, my good fellow; no doubt *you* think they're very important; *I* call them damned twopenny-ha'penny! Now read, my good fellow, read!' As the clerk began to read aloud, the Colonel continued to study his own letters, listening with half an ear and interjecting from time to time 'Pooh! Stuff! Upon my soul! Quite enough too!' When the clerk asked him what he was to say in reply to some applicant or critic, the Colonel became testy and scornful: 'Say to him? Tell him to go and be damned, my good fellow!' While doubtless encouraging personal initiative, this custom of the Colonel's greatly increased the burdens of his junior staff. On the whole,

Colonel Maberley was easy and good-natured, but, we are told by one of his former underlings, 'he could assume an air of *hauteur* and be uncommonly unpleasant at times'. The feckless appearance and slipshod work of young Trollope were calculated to arouse the Colonel's wrath.

Like most persons who feel themselves put upon, or harbour a grievance against life, Anthony Trollope was, both in these days and forever after, excessively touchy. On one noteworthy occasion, Anthony had opened a letter containing banknotes, and had placed it on Colonel Maberley's table. The Colonel left the room some minutes later and when he returned the letter and the banknotes had disappeared. Young Trollope was summoned and found the Colonel engaged in frantic speculation with a chief clerk as to the lost letter's fate. The Colonel turned on Trollope in a fury and shouted: 'The letter has been taken, and, by God! There has been nobody in the room but you and I.' To emphasize his point he banged his fist upon his desk. Thinking himself to be accused of stealing the banknotes, young Trollope lost his temper too, and yelled: 'Then, by God!, you have taken it!' and he, too, banged his fist in a rage; but by accident he did not hit the table, but the Colonel's portable writing desk on which sat a bottle full of ink. The ink flew up into the Colonel's face, and drenched his shirt-front. The chief clerk seized a quire of blotting paper and began to clean up Colonel Maberley who, in agony one may imagine from the ink in his eyes, hit out through the blotting paper at the chief clerk's stomach. At this juncture the Colonel's private secretary came into the room, holding the missing letter and the banknotes in his hand. This incident, though rather exceptional and not of a run-of-the-mill nature, can have done nothing to enhance Colonel Maberley's opinion of his least favourite clerk.

(iii)

Under Colonel Maberley's regime the Secretary's office was staffed by some fifty clerks, who were underpaid and sometimes overworked. There was a general feeling amongst them that their activities were not sufficiently recognized by the general public which 'never seemed to give any heed to the huge amount of ability, patience, experience and technical knowledge required to insure the prompt and proper delivery of their mails'. For these fifty men in the Secretary's Office were responsible for the whole network of post offices, postmen and postal deliveries throughout the United Kingdom, for the services linking Great Britain to her Colonies and to foreign countries, for contracts with the great steamship companies and for much more as well. The Mail-Coach Office formed another vital department at St Martins-le-Grand, and the departure of the night mails was one of the romantic sights to which eminent visitors to London were treated. Forewarning that these privileged persons would be coming on such-and-such a night was ordinarily given to the Secretary's Office and plans appropriate to their status were made to entertain them. On one occasion, however, the Queen of Saxony, attended by two German gentlemen and a lady-in-waiting, appeared in royal glass coaches at St Martins-le-Grand at midnight, as if by magic, and without notice. It happened that Anthony Trollope was doing his turn of night duty, and it fell to him, a mere junior, to show the visiting royalty round. This he considered that he had done to perfection, walking clumsily backwards up staircases and along corridors. When the Queen and her suite left, one of her gentlemen affronted Trollope by tipping him half-a-crown.

The office hours which Trollope often failed to keep strictly ran from ten in the morning until half-past four. His first biographer explains that 'the lads with whom he was thrown counted for lost every odd half-hour not spent in drinking, smoking and card-playing'. Certain of the clerks lived in the Post Office itself, and would give evening parties in their quarters, with tobacco, spirits-and-water and cards. The atmosphere of the juniors' department was distinctly larky, and even Anthony managed to relax somewhat amongst his cheerful colleagues. Hot lunches used to be sent in from neighbouring chophouses until Colonel Maberley put a stop to it, since he resented the daily invasion of 'strange persons wandering through the lobbies, balancing tin-covered dishes and bearing foaming pewter-pots'. A 'marvellously elastic' quarter of an hour for lunch outside the office was substituted. The senior, and therefore better-paid, clerks lunched at Dolly's Chophouse or at the Cathedral Hotel in St Paul's Churchyard. The impecunious juniors would go to Ball's Alamode Beef House in Butcher Hall Lane, or to one of the Crowley's Alton Ale houses which sold beer, ham sandwiches or bread and cheese 'all of the very best'. Another cheap and popular eating house was on Addle Hill near the Doctors' Commons; but on the whole lunching out in London inexpensively was very much the problem it has always been.

There seems to have been an amiable laxity about public access to the rooms in which the Post Office clerks worked, although in Trollope's case it was enemies rather than friends who would bother him at his desk. The money-lender from the little street behind Mecklenburgh Square would come and hover at his shoulder as he worked, begging him to 'be punctual' in his repayments. Sheriff's officers 'with uncanny documents' which he never understood would also surface from time to time; and on one unforgettable day of horror the mother of a country girl who wished to marry him stalked into the room wearing a huge poke bonnet and carrying a basket and asked in a penetrating voice: 'Anthony Trollope, when are you going to marry my daughter?'

Amongst the several aspects of his London youth on which Anthony Trollope does not enlarge in his autobiography is what he did with his evenings. He does tell us that 'no allurement to decent respectability' came his way and that 'there was no house in which I could habitually see a lady's face and hear a lady's voice'. He likewise mentions 'temptations of loose life' to which he would shamefacedly give way. Michael Sadleir, in his *Life* of Trollope published in 1927, takes pains to persuade us that Anthony's loose life was hardly loose at all; but, since most of his statements in the *Autobiography* are straightforward and convincing, doubts on this subject seem unmerited. Moreover, the very detailed knowledge of sleazy taprooms and of tawdry boarding-house romances which he displays in such books as *The Three Clerks* and *The Small House at Allington* must certainly have been based on direct experience. A vigorous and hefty youth, alone in London from the age of nineteen to that of twenty-six, is unlikely to have led a life of monastic virtue—and, as we now know, there was no city in Europe which could compete with Queen Victoria's London in catering for every vice. A sentence from the *Autobiography* seems relevant here: 'Could there be any escape from such dirt? I would ask myself; and I always answered that there was no escape.'

(iv)

The distinctly uneven tenor of Anthony Trollope's early years at the General Post Office was twice interrupted by illness—in 1838 and 1839. In the former year a severe influenza epidemic swept through London, and claimed Mrs Trollope, Cecilia and Anthony amongst its victims. Anthony was at this moment living briefly with his family in the London house taken for Cecilia's forthcoming marriage. Cecilia, who was always delicate, fainted on trying to stand up after two days in bed, and Anthony was so weakened that he could not lift his sister off her bedroom floor. In February of the next year, when he was back in lodgings, he developed a mysterious, unidentified and probably psychosomatic illness, from which his brother tells us that he nearly died. His doctors were prepared to give up all hope, when encouragement came from a most unexpected quarter—that of the Okey girls. These sisters, aged thirteen and fourteen, were nubile cataleptics, who were being treated by magnetism in the private hospital of Dr Elliotson, a fashionable crank who, needless to say, was one of Mrs Fanny Trollope's closer friends. The Okey girls shared one specific and ghoulish gift, that of being able to tell both acquaintances and strangers that they were shortly going to die. They used the expression 'seeing Jack' in these cases, for they would both of them see a form of ghost, which they were quite unable to describe, standing by a patient's hospital bed, or even seated next to a doomed passenger on the omnibus. The disquieting fact was that they seemed always to be right, and that the people they indicated as moribund did in truth die soon afterwards. They seem not to have been very strictly confined in Dr Elliotson's hospital, for they would roam about London looking in on invalids in the hope of 'seeing Jack'. For some reason we do not know, Anthony Trollope's lodging house behind the Marylebone workhouse was on the Okey girls' circuit; it is of course likely and even probable that Mrs Trollope, who took up spiritualism in her old age and had anyway cherished a lifelong interest in the bizarre, may have dispatched them to Anthony's sick-room. In any case they returned with the cheering news that they had indeed seen Jack at Anthony's side 'but only up to his knees'. This partial manifestation convinced the sisters that Anthony was intended to recover, and recover he did. Perhaps at the instance of the other inmates, the Okey girls were ultimately expelled from Dr Elliotson's hospital, and their further history remains unknown. Many years later a daughter of Jane Okey worked as a housemaid to the Anthony Trollopes in their house at Waltham Cross.

Both in youth and in age, Anthony Trollope was physically robust; his worst illnesses in later life consisted of pus-filled carbuncles, or anthrax, on the forehead. The pent-up energy which he later worked out upon the hunting-field, and in riding about Ireland and western England as a postal surveyor, he expended in his London youth by forming with two friends a 'Tramp Society'. This small club was governed by a set of statutes, one of these being that the three of them should never spend more than five shillings a day during their pedestrian excursions. Their marathon walks took them all over Buckinghamshire and Hertfordshire; the farthest point they ever reached on foot was Southampton. 'These were the happiest hours of my then life,' Anthony writes, '—and perhaps not the least innocent, although we were frequently in peril from the village authorities whom we outraged.' These weekend rambles formed a refreshing change from evenings spent in public houses, or in drifting sombrely about the gas-lit London streets.

During his London youth, Anthony Trollope seems to have taken a perverse and sedulous care to avoid what was then considered good society, or the company of intelligent men. In his autobiography he bemoans his lack of access to the drawing-rooms or dinner-tables of well-bred persons, but his first biographer, Thomas Sweet Escott, asserts that he always refused invitations. Sir Henry Taylor, the author of *Philip van Arte-veldt* and a permanent secretary at the Colonial Office, told Escott that he could never persuade young Trollope to come to his house, which was filled with Taylor's daughters. John Forster, the editor, friend and biographer of Dickens, made the same complaint. Mrs Clayton Freeling herself could seldom lure him to her house. Escott remarks that had he given the slightest sign of life to his numerous family connections many doors would have been opened to him, beginning with that of Sir John Trollope, the Member for the southern division of Lincolnshire and his wife, and it is to be presumed that Sir John, as head of the family, would have invited his young cousin to stay, as the Trollope parents had often stayed, at his country house, Casewick. It may have been shyness that kept Anthony away from a world which he later so much relished depicting, or it may have been such practical considerations as a lack of evening clothes, or of expensive shirts and shoes. It may also have been self-consciousness about his somewhat menial job; the secondary hero of *Marion Fay* (which was published in 1882 and deals as we have seen with the problems of a consumptive and en-amoured Quaker) holds just such a junior clerkship in the General Post Office as did Anthony in his youth. As young Lord Hampstead's closest friend, he loves and is loved by Hampstead's beautiful and aristocratic sister, Lady Frances Trafford. Lord Hampstead's stepmother, the designing Marchioness of Kingsbury, finds both her stepson's choice of a friend and her stepdaughter's love degrading, and she affects to believe that the young aspirant is on a social level with the postman who delivers the mail. Whatever the reasons for it—shyness, penury or snobbery—Anthony's sordid isolation did at least enable him to feel more sorry for himself than ever.

(v)

There are inevitable discrepancies between Anthony Trollope's own account of his drudgery at the General Post Office, and the account which he would give verbally to his friends of later years. Thus Escott declares that Trollope had told him of how on a certain day 'when there were no high jinks with his brother clerks' he began idly to delve into a heap of musty documents which proved to be old Tudor records concerning successive Masters of the Posts, who had held what was then purely a court appointment. According to Escott, Anthony is alleged to have described the effects of this haphazard discovery on himself:

'As I pieced these fragments together into a continuous story, I found myself, not for the first time, but more unmistakably than I have ever felt before, realizing that a Post Office clerk's career might be one of profit to himself as well as of usefulness to his fellow creatures in all their concerns and interests, whether as citizens or as family breadwinners. From what I saw had been done in the past, I mentally constructed a scheme of possibilities for the future.'

Escott tells us that Anthony 'gradually became conscious of associations with the national life and movement' and anxious to contribute his own mite of effort to improving the postal services of the United Kingdom. This is certainly a very different attitude to the Post Office from that which Trollope gives us in his own life story, and at one point in Escott's reminiscences he really does tax our credulity too far: 'A romantic instinct had already invested the whole system which gave him employment with a poetry of its own.'

As a matter of fact, the period of its history in which Trollope first set foot inside the General Post Office was an enterprising and, potentially, an exciting one. The new building at St Martins-le-Grand was only five years finished when he took up his job there, and a vast reorganization of the postal services had been undertaken by Sir Francis Freeling at the instigation of the then Postmaster-General, the Duke of Richmond. Thirty-nine specific reforms were tabulated and carried out, recasting the whole system of mail packets and making 'deliveries from foreign parts as safe as those within the United Kingdom'. The new railways which were beginning to fan out across the face of England were also taken into account as a speedy means of getting mail out to the cities and country towns, although it was not until 1854 that the Mail-Coach Office became obsolete and was abolished.

When Anthony Trollope had worked at St Martins-le-Grand for seven years, always, he tells us, hating his position there, he unexpectedly found 'a way of escape'. Amongst the most recent administrative reforms was the creation of a new body of officers called surveyors' clerks. There were then seven surveyors in England, two in Scotland and three in Ireland. The new clerks were destined to be aides-de-camp to the surveyors, and to 'travel about the country under the surveyor's orders'. The terms of employment were distinctly good: a salary of one hundred pounds a year, with an additional fifteen shillings a day for every day spent away from the surveyor's base and sixpence for every mile travelled on postal business. This was said to tot up to the considerable aggregate of four hundred pounds a year. Anthony and his fellow-clerks used half-heartedly to discuss the possibility of themselves taking up such clerkships, but they came to the general conclusion that these posts were derogatory. It was rumoured in St Martins-le-Grand that the first surveyor to receive a clerk had sent him out to get his beer, and that another had ordered his clerk to take his dirty linen to the laundry. In the end no one from the General Post Office volunteered, and all the jobs were filled by outsiders. In August 1841, however, a report from Ireland reached the office, and was, by chance, allotted to Anthony to open and read. It was a complaint from the Post Office surveyor at Banagher in the King's County complaining that his new clerk was 'absurdly incapable', and asking for a replacement. At that moment Anthony Trollope was up to his ears in debt, and still engaged in squabbling with—and contradicting—the good old Colonel-Secretary. He also had 'a full conviction that my life was taking me downwards to the lowest depths'. To Colonel Maberley's delight Trollope volunteered for the vacant job. The Colonel expressed an enthusiastic agreement. Such friends as Trollope had shook their heads over this decision; Mrs Trollope and Tom were abroad and 'were not consulted; did not even know my intention in time to protest against it'. Borrowing two hundred pounds from 'a dear old cousin, our family lawyer', Anthony Trollope set off by sea to Dublin. He landed in Ireland on September 15th, 1841. 'This,' he remarks, 'was the first good fortune of my life.'

On his first evening in Ireland Anthony Trollope at once felt that elation which the sense of being utterly isolated in a foreign country will often bring. He took a room for the night in a musty Dublin hotel, ordered his 'tea', and after the meal indulged himself with whiskey punch. 'There was an excitement in this,' he recalled, 'but when the punch was gone I was very dull. It seemed so strange to be in a country in which there was not a single individual whom I had ever spoken to or ever seen.' As he sat there with his empty glass before him, he began to find his immediate prospects daunting, for he was aware that his new job would primarily involve inspecting and helping to balance rural postmasters' accounts. Now at Harrow, Sunbury and Winchester he had never been taught the multiplication tables or been made to do a simple sum in long division. Of Banagher, his future home and headquarters, he knew nothing save its location on the map and that it had once been conquered by Oliver Cromwell. The next morning brought him no encouragement, for, on calling upon the Secretary of the Irish Post Office, he learned to his chagrin that he was still within reach of the long arm of Colonel Maberley, who had sent a devastating private report to Dublin. This document described Anthony Trollope as 'worthless' and predicted that sooner or later he would have to be sacked. The lenient Irish Secretary, however, told the young man before him that he proposed to judge him on his own merits: 'From that time to the day on which I left the service, I never heard a word of censure ... Before the year was over, I had acquired the character of a thoroughly good public servant.' The benign influence of Irish life upon Anthony Trollope was immediate. His sense of being unpopular, insecure and degraded faded away as speedily as the white morning mists along the River Shannon. 'From the day on which I set foot in Ireland all these evils went away from me,' he writes. 'Since that time who has had a happier life than mine?'

Trollope's knowledge of Ireland, before he went to live there, was as sketchy as his knowledge of Banagher itself. 'Ireland,' he wrote in a short story published in 1867, 'is not very well known now to all Englishmen, but is better known than it was in those days.' He had supposed Ireland to be a rattling country 'flowing with fun and whiskey', unconventional and loud with brawls.

What he found there was very different to these roseate previsions. The Irish peasantry was and had always been the poorest in Europe; their condition was described by a German contemporary of Trollope's as worse than 'the state of the Negro in his chains' and worse than that of the Letts in Livonia. 'There never was a country in which poverty existed to the extent it exists in Ireland,' wrote the first Duke of Wellington, himself a native of County Meath. The country people lived in windowless mud cabins; furniture such as beds, tables and chairs was the rarest of luxuries. The staple food of the Irish and their pigs was the potato, upon which, as the Famine soon showed, their very survival most unequivocally depended. They cherished a bitter hostility towards all British officials—of whom Trollope was now one—and towards the British soldiers who were stationed in barracks all over the country.

At the period in which Anthony Trollope began his Irish life the number of British troops in Ireland was larger than the whole British garrison of India. During an occupation of seven hundred years the Irish had never succumbed to their oppressors and they had never been assimilated. Ireland remained an alien country under a foreigner's rule. Yet in spite of their hopeless circumstances the innate gaiety of the Irish was never, until the Famine, vanquished. They sang and danced, played the fiddle, related old legends and forever indulged in what was once called the chief industry of Ireland—talk. There was even an unexpected *dolce far niente* about Irish peasant life. Gingerly venturing for the first time into the wild and lawless Province of Connaught beyond the Banagher bridge, Trollope was amazed to find that able-bodied men in the Galway towns and villages were to be seen 'at all hours of the day' standing about the streets talking, their knee-breeches unbuttoned, their stockings rolled down over their brogues and wearing swallow-tail coats of frieze. 'Nor,' he added, 'though thus idle, did they seem to suffer any of the distress of poverty, There were plenty of beggars, no doubt ... but it never struck me that there was much distress in those days. The earth gave forth its potatoes freely, and neither man nor pig wanted more.' He soon discovered that the Irish were good-humoured and clever—'the working classes very much more intelligent than those in England'. They were not, as they were reputed to be, spendthrifts, but were economical, hospitable and kind. Their chief defects, he judged, were that they could switch to being very perverse and very irrational, and that they were 'but little bound by the love of truth'.

Although very much smaller than the town of Birr, which is only eight miles away, Banagher had all the same been chosen as the base for a Postal Surveyorship, probably because its position on the Shannon offered easy access by canal boat to Dublin or to Limerick. The town was ancient and had witnessed much fighting in the Cromwellian, the Williamite and the far earlier inter-clan wars, for, besides having a very substantial stone bridge across the Shannon, Banagher was also built at one of the river's few fords, and lay on the direct highway from Leinster and Munster into the ominous lands of Connaught. The town had a long history of loyalty to the house of Stuart. Charles I had granted Banagher rents for the upkeep of a Royal Free School and by another charter he had empowered them to hold the famous Banagher Great Fair, at which everything from cattle and sheep to boots and basket chairs was on sale. This Fair, the greatest in all the Irish Midlands, began on September 15th, and lasted four days. The line of horses tethered on each side of Banagher Main Street stretched from the Shannon river bridge to the crossroads two and a half miles outside the town known as Tailor's Cross. Anthony Trollope, who would have left Dublin by the canal boat to Shannon Harbour on September 16th, 1841, must thus have had a festive, gay first impression of his new home. Owing to his height he found the small canal-boats cramping, and complained that he could not stretch his legs.

The month of September in Banagher, and all along the Shannon banks, is visually a glorious one, with golden autumn mornings, the low sun making long shadows of the houses in the street. At dusk the whole river reflects the varied sunsets as the days draw in—effects of palest pink, for instance, striped by cloudy lines of green, or an horizon aflame with scarlet and orange light.

Banagher, in the last years before famine and pestilence scoured the land, was at its peak of prosperity, a bustling, busy little place which even the presence of strong contingents of British redcoats in the barracks by the bridge could not anglicize in any way. It had only begun to flourish with the construction of the Grand Canal, which, in the eighteenth century, opened up the Shannon to boats from Dublin. Besides its annual Great Fair, Banagher had a weekly corn-market which was the biggest in the country, and could also boast a distillery, a brewery, two tan-yards, a malt-house and corn mills. There were likewise home industries such as weaving, dyeing and coopering. The women of Banagher were so noted for their skill at the loom that youths from neighbouring counties would make a special trip thither to choose a wife. In 1846, the first year of the Famine, the town was estimated to have a population of three thousand souls. Yet, in Trollope's words, Banagher then seemed 'little more than a village'. It retains a quality of friendly village life to this day and can have changed little since Trollope's time, save that its population has declined to eleven hundred. Underfoot there are now no cobblestones with grass growing up between them, and there are no longer the old, smoky and smelly paraffin lamps which used to be hung out along the main street after dark. This long main street, in fact, can hardly have changed at all. It slopes downwards to the bridge over the Shannon. At the top of the incline stand two spired churches, Roman Catholic and Church of Ireland, and the vicarage in which Charlotte Brontë's widower used to live. Up at that end also is the old post office, evidently in much the same condition that it has always been, and next to this is a small bungalow which Anthony Trollope and his superior used for transacting business. Along this main street, as you walk down to the river, there are shops, bars and private houses—some of the last of very considerable size, dignity and architectural interest. Just outside the town stand the ruins of Cuba Court, a fine example of an Irish country-house of the mid-eighteenth century in the manner of the Dublin architect Pierce. In Trollope's day this building, which contained two circular rooms, housed the Royal School, and an avenue of lime trees led to the front door. Like too many of Ireland's great houses, Cuba Court is now being slowly but deliberately demolished. The lime trees have long been hacked down.

At the lower end of Banagher are some more big houses, one of them now a hotel. All such houses in small Irish towns have an unexpected and very long garden (or 'yard'), at the back; one of those in this lower region of Banagher has a great arched carriage gateway and, behind it, four acres of orchards and fields. The bridge itself, a handsome structure of seven stone spans, replaces an earlier bridge which was demolished while Trollope was first in Banagher, the new bridge being built by the Commissioners for the Improvement of Navigation on the Shannon and opened in 1843. In the very centre of the bridge you pass from County Offaly into Galway or, if you prefer, from the province of Leinster into that of Connaught. At the Banagher end of the bridge are the ruins of the former British barracks, and the picturesque Old Maltings—great grey-brown warehouses with reddish roofs standing upon the river's brink. On the Connaught side is a defensive fort of uncertain date, and a Martello tower. The bridge at Banagher affords a splendid view over the level reaches of the river, which here flows glassily between a countryside as flat as that in some Dutch picture. In winter-time the flooded river spreads across these meadows to create an inland sea. In spring and early summer kingcups bloom amongst the sedge and reeds along the Shannon's bank, wild yellow irises abound and cowslips also. In early summer, too, plumes of mauve and purple lilacs hang over the white walls of the yards of Banagher, and the whole countryside beyond the town displays brilliant variations of the 'forty shades of green'.

In Banagher Anthony Trollope established himself in a hotel —a long, plaster-fronted, roomy house a few hundred yards from the bridge over the Shannon. As is the case with several other houses in Banagher, and also in the county capital of Tullamore and in nearby Ballinasloe, the front door and hallway of the hotel jutted out on to the cobbled street, and had a pretty fanlight over it. It is at the other end of the town to the uphill post office but only a matter of minutes on foot. Next to the post office is the two-roomed bungalow, again with a fanlight over its door, which was used by the Postal Surveyor and his new deputy as their working headquarters.* The Surveyor whom Anthony was to serve lived with his wife and her sister in another house down the street. This family group were waited on by a slatternly little Irish girl who wore no shoes or stockings —a fact which shocked Tom Trollope when he called on his brother's employer during a short holiday visit to Banagher. Tom found that Anthony stood high in the Surveyor's good graces, since he was working so hard that there was little left for his superior officer to do. The Surveyor, while not himself a hunting man, kept the local pack of hounds in kennels (still to be seen today) on Church Lane, just opposite the grave hummocks of the Old Burying Ground and its little roofless chapel. It was through the presence of this pack of hounds in the King's County that Anthony Trollope first developed his lifelong passion for fox-hunting. He immediately bought an expensive hunter and kept this, and the horse he used for his

* This bungalow, which now belongs to an ex-Garda, Mr Ivory, is erroneously considered to have been the residence of Trollope himself.

postal journeys, in stables at the back of his hotel. He also obtained the services of a young groom, Barney MacIntyre. Barney became a permanent feature of Anthony Trollope's establishments, both in Ireland and, later on, in England too. 'I do not know that I ought not to feel that I owe more to him than to any one else for the success I have had,' Anthony wrote in his *Autobiography*. This arcane supposition he clarified by explaining that it was to Barney MacIntyre, during his master's later years of industrious success, that there fell the duty of calling him early every morning with coffee and bread and butter, so that the novelist could be at work at his desk, fully dressed, at five-thirty. Trollope relates that neither he nor Barney—by then changed by the lapse of years into 'an old groom'—ever allowed themselves 'any mercy' as to rising at this unholy hour. Trollope paid MacIntyre an extra five pounds a year for this additional work: 'During all those years at Waltham Cross he was never once late with the coffee.' Annie Thackeray, who would sometimes stay at the house at Waltham Cross in which Anthony Trollope and his family lived from 1859 to 1871, commented in her journal on the noise which signalled this spartan beginning of her host's day: 'I can also remember in the bitter cold dark morning hearing Mr Trollope called at four o'clock. He told me he gave his man half a crown every time he (Mr Trollope) *didn't* get up! 'The labourer is worthy of his hire,' said Mr Trollope in his deep cheerful lispy voice.' It would seem likely that, when the Trollopes moved into a London house and left Waltham Cross in 1871, Barney returned to Ireland. But in January 1882, the year of his old friend and employer's death, Barney was once more summoned, for the Trollopes were again living in the English countryside, this time at Harting near Petersfield. 'Barney has turned up again as fresh as paint,' Anthony wrote to his eldest son. 'We wrote to the Protestant parson, and he says he saw him walking about Banagher every day,—only just a little the worse for wear.' In Banagher the MacIntyre family are now extinct.

(ii)

Anthony Trollope soon twigged that his superior officer at Banagher did not much care for his clerk's owning a hunter, but 'could not well complain'. By that winter the newcomer from London (whose 'upright and elastic' figure at this period of his life, and indeed until he was overtaken by a bulky, early middle age, showed 'to special advantage in the saddle') had become a welcome character on the hunting fields of Galway and the King's County. For an alien in the West of Ireland, hunting was the quickest and the easiest way to ingratiate oneself with the local gentry and the impoverished yeomen farmers who regularly attended meets. In a short story, *The O'Conors of Castle Conor*, which he based on a personal experience of his own, Trollope relates how, a stranger at a meet in County Mayo, he was immediately asked to come over to stay at Castle Conor that very night for a dance which the family were giving. Even in the more hieratic world of fox-hunting in Victorian England there was then, at meets, a sense of *camaraderie* and of sham equality amongst fox-hunting folk which, though it would certainly not be extended to other humdrum days of the week, was recognized by social aspirants as useful. At Waddesdon in the Vale of Aylesbury, for example, Baron Ferdinand de Rothschild kept a famous pack of hounds and a string of hunters, thus making his mark with reclusive Buckinghamshire county families, who tended in general to ignore foreigners and millionaires alike.

In a great many of Trollope's novels there is much evidence of the social possibilities of hunting, as well as of the sheer zest of pursuing the fox on horseback. Confessing to a passion for the writing of hunting scenes, he declares, in his *Autobiography*, that he had always felt himself 'deprived of a legitimate joy when the nature of the tale has not allowed me a hunting chapter'. He says that on no other subject had he written 'with such delight as that on hunting. I have dragged it into many novels—into too many no doubt.' For those who are not themselves devotees of blood sports, the wealth of hunting scenes, of stable lore, of foxy talk over the port when the ladies have withdrawn, can form a strong incentive to skip the next sixty pages and get on with the story. Yet, if persevered with, these chapters are found to contain some of the freshest and happiest episodes in the whole corpus of the Trollope novels. Through such passages there seems to blow the clean sweet air of an English October morning, or the crisp chill of a December twilight glimmering over the unspoiled beauty of English fields, bare hedgerows and skeletal winter wood and copse. It is in these passages that Anthony Trollope's sometimes cumbrous style of descriptive prose takes wing and displays a rural poetry all its own. It is also a tactical mistake to scurry through or skip the hunting scenes, for you may thereby miss an essential link in the story itself; it is with a truly amazing ingenuity that, determined to indulge himself in a hunting passage, Trollope manages to entangle therein the loves, the hatreds, the snobberies and the lost chances of some of his main characters. Much more than the mere chasing of foxes, he indicates, could happen to you on the hunting-field. It might help you, as it helped Phineas Finn, to take a header into a muddy ditch just in front of Madame Max Goesler on her elegant little horse Dandolo. Madame Max can thus naturally renew her earlier intimacy with Phineas by fussing over him as they amble in solitude along the leafless rides of Broughton Spinnies. In *Orley Farm* the ugly young lawyer Felix Graham has the unheard-of good luck to smash his bones badly while out hunting as a Christmas guest of Sir John and Lady Staveley at Noningsby—for Felix, who is in a state of undeclared love with their nineteen-year-old daughter Madeline, has to remain a bed-ridden invalid in her parents' country house for many weeks. In *The American Senator* Arabella Trefoil assumes a false zeal for hunting in order to beguile into a marriage snare the rich and handsome sporting peer, Lord Rufford of Rufford Park. Even Lady Eustace, whose attempts at riding to hounds are both timorous and insincere, buys a pair of expensive hunters and briefly frequents an Ayrshire hunt to impress her guests at Portray Castle, and in particular her 'corsair' Lord George de Bruce Carruthers. In *The American Senator* Trollope does not actually go so far as to allege that a good run with the hounds offers the perfect opportunity for 'real lovemaking', yet he explains that

'very much of preliminary conversation may be done [in the hunting-field] in a pleasant way, and intimacies may be formed. But, [he continues, referring to Lord Rufford and Miss Trefoil] when lovers have already walked with their arms round each other in a wood, riding together may be very pleasant, but can hardly be ecstatic. Lord Rufford might, indeed, have asked her to be Lady R. while they were breaking up the first fox, or as they loitered about in the bog wood;—but she did not expect that. There was no moment during the day's sport in which she had a right to tell herself that he was misbehaving because he did not so ask her.'

Besides 'dragging' hunting scenes into so many of his novels, Anthony Trollope published, in the *Pall Mall Gazette* for 1865, a set of eight *Hunting Sketches*. These brief essays are light-hearted if desultory, and are classified under such sub-titles as *The Man Who Hunts and Doesn't Like It, The Lady Who Rides to Hounds, The Man Who Hunts and Never Jumps* or

The Hunting Parson. In the second of these just listed, he attacks ignorant people who do not hunt for thinking hunting 'wicked', and in particular for thinking it an inappropriate pastime for women. These persons connect the hunting-field with flirtation, but this is a misjudgment which Trollope staunchly rejects: 'As girls are brought up among us now-a-days, they may all flirt, if they have a mind to do so; and opportunities for flirting are much better and much more commodious in the ballroom, in the drawing-room or in the park, than they are on the hunting-field.' He also rejects the assumption that hunting ladies or hunting girls are led into 'fast habits,—to ways and thoughts which are of the horse horsey,—and of the stable, strongly tinged with the rack and the manger'. He said that he himself very much liked to see a few ladies in the field—so long as they were not imperious and could look after themselves without distracting their male companions, or making tiresome demands upon the gentlemen's time. In his day there was indeed an elegance about hunting ladies, seated side-saddle as they cantered after the hounds, the long veils wreathed round their small top-hats floating out behind them as they rode.

On his own admission, and on the testimony of many of his friends, we know that hunting, together with writing novels and working at his new, peripatetic form of postal job, became one of the three dominating passions of Anthony Trollope's life:

'I have ever since [his Banagher days] been constant to the sport, having learned to love it with an affection which I cannot myself fathom or understand. Surely no man has ever laboured at it as I have done, or hunted under such drawbacks as to distances, money and natural disadvantages ... Nor have I ever been in truth a good horseman ... Nothing has ever been allowed to stand in the way of hunting—neither the writing of books, nor the work of the Post Office, nor other pleasures.'

To us, with our knowledge of his family and of his wretched schoolboy life, of his sense of being unwanted and of having been banished to a nether world of contempt, it may seem a most unlikely passion for Anthony to have developed. But is it not probable that in the concentrated joviality of the hunting-field he first found the uncarping acceptance and uncritical recognition for which he had yearned from childhood? Although we shall presently revert to his sturdy prowess on the hunting-field, we had now best consider the nature and the lenient routine of his Post Office work in the West of Ireland. While making his rounds through the Irish country lanes on horseback, he was all the time exercising those uncanny powers of observation, and that eagle eye for detail which he put to fine use in his first and second novels—both of them, as we know, with West of Ireland themes. An intelligent Dublin lady, who knew Anthony Trollope well in these earliest Irish days, used reminiscently to say that 'his close looking into the commonest objects of daily life always reminded her of a woman in a shop examining the materials for a new dress'.

(iii)

'It was altogether a very jolly life that I led in Ireland'—such was old Anthony Trollope's verdict as he peered back through his gold-rimmed spectacles across the gulf of more than thirty years. For the harassed postmasters or postmistresses of townships and villages within the Banagher Surveyor's far-flung postal district, Mr Deputy-Surveyor Trollope's unheralded visitations cannot have been jolly at all. These untutored holders of the local Post Office monopoly were usually the owners of some small general-goods shop, in the cluttered dim back-room of which the postal cage and counter lurked. In those days the system by which such rural post offices were supposed to function involved the filling in of many intricate printed forms. During his first fortnight in Banagher, Trollope, who had been in this respect so daunted by his own ignorance of simple mathematics and accountancy, was trying to learn the ropes of his new job. But in his third week in Banagher luck came his way. He was sent down to a little town in the far west of County Galway 'to balance a defaulting postmaster's accounts, find out how much he owed, and report upon his capacity to pay'. He had never balanced an account in his life, and he did not understand the Post Office forms. On this Galway assignment he determined to learn it all at one fell swoop and he 'went to work ... and made that defaulting postmaster teach me the use of those forms'. Once it had been explained to him, he found no difficulty in balancing the account. Back in Banagher he reported that the Galway defaulter was totally unable to pay his debt. 'Of course he was dismissed,' Trollope tells us in his unattractive way, '—but he had been a very useful man to me. I never had any further difficulty in the matter.'

Ebullient in the Irish hunting-field, Anthony, in his official capacity in the Banagher postal district, 'combined much of youthful crudity with civilian stiffness'. Escott, who must have been told this by King's County people old enough to remember the new Deputy-Surveyor's regime, thought that Trollope had unconsciously copied the manner of his colleagues at St Martins-le-Grand and that, as the Irish years rolled by, he had superimposed on this stiff groundwork the peremptory, sharp and severe official manner of his own. These gruff, rebarbative exercises in authority Escott thought had ended by becoming 'part of the man himself', but in reality 'veiled a more than feminine self-consciousness'. Certainly Trollope's manner to his underlings was aggressive and offhand, nor can the western Irish, famous then as now for their kindness and enduring charm, have relished what Trollope's friends used to call his 'abrupt bow-wow way' of addressing them.

We are more or less able to reconstruct the effect on the inhabitants of King's County, or Galway, or the Meaths or Clare, of Anthony Trollope's habit of cantering hither and thither on horseback, checking harshly on letter delivery systems, answering complaints or catching out defaulting postmasters, but we do not really know what he looked like at this time—his late twenties. All his life he hated photographs: 'I do not like photographs, and dislike my own worse than all others', he once wrote to a fan, and it is interesting to observe in passing that the *carte-de-visite* photograph—that ubiquitous and classless expression of mid-Victorian intimacies—plays hardly any part in his own novels. Mr Gager, a plain-clothes detective in charge of the police investigations into the real and final theft of Lady Eustace's diamonds, has kept for himself the photograph of a pretty girl which he found on the person of her ladyship's tall footman, searched after the alleged burglary at Carlisle. This appealing photo is of Lady Eustace's lady's-maid, Patience, who has left her service with suspect speed but is tracked down by Gager to a Ramsgate inn; he there persuades her to marry him and turn Queen's evidence. But this is almost a single instance of a cherished photograph in the Trollope novels—and even this carries with it the implication that sentimentality over photos is confined to the lower orders and carries a below-stairs stigma. The only established case of an exchange of photographs between people who should have known better is in *Phineas Finn*, that of the Duke of Omnium and Madame Max Goesler in the early stages of their acquaintanceship, when the old Duke is already falling in love:

'After a time, the photograph was brought forth from his Grace's pocket. That bringing out and giving of photographs, with the demand for counter photographs, is the most absurd practice of the day ... Words were spoken that were very absurd. Madame Goesler protested that the Duke's photograph was more to her than the photographs of all the world beside; and the Duke declared that he would carry the lady's picture next to his heart—I am afraid he said for ever and ever. Then he took her hand and pressed it, and was conscious that for a man over seventy years of age he did that kind of thing very well.'

In any case, to revert to Trollope's physical appearance as he strode down Banagher's grey, cobbled main street, we are really unable to know, at this distance of time, what he looked like as a young man. The discoveries of Fox Talbot and Daguerre, which in the mid-1840s suddenly bloomed upon a startled European public, must have reached Dublin, but surely not the King's County, before Anthony finally left Ireland in 1859. We simply know about that elastic figure, that burly presence, those sharp yet near-sighted blue eyes, his chestnut-coloured hair and blonde beard.* Escott uses the old-fashioned phrase 'he stood six feet high in his socks', and adds that Trollope's complexion was fresh. The same writer reminds us that 'during the earlier years of his long sojourn amongst them, the Irish classes and masses knew Trollope, not as a writer, but as the impersonation of the severest officialism'.

At some unspecified date, most probably in 1842 or 1843, when Anthony had been visiting his family in Cumberland, his brother Tom came back with him to stay awhile in Banagher. From the moment of landing upon the shores of Ireland, Tom was much struck by the marked contrasts between England and Ireland. The sense of entering a foreign country, which recalled his sensations on first visiting France, remained with him throughout his stay in Banagher and his walking tour with Anthony in Connemara. At Penrith the Trollopes had all found

* Some confusion has in the past arisen as to the colour of Anthony Trollope's eyes, hair and beard. Escott, who knew him well and published the first biography of Anthony in 1913, describes his eyes as bright blue. The Spanish consul in Jamaica also called the eyes blue, and the beard chestnut-colour. Sadleir, following an account by Julian Hawthorne, states in *Trollope, A Commentary* (Constable, London, 1927) that the eyes were black, and the beard black as well. Samuel Laurence's sketch (1864) shows the eyes to be light and clear, as does the O'Neill portrait in the Garrick Club. A member of the Garrick has left on record the fact that Trollope's beard was 'blonde', giving him the look of a German physician.

their ugly duckling, Anthony, 'a very different man from what he had been in London'. In Banagher Tom went to call on the Surveyor, and, as we have seen, was shocked that the door should have been opened for him by a ragged, shoeless, bare-legged brat. He liked the Surveyor and found that his brother 'stood high in his good graces by virtue of simply having taken the whole work and affairs of the postal district on his own shoulders. The rejected of St Martins-le-Grand was already a very valuable and capable officer.' Anthony regaled Tom with excellent stories of his official experiences in Ireland—so much so that Tom said afterwards that he felt himself 'tolerably competent to write a volume of *Memoirs of a Post Office Surveyor*'. Tom, perhaps unfortunately for us, relates only one of these anecdotes, but this shows Anthony in a triumphant and a vengeful mood. He had recently been visiting a certain postmaster in the south-west, and, during his interview, had observed that the man carefully locked a large desk in his office. Two days later there came from Dublin an urgent inquiry about a lost letter of some value. This inquiry reached the Banagher Surveyor late at night, who handed it on to Trollope for action; but there was no way of getting transport to the place in question before the next morning. Anthony, however, leaped on to his horse and rode all the way out there, hammering on the post-office door in the small hours. He stamped straight into the house and shouted: 'Open that desk!' Told that the key had been lost some time since, he said nothing—but stepping up to the desk smashed it open with one hefty kick. Needless to say the missing letter and money were found in it. These rough and ready methods evidently paid off, but they can scarcely have been found endearing. It is sad to have to conclude that, however much Trollope, unlike his own countrymen, admired and esteemed the Irish people, his attitude towards them did not in practice differ so very much from that of the arrogant contingents of British troops and their officers posted in so many Irish towns, including those in the barracks near the bridge in Banagher itself.

As we all know well, many people who, in childhood and youth, especially resent some unpleasing trait of a parent's character themselves develop a somewhat similar trait as they themselves grow older. We have seen how much Anthony, his mother and his brothers—and his sisters as well—had suffered from old Mr Trollope's insensate outbursts of rage. This capacity for quick anger was inherited, although in a sane rather than a demented manner, by Anthony Trollope himself. In Ireland he gave it full rein. Throughout their seven centuries of military and civil occupation of Ireland, English administrators, clerics, landowners and military men had found the subject race exasperating to deal with, for, like the Negro slaves in the West Indies, the captive Irish had over the generations perfected a form of silent resistance to their conquerors. This ranged from pretending not to understand orders given in English to the exasperating obstructionist tactic of sending exhausted and rain-drenched British strangers in the wrong direction to that in which they wished to go, and of minimizing vast distances by kindly explaining that some remote town was but three or four miles off. These were subversive activities with which a short-tempered English official such as Mr Deputy-Surveyor Trollope could not readily sympathize. Nor was he accustomed to the sharing of public-house bedrooms in wayside hamlets, which was merely the result of a chronic shortage of space, itself an out-crop of the poverty and squalor in which the Irish peasants were obliged to live.

In another Irish short story, *Father Giles of Ballymoy*, which, like *The O'Conors*, was based on his own experience, Trollope, writing in the first person as 'Mr Green', relates how, arriving after dark at this village, he put up at a so-called inn. On going to bed he saw that in the room allotted to him there were two beds, but thought nothing of it. Awakened by a noise in the night, he saw by the light of a candle a heavy, elderly person getting ready for bed, and coolly brushing his coat with Trollope's own clothes-brush. Leaping out of bed in a fury, he accosted the intruder and, wrenching open the bedroom door, slung him head first out. It unluckily happened that the doorway gave straight onto a steep ladder-like flight of stairs. Anthony's physical violence was such that the old man fell headlong down the stairs and lay as though dead on the floor below. Roused by the din, the people of the inn shrieked out that the Englishman had killed Father Giles, the parish priest. A dangerously angry crowd collected. Then a British revenue officer appeared and, to Trollope's amazement, marched him off to the police-station cell for the night. Next morning his furious expostulations were quelled by this officer, who told him that had he not taken him into safe custody, Mr Trollope might well have been lynched by Father Giles's infuriated flock. He also learned that the bedroom was in fact Father Giles's own bedroom, and that he had courteously allowed Trollope to use the spare bed. It says much for Anthony, whose fits of temper, though very violent while they lasted, seldom endured, that he apologized to the old priest, who was badly bruised, made friends with him, and, in after years, often had him over to stay with himself and his family when they were living at Waltham Cross. Anthony Trollope's bow-wow bark was always worse than his bite.

(iv)

In these years before the Great Famine, there were no railways at all in Ireland. They were only introduced some years later, as yet another English palliative for Ireland's ills. The jaunting car was one of the few means of transport between small villages and little towns. On this vehicle, which was open to all weathers, the passengers sat back to back the whole length of it, with their feet dangling over the edge, their legs protected by a soiled canvas 'apron' in wet weather. Trollope records how uncomfortable he had been riding in County Cavan (which was actually outside his own postal district) on a jaunting car in a snow-storm at night. Political candidates in Irish parliamentary elections depended very largely on hired jaunting cars to bring the people from outlying districts to the polling stations. This was a costly system, and one of the two Members elected for the King's County in 1859 lost his seat at the next election because of the unpaid bills he already owed to the men who hired out the local jaunting cars. The rivers such as the Shannon—which as we may remember was now linked to Dublin by the new Canal—were, of course, much used both for passengers and for freight. In a chapter of his second Irish novel *The Kellys and the O'Kellys* (published in 1848) Trollope gives a memorable account of a twenty-hour journey on board one of these 'floating prisons'—in this case the canal boat from Dublin to the town of Ballinasloe in County Galway, well-known for its big sheep market. He describes how impossible it was for anyone on board 'to occupy or amuse' his mind. The passage is worth quoting at some length, not only for its relevance here, but because it exemplifies Trollope's outstanding and almost journalistic gift for direct description—a gift which makes his later travel-book *The West Indies and the Spanish Main* (1859) one of the best ever written in that peculiarly English genre. He declares 'the *vis inertiae* of patient endurance' as 'the only weapon of any use in attempting to overcome the lengthened ennui of this most tedious transit' and continues:

'Reading is out of the question. I have tried it myself and seen others try it, but in vain. The sense of the motion, almost imperceptible but still perceptible; the noises above you; the smells around you; the diversified crowd of which you are a part; at one moment the heat this crowd creates; at the next the draught which a window just opened behind your ears lets in on you; the fumes of punch; the snores of the man under the table; the noisy anger of his neighbour who reviles the attendant sylph; the would-be witticisms of a third, who makes continual amorous overtures to the same over-tasked damsel, notwithstanding the publicity of his situation; the loud complaint of the old lady near the door, who cannot obtain the gratuitous kindness of a glass of water; and the baby-soothing lullabies of the young one, who is suckling her infant under your elbow. These things alike prevent one from reading, sleeping or thinking. All one can do is wait till the long night gradually wears itself away, and reflect that, *Time and the hour run through the longest day* ... I believe the misery of the canal-boat chiefly consists in a preconcieved and erroneous idea of its capabilities. One prepares oneself for occupation—an attempt is made to achieve actual comfort—and both end in disappointment; the limbs become weary with endeavouring to fix themselves in a position of repose, and the mind fatigued more by the search after, than the want of, occupation.'

Such was the effect of a canal-boat journey on a sensitive mind. Trollope explains however that his ambitious young hero Martin Kelly, son of the widow Kelly who has a shop in Dunmore, neither resented nor even noticed these conditions.

'He made great play at the eternal half-boiled leg of mutton, floating in a bloody sea of grease, which always comes on the table three hours after the departure from Porto Bello. He, and others equally gifted ... swallowed huge collops of the raw animal and vast heaps of yellow turnips, till the pity with which a stranger would at first be inclined to contemplate the consumer of such unsavoury food, is transferred to the victim who has to provide the meal at two shillings a head ... [Martin] ate out his money with the true persevering prudence of a Connaught man, who firmly determines not to be done. He was equally diligent at breakfast; and, at last, reached Ballinasloe at ten o'clock the morning after he had left Dublin, in a flourishing condition. From thence he travelled by Bianconi's car, as far as Tuam, and when there he went at once to the hotel, to get a hack car to take him home to Dunmore.'

Apart from these two modes of travelling, the jaunting car for the insignificant smaller places, the river-traffic for the towns like Banagher or Athlone, and for such cities as Limerick, there was, however, one popular and comparatively speedy method of road transport between all the more important towns of the south and west: Bianconi's 'long-cars' one of which Martin Kelly took to Tuam. A clever Milanese expatriate who had settled at Clonmel, Carlo Bianconi had, in 1815, fancied that he could make a good profit by running horse-drawn 'cars' from Clonmel to Cahir and back again. Succeeding in this modest venture, he soon began to operate on a much more ambitious scale. By 1841, the year of Anthony Trollope's arrival in Ireland, he was operating a sufficient number of cars to link, at short regular intervals, all the market towns in the southern and western areas. The 'daily total of the collective miles covered by them' was estimated, in 1841, at three thousand six hundred, and the horses were said to be 'enough to mount a cavalry regiment'. Trollope, who evidently got to know the old Italian well when he himself was moved from Banagher to Clonmel in 1845, was so impressed by the secret of Bianconi's success that he copied him when, in 1851, he was asked to reorganize the postal services of Ireland. Bianconi's secret, which he readily told to Trollope, had been the somewhat obvious one of seeking out the shortest cuts between the towns he serviced, while 'ensuring to his vehicles a maximum of speed with a minimum expenditure of motive power'.

Bianconi's cars, however, only linked major towns and chance villages which happened to be on their route. They were also comparatively expensive and were quite beyond the average peasant's means. There remained, for the greater part of the population who for one reason or another wished to make journeys, the jaunting cars and, above all, for long distances, the network of canals. Three miles from Banagher is the now deserted canal station, Shannon Harbour. Today it contains a handful of houses, some miniature dry-docks, a pub and the impressive shell of the Georgian Canal Hotel, the gaping, doorless façade of which is approached by a flight of grand stone stairs. It can still be sensed that the Canal Hotel at Shannon Harbour was, in its heyday, a flourishing and highly commodious building, with three floors of guest-rooms. Like all ruins in Ireland, ancient or modern, the hotel's empty window-frames and crumbling walls are sheathed in a lush, ebullient mass of bright-green ivy; small trees have planted themselves in what were the reception rooms, and the whole effect today is irresistibly lonely and romantic. The narrow greenish canal, almost choked at some seasons by reeds and water-flowers, joins the great Shannon river a few hundred yards beyond the sheds and dry-docks of Shannon Harbour. Close in against one of the canal's banks a huge and wily old pike has, for many years, been said to lead a life of quiet, skilful ease. There are two tall houses, like town-houses, both painted pink. Even the little modern school which stands back from the canal does not impair the sense of death and the silence that pervade Shannon Harbour.

When Trollope came to Banagher, passengers for that town left the Dublin boat and its weary draught-horses at Shannon Harbour, refreshed themselves at the bar of the busy, humming Canal Hotel, and trundled off on their way to Banagher in carriages or jaunting cars or, in the case of the more prosperous, were met there by a groom with a horse. Nowadays as moribund as the Dead Ports of Zuyder Zee, Shannon Harbour was once all self-important bustle and confusion. During and after the Famine the little place took on a new and different significance, for it was from here that the sickly, starving emigrants to Canada and to the United States would take the boat to Dublin, another to Liverpool and be then herded into the 'coffin-ships' —many of them former slave-traders—to endure a voyage across the Atlantic for seven endless-seeming weeks. The emigrants were usually supplied with five pounds by a landlord wishing to get rid of his plague-ridden, gaunt and emaciated tenants, and this sum was supposed to suffice them for their whole journey. Often the shipmasters in Liverpool would not charge them for the transatlantic crossing, since their use as human ballast crammed into empty ships crossing the ocean was soon recognized. At Shannon Harbour at that time cakes or, rather, lumps of heavy corn-and-oatmeal bread, as dry as hard tack, were made in special bakeries and sold to the refugees. On this, and on water chancily supplied in the Liverpool ships, the emigrant families were expected to live until they reached the coastal ports of the New World, where they spread the lethal germs of plague and fever and became both a medical problem and a health hazard to Canadians and New Englanders. Once past the quarantine, these wretched creatures sank at once into the lowest, foulest depths of the transatlantic community, huddling together in damp basements, forming putrid ghettoes and living on home-brewed poteen, rum and scraps of food from sidewalk trash-bins.

Shannon Harbour is by no means the only place of romantic beauty in the immediate neighbourhood of the Shannon at Banagher. A little to the south of the town a canal passes through the Victoria Lock, which, like the town bridge, was constructed in 1843. Save for an occasional canal-boat, this lock and its immediate surroundings are so unfrequented that even fishermen do not trouble to go there. Here the banks of the canal and of the Shannon itself sustain a vegetation so rich and wild, so tangled and impenetrable too, that you are reminded of some tributary of the Niger at Old Calabar or Bonny, or of the tropical setting of the mountain torrents of Jamaica and Dominica. Only the wild swans or the geese in flight, the meandering presence of a donkey and her inquisitive, velvet-snouted foal, or the enthusiastic barking of a collie dog, pleased perhaps to see a stray human being at last, remind you that you are in Ireland.

Banagher is situated in the region called the Irish Midlands, which are in every sense the antithesis of the English Midlands for they are sumptuously rural, with many of the roads lined by tall and splendid beech trees, horse chestnuts and aged oaks. Great flat stretches of the bog are, in summertime, sprinkled with feathery white and yellow flowers; many of the roads crossing the bog have become switchbacks from subsidence caused by the bog-water on which they are laid down. But, apart from their natural beauties, the Midlands abound in well-preserved ruins of abbeys, friaries, forts and castles, which seem from a distance, moored in the bogs and meadows. Here flocks of gregarious sheep and more solitary cows and bullocks mooch and graze on the coarse green grass spattered with buttercups and daisies beneath the windswept Irish sky. It is unlikely that Anthony Trollope had strictly antiquarian interests, but in his peregrinations through this countryside he can scarcely have failed to dismount to examine such lofty relics of the Irish Middle Ages as the ruins of Kilconnel Friary, which still shelter some of the most spectacular medieval tombs in the whole country, nor those of the fifteenth-century castle of Clonony, where a tombstone records the death of two exiled cousins of Anne Boleyn. Within walking distance of Banagher—and Anthony like his brother Tom was avid for long country walks—there stands in its leafy graveyard the twelfth-century Abbey of Clonfert, a community first founded by St Brendan in A.D. 557. Clonfert, which has been Protestant since its seizure in the reign of Queen Elizabeth the First, has what is reckoned to be the finest ornate romanesque doorway in all Ireland; it is near the edge of the bog, and people living in the Bishop's House behind it (now burned down) would be wakened in the morning by the cry of the curlew and a chorus of the other birds of the marsh. A similar doorway is to be seen in the town of Roscrea to the south of Banagher, and there, moreover, is one of the Round Towers of Ireland, those tall, pencil-shaped edifices within which the monks would take refuge against the marauding parties of Vikings, who would sweep smoothly and without warning up the Shannon River to burn and plunder monastery and town. A few miles to the east of Banagher, beyond Shannon Harbour and Shannon Bridge—a place heavily fortified against invaders from the Connaught side—are the famous remains of the sixth-century Cathedral of Clonmacnois. There two round towers rear themselves in protection of what has been described as 'a monastic city', and there also is the great runic Cross of the Scriptures. The position of Clonmacnois, on an eminence above an S-turn in the Shannon River, was admirably chosen for its strategic value, and from its ruins today you can survey the whole bog and plain upon the further shore of the river as far as the horizon. There are more abbey ruins at Clantusket and, at Portumna, the colossal shell of the Jacobean palace of the Earls of Clanricarde, built in 1618 and accidentally burned down some fifteen years before the date of Trollope's arrival in Ireland.

Today, of course, in County Offaly several of the large country houses which Trollope would certainly have visited are themselves, in their turn, ruins, either burned out during the Troubles, or abandoned by their owners. The Eyres of Eyre Court, a nearby house which Trollope must have known well, and which dates from the reign of Charles II, are a case in point of a family who, in this present century, finding the house too grandiose to keep up, simply emptied it of furniture, turned the key in the front door and left it, never to return. The walls of Eyre Court are by some miracle still standing, and the ground is littered with pieces of carved woodwork and corbels, but the roof is off and the customary billowing ivy is now in full control.

The Irish landed society in which Anthony Trollope would have been welcomed consisted of such plantation families as the Eyres of Eyre Court, the Lloyds of Gloster, the Dawson-Damers of Damer House (a stately example of a seventeenth-century town house, built into the walls of Roscrea Castle, and now degraded to serving as a Fire Brigade Headquarters) and many others. Sir William Gregory, who had despised Anthony at Harrow, always welcomed him cordially at Coole, from which house he would hunt with the West Galway; he would also have had friends amongst the British army officers in Banagher and also in Birr, where the Galway Blazers kept their hounds. It was contacts such as these, rather than his own struggles with provoking Irish postmasters, that made Anthony remember the Banagher years as so very jolly. It was also, we may recall, at Banagher that he commenced *The Macdermots of Ballycloran*, his first published book. He did not find the beginning of his literary career in any way facile: 'I commenced the book in September 1843,' he tells us, 'and had only written a volume when I was married in June 1844.'

Anthony had met his future wife at the watering-place of Kingstown near Dublin during his first year as Deputy-Surveyor at Banagher, and for the next two years they were secretly engaged. Self-conscious as ever, Anthony was persuaded that his friends round Banagher resented his bringing back an English wife. This made him feel uncomfortable in the King's County:

'On my arrival there as a bachelor I had been received most kindly, but when I brought my English wife I fancied that there was a feeling that I had behaved badly to Ireland generally. When a young man has been received hospitably in an Irish circle, I will not say that it is expected of him that he should marry some young lady in that society;—but it certainly is expected of him that he shall not marry any young lady out of it. I had given offence and I was made to feel it.'

Owing to her husband's habit of destroying letters and also to his cult of personal reticence about his emotions, Miss Rose Heseltine, the bank manager's daughter from Rotherham, only survives for us in a species of chiaroscuro, a small-limbed, shadowy presence behind her husband's burly back. But the little we do know of her could suggest that what his Irish friends may have resented was less his choice of a bride who was English so much as his choice of that particular English girl. She may well have felt, and shown, a certain distaste for her husband's inglorious position at Banagher—an attitude of mind almost endemic to the wives of minor Crown Colony officials in days not so very long gone by. In June of 1882, the year of his own death, Anthony Trollope was once more travelling around Ireland, this time with his wife's niece Florence Bland, who acted as his secretary. Writing a note to his 'Dearest Love' (as he would usually address his wife), the old and ailing novelist inserted what was evidently a private joke from the very distant past: 'I will give up being Surveyor's clerk as you dont seem to like it, but in that case must take to being guide at Killarney.' To appear to think that her twenty-nine-year-old husband was wasting his time at Banagher would not have been the way for an English bank manager's prissy daughter to keep Irish eyes a-smiling, nor to set Irish hearts a-glow.

Kingstown, the fashionable watering place near Dublin, was in those days a reduced, Irish version of Brighton. In 1842, when she first met Anthony Trollope there, Miss Rose Heseltine, who was nineteen or twenty,* would have been on holiday with her father, who was forty-three, her stepmother, formerly a Miss Platts, and her two sisters. The three Heseltine girls were locally known in Rotherham as 'the three graces', and were given to such skittish jokes as sewing lace round the bottoms of their father's trousers while he was asleep in his armchair. They would have been holidaying at Kingstown since it was, for English middle-class families of modest means, a less expensive resort than any similar place on the Continent. Edward Heseltine, the father of Rose and her sisters, officially had no other money than his salary and was unable to give his daughter Rose a jointure. He was manager of the Rotherham office of the Sheffield and Rotherham Joint Stock Banking Company, and was a respected member of the Rotherham community. When he retired from this position in 1853, however, deficits of many thousands of pounds were revealed. On being cross-examined by the directors, Mr Heseltine pleaded ill-health, deterioration of the brain and loss of memory. When it became apparent that a criminal case was about to be brought against him at York, he fled to Le Havre, where he died in the autumn of 1855. What Anthony Trollope thought about his father-in-law's rather startling and pitiful career we do not know. 'The engagement took place,' writes Anthony in a maddeningly reticent passage of the *Autobiography*,

'when I had been just one year in Ireland; but there was still a delay of two years before we could be married. She had no fortune, nor had I any income beyond that which came from the Post Office; and there were still a few debts which would have been paid off no doubt sooner, but for the purchase of the horse. When I had been nearly three years in Ireland we were married on the 11th of June 1844;—and perhaps I ought to name that happy day as the commencement of my better life,

* Even the date of Rose Heseltine's birth cannot be verified, but when she died in 1917 she was said to be ninety-five. This indicates that she was born in 1822, but in what month we do not know. She was, in any case, seven years younger than her husband.

rather than the day on which I first landed in Ireland ... My marriage was like the marriage of other people and of no special interest to any one except my wife and me. It took place at Rotherham in Yorkshire ... We were not very rich, having about £400 a year on which to live. Many people would say that we were two fools to encounter such poverty together.'

When, in *The Bertrams*, Caroline Waddington makes a marriage of reason with the rich Sir Henry Harcourt, Trollope writes of such worldly unions in a pitying tone, contrasting them with the excitement of marrying on slender means:

'It would seem that the full meaning of the word marriage can never be known by those who, at their first outspring into life, are surrounded by all that money can give. It requires the single sitting-room, the single fire, the necessary little efforts of self-devotion ... One would almost wish to be poor, that one might work for one's wife; almost wish to be ill-used, that one might fight for her.'

These aspirations must have been Anthony's own when he brought his bride back to Banagher.

So far, so good. Lack of coin will as a matter of course extenuate the tedium of a long engagement. Yet Anthony's Post Office stipend when they finally did get married was precisely the same as it had been when they had got engaged; a few trifling debts in Banagher can hardly have taken more than two years to pay off. Odder still is the fact that Anthony kept the engagement a secret from his mother and his brother Tom, then resident in Florence. 'In the spring of 1844,' writes Mrs Tom Trollope in the *Life* of her mother-in-law from which I have already quoted,

'the first tidings reached Casa Berti of the engagement of Mrs Trollope's son Anthony to Miss Rose Heseltine. His marriage took place on the 11th of the following June ... In May, Mrs Trollope and her son went to England, chiefly in order to pay a visit to the Tilleys in Cumberland, and, also, doubtless, for the purpose of seeing her new daughter-in-law. Anthony and his bride arrived at Carlton Hill in the course of the summer.'

Now Carlton Hill is near Penrith, and the distance by rail from Penrith to Rotherham would have been no deterrent to the peripatetic Tom and his indefatigable mother. There must have been some very cogent reason that prevented them from going to Anthony's wedding. It may have been that he did not want his famous mother to attend the simple Yorkshire ceremony, and scare or overwhelm with her eager cosmopolitan manner the family of a Rotherham bank employee. It would seem more probable, however, that Mrs Trollope, who was distinctly a snob and would later refer to Rose condescendingly as 'Anthony's excellent little wife', did not think much of her son's unworldly choice of a bride. That he feared that this would be his mother's attitude would surely explain why he kept his long engagement secret, and only sprung it on her a few weeks before the actual wedding ceremony took place?

Whatever the true motives for the protracted and secret engagement of marriage between Anthony Trollope and Rose Heseltine, many passages in the novels indicate that it may have been very much to his taste. The period between the successful proposal and the festive nuptials in the flower-decked village church at the end of many of his books, is frequently represented by the novelist as having a poignant sweetness all its own, and never, after marriage, to recur or be recaptured. 'During those lovely summer evening walks along the shores of Loch Derg, Phineas was as happy as he had ever been in his life'—and Phineas was then spending the first week of his engagement to Mary Flood Jones of Floodborough at his home town, Killaloe. On social grounds Trollope later regretted this particular piece of hasty match-making: 'As I fully intended to bring my hero back into the world, I was wrong to marry him to a simple, pretty Irish girl who could only be felt to be an encumbrance on such a return ... I had no alternative but to kill the simple, pretty Irish girl, which was an unpleasant and awkward necessity.' Nevertheless, those summer evenings at the southern end of Loch Derg did heal the much-scarred heart of Phineas Finn, who, after his varied emotional escapades in the burnished world of London Society found calm and happiness in an acknowledged engagement. He, at any rate, could not know that his little Mary was already doomed to a remarkably early death in childbirth. To Trollope's heroes an engagement is usually a time of unalloyed bliss, rendering them oblivious to their surroundings. In *Orley Farm*, for example, we are told: 'So Graham wandered about through the dry March winds with his future bride by his side, and never knew that the blasts came from the pernicious east.' His heroines, such as Lily Dale in *The Small House*, rejoice in a happiness almost indiscreetly public:

'And then she gently rose again, smiling, oh, so sweetly on the man she loved, and the puffings and swellings went out of her muslin. I think there is nothing in the world so pretty as the conscious little tricks of love played off by a girl towards the man she loves, when she has made up her mind boldly that all the world may know that she has given herself to him.'

Very occasionally there are specimens of an engagement without love, such as that at the opening of *Is He Popenjoy?* when Mary Lovelace, to please her father, the socially climbing Dean of Brotherton, accepts as her husband Lord George Germain, the childless Marquess of Brotherton's younger brother. Miss Lovelace is given three months to get ready for this wedding:

'Of course she had much to do in preparing her wedding garments, but she had before her a much more difficult task than that, at which she worked most sedulously. It was now the great business of her life to fall in love with Lord George.'

In other, darker and more cynical descriptions of marriage engagements, Trollope emphasizes the public triumph of the happy girl and the sudden, almost castrated, powerlessness of her accepted lover. In *Ayala's Angel,* the red-headed Colonel Jonathan Stubbs genuinely adores Ayala Dormer, one of Trollope's more fractious and headstrong heroines, but all the same 'it is probable that the Colonel did not enjoy his days at Stalham before his marriage ... There is always on such occasions, a feeling of weakness, as though the man had been subdued, brought at length into a cage, and tamed ... whereas the girl feels herself to be the triumphant conqueror, who has successfully performed this great act of taming.'

In Trollope a betrothal can also quickly turn into a dangerous form of the truth-game, for the man tells the girl the names of all the women whom he had imagined he loved in the past, but had never indeed loved as he loves her now:

'A man desires to win a virgin heart, and is happy to know— or at least to believe—that he has won it. With a woman every former rival is an added victim to the wheels of the triumphant chariot in which she is sitting'

—and this comment is evoked by the unconcealed delight of meek Mary Flood Jones, who is quite persuaded, during those strolls at Killaloe, that she is superior to Lady Laura Standish, Miss Violet Effingham and Madame Max Goesler, three influential London ladies each of whom Phineas confesses that he had thought he loved. Some heroines become almost distastefully familiar and dictatorial during their engagements—Madeline Staveley, the judge's daughter at Noningsby Park may be taken as an example of these:

'You are not to go away from Noningsby when the trial is over, you know. Mamma said that I had better tell you so.' It was thus that Madeline had spoken to Felix Graham as he was going out to the judge's carriage ... and as she did so she twisted one of her little fingers into one of his button-holes. This she did with a prettiness of familiarity, and the assumption of a right to give him orders ... And why should she not be familiar with him? Why should she not hold him to obedience by his button-hole? Was he not her own? Had she not chosen him and taken him up to the exclusion of all other such choosings and takings?'

Does not this rather unnerving description towards the close of *Orley Farm* seem, somehow, to lend to Anthony Trollope's views on marriage a certain affinity to those of James Thurber?

One further random excerpt (in this case from *The Small House at Allington*) is more explicit and goes much further than any of those already quoted. It is not humorous, and ostensibly it concerns Trollope's 'pet' Lily Dale:

'And now Lily Dale was engaged to be married, and the days of her playfulness were over. It sounds sad, this sentence against her, but I fear that it must be regarded as true. And when I think it is true ... it becomes a matter of regret to me that the feminine world should be in such a hurry after matrimony. I have, however, no remedy to offer for the evil; and, indeed, am aware that the evil, if there be an evil, is not well expressed in the words I have used. The hurry is not for matrimony, but for love. Then, the love once attained, matrimony seizes on its own, and the evil is accomplished.'

Most of the novels close before the honeymoon. The reader is dismissed under the lych-gate along with the dispersing wedding guests and is seldom invited to accompany the closer relatives, more intimate friends and hand-picked bridesmaids to the sumptuous wedding breakfast in 'the big house'. At the end of *Mr Scarborough's Family*, however, we are given a furtive glimpse of the honeymoon of Florence Mountjoy and her husband Harry Annesley (whom she has married despite the regulation disapproval of her own family). They are spending their honeymoon amongst the alpine flowers and clanking cow-bells of the Bernese Oberland; Florence is riding a pony, her arm symbolically round the neck of Harry, who is wearing 'highlows' or hobnail boots:

'"Well, old girl!" he said, "and now what do you think of it all?"

'"I'm not so very much older than I was when you took me, pet."

' "Oh yes, you are. Half of your life has gone; you have settled down into the cares and duties of married life, none of which had been so much as thought of when you took me." '

They jokingly discuss the clothes he wore before their engagement—'You knew that they were the boots and the clothes of a man making love, didn't you?'—and Harry remarks that had he worn highlows then, she would have judged him to be 'such an awkward fellow':

' "But now you must take my highlows as part of your duty."
' "And you?"
' "When a man loves a woman he falls in love with everything belonging to her. You don't wear highlows. Everything you possess as specially your own has to administer to my sense of love and beauty."
' "I wish, I wish it might be so."
' "There is no danger about that at all. But I have come before you on such an occasion as this as a kind of navvy ... And then there is ever so much more," he continued, "I don't think I snore."
'Indeed no! There isn't a sound comes from you. I sometimes look to see if I think you are alive." '

The pony stumbles over a stone, and Harry warns his bride that 'that brute'll throw you':

' "One has to risk danger in the world, but one makes the risk little as possible, [Florence replies] ... You chose the pony but I had to choose you. I don't know very much about ponies, but I do know something about a lover;—and I know that I have got one that will suit me." '

So concludes *Mr Scarborough's Family*. Once more it is the girl who selects her man, and thus, initially, gains the upper hand.

(ii)

It is thus clear that, in Anthony Trollope's opinion, romantic love hardly survives the honeymoon, hardly indeed the wedding altar, a view which must basically reflect upon his own experience as much as on his observation of the world around him. In an equable state of married happiness he faithfully believed, for he himself was happy in his marriage. Writing to a friend in April 1861, when *Orley Farm* was coming out in monthly numbers, he makes his position entirely clear. The letter which he is answering does not survive, but it would seem to have been critical of his own differentiation between youthful romance and happy marriage. It is worth quoting in full:

I must consider your letter as in some degree special, and give it a special answer.

You take me too closely *au pied de la lettre* as touching husbands and lovers. As to myself personally, I have daily to wonder at the continued run of domestic & worldly happiness which has been granted me;—to wonder at it as well as to be thankful for it. I do so, fearing that my day also of misery must come; for we are told by so many teachers of all doctrines that pain of some sort is man's lot. But no pain or misery has as yet come to me since the day I married; & if any man should speak well of the married state, I should do so.

But I deny that I have done other. There is a sweet young blushing joy about the first acknowledged reciprocal love, which is like the bouquet of the first glass of wine from the bottle—It goes when it has been tasted. But for all that who will confuse the momentary aroma with the lasting joys of the still flowing bowl. May the Bowl still flow for both of us, and leave no touch of headache.'

A piquancy is added to this plain and convincing statement when we know that the man to whom he was writing, and for whom he wished the bowl to go on flowing, was his friend G. H. Lewes, who had left his own wife and family seven years earlier to live in a state of public and connubial love with the literary spinster Marian Evans, known to her contemporaries and to posterity as George Eliot.

It seems in keeping with Rose Trollope's determination not to survive as an interesting figure for posterity that we find only the rarest accounts of her appearance in contemporary memoirs. Annie Thackeray assures us that she was always fashionably dressed—and so it would seem that her interest in this aspect of London life enabled her to help her husband with his meticulous accounts of the clothes of women of all classes in his novels. Augustus Hare was struck by her beauty when she was fifty-five. He encountered her at one of Lord Houghton's distinguished yet indiscriminate evening parties in Upper Brook Street, which, Hare comments, reminded him of Madame de Staël's criticism of such social gatherings—'*une société aux coups de poing*'. This was in May 1877, and Hare wrote in his journal: 'every one there, from Princess Louise to Mrs Anthony Trollope, a beautiful old lady with snow-white hair turned back'. Her hair seems to have gone white long before this, for another account describes her as having lovely white hair above a youthful face. That she was diminutive we do know. We also know that she liked country life as well as the London world, that *Henry Esmond* was one of her favourite books, that she used to buy great bottles of eau-de-Cologne in the Rue de Rivoli and keep them to mature for a year or two, that she was subject to 'dismal' attacks of depression when her husband was away on his travels, that she had a talent for embroidery which won her a bronze medal at the Great Exhibition of 1851 (to which she had submitted a three-fold screen designed and embroidered by herself), and that she liked going to picture galleries. She bore her husband two sons, Henry and Frederick, born respectively in 1846 and 1847 in Clonmel, County Tipperary. She also acted as his amanuensis, copying out each novel in her even hand before it was submitted to the publisher; when her husband was abroad she handled his London publishers competently.

Amongst the descendants of her brother-in-law Tom Trollope there survives a tradition that she was not much liked by that side of the family, and that she was considered 'bossy' and generally unsympathetic. That she was an ideal wife for Anthony himself it would be hard to deny. Elegant, thorough-going and highly domestic, she evidently gave him exactly the background which he needed for his life and work. He would never have dared to propose to, or indeed been attracted by, a girl who was not at least as impoverished as himself, and when fame and wealth came to him Rose must have felt that her own choice of husband had been both a lucky and rewarding one. She completely subjugated herself to Anthony's habits and interests. One of her few surviving letters was written to her husband's platonic friend Kate Field, the Boston blue-stocking. Part of this reads:

'He—my husband ... has gone to hunt and on such days I always write heaps of letters because I dont like to be out of the way never knowing at what hour he may be in—Well at any rate if you are angry with me [Kate had not written to the Trollopes for some weeks] I am not going to care and shall torment you when the fit comes on ...'

It is sad to think that of Mrs Anthony Trollope's 'heaps of letters' barely a dozen survive, thus depriving her husband's biographer of invaluable source material. Rose Trollope also performed the duty of being sole reader (and, perhaps, sole censor?) of her husband's novels—of which in any case she made, as we have seen, fair copies. 'She, I think, has so read almost everything to my very great advantage in matters of taste. I am sure that I have never asked a friend to read a line; nor have I ever read a word of my own writing aloud—even to her.' The matters of taste on which he took his wife's advice are of course unknown to us at this distance in time; but Frederick Harrison, the author and positivist, whose essay on Trollope in *Early Victorian Literature* (1902) is one of the best assessments of the novelist ever published, writes in it of his old friend: 'Sometimes, but very rarely, Trollope is vulgar,—for good old Anthony had a coarse vein: it was in the family.'

To sum up: we know extremely little about the pretty Yorkshire girl whom Anthony Trollope met at Kingstown near Dublin in the summertime of 1842, to whom he was engaged for the best part of three years, and whom he finally married. What we do know is that for nearly four decades she made him perfectly happy, looked after his comfort and made his interests her own. It may well be that those who love Trollope's novels should acknowledge that they owe Rose Heseltine a considerable posthumous debt.

(iii)

Their honeymoon over (where, he does not reveal), Anthony Trollope and his bride proceeded to Cumberland, to stay with John Tilley and his wife, who was, we may recall, Anthony's sole surviving sister. The Tilleys were now living at Carlton Hill, the house which Mrs Fanny Trollope and Tom had built in 1842, only to abandon it less than a year later. Also visiting the Tilleys were Tom and his mother, who was now an energetic sixty-three, and still an enthusiast for picnics and for long mountain walks. She got up very early in the morning, made her own tea, and settled down at her desk to continue her current novel. The garden at Carlton Hill, which Tom had laid out, was by now well advanced; having completed 'the allotted task of so many pages', Mrs Trollope would then trot out on to the lawn with basket and secateurs and bring back roses for the dining-room table and the vases and bowls in the drawing-room. All this she achieved before the bell rang for family breakfast.

For Rose Trollope that first meeting with her mother-in-law and her husband's brother and sister must indeed have been nervous work. Mrs Fanny Trollope's literary reputation was still in the ascendant. Having attacked the American scene in *Domestic Manners* in 1832, she had lately turned her attention to the horrors of English industrial society in the Hungry 'Forties. Two novels, *Michael Armstrong*, a diatribe on Lancashire mill-owners and on child labour, and *Jessie Phillips*, a violent denunciation of the New Poor Laws and illustrated by John Leech himself, had made her almost as unpopular at home as she had ever been in the United States. To fame she had now added notoriety, and had allied herself with Lord Shaftesbury who had given her letters of introduction to Lancashire philanthropists. The knowledge of all this literary activity, combined with the consciousness of her lengthy, hole-in-corner engagement, must have rendered Rose Trollope apprehensive as the train drew in to the railway station at Penrith. But to her delight, the celebrated mother-in-law welcomed her with an unfeigned warmth of manner. 'Nothing could have been kinder or more affectionate than the way she received me,' Rose remembered in her own old age, '—kind, good, and loving, then and ever afterwards.' 'I thought her the most charming old lady who ever existed,' Rose stated in another part of her recollections of her mother-in-law. 'There was nothing conventional about her, and yet she was perfectly free from the vice of affectation; and was worlds asunder from the "New Woman" and the "Emancipated Female" School. I do not think she had a mean thought in her composition ... She could say a sarcastic word, but never an ill-natured one.' Anthony, too, must have been relieved at the success of this first meeting between his wife and his mother. In Rose he had for the first time in his life a confidante with whom he could discuss the miseries of his childhood and youth, and his persisting belief that he had been treated as an outcast by his family. Further, he now had in his own private possession a prototype of all those English girls who would animate his novels and with whom Henry James suggested that Anthony Trollope was always paternally in love.

His leave of absence over, Anthony now went back with his wife to Ireland. We dare not speculate on the reactions of this fashionably dressed English girl, with her crinoline and her parasol, to the nauseous canal boat which brought them at a snail's pace from Dublin to the hotel at Shannon Harbour. Nor can it be supposed that she was much impressed by the hotel at Banagher, where her husband would have taken fresh, larger rooms. Rose did not hunt, and her husband was away a great deal on his postal duties—duties vital to the Trollopes' own domestic economy, since the farther afield he went the larger was the increment to his pay. Rotherham may have been provincial, but Banagher in 1844 must have struck Rose as the back of beyond. Her conclusions were probably not unlike those of her contemporary, Charlotte Brontë, ten years later. Charlotte Brontë's husband, the Reverend Arthur Bell Nicholls, was a native of Banagher, and he took his wife there for a part of their honeymoon, during which they stayed at the Royal College at Cuba Court, of which a cousin of his was then headmaster. Mrs Nicholls disliked both Banagher and its inhabitants, although she greatly admired the surrounding countryside. Neither Mrs Nicholls nor Mrs Anthony Trollope had, in fact, to endure Banagher for long. Charlotte Brontë's husband took her back to England where, within a few months of their return, she died. For Rose there was a less drastic order of release, for Anthony Trollope very soon got a new appointment, as Deputy-Surveyor in the town of Clonmel on the Waterford–Tipperary border. The coldness with which he and his English wife seemed to themselves to have been received by his cronies and his dancing partners in the Banagher locality is quite likely to have been genuine rather than a figment of Anthony's morbid imagination. Even to those Irish families who loathed the British most, an unmarried British official or army officer was regarded as the rightful prey of bright-eyed Irish girls. To marry an Englishman was, indeed, the only way of escape from a poverty-stricken marriage with an Irish squireen, or else from the fate of becoming a nun or a fanatically religious old maid. In *An Eye for an Eye*, while Father Marty, the parish priest of Liscannor on the cliffs of Mohir, is discussing with her anxious mother Kate O'Hara's incipient love for the handsome young English lieutenant, Fred Neville (stationed at Ennis), the priest reassures Mrs O'Hara in these terms: 'Let her keep her heart till he asks for it; but if he does ask her, why shouldn't she be his wife? How many of them young officers take Irish wives home with 'em every year. Only for them, our beauties wouldn't have a chance.' In another passage in which he analyses Father Marty's attitude towards Fred Neville, Trollope remarks that the priest 'regarded a stranger among them, such as was Fred Neville, as fair spoil, as a Philistine to seize whom and capture him for life on behalf of any Irish girl would be a great triumph—a spoiling of the Egyptian to the accomplishment of which he would not hesitate to lend his priestly assistance, the end to be accomplished, of course, being marriage ... Father Marty was no great politician, and desired no rebellion against England. Even in the days of O'Connell and repeal he had been but lukewarm. But justice for Ireland in the guise of wealthy English husbands for pretty Irish girls he desired with all his heart ... So little had been given to the Irish in these days, that they were bound to take what they could get.'

The very existence of Rose Trollope and her presence in Banagher may thus have been felt locally to be an affront—and one with which she would have been in no way equipped to deal. Anthony, unwieldy as he already was, still loved to dance. He may well have given rise to unjustified hopes amongst one or more of his young dancing-partners in the King's County. He would hardly have been regarded as a great matrimonial catch— but in Ireland, at that time, four hundred pounds a year went much further than it did in England. In any case an Irish Mrs Anthony Trollope would have been felt to have a husband with a future, as well as the opportunity of leaving for good some decayed parental roof.

(iv)
It is obvious, although he does not specifically say so, that amongst the other confidences that Anthony Trollope made to Rose both before and immediately after their marriage was his private ambition to become a novelist, and thus to turn to practical use his habit of day-dreaming in detail. We have seen how the germ of the plot for his first novel, *The Macdermots of Ballycloran*, had infected him during an autumn ramble with an English friend outside Drumsna in County Leitrim. The story was, we may remember, inspired by their speculations about 'the modern ruins of a country house' which they had strayed on in their walk. Today the ruins of Ballycloran House are still standing in what is now a bleak stony meadow near Drumsna. Destroyed by ivy, and also by gales, two of the four walls of the roofless old house have fallen in. The mysterious woods through which Trollope and his friend Merivale wandered are long felled. But, as in their day, the landscape of County Leitrim is one of the most barren in all Ireland, consisting of bog and scrub and rocks, with blocks of yellow furze in springtime and purple heather in the late summer. Miniature lakes, strewn in haphazard fashion, reflect the windswept Leitrim sky.

Trollope began to write this book in September 1843, but had only written one volume of it in a desultory fashion by the date of his marriage in June 1844. He had found himself constantly procrastinating over the novel, keeping late hours when he was not working at his postal duties, hunting, drinking whiskey punch and enjoying 'the rattling Irish life' to the exclusion of any sustained effort at creative writing. But now the stability of married life, and, probably, an anxiety not to let his young wife see how little he was doing towards the achievement of his pet ambition, combined to make him work seriously at the book. In June 1845—almost a year after their wedding—he gave his wife the completed novel to read. That July, with the manuscript neatly packaged inside his portmanteau, they once again traipsed across the Irish Sea to spend some weeks of leave with the Tilleys and the Trollopes at Carlton Hill. There he suffered yet another swingeing snub from his family.

Mrs Fanny Trollope, Tom, and Cecilia and John Tilley had been gratified by the change in his demeanour which had resulted from Anthony's years in Ireland. They had, despite the furtive nature of his engagement, genuinely welcomed Rose Heseltine as his wife. The astonishing new fact that Anthony had apparently always cherished literary ambitions, which he had never bothered to reveal to them, was, however, quite another matter. And that he should turn up for his holiday with a manuscript novel as well as a wife seemed to them totally out of keeping with their own very modest assessment of his gifts. His mother volunteered to offer the manuscript to a London publisher, but said that she felt sure that Anthony would agree with her that it would be much better that she should not first read it herself: 'She did not give me credit for the sort of cleverness necessary for such work.' Poor Anthony relates that he could 'see in the faces and hear in the voices of those of my friends who were around me at the house in Cumberland—my mother, my sister, my brother-in-law, and, I think, my brother —that they had not expected me to come out as one of the family authors'. They found it 'almost absurd' that Anthony should wish to intrude himself amongst the number of the writing Trollopes. There was his father, who had diligently but most unsuccessfully compiled that Ecclesiastical Dictionary. There was his mother, 'one of the most popular authors of the day'. There was Tom, who was already being well-paid for travel-books. There was even Cecilia Tilley, who had in her drawer the completed manuscript of her one and only work of fiction, afterwards published anonymously under the title *Chollerton*. 'I could perceive,' writes Anthony ruefully, 'that this attempt of mine was felt to be an unfortunate aggravation of the disease.' It must have been as humiliating an experience as any in the long chain of those which his own immediate family had ever inflicted upon him—and it was made worse still by the presence of a doting, admiring and credulous young wife. Is it surprising that the Anthony Trollopes only saw 'the Mammy' four times more before she died—once, when she paid them a very exhausting visit in Mallow, County Cork, and on three other occasions when they travelled, for brief family reunions, to Italy?

Fanny Trollope was, of course, as good as her word, and had soon badgered Mr Newby of Mortimer Street to publish the unpruned novel, with its endless dialogues in broadest Irish brogue, at his own expense, granting the author half profits on the venture. The book came out in May 1847 and was reviewed, but Anthony says he neither saw the reviews nor ever heard again from Mr Newby, whom he assumed could hardly have sold fifty copies.

It is extremely hard to believe that, as Trollope himself asserts, he never saw a review of *The Macdermots of Ballycloran*, for, with one solitary exception, the critics of the day (all of whom, of course, wrote anonymously) were, with reservations, enthusiastic, In *John Bull* it was called 'a work of singular merit'; the *Athenaeum* thought it 'clever'; *Douglas Jerrold's Shilling Magazine* said that the novel augured well for a successful career in fiction-writing. Inevitably, *The Macdermots* was praised for showing signs of an inherited 'keenness of observation and power of narrative', while a critic in *Howitt's Journal* expressed the opinion that 'the son assuredly inherits a considerable portion of the mother's talent'. The *Spectator*, at that time a very much respected organ, went even further, and proclaimed that there was 'more of mellowness in the composition of Mr A. Trollope, and less of forced contrivance in the management of his story, than the fluent lady has ever displayed'. Both the Tilleys at Penrith and the Trollopes in Florence would have subscribed at least to the *Spectator*, and it seems strange, if it is true, that none of them sent a clipping on to Anthony in Ireland. The *Autobiography*, as I have tried to show, is by turns reticent and, in its earlier chapters, full of self-pity. We should never forget when reading it that it is indeed the memoirs of a novelist. Its theme and its structure are that of a success story— a miserable boyhood, a dreary youth, an ignored first novel, the whole building up to fame and fortune. To present this sequence of events (or, rather, of sensations) in the most emphatic way it was essential that the dark years should be made yet more umbrageous, the chrysalis more constraining. There still clung to

Anthony, now in his early thirties, a mulish conviction that any book he might write would be neglected by the reading public and by the critics alike. This masochistic stance was a left-over from his earlier youth. Of *The Macdermots* he declares that he was

'sure that the book would fail, and it did fail most absolutely. I never heard of a person reading it in those days. If there was any notice taken of it by any critic of the day, I did not see it. I never asked any questions about it, or wrote a single letter on the subject to the publisher ... I do not remember that I felt in any way disappointed or hurt. I am quite sure that no word of complaint passed my lips. I think I may say that after the publication I never said a word about the book, even to my wife.'

I think we have the right to discountenance this latest statement.

In form, *The Macdermots of Ballycloran* is an inchoate work, and, naturally enough in a lengthy first novel, it lacks discipline. But then it deals with a society in conditions of disruption— that chronic Irish state of disruption which had always persisted through the long centuries of British rule, and which has only ceased in the Irish Republic in the last fifty years. There is already much evidence of what Henry James callld Trollope's 'good ear'. The speech and the behaviour of the Irish characters swarming through the novel is admirably and meticulously reproduced; but there is far too much of both. It is as though everything that Anthony Trollope had seen and heard in his three years of Irish living had been stored up in a mental reservoir which, as he began to write his novel, burst its banks and became a torrent or a flood. Some writers on Trollope have, I think wrongly, denied him any sense of place, or powers of describing scenery. This may be true of some of his pot-boilers such as *Kept in the Dark* or *Marion Fay*, but certainly not of any of his major and enduring works. It is interesting, therefore, to note in his very first novel such talented evocations as that of the big, shoddy and yet newly built house of the Macdermots, or of the windowless mud cabins of the peasants of Mohill. These accounts are not only convincing but thoughtful. Of the squalor of the town of Mohill, he writes:

'The miserable appearance of Irish peasants, when in the very lowest poverty, strikes one more forcibly in the towns than in the open country. The dirt and filth around them seems so much more oppressive on them; they have no escape from it ... On a road-side, or on the borders of a bog, the dusty colour of the cabin walls, the potato patch around it, the green scraughs or damp brown straw which forms its roof, all the appurtenances, in fact, of the cabin, seem suited to the things around it … Poverty, to be picturesque, should be rural.'

In *The Macdermots* we encounter Anthony Trollope's very first heroine, one Euphemia Macdermot, or Feemy, as she is called by her family and in the neighbourhood. Feemy, who is 'about twenty', is a deftly drawn character, and in every way the antithesis to those country house or vicarage 'English maidens' whom Henry James so much appreciated in Trollope's later novels. The description of Feemy, who 'walked as if all the blood of the old Irish princes was in her veins', shows to what a degree Anthony was already a master of close observation. He describes the beauty of her large dark eyes, her 'long soft shining dark hair', her nose, her mouth, her chin and her complexion, but at the same time he emphasizes the helplessness of being an Irish girl of good but penniless stock. No one in the book, except for the village priest, Father John, who is a bibliophile and has lived much in France, has any standard of comparison whatever, nor is cleanliness at all their strongest card:

'In all, Feemy was a fine girl in the eyes of a man not too much accustomed to refinement. Her hands were too large and too red, but if Feemy got gloves sufficient to go to mass with, it was all she could do in that way; and though Feemy had as fine a leg as ever bore a pretty girl, she was never well-shod,—her shoes were seldom clean, often slipshod, usually in holes, and her stockings—but no! I will not further violate the mysteries of Feemy's wardrobe.'

Her family consists of a father entering on his dotage, and her brother Thady, who acts as agent and rent-collector on his father's unprofitable land. Feemy could be as ardent and as energetic as her brother, 'if she had aught to be ardent about; she was addicted to novels, when she could get them from the dirty little circulating library at Mohill; she was passionately fond of dancing, which was her chief accomplishment; she played on an old spinet which had belonged to her mother'. Idle, perforce, and in her trashy way romantic, Feemy is an obvious prey. She is seduced by Captain Myles Ussher, a British police sub-inspector in County Leitrim, head of a squad of men whose duty it is to ferret out and arrest anyone illegally brewing poteen. As Ussher is about to take her away with him to Dublin as his mistress they are surprised by Feemy's brother Thady, who kills the Captain, goes into hiding, gives himself up and is tried and hanged in Carrick-on-Shannon. During the trial Feemy, secretly pregnant, dies in a side-room of the Assize court. The Macdermots of Ballycloran are thus totally extinguished by their chronicler's unpractised but ruthless hand.

(v)

Undeterred by the total failure, financially if not critically, of *The Macdermots of Ballycloran*, Anthony Trollope continued at Clonmel to work on his second novel, *The Kellys and the O'Kellys*, which was accepted by his mother's publisher Colburn and appeared in 1848. Only one hundred and fifty copies of this book were sold, and it made a net loss of the peculiar sum of £63. 10s. 1½d. The reviewers called the style fluent, but the story coarse. 'It is evident that readers do not like novels on Irish subjects as well as on others,' Colburn wrote to the author. 'Thus you will perceive it is impossible to give any encouragement to you to proceed in novel-writing.' Colburn also told him that 'the greatest efforts' had been used to sell *The Kellys*—'but in vain'.

Writers on Trollope have in the main followed the lead of the late Michael Sadleir in dismissing the two novels of Irish life 'as pamphlets in fictional guise' and bluntly excluding them from the true *corpus* of Trollope's subsequent work. Sadleir calls them 'the products of a wholly different mental attitude alike to life and to authorship. And that is why the starting of *The Macdermots* was no significant event in Trollope's life. It did not mark the rising of the Trollopian sun; it was a false dawn.' In point of fact the evidence of the closest observation, as well as the ease of the dialogue, in *The Macdermots* surely foreshadows Trollope's later achievements, while in *The Kellys* we find almost all the ingredients of his subsequent, more famous, novels. *The Kellys* is constructed with a mature assurance, and in this second novel the author does not get bogged down in irrelevant detail about land-rents and Irish poverty. Ignored though it was, and at present remains, *The Kelleys* is a fast-moving, riveting tale and in its own way quite as important as the Barchester and Palliser sagas. Unlike *The Macdermots*, this second novel has the double plot which became so very much too dear to Trollope's heart, but here the two plots dovetail perfectly. The two heroines, the patrician Fanny Wyndham who loves Lord Ballandine, and the ill-educated Anastasia Lynch, who is loved for her money by Martin Kelly, a tenant and very remote blood connection of Ballandine, are both interesting characters. With the creation of Fanny Wyndham, Trollope for the first time tried his hand at producing an aristocratic English girl. Grey Abbey, the gloomy domain near the Curragh owned by Fanny's guardian, Lord Cashel, is likewise Trollope's first attempt to explore the interior of a large country-house—in this case such an Irish house as he must often have visited during his postal duties or as a guest at dinner. Lord and Lady Cashel and their daughter Lady Selina are entirely vivid and convincing.

The Kellys, moreover, contains Trollope's first account of a hunt, of the antics of a spendthrift heir to a great estate, of an incurable alcoholic, of a lawyer's office and of life in a tiny village inn, where Mrs Kelly reigns and rules. Even more significant, his favourite theme of the importance attached to money and of the efforts made to obtain it by marrying a rich heiress, appears for the first time. Candidly and subtly, Trollope makes us see that even an upright, if tedious, old man of Lord Cashel's standing will not scruple to try to get his debt-laden son to marry the rich Wyndham heiress who is Lord Cashel's ward. In the sub-plot, the handsome young farmer, son of the widow innkeeper, pays court to a spinster ten years his senior in order to get hold of her four hundred pounds a year—to the Kelly family untold wealth—but, as he gets to know her, he finds that he has fallen in love with her. There are also racing and betting elements in *The Kellys*, ways of losing money and ways, by a rich marriage, of paying such debts. What with its double plot, its pictures of both country-house and village-pub life, its mercenary characters as well as its unworldly ones, its hunting scenes, its legal complications, *The Kellys* can be regarded as an examplar for all the rest of Anthony Trollope's work. The book also displays, for the first time, that coarse-grained snobbery which Anthony most probably inherited from his 'hen-wife' mother. As sooner or later we shall have to tackle this unpleasing aspect of the Trollope novels, we may as well do it here.

Anthony Trollope's portraits of established aristocratic women—Lady Glencora Palliser, Lady Lufton and a myriad others—have in them no jarring tone. But when it comes to girls who aim at marrying marquesses, earls or viscounts, Trollope's attitude is as ambivalent as that of a worldly middle-class uncle. Unfortunate phrases such as 'she looked every inch a countess' are frequent, and these are the author's own asides to the reader and not the spoken words of some ambitious character. As he saw more of the world, Trollope did not much care for the aristocracy; his *beau idéal* was the English country gentleman or a younger son with a meek wife and two or three well-brought-up daughters. But sometimes his ear was at fault—we cannot, for instance, suppose that even a mid-Victorian earl would in private address his son Adolphus as 'Lord Kilcullen'—yet this is what the Earl of Cashel does in *The Kellys*. While being perfectly aware that class-snobbery, that specifically national vice, was then far more rampant in the United Kingdom even than it is today, we cannot but find the obsequiousness of many Trollope characters to persons of rank very perplexing. It is not that he takes sides with the aristocracy—the ladies at Courcy Castle, or the Countess Lovel (Lady Anna's mother in the novel of that name) are shown to be as shallow and scheming as anybody else. To quote once more from Henry James's valedictory essay on Trollope:

'He evidently took a good deal of pains with his aristocracy ... It is difficult for us in America to measure the success of that picture [James is writing of Lady Arabella de Courcy] which is probably, however, not absolutely to the life. There is in *Doctor Thorne* and some other works a certain crudity of reference to distinctions of rank—as if people's consciousness of this matter were, on either side, rather inflated. It suggests a general state of tension. It is true that if Trollope's consciousness had been more flaccid he would perhaps not have given us Lady Glencora Palliser and Lady Lufton. Both of these noble persons are as living as possible ...'

Frederick Harrison, who in a clear-sighted manner greatly admired Anthony's work, has written that what makes his old friend's achievement 'so strange' is the fact that 'when he began to write novels, Trollope had far less experience than have most cultivated men of cathedral closes, rectories and county families ... till past middle life he had never had access to the higher grades of English society. He never at any time ... had any footing whatever in clerical circles, and but little intimate acquaintance with young ladies of birth and refinement in country homes. He never was much thrown with the young bloods of the army, of the universities, or of Parliament. He rarely consorted with dukes or county magnates, and he never lived in the centre of the political world.'

And yet there have been serious critics who have condemned Anthony Trollope for lack of imagination.

The Trollopes moved to Clonmel late in 1844. The town's Gaelic name can be loosely translated as 'honey-meadow'. The move south made a considerable difference to their lives, and to Rose Trollope it must have seemed a godsend after their restricted social circle in the King's County. Clonmel lies in the idyllic little valley of the Suir, which runs through the town under old bridges and yields a good many salmon and sea-trout. It is the capital of the richly agricultural South Riding of Tipperary, a county first established in the reign of King John. Clonmel was once a heavily fortified place. Substantial parts of the old wall which ringed it have survived, but the four gates are gone. The West Gate, however, was taken down and rebuilt, allegedly in replica, during the reign of William IV, and, although a fake, has quite an air of authenticity about it. A good seventeenth-century guard house, with a cupola, and known as the Main Guard, was completed in the year 1667, and is reputed to have been copied from drawings by Wren. Beyond the West Gate is a section of the town still known as Irishtown, for at nightfall the Irish manual workers in Clonmel used, for security reasons, to be thrust back through the closing gate to their hovels outside the walls.

Clonmel boasts certain rather tenuous literary associations. Laurence Sterne, whose father was a subaltern in the British regiment then garrisoning the town, was born there in 1713. George Borrow went to the school there which he has described in the early chapters of *Lavengro*. Surprisingly enough, one of the pools in the Suir river is traditionally known as 'Lady Blessington's Bath'. It seems indeed a far cry from the South Tipperary mountains to the sophisticated salon life of Gore House; but Marguerite Power was born at Knockbrit, just five miles from Clonmel, and lived in the town with her first husband. Like most ancient Irish towns, Clonmel has a long history of feud and bloodshed behind it, but by far its most illustrious episode was its celebrated defence in 1650 by Owen Roe's nephew, Hugh Dub O'Neill, against nine thousand veterans of the Model Army under Oliver Cromwell himself. O'Neill's troops and the Clonmel townspeople managed to hold out for five weeks, but finally, as they had run out of ammunition, O'Neill and his men stealthily withdrew by night, leaving the townspeople to capitulate on exceedingly favourable terms.

In one of the lanes or wynds which seem characteristic of Clonmel town, a small low door with an iron-work lantern-holder above it gives entry to the grand and now dilapidated house in which Cromwell stayed when the town had surrendered. Today threatened with demolition, the house has walls three or four foot thick, with deep window embrasures. A fine carved oak staircase with low, broad treads leads up to the *piano nobile*, which overlooks what used to be called the High Street of Clonmel. It was in this house, and, we may presume, on the first floor of it, that the Anthony Trollopes took furnished rooms when they came to Clonmel in 1844. Here, on March 13th, 1846, their first child and eldest son was born. He was christened in St Mary's by a Church of Ireland clergyman, Mr J. B. Gordon, eleven days later. The boy was named Henry, after the brother of Anthony who had died nearly twelve years before in Bruges, and Merivale, after his father's old friend John Merivale.

Living in spacious quarters in a bustling Tipperary town should have been exceedingly agreeable to the Trollopes. Clonmel was then a prosperous place, situated in the country's Golden Vale; it was a centre for horse sales, and on either side of the Suir it contained grain mills four stories high, many of which are still used as warehouses today. But their move to Clonmel coincided with the first ominous signs of the Great Hunger; and, later on, Anthony Trollope, riding on his postal duties through the very worst famine regions—the western parts of Cork, Kerry and Clare—saw many devastating scenes, some of which he later reproduced in *Castle Richmond*, a famine novel written in 1859 and published a year later. One of the fiercest, most justifiable and never-forgotten grievances of the Irish was and is that, all through the period of the famine, foodstuffs, dairy produce and meat were streaming out of the Irish ports to England. Within the walls of Clonmel this scandal was fully recognized by the people. Laden barges were filled up at the Clonmel grain mills, and set off every week for Carrick-on-Suir, protected by a British force of two guns, fifty cavalry and eighty infantry, for the starving people, who tried to set fire to the mills and once, in 1848, raised the red flag on one of them, would attempt to intercept and plunder the grain barges as they left the town. Harrowing though the famine might seem, British officials like Anthony Trollope, local land-owners like the Powers at Gurteen, the Church of Ireland clergy, and the

British officers and men of the Clonmel garrison were, of course, unaffected by any food shortage.

The valley of the Suir, and the country all round Clonmel, is singularly picturesque. The valley itself is sheltered by three small mountain ranges—the Comeragh, the Knockmealdow and Slievenamon. This last range contains a mountain nearly two and a half thousand feet high. It is famous in legend, and has caves reputedly the residence of fairies and of giants. Up in the mountains, too, is Palliser's Castle,* a formation of rock which has been celebrated by the Clonmel poet, C. J. Boland:

> 'Oh, Palliser's Castle, above on the Hill,
> I am far, far away, but I dream of you still,
> And as scenes very distant are longest in view,
> Most vivid in dreams are my childhood and you!
>
> Who has quaffed the cool Ragwell, or bathed by the Green,
> Who has plunged from the Boat-house, or fished to Gurteen,
> Who has heard the hoarse weir by the old Manor Hill,
> That loves not the Castle above on the Hill?'

The distant views of Slievenamon and of another landmark, Knockanafrin, are—like the cool green banks of the Suir—features of the Golden Vale which must indeed, in pre-Famine days, have made Clonmel a delectable place in which to live. 'In Tipperary a stranger is a King' says an adage current in Clonmel.

(ii)

However picturesque Clonmel might be, and however spacious and snug their quarters in the rambling old house on the High Street, Anthony Trollope of course continued his postal investigations and was often away from home. By 1846, however, these rides about the countryside had ceased to be either stimulating or quaint. The Deputy-Surveyor's jaunts now took him into a macabre world of mud cabins peopled by skeletal beings who soon became plague-stricken as well. All around beneath the

* It would seem probable that Trollope remembered this name when he began his series of Palliser novels. In the same way he called Burgo Fitzgerald after the Burgo who once owned all the land in Clonmel, while the de Courcys of Courcy Castle in Doctor Thorne and other Barsetshire books were obviously named after the extinct family of de Courcy, Earls of Ulster.

hedgerows and the stone walls lay withered, shrunken corpses. In the ditches evicted families lived (or, more correctly, died) in holes in the ground, or 'huddled together in wigwams pitched under park walls'. The skin of these starving peasants was so tightly drawn that the skull, elbows and rib-cage showed through it. Plague took a swift and easy hold upon the victims of starvation; one of its first signs was that the taut faces became covered with small light hairs, 'as of those on a gooseberry'. The 'rattling' Ireland that Anthony had so enjoyed was now becoming one vast green charnel house or open-air morgue. Owing to the lack in those days of any reliable Irish census, or of any system of registering births, it has never been certain how many of the Irish died in the Great Hunger and its aftermath, but the lowest figure rates these at one and a half million souls, while between 1846 and 1851 nearly a million more emigrated to Canada and the United States. In January 1847 Lord John Russell declared that the Irish famine was on a scale 'such as has not been known in modern times; indeed I should say it is like a famine of the thirteenth century acting upon a population of the nineteenth'.

Through this nightmarish landscape, peopled by figures which might have served Holbein as models for his woodcuts of the Dance of Death, Anthony Trollope rode stolidly on, improving postal arrangements between garrison towns, or from country house to country house. The famine deaths did not affect his role or duty, for the million and a half who died were illiterates anyway. In *Castle Richmond*, which he wrote as a weird farewell to Ireland, he admits that: 'They who were in the South of Ireland during the winter of 1846–47 will not readily forget the agony of that period ... the greater part of eight million human beings were left without food.' To a mind as sensitive and observant as was Trollope's, the famine scenes were especially hideous, yet, in his doctrinaire way he believed that 'the efforts—I may say the successful efforts—made by the Government to stay the hands of death will still be in the remembrance of many ... The people themselves wished of course to be fed without working.' Few intelligent persons at that time or ever since have thought much of Sir Charles Trevelyan's skimpy salvage operations, a part of which was the import of Indian corn (or maize) which should have been ground in mills, had there been sufficient mills to grind it. Millers and dealers made fortunes out of the corn, which in many of the mills was ground up with the husks, increasing the weight and bulk but rendering the corn spiky and inedible.

In *Castle Richmond* you may find a vivid description of a typical soup-kitchen open to feed the poor at Gortnaclough, on the FitzGeralds' estate near Kanturk. Lady Clara Desmond, the limp, wan heroine of the novel, goes to help serve in this soup-kitchen which was a soup-kitchen only in name, for in reality it served as an improvised shop for selling hard corn to the starving tenants—the theory being that it was essential not to give the people food for nothing, since they would only appreciate what they paid money for. Lady Clara and her friends Emmeline and Mary FitzGerald, delightful sisters of Clara's future husband Herbert FitzGerald, go up to dress for dinner after their day at the Gortnaclough shop. While dressing in Emmeline's bedroom they discuss the question of the Indian meal:

' "I wish we could get them to like it," said Clara, standing with one foot on the fender, in the middle of the process of dressing, so as to warm her toes; and her friend Emmeline was standing by her, with her arm round her waist.

' "I don't think we shall ever do that," said Mary, who was sitting at the glass brushing her hair; "it's so cold, and heavy, and uncomfortable when they get it."

' "You see," said Emmeline, "though they did only have potatoes before, they always had them quite warm; and though a dinner of potatoes seems very poor, they did have it altogether, in their own houses, you know; and I think the very cooking it was some comfort to them."

' "And I suppose they couldn't be taught to cook this themselves, so as to make it comfortable in their own cabins?" said Clara despondingly.

' "Herbert says it's impossible," said Mary.

' "And I'm sure he knows," said Clara.

' "They would waste more than they would eat," said Emmeline. "Besides, it is so hard to cook it as it should be cooked; sometimes it seems impossible to make it soft."

' "So it does," said Clara, sadly; "but if we could only have it hot for them when they come for it, wouldn't that be better?"

' "The great thing is to have it for them at all," said Mary the wise.'

The Gortnaclough store is Lady Clara Desmond's first experience of dishing out Indian corn. 'A gaunt tall creature with sunken cheeks and hollow eyes' comes storming into the shop, carrying two children and followed by another four. She forces her way through the crowd until she is standing at the counter behind which the three girls are serving. Opening a dirty hand-kerchief she points to the mess which it contains:

' "Feel of that," said the woman: "would you like to be 'ating that yourself now?"'

' "I don't think you have cooked it quite enough," said Clara, looking into the woman's face, half with fear, half with pity, and putting, as she spoke, her pretty delicate finger down into the nasty daubed mess of parboiled yellow flour.

' "Cooked it!' said the woman scornfully ... "would you like to be putting sharp points like that into your children's bel-lies?" '

Clara's mother, the Countess of Desmond (of Desmond Court on the banks of the Desmond River) consults Herbert FitzGerald about a boiler for her own famine-relief efforts at Clady. This boiler gives young Herbert a chance to go fre-quently to Desmond Court, where, on one such occasion, he proposes to Lady Clara and is accepted by the nervous girl and her enraptured mother. *Castle Richmond* is far from being a good novel, for its plot is not credible and certain chapters wholly consist of pontifical commentary on famine-relief; but it is an example of its author's resourcefulness in even concoct-ing a plot which is, so to speak, shored up by the famine and the young enthusiasts' plan for local relief. In the book Trol-lope explains that 'the hardest burden which had to be borne by those who exerted themselves at this period was the ingratitude of the poor for whom they worked; or rather I should say thanklessness ... It would have been unreasonable to expect that they should be grateful. Grateful for what?'

When the famine had ended, Trollope wrote five articles for the *Examiner*, then edited by John Forster. He worked hard at these, but he was not paid for them. They were inspired by his irritation at the widespread criticism in England of the Govern-ment's incompetence over famine relief—for, as an official him-self, he detested philanthropists who thought they knew better than the Government. In an interesting passage in *Castle Rich-mond* he becomes fierce, also, about the sham Irish gentlemen who were in fact merely the agents for absentee landlords:

'We used to hear much of absentees. It was not the absence of the absentees that did the damage, but the presence of those they left behind them on the soil ... It is with thorough rejoic-ing, with triumph, that I declare that the idle, genteel class has been cut up root and branch, has been driven forth out of its holdings into the wide world, and has been punished with the penalty of extermination.'

In one of the *Examiner* articles he defended Lord John Russell against the abuse heaped on his name by just these people—'a class of men not to be surpassed in the pride of station or in the want of refinement'. At the same time he was convinced that the Irish could never govern themselves. 'I find it impossible to believe,' he wrote in his final article, 'that the Irish are gifted with those qualities which are required to support a stern struggle for constitutional liberty.' Writing to his mother in 1848, the year of the Young Ireland uprising which speedily ended with the trial in Clonmel court-house of William Smith O'Brien and his fellow conspirators, Anthony reassured the old lady that there could never be an Irish revolution. 'Here in Ireland,' he told her, 'the meaning of the word Communism—or even social revolution—is not understood . . . Revolution here means a row.' Anthony Trollope lived long enough to see Ireland in turmoil over the Landleaguers (he was completing a novel upon them when he died), but he seems never to have lost completely the exasperating condescension which has always tainted an Englishman's attitude to Irishmen and Irish ways.

(iii)

For the upper classes, the British officials and the soldiery, daily life, then, continued normally in the very teeth of the famine. Anthony Trollope hunted in Waterford and Tipperary, he and his wife would drive up to see the local slate quarries in the foothills of the Comeragh mountains, and long evenings were doubtless spent playing Anthony's favourite card game, whist. There were hospitable friends to be made amongst such of the gentry as were not absentees, but whose bucolic private lives sometimes exploded into drama. Mr Power, for instance, who was the Master of Gurteen, a riverain estate four miles from Clonmel, shot himself, leaving a young widow and an infant heir. On a final visit to Ireland in 1882, the year of his own death, Anthony Trollope stayed at Gurteen with the very 'gracious and civil' Master, who was the son of the suicide, a Count of the Holy Roman Empire, and had changed his family surname back to its older form, Le Poer.

In the autumn of 1847 Rose Trollope gave birth to a second son, Frederick James Anthony Trollope, who was born in the old house in the High Street on September 27th. The births of his two sons are not mentioned in their father's autobiography until half way through the fifth chapter, and even then with restraint: 'While we were living at Clonmel two sons had been born, who certainly were important enough to have been mentioned sooner.' After Freddie's arrival the Trollope couple had no more children.

We can no longer know much about Anthony Trollope's attitude to his two sons, but at any rate we may be sure that he provided them with a happier childhood than that which he had endured himself. References to them in his letters are sparse and not particularly interesting. 'Harry and Freddie are quite well and are very nice boys,' he wrote to his mother in 1852, '—very different in disposition, but neither with anything that I could wish altered.' 'Harry came home from Cork today,' he wrote, again to his mother, in 1854, '—and with such a Cork brogue—& such a pair of cheeks—& no shoes to his feet ... Fred is somewhat delicate—he is so miserably thin—he is like a skeleton—but full of life & spirits—a horse threw him last week and trod on his hand—how he escaped is marvellous—but he only had one nail squeezed.' The fact that at the age of eighteen Fred insisted on migrating to sheep-farm in Australia does not, perhaps, suggest a very close relationship with either parent. Harry, on the other hand, was bought a partnership in Chapman and Hall's publishing firm when he was twenty-one, but did not make a success of it. As he grew up his relationship with his father seems to have become closer, but there is reason to suppose that Anthony Trollope was disappointed in any hopes he may have harboured of his sons proving to be distinguished or remarkable men.

Not long after the birth of Fred Trollope, his father's posting was changed once more. The little family now settled in a tall Georgian house in the High Street of Mallow, a busy market town on the northern bank of the River Blackwater in County Cork. It was the first time that the Trollopes had had a house of their own, and, since Mallow was in the centre of hunting country, Anthony tells us that he found it 'very pleasant'. For those who do not hunt, Mallow is not a specifically attractive town. Its narrow High Street is crowded, and the old Georgian houses and shop-fronts that line it are not well kept, for on many the paint is flaking off and the upper windows are, in cases, opaque with dust and grime. It is a town which seems dominated aurally by the harsh and at times unintelligible Cork brogue and visually by the soft persistent rain of the south-west of Ireland. Banagher, where as we may remember Trollope started off his Irish career, has, like Dublin, the lowest rainfall in the country; in parts of Kerry you may expect at the very least two hundred days of rain a year; and in County Cork the rate of rainfall is also pretty high. There are, however, compensations for such weather—for the cloud formations are forever changing, now as round and white as giant puff-balls, the next moment turning into horizontal streaks of grey in a rain-swept sky which becomes palely green. Ireland is emphatically a country in which you are always conscious of the sky, which here seems far wider and higher than a sky in England or in northern France. Sunsets on rainy evenings in Tipperary, Waterford or County Cork can combine dark blue, mauve and luminous yellow lights, even though the peaks of the Comeragh and Knockmealdow mountains are swathed in rain-clouds of a threatening grey.

In the old days Mallow was a fashionable spa, to which genteel persons from Cork and other towns of the south-west would flock to take the waters. The Spa House was once the constant meeting-place of the 'Rakes of Mallow' about whose exploits a lilting ballad is still sung:

> *'Beauing, belling, dancing, drinking,*
> *Breaking windows, damning, sinking,*
> *Ever raking, never thinking*
> *Like the rakes of Mallow.*
>
> *Spending faster than it comes,*
> *Beating waiters, bailiffs, duns,*
> *Bacchus' true begotten sons,*
> *Like the rakes of Mallow.'*

The mock Tudor building contains a winding stairway down to the medicinal spring; it is believed that if, on dipping your glass in the waters, you catch a bubble you will be granted one wish. Mallow is a good deal changed since Trollope's time: a gloomy housing estate of khaki-coloured, pebble-dashed terrace villas now smothers a steep hill which was once open country, with a lane leading to a charming low-fronted old house, Rock Cottage, which still stands in its rambling old garden, bright with star clematis and roses. This was the house in which Mrs Henry Wood wrote *East Lynne*.

At the lower end of the town, just short of the bridge spanning the Blackwater, are the Gothic-revival lodge and entrance gates to the park of Mallow Castle. Originally built on the orders of King John, when he was Governor of Ireland, the castle is yet another Irish ruin, having been burned by James II's troops during the Williamite Wars. After the fire the Jephson family, whose descendants still own Mallow Castle, withdrew into the stables which were gradually enlarged, mainly in 1831, and finally completed as a house as late as 1954. In the castle park there roams a herd of thirty head of white deer, with branching antlers that look as though they are coated with white velvet and had been designed by Inigo Jones for some court masque. There is also a herd of brown fallow deer of even more antique lineage; but the white deer of Mallow themselves descend from a pair presented by Queen Elizabeth I to her goddaughter, Elizabeth Norreys, who married a Protestant Major-General, Sir John Jephson, in 1601. The white deer must have become a familiar sight to the little Trollope children. They would also have proved of interest to the beady eye of those children's grandmother, old Mrs Fanny Trollope, who bustled over to Ireland in July 1849 on a short visit to her younger son's family. 'Anthony and his excellent little wife are as happy as possible,' she reported back to Tom Trollope, who had himself just married Miss Theodosia Garrow, a young poetess of mixed Indian and Jewish blood whom he and his mother had got to know in Florence. This marriage had temporarily deprived Fanny Trollope, who loathed travelling alone, of Tom's company. She had, though, come to Mallow escorted by her son-in-law John Tilley. They brought with them a female child of Tilley's whom the Anthony Trollopes had offered to adopt.

(iv)

The irruption of Fanny Trollope upon the Mallow scene was the direct result of yet another family tragedy. Her only surviving daughter, Cecilia Tilley, had, like some of her brothers and sisters, just died of consumption. Cecilia had been ten years married when, in April 1849, she finally succumbed to the disease in her husband's London house in Allen Place, Kensington. She had borne her husband four children: Frances or Fanny, Cecil, Arthur and Edith Diana Mary. Shortly after their mother's death, little Fanny Tilley and one of the boys died of consumption too. It was to Edith Diana Mary Tilley, whose date of birth we do not know, that Anthony Trollope and his wife extended a kind invitation to come over and join their own family in Mallow, and to act as substitute sister to Harry and to Fred. Since Cecilia had long been an invalid and her small children were forbidden, for fear of infection, to go into her room, they seemed to their grandmother unmoved by their mother's death: 'The dear children are too young to understand their loss ... they feel less than I expected they would.'

'Bring mama over here,' Anthony had written to his widower brother-in-law when informed of his sister's death, '—it will be infinitely better for you—for you both—than remaining alone in the house which must for a time be so sad a place for you.' To take on voluntarily the care and the expense of a third child was very good of the Anthony Trollopes, for they were still hard up and Anthony could not afford to go to London for the funeral. 'I could not go without crippling myself with regard to money,' Anthony wrote to the widower, 'in a way which not even that object could justify.'

Cecilia had been ailing for some time, but it was not until August 1847 that her London doctors declared that she must go to live in Italy for two years. A letter telling of this decision had arrived in Florence just as Tom Trollope and his mother were in the midst of their customary social whirl of musical evenings, *conversaziones*, picnics and rubbers at cards. Tom rushed back to England so as to escort Cecilia down to Florence, but found a letter at the Ramsgate *poste restante* to say that owing to her weak state she was travelling by sea to Leghorn. There her mother met the invalid. She found her looking wan and ill, but the London doctors had assured John Tilley that 'Mrs Tilley's lungs were not touched'. Old Mrs Trollope, with her sad memories of such misleading medical verdicts in the past, can hardly have been deceived in Cecilia's case. She and Tom curtailed their festive season, and did their best to look after Mrs Tilley. In October the Florentine homoeopathic doctor, into whose hands her mother had characteristically entrusted Cecilia's fate, suddenly declared that nothing could be worse for his patient than a winter on the Arno. On hearing this Mrs Trollope impetuously decided on Rome, where she took an apartment on the Via delle Quattro Fontane. She had invited Theodosia Garrow, with whom Tom was already in love, to come with them to Rome. Much of the winter was spent sightseeing by the haler members of the party. But as the Roman winter turned into a Roman spring, it was clear that Cecilia Tilley was firmly giving up the good fight. She said that all she now wanted was to return to England to be with her husband and their children until she died.

She sailed to London from Leghorn in May 1848 and managed to keep alive for the best part of a year. Then, in March 1849, her condition became so much worse that Mrs Trollope journeyed back alone to England from Aix-en-Provence, whither she had accompanied Tom and his bride Theodosia who were bent on a sketching tour in upland Provence. 'The long and solitary journey was a dismal trial to my strength of all kinds,' she wrote to them from London. On seeing her mother, Cecilia seemed to improve, but they all knew that there was no longer any hope. It was a cold and backward London spring; the old lady had insomnia and had become, in her own words, 'deplorably thin'. She could not continue writing her current novel because Cecilia's bed had been brought down to the back drawing-room at Allen Place, and the folding doors were kept open day and night. 'I feel that I am almost too old for a rally,' wrote Mrs Trollope, whose heroism was always tempered by a sharp sense of personal discomfort. 'I have, as you well know, my dear Tom, suffered ere now, and very severely; but I almost think the last month has been the most suffering period of my existence.' 'And truly I want some gilding over the future,' she also wrote to Tom, 'to enable me to bear the heavy sorrows of the present.'

Cecilia Tilley died in the first week of April 1849. 'It was as though she had fallen asleep,' her mother wrote, employing the hackneyed Victorian phraseology for Death. '... Sweet soul! She longed—but never with impatience—for the moment of her release.' His mother-in-law admired the fortitude of John Tilley, an autocratic, clever and caustic man—the very embodiment of a civil servant—who was, according to one of his juniors at the Post Office, 'as unimpressionable as an oyster'. Along with the widower and his sickly children, Mrs Trollope developed bronchitis and next believed that she had acquired 'that most painful malady—the *mumps*'. The mumps can have been but of unusually short duration, for four days after the funeral she took John Tilley down to Offham, to stay with the Partingtons. Mrs Thomas Partington had been born Penelope Trollope, a sister of Fanny Trollope's eccentric husband. Also in the house was a Partington daugher, Mary Anne, who had been an intimate friend of her cousin Cecilia—and whom uxorious Mr Tilley married in 1850, less than a year after his late wife's death. In the July following this visit to Offham, Tilley and his mother-in-law crossed to Ireland, taking with them Edith Diana Mary Tilley who, as we have seen, was supposedly destined to be integrated into the little family at Mallow. Even the prospect of Ireland, a country in which she had never before set foot, could not restore Fanny Trollope to her customary state of optimism, which was for the moment in eclipse: 'In July we shall (D.V.) go together to Ireland for a month,' she wrote un-enthusiastically to the Tom Trollopes, for whose company she yearned. Fanny Trollope was, indeed, totally dependent on Tom's devotion and self-sacrifice and also on his wife's affection. She could only see Ireland through their eyes: 'We pleased ourselves mightily while with Anthony and his wife, in plotting and planning a visit to them and their lakes in company with you and Tom,' she wrote to her new daughter-in-law Theo-dosia. '...God bless you, my dear daughter! Had I my will, wish, and way, you should never be very far from me.' Such vociferous plans must have seemed a trifle disappointing to Anthony and Rose, who were making the most strenuous and costly efforts to divert and cosset 'the Mammy', now in her seventieth year.

Rose Trollope's own recollections of her mother-in-law's visit make it clear that this was not an unmitigated success. The old lady certainly admired the lakes at Killarney—'Lord Kenmare's park especially delighted her'—and she walked through the stony Gap of Dunloe 'as easily as if she had been twenty-nine instead of sixty-nine!' When Anthony introduced into the drawing-room an old piper named Spellan, his mother was in-itially dismayed—'but soon tears were rolling down her cheeks from the pathos of his music'. Rather unwisely, Anthony, who was himself tireless, arranged a long overnight jaunt to Glengar-riff in the Caha Mountains, with its beautiful inlet on Bantry Bay. '...We put her on one of Bianconi's cars running to Glengarriff, after much protest on her part against the ram-shackle looking machine,' Rose Trollope recalled. 'Presently, however, after a few jerks, and a dozen "Niver fear, yer hon-our!" from Mick the driver, she almost persuaded herself that she would rather travel through Ireland in that way than any other!' The glen is a very long way from Mallow, and on arrival the old lady was thoroughly exhausted. 'Glengarriff was not a success,' Rose tells us. 'She was tired with her journey; the tea was rubbish; the food detestable; the bedrooms pokey; turf fires disagreeable, and so on. And now looking back on it all, I feel that she had grounds for complaint; and I should vote it—nasty. However the next day was better, when we drove through the Bantry demesne.'

While in Ireland, Mrs Trollope was already arranging to meet

Tom and Theodosia as soon as possible, preferably at the house of her old cousin, Fanny Bent, at Exeter. Her Irish interlude must have proved an ordeal for her host and hostess, who had done their level best to entertain her on their very slender means. In mid-August she and John Tilley sailed from Dublin. They left little Edith Diana Mary behind at Mallow, in the Anthony Trollopes' care. This child-guest only stayed with her aunt and uncle a few months, for Cecilia's successor as Mrs John Tilley wished to have Edith back in the house in Kensington. 'We are very sorry,' Anthony wrote, with unusual emphasis, to his mother, 'but we have no right to complain. Indeed, the incurring the chance of losing her at any moment after we had become fond of her, was the only drawback to the pleasure of taking her.' And so Edith Diana Mary Tilley—who did not die of consumption and who was still in the land of the living in 1875—disappears from our narrative, though her memory must have lingered in her uncle's mind. We might like to recognize her in the winsome Posy Arabin, old Mr Harding's favourite granddaughter in The Last Chronicle of Barset. In very, very few of Anthony Trollope's novels are children either seen or heard. Their presence is only indicated, and, in a sense, felt. 'Frank! Frank! do look at me; pray do, Frank; I am drinking your health in real wine, ain't I, papa?' This squeaky interruption of the general toast at Frank Gresham's coming-of-age dinner at Greshamsbury is our only reminder that Mr Francis Gresham and his wife Lady Arabella have another six portionless daughters in the nursery and the schoolroom, whose existence we take otherwise on trust. Whichever of Frank's little sisters was in fact sipping wine, she makes this shrill, solitary effort to draw attention to herself, and then, so far as we are concerned, she forever holds her peace.

(v)

Random recollections of one of Anthony Trollope's nephews, jotted down for the benefit of the late Michael Sadleir (whose long study of the novelist was published in 1927), imply that his uncle was fond of children. Recalling children's Christmas parties organized by the Anthony Trollopes when they lived at Waltham Cross, he stated that he had only to reread the description of Christmas at Noningsby in Orley Farm 'to live again those childhood days'. As in Orley Farm, there was blindman's buff in the schoolroom after the Christmas lunch, followed by an older girl taking the part of 'ghost', with white muslin across her face, a sheet draped around her body and her hair down over her shoulders. The ghost would enter the twilit schoolroom bearing a huge flaming dish of raisins and nuts, for which the children had to grab smartly without getting their fingers burned. On other days the game of 'Commerce' was always played; Uncle Anthony 'would join all the games, contriving with great ingenuity that at "Commerce" the children got the winning cards'. We have already noted in this context the scarcity of child characters in the Trollope novels. The handful of little boys who hover in the wings of some of the stories are usually unpleasant. Little girls, such as one of the Stavely granddaughters, Marian Arbuthnot in *Orley Farm*, are chiefly praised for their promising adult-potential:

'[Marian] was a beautiful fair little thing, with long soft curls, and lips red as a rose, and large, bright blue eyes, all soft and happy and laughing, loving the friends of her childhood with passionate love, and fully expecting an equal devotion from them. It is of such children that our wives and sweethearts should be made.'

Co-existent with the mid-Victorian sentimentality about death-beds, a cult centring on the charm and innocence of small children was gently fostered amongst the English upper and middle classes. We can find evidence of this everywhere—from the lithographs after Birkett Foster or Millais which would hang in country-house bedrooms, to the many excellent books written for children about other children by such writers as Mrs Ewing. At times—witness Kilvert's diaries or the letters of Lewis Carroll—this cult branched out into the dark fields of psycho-pathology, but on the whole it was as wholesome as it was certainly dominant. Unhappy children, as we all know, were one of Charles Dickens's strongest cards. Yet in the works of Anthony Trollope children appear either as pawns in the game of life enacted by their elders, or to emphasize and enhance atmospheres already thoroughly unpleasant. Only in one novel, and that his last, does Trollope seem to divine those treacherous depths in child psychology explored by Henry James. Save for the one exception, ten-year-old Florian Jones in *The Landleaguers* (posthumously published as an unfinished novel in 1883), Trollope accepts children quite casually, at their rather nasty face-value.

In two novels, *He Knew He Was Right* (1869) and *Is He Popenjoy?* (1878), the main plot is constructed round the existence of a child. *He Knew He Was Right* is in itself a remarkable work. Instead of its author's favourite formula of love triumphing over opposition and ending with the orange-blossom and church-bells of a wedding, this novel begins with a most promising marriage and traces its slow disintegration. Emily, eldest daughter of Sir Marmaduke Rowley, Governor of the Mandarin Islands, has already met and married her rich and handsome husband Louis Trevelyan, and has already borne him a son, Louey, who, at the novel's commencement, seems to be two or three years old. Her husband's unfounded jealousy and her own stubborn pride bring about the collapse of their relationship, and Emily is deserted by her husband and centres all her happiness in her little boy. This child is kidnapped on his father's orders in a dingy Bloomsbury street and taken by him to live in hiding, first in a cottage near Kensal Green Cemetery, and then to an old farmhouse in the countryside beyond the walls of Siena. By this time Louis Trevelyan is patently insane. His determination to keep the child in his own custody—for which he has the law on his side—and Emily's efforts to get her son back make the novel's drama. It was of this book that Henry James wrote in admiration:

'The long slow process of the conjugal wreck of Louis Trevelyan and his wife ... arrives at last at an impressive completeness of misery ... Touch is added to touch, one small, stupid, fatal aggravation to another; and as we gaze into the widening breach we wonder at the vulgar materials of which tragedy sometimes composes itself.'

The very existence and the fate of the boy Louey become the central theme of the novel, but he is only shown to us in snatches as a bewildered, brooding little creature who will not even play with his new toys at the farmhouse at Casalunga:

'The toys remained where the father had placed them, almost unheeded, and the child sat looking out of the window, melancholy, silent and repressed. Even the drum did not tempt him to be noisy. Doubtless he did not know why he was wretched, but he was fully conscious of his wretchedness. In the meantime his father sat motionless, in an old worn-out but once handsome leathern arm-chair, with his eyes ever fixed against the opposite wall, thinking of the wreck of his life.'

Louey Trevelyan is one example of the uses of the pawn-child in Trollope's fiction; and he, at least, is exhibited to us in various stages of puzzlement. Another case is that of Tavo, Viscount Popenjoy, around whose legitimacy the plot of *Is He Popenjoy?* revolves. Was this swarthy, overdressed child born before or after the marriage of his immensely rich father, the Marquess of Brotherton, to his strange-looking Italian wife? If he is not legitimate he cannot inherit the title or estates, which would then fall at the cantankerous Marquess's death to his brother, Lord George Germain, the husband of the novel's heroine. Even the age of the alleged Lord Popenjoy is as baffling to the Marquess's family as it is to the reader. He is carried about by his nurse, but 'Lord George thought that he was big enough to have walked.' Trollope, who always shows himself insular when describing the get-up of French or Italian men and boys, only lets us see 'the ugly, swarthy little boy, with great black eyes, small cheeks, and a high forehead' twice in the book. In one instance little Lord Popenjoy is 'dressed up with many ribbons ... altogether as gay as apparel could make him'; in the other he is smothered in shawls, crammed into a perambulator, and pushed a mile across the park from Manor Cross to the dower-house in which his grandmother and her three spinster daughters are living. The Dowager Marchioness, who is verging on senility, is the only member of the family who chooses to believe that Popenjoy was born after and not before her elder son's marriage:

'The nurse ... held him up to be looked at for two minutes while he still screamed, and then put him back into his covering raiments.

' "He is very black," said Lady Sarah severely.

' "So are some people's hearts," said the Marchioness, with a vigour for which her daughters had hardly given her credit.'

The problem of Popenjoy's legitimacy is never solved, but the death of the Marquess following that of his ailing child clears the decks for Lord and Lady George Germain to become Marquess and Marchioness of Brotherton, and to have a real Popenjoy of their own. This achievement of Mary Germain, who is merely the granddaughter of the keeper of a livery stable, and her rise to the rank of Marchioness seem to have given Trollope as much satisfaction as they certainly gave to her father, the pugnacious Dean of Brotherton. Popenjoy is, however, but a sorrowful example of the pawn-child, for his only contribution to his family's problems is to be born, to look swarthy and to die.

Alongside the pawn-child in the novels there is another, rather closely related, breed, whom we might term specimens of the child-as-ally, or even of the child-as-adjunct. These unfortunate and usually neglected beings are mobilized when needed to further a mother's schemes. In *Barchester Towers*, tiny Julia Neroni—another over-dressed Italianate child—is made use of by her mother the Signora Vesey-Neroni to display her maternal instincts and so to soften the heart of some fresh admirer like old Mr Thorne of Ullathorne. In the brilliant engagement scene early on in *The Eustace Diamonds*, Lizzie Eustace seizes on the existence of her child as an additional weapon when trying to trap Lord Fawn into a proposal. She subtly combines an exhibition of mother-love with a means of letting Fawn know how rich she may really be:

'"I have a child, you know, to bring up."

'"Ah yes, that gives a great interest, of course."

'"He will inherit a very large fortune, Lord Fawn; too large, I fear, to be of service to a youth of one-and-twenty; and I must endeavour to fit him for the possession of it. That is,—and always must be the chief object of my existence." Then she felt that she had said too much. He was just the sort of man who would be fool enough to believe her.'

The guileless Lord Fawn replies to this most unmaternal of widows:

'"It's a comfort, of course, to know that one's child is provided for."

'"Oh, yes; but they tell me the poor little dear will have forty thousand a year when he's of age; and when I look at him in his little bed, and press him in my arms, and think of all that money, I almost wish that his father had been a poor plain gentleman." Then the handkerchief was put to her eyes, and Lord Fawn had a moment in which to collect himself.'

Even Lady Glencora Palliser, whose husband is nephew and heir to the princely possessions and the title of his old uncle the Duke of Omnium, is not above using her own child, Planty Palliser, as a reinforcement in her opening campaign in *Phineas Finn* to prevent the Duke marrying Madame Max Goesler. Lady Glencora intended that

'her little boy, her fair-haired, curly-pated, bold-faced little boy, should be Earl of Silverbridge when the sand of the old man should have run itself out. Heavens, what a blow would it be, should some little wizen-cheeked, half-monkey baby, with black brows and yellow skin, be brought forward and shown to her some day as the heir! What a blow to herself;—and what a blow to all England.'

So, when calling at Madame Goesler's little house in Park Lane at a time when she knows that the Duke is *en tête-à-tête* with that bewitching Viennese, Lady Glencora brings her eldest child with her, as a reminder to the Duke and a grave warning to Madame Max of all that is at stake.

A sidelight on Trollope's fundamental lack of interest in children who could be used neither as pawns nor as allies, may be found in the fact that in the books now known as the Palliser Novels, he gets into a very uncharacteristic tangle about the names and even the numbers of Lady Glencora's progeny, some of which change from book to book. Nor does he introduce us to many of our child acquaintances when they have grown up. Silverbridge, his brother and his sister do as adults dominate *The Duke's Children*; for the rest we have only Henry and Grizzle Grantley and Grace Crawley to satisfy our curiosity about the destiny of the fictional children we meet or learn of by hearsay. Trollope is so percipient about the thraldom of a doting mother to a worthless grown-up son—we have only to think of *Orley Farm* and of *The Way We Live Now*—that we would give much to know what scheming Lady Eustace's son, Sir Florian, really thought about this parent after he had reached wealthy manhood.

In *The Warden* the three boys of the Archdeacon, Dr Grantley, fall into another category—that of wily children who know how to make their father's opponents feel thoroughly uncomfortable. Like the Lovel offspring at Yoxham Rectory in *Lady Anna*, they are, by embodying their parents' prejudices, capable of being either stand-offish or downright impertinent to a newcomer whom they know to be officially disliked. 'Dr Grantley,' we read, 'was blessed with a happy, thriving family'; Trollope then proceeds to satirize each of the Archdeacon's three sons in turn.

'Charles James was an exact and careful boy; he never committed himself; he well knew how much was expected from the eldest son of the Archdeacon of Barchester, and was therefore mindful not to mix too freely with other boys.'
The second:
'... was the Archdeacon's favourite son, and Henry was indeed a brilliant boy ... The ring was the only element in which he seemed to enjoy himself; and while other boys were happy in the number of their friends, he rejoiced most in the multitude of his foes ... though he could fawn to the masters, and the Archdeacon's friends, he was imperious and masterful to the servants and the poor.'

The Grantleys' third son, called after Bishop Wilberforce,

again has few redeeming features:

'... perhaps Samuel was the general favourite; and dear little Soapy, as he was familiarly called, was as engaging a child as ever fond mother petted ... To speak the truth, Samuel was a cunning boy, and those even who loved him best, could not but own that for one so young he was too adroit to choose his words, and too skilled in modulating his voice.'

In his own bleak childhood, Anthony had admittedly had no chance of intimate friendship with other children. We could have assumed that when he became himself the father of two 'very nice' boys he would have been stirred to depict male children more sympathetically, but for some reason or other he did not.

I have already said that in his last novel, *The Landleaguers*, Anthony did, at length, create a complex and secretive child. Little Florian Jones would, in fact, have felt quite at home at Bly with Miles and Flora in *The Turn of the Screw*. Florian, the last and by many years the youngest of the beautiful, doomed youths who crop up from time to time in Trollope's novels, is just ten years old. He lives with his father, his elder brother and his two sisters, Ada and Edith, at Morony Castle near Ballintubber in County Galway and not far from the shores of Loch Corrib. His father, Mr Philip Jones, is a meticulous Protestant landlord, much regarded in the county. Mr Jones idolizes his son Florian, and does not even criticize him when the lad, under the influence of the local priest, becomes a rather self-conscious Roman Catholic. Florian's sisters spoil him, but they have much to bear, for phrases such as 'we Catholics don't like telling lies' trip off the juvenile convert's tongue. None of the family raises an objection when Florian sets off to Sunday mass while his close relatives attend the Church of Ireland service. Trollope implies that Florian's change of faith was just a form of self-assertion and a way of irritating his family. A side effect of Florian's change of religion is that the surrounding peasantry take him to their hearts and look upon him as one of themselves.

A local man, Pat Carroll by name, works off a grudge against Mr Jones by opening the floodgates of the Ballintubber marshes, thus putting eighty acres of reclaimed land under water, and costing the landlord five hundred pounds. By sheer chance, Florian happens to have seen the men opening the floodgates. Luring Florian into a cottage at nightfall, the malefactors force him to swear on oath that he will not give their names to his father, threatening that if ever he did so he would be 'holed' just like a certain Mr Bingham who had recently been murdered. Florian is thoroughly frightened by a masked man, who stands in the shadows of the room, and who explains that it is he himself who will, if need be, kill Florian Jones. Yet although terrified, Florian feels that the threat adds a new dimension to his life. It makes the boy feel important:

'To tell the truth of Florian, he felt rather complimented in the midst of all his horrors in being thus threatened with the fate of Mr Bingham. He had heard much about Mr Bingham, and regarded him as a person of much importance since his death. He was raised to a level now with Mr Bingham. And then up to now his immediate position was very much better than Bingham's. He was alive, and up to the present moment— as long as he held his tongue and told nothing—he would be regarded with friendly eyes by that terrible man in the mask.'

Florian's father and his two sisters are convinced that he knows who caused the submersion of the meadows. The boy remains sullen and secretive, blushing ruby-red when questioned. In the end he is trapped into a confession by Captain Yorke Clayton, a young magistrate in love with Florian's sister, Edith Jones. He signs a statement to be read at Carroll's trial, for Captain Clayton has Pat Carroll arrested and charged. Breaking his oath frightens Florian far more than swearing it had done. His father would have liked to send him to safety in England, but lacks the means. When driving with Florian and an old servant, Peter, along a country lane between high banks, Mr Jones sees a face in a mask above them. In a trice young Florian is shot through the head. The father and the magistrate are morally to blame for the boy's death. Trollope's description of poor Florian's dilemma is an eminently subtle piece of child psychology, for the boy feels guilty at concealing the truth from his doting father; at the same time he is sure that after confessing his secret, he will without any question be 'holed'. He is.

(vi)

One might well assume that by the summer of 1848 (when *The Kellys and the O'Kellys* was so unprofitably published), the pattern of Anthony Trollope's life was more or less established. He was now thirty-three, happily married with two children, living in a house in Mallow, hunting with a zestful regularity, and determined to be a successful writer. In fact, he was suffering from a lack of judgment about his own work—and this, in some ways, he never lost. The failure of *The Kellys* perhaps unnerved him more than, in his *Autobiography*, he leads us to believe. He next tried his hand at the historical novel, producing *La Vendée*, for which he got a meagre twenty-pound advance; this he followed up with an historical play, *The Noble Jilt*, and intermittently 'spent six or eight months' compiling a guide-book to Ireland, which he believed that John Murray had commissioned. To his chagrin, the publisher never read this guide-book —or rather such parts of it as were completed—which is to say an account of Dublin, and of the journey thence to County Kerry. The roll of manuscript was returned to him by the publishers unopened. It seems strange that Murray or anyone else really wished for a tourist-guide to an Ireland still suffering from the effects of the famine, still without good roads and without railways. Evictions by the police, aided by British soldiers, continued to be a daily Irish occurrence; the peasants' houses were demolished with battering rams, while red-coated infantry and the mounted Hussars clad in blue and gold stood guard. Many of these evictions were for arrears of rent. Many were due to the exalted ideas of distant British landlords, who swept away hovels and whole villages in order to lay out a park with a view. In any case, tourism in Ireland one hundred and twenty years ago was unedifying, uncomfortable and, with the English, improbable and unpopular. Swizerland was safe and attractive, and much patronized by Victorian honeymooners. Who would go for a honeymoon to Ireland? With some temerity Queen Victoria and Prince Albert visited Cork and Dublin in 1849, when considerable trouble was taken, on the Viceroy's orders, that they should be shielded from any sight of misery or squalor. For their benefit Viceregal Lodge was refurbished at great expense and was heavily guarded. The Duke of Leinster entertained the royal couple at Carton. The whole visit was rated to be a minor triumph. It was the Queen's first sight of her alien and unwilling Irish subjects. She found Cork 'not at all like an English town' and 'rather foreign'. 'The crowd is a noisy, excitable, but very good humoured one,' she wrote in her diary, 'running and pushing about, and laughing, talking and shrieking.' Even this Royal junketing did not persuade the British that Ireland was a suitable holiday centre. Their views on that sad country were as vague and as suspicious as those of Lady Eustace herself in *The Eustace Diamonds*:

' "Ah!—I myself am a poor man;—for my rank, I mean," said he [Lord Fawn].

' "A man in your position, Lord Fawn, and your talents and genius for business, can never be poor."

' "My father's property was all Irish, you know."

' "Was it indeed?"

' "And he was an Irish peer, till Lord Melbourne gave him an English peerage."

' "An Irish peer, was he?" Lizzie understood nothing of this, but presumed that an Irish peer was a peer who had not sufficient money to live upon.

' "... He was then made Lord Fawn of Richmond, in the peerage of the United Kingdom. Fawn Court, you know, belonged to my mother's father before my mother's marriage. The property in Ireland is still mine, but there's no place on it."

' "Indeed!"

' "There was a house, but my father allowed it to tumble down. It's in Tipperary;—not at all a desirable country to live in."

' "Oh, dear no! Don't they murder the people?" '

For whatever reason Mr John Murray rejected Trollope's draft guide-book, it cannot have been that it was bad, since no one in Albemarle Street had bothered to read it, or even to unpack the parcel in which it had been posted. By this time its author knew Ireland exceptionally well, and we can suppose that it was well-written and competent. Neither adjective can be applied to his next work, *La Vendée*, which was published in the summer of 1850. Trollope obstinately tells us that he had reread the book lately, and was 'not ashamed of it', while admitting that when he wrote it he 'knew, in truth, nothing of life in the La Vendèe country'. Possibly his mother had suggested the theme—or it may have been that 1848, the Year of the Revolutions, caused him to read such memoirs of the 1790s as those of Madame de Larochjáquelin, who was a participant in the Breton rising. One reviewer wrote that Trollope's book showed 'want of energy and imagination'. Another proclaimed that the events in *La Vendée* were already only too well known to English readers, and that a new novel on the subject lacked point.

Undeterred, Anthony next set to and composed a costume drama, partly in blank verse and partly in prose. This play was set in Bruges, and, like *La Vendée*, dealt with the events of 1792. Called *The Noble Jilt*, the piece was neither acted nor published; it has since been issued in a limited edition, arranged by Michael Sadleir, in 1923. The play consists of five long acts and is totally devoid of merit. That any intelligent man in his early thirties could have perpetrated it is very hard to comprehend. The kindest thing to say about *The Noble Jilt* is that it might have been contrived by a scholarly yet unskilled adolescent.

In certain ways, *The Noble Jilt* is reminiscent of Bulwer-Lytton's theatrical successes—*The Lady of Lyons* and *Richelieu*—but, in 1850, these had been successes more than a decade ago. Trollope's play is littered with 'twoulds and 'tises. Neither is it devoid of is'ts:

> ' "Is't true the Austrians have left the city?" '

nor of e'ens:

> ' "love's not enough to fill a human heart.
> E'en though it beat within a woman's breast." '

There is also a good measure of 'Tush, tush, child', as well as the free use of archaic phrases such as 'What, all amort, Meg?' For Trollope enthusiasts, *The Noble Jilt* has a certain esoteric interest for, having sent it to his mother's old friend George Bartley, a well-known actor-manager then in retirement, Anthony received a letter so condemnatory that he happily never ventured to pen a play again. '. . . I must reluctantly add that, had I still been a manager, "The Noble Jilt" is not a play I could have recommended for production.' This was one of the few letters Trollope ever kept, although he sneakingly disagreed with it, calling it in his own autobiography 'a blow in the face'. 'But I accepted the judgment loyally,' he adds, 'and said not a word on the subject to anyone. I merely showed the letter to my wife, declaring my conviction that it must be taken as gospel. And as critical gospel it has since been accepted.' He destroyed neither George Bartley's epistle nor the fair-copied text of the play; rather detrimentally he used the plot in later life when he began to write the story of an ignoble or at least a boring jilt, Alice Vavasor, the flaccid heroine of *Can You Forgive Her?* He also amused himself (and us too) by introducing an imaginary first night of *The Noble Jilt* into *The Eustace Diamonds*, on an evening in which Lady Eustace is going to the Haymarket Theatre with her American friends Mrs Carbuncle and a Carbuncle niece, the hysterical Lucinda Roanoke:

'Mrs Carbuncle was very fond of the play, and made herself acquainted with every new piece as it came out . . . The three ladies had a box at the Haymarket taken for this very evening, at which a new piece, "The Noble Jilt" from the hand of a very eminent author, was to be produced. Mrs Carbuncle had talked a great deal about "The Noble Jilt" ... She was very anxious for the success of the piece, which, as she said, had its merits; but she was sure that it wouldn't do ... Lucinda, also, was determined that she would see the new piece ... "I daresay the play may be very bad," she said, "but it can hardly be as bad as real life." ... The play, as a play, was a failure.

Analysing the piece in the carriage on their way back from the theatre, the three ladies proclaim differing views. As usual in that forceful novel, it is Lizzie Eustace who shows a clear, amoral common sense:

' "A noble jilt, my dears," said Mrs Carbuncle eloquently, "is a contradiction in terms. There can be no such thing ... The delicacy of the female character should not admit of hesitation between two men. The idea is quite revolting."

' "But may not one have an idea of no man at all?" asked Lucinda. "Must that be revolting also?" ...

' "If she finds that she has made a mistake——?" said Lucinda fiercely. "Why shouldn't a young woman make a mistake as well as an old woman?"

' "My dear, such mistakes, as you call them, always rise from fantastic notions. Look at this piece. Why does the lady jilt her lover? Not because she doesn't like him. She's just as fond of him as ever."

' "He's a stupid sort of fellow, and I think she was quite right," said Lizzie.'

Hurt by Bartley's professional criticism of *The Noble Jilt*, discouraged by Murray's offhand attitude to the Irish guide-book and by the failure of *La Vendée*, Anthony Trollope was saved from the doldrums by his sudden recall to his own country, to the highly important assignment of reorganizing the postal districts and methods of the whole West Country. This work took up so much of his time that he wrote nothing of his own for the best part of two years. But when he did sit down to his desk again he produced a short novel which has ensured his immortality: *The Warden*. Having seemingly failed in his delineations of Irish, and then of Breton life, he now invented a quite new and ageless county of his own—that of Barsetshire. It all began one solitary summer's evening, on the greensward of Salisbury Cathedral close. What was it that engendered such a change?

Anthony Trollope's new official assignment—that of reorganizing the postal services of the south-west of England—proved unexpectedly agreeable: 'I spent two of the happiest years of my life at the task.' It was his ambition to 'cover the country with rural letter-carriers', none of whom were to be obliged to walk more than sixteen miles on foot a day, and whose work was much facilitated by Trollope's passion for working out intricate short cuts across the English fields. Accompanied by Barney Macintyre, the Banagher groom, Trollope visited every house in the large district assigned to him, riding all over the country and carefully measuring the distances which the letter-carriers were instructed to cover. Somewhat typically, he would try to catch these letter-carriers out, and he admits that he was 'sometimes a little unjust to them'. He began his work down in Devonshire, minutely exploring 'every nook in that county', and continued in Cornwall, Somersetshire, Dorset, the Channel Islands and parts of Oxfordshire, Wiltshire, Gloucestershire, Worcestershire, Herefordshire, Monmouth and the six south Welsh counties.

For Rose Trollope, tagging about behind him and perching in furnished rooms or in hotels, it cannot have been a very contented period, for the children had to be moved from city to city with their parents, and the question of the two boys' education would not have been an easy one in the midst of so nomadic a life. Exeter, Bristol, Carmarthen, Cheltenham and Worcester were but some of the places in which they pitched their tent during these two years. For Anthony, although he was too absorbed in his postal activities to write a book, the experience of these years proved beyond price; for by no other means could he have forced an entrance into every and any West Country manor-house or vicarage, farm cottage or village shop. As is often the way with novelists, he seems to have taken in more impressions than he was himself aware of. Staying with the historian E. A. Freeman only a few weeks before his own death, Anthony was taken on walks down the Somersetshire lanes, over hill over dale into the fields, and through the woods where, in spring, bluebells glimmer. Freeman and their companion, the agile Bishop of Clifton, who managed to haul old Anthony over the stiles, were determined to get the novelist to admit that when writing about Barchester Cathedral he had had that of

Wells in mind—Wells Cathedral with its two towers like those of Barchester, and its old charity for woolcarders almost identical with Hiram's Hospital in *The Warden*. The old author became testy and declared that it was not Wells he had in mind at all, but Winchester, and that he had never heard of the Wells woolcarders in his life. His companions assumed that he had merely forgotten his knowledge and his impressions of Somerset thirty years before.

It always exasperated Trollope to be asked such questions about his own books. Moreover, he took a perverse pride in publicly declaring that he had had no knowledge of life in a cathedral close. He had simply applied to the Barsetshire clergy the characteristics, vanities and muddled intentions of people in other professions about whom he knew more. 'I never lived in any cathedral city,—except London,' he tells us, 'never knew anything of any Close, and at that time had enjoyed no peculiar intimacy with any clergyman. My archdeacon, who had been said to be life-like ... was, I think, the simple result of an effort of my moral consciousness.' Just as he wanted to prove that the writing of fiction was a mechanical trick which anyone could, with application, perform, so was he anxious to persuade himself and others that the whole Barsetshire series had evolved from his 'moral consciousness'. It is hard to equate his assertion about never having lived in a cathedral city with his own account, in this very same autobiography, of schooldays in Winchester, and his reference to spending time in lodgings in Exeter and then in Worcester. His childhood memories of his mother's father, the courteous and eccentric old vicar of Heckfield in Berkshire, with his ideas for patent carriages and for plates on which your knife did not squeak, must certainly have helped him in creating, for instance, Mr Harding in *The Warden*. Escott, who used boldly to talk to his friend about the possible originals for the clergy in the Barsetshire series, had seen portraits of this Berkshire grandfather, the Reverend Mr Milton, and declared that these alone could have suggested to Anthony 'particular features and whole personages for the Barchester gallery'. To Escott Trollope did agree that he had, in his own words, 'seen a certain amount of clergymen on my Post Office tours, just as I had seen them before at Harrow or Winchester ... But what I am conscious of is having depicted the Platonic idea of a cathedral town. Human nature varies infinitely in its outer garb; its inward heart is much about the same everywhere.' He likewise told Escott that *The Warden* and *Bar-*

chester Towers 'grew out of *The Times* correspondence columns during a dull season of the 'fifties'.

Personally, I do not find that it adds one iota to my enjoyment of the Barsetshire novels to know whether their fictive county capital was or was not modelled on Winchester. Their creator thought the same: 'Take my Barchester,' he remarked one day to Escott. 'Here and there may be detected a touch of Salisbury, sometimes perhaps of Winchester.' Instead of such unprofitable speculations, it seems of more use and more relevance to recognize the immense, and to us today quite incomprehensible, influence of the Church of England in the 'forties, 'fifties and 'sixties of the last century. Morning prayers and Sunday sermons, both in church and at home, grace before meals, Evensong, benefices, preferments, formed, in the countryside, thick strands of the warp and woof of English upper- and middle-class life. It is the subtle interaction of the social and the clerical elements constituting the apparently stable and immutable pattern of life in cathedral cities and in the houses of the country gentry, which makes Trollope's Barsetshire novels so fascinating. Frederic Harrison wrote:

'There was scarcely an English village without a rectory or a house whose occupant could not have passed for Lord Lufton or Mark Robarts ... The rectory, the country, and the castle, like the inmates of each, described in *Framley Parsonage* exactly reflect all that was most distinctive of the 'sixties, and therefore invest the story with something of the usefulness to the historian of the future possessed by Jane Austen's novels, or discerned by Lecky and Macaulay in Fielding and Smollett.'

But beneath its superficial assurance, the middle of the last century was becoming, religiously speaking, a time of grave disquiet for Anglican clergy and laymen alike. On the one hand there was the defection of such influential Oxford men as Newman and Manning, who became Roman Catholic converts in 1845 and 1851 respectively. For many Protestants Oxford had itself become a word of menace. ' "Well he has just come from Oxford, you know," said Mr Townsend [a bigoted clergyman in *Castle Richmond*, speaking of the young heir to that property], "and at the present moment Oxford is the most dangerous place to which a young man can be sent." ' On the other hand Lady Lufton, in choosing Mark Robarts for her living of Framley, chiefly selected him because of his Oxford education and views:

'Lady Lufton was a woman who thought much on religious

matters, and would by no means have been disposed to place anyone in a living, merely because such a one had been her son's friend. Her tendencies were High Church, and she was enabled to perceive that those of young Mark Robarts ran in the same direction ... Lady Lufton did not carry her High Church principles so far as to advocate celibacy for the clergy.'

People of lesser station than Lady Lufton, and not so lenient to clergymen, helped to defend the Church's *status quo* by a suffocating routine. Good old Miss Jemima Stanbury, the richest spinster in Exeter, owning much property on the cathedral close, exacted from her impoverished little niece (the secondary heroine of *He Knew He Was Right*), a promise to attend an almost perpetual series of church services:

' "Come it's a fine evening, and we'll go out and look at the towers. You've never seen them yet, I suppose?"

'So they went out, and finding the verger ... they walked up and down the aisles, and Dorothy was instructed as to what would be expected from her in regard to the outward forms of religion. She was to go to the Cathedral service on the morning of every week-day, and on Sundays in the afternoon. On Sunday mornings she was to attend the little church of St Margaret. On Sunday evenings it was the practice of Miss Stanbury to read a sermon in the dining-room to all of whom her household consisted. Did Dorothy like daily services? Dorothy ... said that she had no objection to going to church every day when there was not too much to do.

' "There never need be too much to do to attend the Lord's house," said Miss Stanbury, somewhat angrily.'

In *Phineas Finn* the fact that Lady Laura Kennedy, in love with that attractive Irishman, adamantly refuses to go to church twice a day on Sundays is her opening volley in what soon becomes internecine warfare with her rich, strict newly-wed husband.

Another menace to the Church of England at this time was the growth of Methodism, even in the rural districts. This was a subject which Anthony Trollope never seriously tackled, partly because it was his mother's favourite stamping-ground and partly because, as he says, he knew nothing whatever about Methodists. In *The Vicar of Bullhampton*, however, the vicar's landlord uses a group of local Primitive Methodists as a species of anti-missile missile launched against his own incumbent. The Vicar has defended the family of a Bullhampton miller, whose son is suspected of murder, while one of the daughters, Carry Brattle, has become a London prostitute. The landlord, the Marquess of Trowbridge, demands their extradition from his neighbour—they do not actually live on the Marquess's land. The Vicar sides with his friend the nearby squire to save the family and their home. Lord Trowbridge becomes incensed by such behaviour in the holder of his church living, and he gratuitously offers to the Primitive Methodist Minister a triangle of ground immediately opposite the vicarage gates, and urges him to build on it a chapel for his small, solemn-faced flock. In the end the ground is proved to be glebe-land, and the triumphant vicar sees the Methodist Chapel demolished. As a tale *The Vicar of Bull-hampton* is, in its own author's words, 'not very bad, and it certainly is not very good'. Written to arouse sympathy for Carry Brattle, the miller's prostitute daughter, the book demanded a second and quite stainless heroine, whom Trollope provided in the insipid person of Mary Lowther, yet another of his indecisive young ladies who cannot bring themselves to decide between two suitors.

Laid out according to this well-thumbed formula, the book was not even in its author's eyes especially gripping: 'As I myself have forgotten what the heroine does and says—except that she tumbles into a ditch—I cannot expect that anyone else should remember her. But I have forgotten nothing that was done or said by Carry Brattle.' Yet, all the same, *The Vicar of Bullhampton* remains of interest, not only as witness to the normal attitude to the 'fallen woman' then current, but also as registering Anglican alarm over the spread of Methodism. The Vicar's wife, in every other way a charming and most competent young woman, becomes distraught when she hears the tinkle of the new Methodist Chapel bell, and declares that she will never be able to go out by her front gate again. We find in most of Anthony Trollope's novels the obesssional mid-Victorian fear of encroachment upon established English beliefs and ways, a process of erosion of which he became more and more aware towards the end of his life. This fear, and his conviction that it was justified, give to his later novels a tone of murky pessimism.

With Roman Catholicism and Anglo-Catholicism flourishing at the older universities, and with Methodism taking over the new industrial cities of the midlands and the north, there were elements both lay and clerical within the Church of England's fold who felt that the time had come to deal with at least some of the old abuses and ancient anomalies which had long disfigured that institution. Before Trollope decided to write *The*

Warden, certain of these had been under attack in the correspondence columns of *The Times* during that 'dull season of the 'fifties'. The one which caused most uproar, and which was not legally settled until 1857, concerned the beautiful old medieval almshouses on the edge of the city of Winchester, and known as St Cross. The case concerned the Earl of Guildford, in whose gift the wardenship of St Cross and of its aged gentlemen lay. We need not go into the details of this controversy, but, like others of the same nature, it concerned the problem of whether it was justifiable for an appointed warden to accept as his own sinecure a large income from the lands of the charitable trust of St Cross—this income having grown during four centuries to a sum undreamed of by its founder. Should not such monies, under the terms of the trust, be distributed amongst the inmates and not pocketed by Lord Guildford's nominee?

Anthony Trollope, who had been following this controversy in *The Times*, was impressed by the arguments against such misuse of a charitable trust, but at the same time he was irritated by the virulence with which the present incumbent of St Cross was arraigned in the newspaper columns. To him it seemed that, while the system certainly needed revising, no one could blame the wretched man personally for having accepted a lucrative office and easeful living conditions which to himself and everyone else had seemed sanctioned by an immemorial tradition. It was while reflecting on this subject that Trollope conceived the existence of an unworldly, mild and elderly Warden of an alms-house, who had never questioned the preferment given to him by the bishop, nor his own right to a charming house and eight hundred a year, while the twelve old bedesmen who were nominally in his charge received, from the charity's monies, one shilling and fourpence a day. Trollope's notion was that, once this Warden was convinced that the newspapers' attacks on him were justified, he would resign all his emoluments, move out of the Warden's house, and decide to live in obscurity and poverty for the rest of his life.

This was the plot which surfaced ready-made from the depths of Anthony Trollope's moral consciousness as he leaned upon the parapet of the little bridge that spans the stream by Salisbury Close, one midsummer's evening of the year 1851. He tells us that, as he stood there, he saw it all in his mind's eye, and made out to his own satisfaction the exact spot on which Hiram's Hospital should stand. 'Certainly,' he testifies, 'no work that I ever did took up so much of my thoughts.'

More than twelve months after his flash of insight in Salisbury Close Anthony Trollope settled down, on July 29th,
1852,* at Tenbury in Worcestershire, to write *The Warden*, or
as he entitled it before his publisher intervened, *The Precentor*.
He later put the book to one side and did not finish it until the
autumn of 1853, in Belfast. With his inherent inability to judge
his own best work, and with his bluffly propounded theory of
the novelist as journeyman, he did not perceive that this leisurely
speed of creation greatly helped to make *The Warden* as good as
it is: 'It was only one small volume, and in later days would
have been completed in six weeks,—or in two months at the
longest if other work had pressed.' In later days, more than
probably, *The Warden* would thus have turned out as flimsy as
Kept in the Dark (1882) or that unpersuasive tale of the Australian bush, *Harry Heathcote of Gangoil* (1874).

Published by Longmans in January 1855, the novel was
given serious attention by such critics as John Forster and H. F.
Chorley—although at that time all reviews were, of course,
anonymous. In a notice in the *Examiner* attributed to Forster,
the book was called 'a clever novel, though we are not quite
content with it', while Chorley, in the *Athenaeum*, described it
as 'a clever, spirited, sketchy story, upon the difficulties which
surround that vexed question, the administration of the charitable trusts in England ... The whole story is well and smartly
told, with too much indifference as to the rights of the case.'
The author was also accused of needing 'a much stricter education of his taste. It sometimes serves him admirably, for it does
not lack acuteness, but for lack of proper training it is apt to go
astray.' Chapter Fifteen of *The Warden*, with its clumsy caricatures of Charles Dickens ('Mr Popular Sentiment') and of
Thomas Carlyle ('Dr Pessimist Anticant') were included in
these breaches of taste. To us these passages mar *The Warden*,
not as breaching taste but as falsifying the book's otherwise con-
sistent tone.

It must have been to such noisy interruptions as these that
Frederic Harrison was referring when, as we have seen, he admitted that 'good old Anthony had a coarse vein; it was in the
family'. We shall find many more examples of this coarseness in
his other novels. Why he should have, for a few pages, sus-

* In his autobiography, which not surprisingly contains other
chronological errors, Trollope writes of beginning the book in July
1853.

pended the flow of narrative in *The Warden* to hold Dickens and Carlyle up to ridicule it is hard to understand. In earlier days he had admired Thomas Carlyle, but having in 1851 bought and read *Latter-Day Pamphlets*, he discarded him utterly. 'I look on him as a man who was always in danger of going mad in literature and who has now done so. I used to swear by some of his earlier works. But to my taste his writings have lost their pith and humour,' he wrote in a letter to his mother, and in another context he called Carlyle 'silly and arrogant'. He was, at least, mercifully far from the veneration with which Dickens treated the Sage of Chelsea—a veneration which was, indeed, responsible for that misguided novel *A Tale of Two Cities*. Trollope's scornful attitude to Charles Dickens who, when *The Warden* was published, was at the very height of his fame and success, sprang from his detestation of humanitarians and reformers; but may it not also have been tinged with jealousy? The flamboyant, wealthy life which Charles Dickens, only three years Anthony's senior, was leading, must indeed have been galling to so slow a starter in the fields of literature as the Deputy-Surveyor of provincial post-offices. Carlyle, too, was revered, and was treated as an oracle both by London society and by the English public. The contrast would have been made more bitter by the fact that before he had finished writing *The Warden*, Trollope was posted back to Ireland, and had to complete his novel in the dread, grey, alien city of Belfast. He was doomed to live in the north of Ireland from the autumn of 1853 to that of 1854, when he and his wife were reprieved by the postal authorities and could take a house at Donnybrook near Dublin for the next five years.

Oddly enough, *The Warden* did not at first catch on. From Longmans in 1855 Trollope received a cheque for nine pounds odd, at the end of 1856 he received a cheque for £10. 15s. 1d.: '... as regarded remuneration for the time', he observes, 'stonebreaking would have done better'. *The Warden* sold but seven hundred copies in five years; the remainder of the original printing of one thousand was then rebound as a cheap edition. It was not until the success of *Barchester Towers* and its Barsetshire sequels that *The Warden* achieved a reading public and came into its own. Its author was, therefore, once more disappointed and once more denied success. But this time he had begun to understand the special quality of his own gift. He termed this 'the most useful' gift any author could have—and assessed it as having a power to realize to himself a series of portraits, and the ability 'so to put them on the canvas that my readers should see that which I meant them to see'. The harvest of those long hours of his boyhood and youth, spent peopling for himself 'a world outside the world', could now at length be garnered. The characters of Barchester Close and Plumstead Episcopi were, so to speak, clamouring to get out. Not that one can connect any great resonance of clamour with Warden Harding or the enfeebled and well-intentioned old bishop. But Archdeacon Grantley, his wife and, briefly, their odious children had become, to their creator and to his readers, emphatic characters to be reckoned with, and so had Eleanor Harding and her lover, John Bold. Contemporary reviewers judged Trollope's attitude to John Bold, 'the Brutus of Barchester', to be ambivalent, perhaps rightly labelling the results of Bold's reforming zeal 'inconclusive' and thus 'a grave drawback' to the story of *The Warden*. However that may be, and although Trollope lets Bold marry Eleanor Harding, he kills him off in some mysterious way before the opening of *Barchester Towers* so that Eleanor, a rich and attractive young widow with a baby, may become a target for the bachelor fortune-hunters of the town.

Anthony Trollope's analogy of his gift for characterization with that of painting a series of portraits on canvas which his public could then see, is not a happy one. His highest talent, which had emerged even in *The Macdermots of Ballycloran* and, more sharply, in *The Kellys and the O'Kellys* is the marvellous skill of allowing his diverse personages to reveal their inmost natures in simple everyday speech. To Jonn Bold, for instance, who has taken on himself the public duty of proving that Mr Harding has no right to his own house or to his own income, the Warden replies with a transparent honesty and absence of all rancour:

' "I presume you think I am not entitled to the income I receive from the hospital and that others are entitled to it ... pray do what you consider to be your duty; I can give you no assistance, neither will I offer you any obstacle. Let me, however, suggest to you, that you can in no wise forward your views nor I mine, by any discussion between us. Here comes Eleanor and the ponies, and we'll go in to tea." '

That touch of Eleanor and the ponies and the waiting teatable is, we are convinced, exactly the way in which the Warden of Hiram's Hospital would put an end to an awkward and vexing conversation.

We would have supposed that, after inventing Barchester in

The Warden, and after recognizing his own particular bent for producing lifelike characters moving in probable situations, Anthony Trollope would have gone straight on to write *Barchester Towers*. He did, in fact, write to Longmans from Dublin in February 1855 explaining that he was at work on an unnamed sequel to *The Warden*. According to Michael Sadleir, 'the reply was discouraging; the sequel to *The Warden* was abandoned'—although it would seem more likely that it was merely put away in a drawer, to re-emerge presently as the opening chapters of *Barchester Towers*. Thus deterred, Trollope plunged into an activity which can only be characterized as both inexplicable and idiotic. Having trounced Carlyle in *The Warden*, he now tried to surpass him at his own game, writing a book which he called *The New Zealander*. The title was intended to refer to Macaulay's 'New Zealander standing on the ruins of London Bridge', and the book's purport, it seems, was to excoriate most current British institutions, and to show just how the country could be kept from total collapse. From Donnybrook outside Dublin he sent the manuscript to William Longman, whose reader stood amazed:

'If you had not told me that this work was by the author of *The Warden* I could not have believed it. Such a contrast between two works from the same pen was hardly ever before witnessed. The object of the work is to show how England may be saved from the ruin that now threatens her ! ! ! ...

With this view the author goes through all the leading influences and institutions of the State and pours out the vial of his wrath upon them. This he does in such a loose, illogical and rhapsodical way that I regret to say I would advise you not to publish the work on any terms.

All the good points in the work have already been treated of by Mr Carlyle, of whose *Latter-Day Pamphlets* this work, *both in style and matter*, is a most feeble imitation.'

This extraordinary aberration is not even mentioned in the *Autobiography*, and would never have been heard of had not Sadleir unearthed the reader's report and a letter of Trollope's own in the archives of Messrs Longmans, Green (since destroyed in the Second World War). In writing *The New Zealander* Trollope may have been motivated by the success that Carlyle could so effortlessly achieve—on the 'if-you-can't-beat-them-join-them' principle. Anthony Trollope perpetrated the book on the verge of his fortieth birthday. Whether he pretended so or not, he very much minded his own state of continual nonentity, and it is reasonable to fancy that, in a childish mood, he thought that he might flame over the reading public as a new prophet and politico-philosophical firebrand. If Carlyle, whom he had once described as having a 'grain of commonsense smothered up in a sack of the sheerest trash', could sear and scorch the British reading public, who only came back to him for more, why shouldn't Anthony himself do as well, and spring—at one starry leap—to fame? In a passage of disarming candour he informs us:

'To be known as somebody,—to be Anthony Trollope if to be no more,—is to me much. The feeling is a very general one, and I think it beneficient. It is that which has been called the 'last infirmity of noble mind'. The infirmity is so human that the man who lacks it is either above or below humanity. I own to the infirmity.'

And what, by the age of forty, had Anthony Trollope publicly achieved? He had published four novels, one of them interesting, one of them good, one of them destined to become a deathless classic in due course. He had at last, in 1854, been promoted to a full Surveyorship at seven hundred pounds a year. For some reason—his inability to get on well with colleagues and underlings perhaps—he had been passed over for promotion again and again. 'The more I see the way in which the post-office work is done, the more aggrieved I feel at not receiving the promotion I have a right to expect,' he had written to his mother in the autumn of 1852. That winter he had applied to Lord Hardwicke, the Postmaster General in Lord Derby's ministry, to be made the new Superintendent of Mail Coaches. 'I have been 18 years in the service,' he wrote, 'and I believe I may confidently refer your Lordship to any of the officers under whom I have served, and especially to Col. Maberley, as to my fitness for the situation.' Lord Hardwicke may indeed have referred himself to Colonel Maberley, for this important post was given to some other applicant.

Aggrieved about promotion he might feel, but in other ways he was contented. He told his mother that his perennial lowly status did 'not really annoy' him: 'I can't fancy any one being much happier than I am,—or having less in the world to complain of. It often strikes me how wonderfully well I have fallen on my feet.' None the less, a generally unrecognized gift—or, as Henry James frankly termed it, a genius—for writing gripping English fiction was still a harsh burden to bear. One reason for the positive spate of novels which he wrote once he was rich and famous may have been an anxiety to make up for lost time. Forty is a very dangerous age for an ambitious man to find that he is still unknown.

(iii)

It is a sombre and a sobering thought that Belfast must be accepted as the birthplace of Barsetshire. 'Where shall we live?' Anthony had written in his letter telling his mother of his promotion to Surveyorship. 'We both dislike the north—& the districts may all be changed ... We won't buy our furniture at any rate till we have discussed with you the colour of the drawing-room curtains.' 'I should prefer the South to the North of Ireland,' he wrote to a Bristol acquaintance in November 1854, 'preferring on the whole papistical to presbyterian tendencies. I shall hope to leave this district some day, but till then shall endeavour to make myself contented ... In the meantime, tho' the North of Ireland is not the choicest permanent residence, it has some charms for the tourist ... My present residence is Belfast, but I hope to be enabled to move to Dublin which is a nice city enough.'

Having escaped from Belfast after twelve months there, the Anthony Trollopes settled with satisfaction into a large house in Seaview Terrace, Donnybrook, now a suburb of Dublin but in those days a village on its own, within easy reach of the Irish capital, where the Queen's representative, the Lord-Lieutenant, held semi-royal court in the Castle, and went under heavy guard to Sunday service in the city. At Donnybrook, in April 1855, Trollope started to write *Barchester Towers*. The manuscript was completed by November 1856, and published in London in the spring of the following year. In this splendid novel the Barsetshire world is widely extended, and yields many more and diverse inhabitants of what Trollope once called 'the dear county', of which, while writing *Framley Parsonage*, he made a sketch-map.* And it is not, in this second Barsetshire novel, only a matter of our meeting numerous new characters, but of being shown new places within the shires. Anthony wrote:

'I had it all in my mind,—its roads and railroad, its towns and parishes, its members of Parliament, and the different hunts which rode over it. I knew all the great lords and their castles, the squires and their parks, the rectors and their churches.'

In a passage at the very beginning of *Doctor Thorne*, Trol-

* See endpaper map.

lope wrote of his imaginary county with a lyrical affection:

'There is a county in the West of England ... very dear to those who know it well. Its green pastures, its waving wheat, its deep and shady and,—let us add—dirty lanes, its paths and stiles, its tawny-coloured, well-built rural churches, its avenues of beeches, and frequent Tudor mansions, its constant country hunt, its social graces, and the general air of clanship that pervades it, has made it to its own inhabitants a favoured land of Goshen.'

Anthony Trollope's expanding vision of Barsetshire in the six novels devoted to the denizens of that county can be likened to the opening of some great theatrical spectacular. As the curtain rises, the audience sees nothing but a pitch-dark, empty-seeming stage, with a single spotlight on a cathedral façade. But as the stage slowly lightens, you realize that it is not empty at all but crowded with actors and actresses, standing in groups within a varied architectural setting. In *The Warden* Trollope only saw Barchester Close, and, briefly, Plumstead Episcopi. He had heard of both Crabtree Canonicorum and of Crabtree Parva, but had never seen either. Next, while writing *Barchester Towers*, he found that the county was more populated than he had ever dreamed it to be—found, for example, that it contained the fine old Elizabethan pile of Ullathorne, home of the ancient family of Thorne, of Ullathorne. The Bishop of Barchester, an ineffectual old gentleman, expires in the first chapter, to be replaced by another equally ineffectual prelate, who is dominated by his wife Mrs Proudie in much the same way that Bishop Grantley had been dominated by his son, the Archdeacon; the episcopal palace, every room in which Trollope knew, now becomes a major scene of action. Hiram's Hospital, with no warden and scarcely any bedesmen left, stands deserted in its weed-grown garden.

There is much more of town life than in *The Warden*. The main theme of the novel is, basically, the impact on town and county of two strange and disparate women; the bishop's wife, Mrs Proudie, and the Signora Vesey-Neroni, whose Italian husband has deserted her. The Signora's father, the Reverend Doctor Vesey Stanhope, is the incumbent of Crabtree Canonicorum, but usually lives with his son and his two daughters on the Italian lakes, using the revenues of his parish. The effect of the Signora Vesey-Neroni upon the clergy and also the laity of Barchester may be compared to that of Zuleika Dobson on the Oxford undergraduates. The very knowledge that Madeline is a cripple, and receives gentlemen visitors who have to sit close up to the sofa on which she permanently lies, gives her, in the eyes of part of Barchester, an additional exotic charm. The fact that the husband who had crippled her and then deserted her was an Italian, and that Madeline herself is a feline, sophisticated, Italianate flirt, sets her apart from the ladies of Barchester but makes her a centre of sinister attraction to Barchester men.

Anthony Trollope, although he wrote a few short stories about Vienna or Venice or the Pyrenees and loved to travel abroad, was himself singularly insular and English. The very idea of Italy seems to have unnerved him, for whenever that country or its people come into his novels it is, generally, on a pejorative note. Italy is the refuge of erring husbands, such as Louis Trevelyan in *He Knew He Was Right*. Italy is a country notably careless about certificates of marriage or of birth—witness overdressed little Lord Popenjoy and his sallow Italian mother. Trollope's many honeymooners tend to go to Switzerland rather than to Italy. It was in Italy that that evil debauchee Lord Ongar died of drink, after trying to force his wife Julia (born a Brabazon) to sleep with his dissolute friend Count Pateroff. It is to Italy that the amoral old Duke of Omnium (in *Phineas Finn*) wishes to lure Madame Max Goesler, but that Viennese lady is too many for him:

' "Marie," said the Duke, "you will go abroad when the summer is over."

' ... "Yes, probably; to Vienna. I have property in Vienna, you know, which must be looked after."

' "Do not mind Vienna this year. Come to Italy."

' "What; in summer, Duke?"

' "The lakes are charming in August. I have a villa on Como which is empty now, and I think I shall go there. If you do not know the Italian lakes, I shall be so happy to show them to you."

' "I know them well, my lord. When I was young I was on the Maggiore almost alone. Some day I will tell you a history of what I was in those days."

' "You shall tell it me there."

' "No, my lord, I fear not. I have no villa there."

' "Will you accept the loan of mine? It shall be all your own while you use it."

' " ... No, Duke; it behoves me to live in houses of my own. Women of whom more is known can afford to be your guests."

' "Marie, I would have no other guest than you."

' "It cannot be so, Duke."
' "And why not?"
' "Why not? ... Because the world would say that the Duke
of Omnium had a new mistress, and that Madame Goesler was
the woman. Do you think that I would be any man's mistress;—
even yours?" '

It will be relevant at this juncture to consider the Anthony
Trollopes' first visit to iniquitous Italy. This had taken place in
April 1853. Had they not crossed the Alps that spring and gone
to stay at the Villino Trollope in Florence, we should never
have had the doubtful pleasure of meeting the Signora Vesey-
Neroni in Barchester at all.

Life at the Villino Trollope was the acme of agreeable expatriate living. Tom Trollope, whose chief interest in life was
money, and after that works of art, had adjusted himself perfectly to the Anglo-Italian scene beside the Arno with his wife,
the ethereal Theodosia, and his mother Fanny Trollope. Also
part of the household were Theodosia's father, Mr Garrow, a
partially Indian widower, and Theodosia's month-old baby,
Bice, who had been born, after five childless years, that same
March. Florentine gossip whispered that baby Bice was not a
Trollope at all, but this was never suspected inside the family
circle. Theodosia Trollope was an ardent exponent of Italian
unity, in girlhood had not escaped being flattered and petted by
old Landor, and was herself the writer of harmless verse, as
these lines from a sixteen-stanza panegyric about her baby
daughter will testify:

In the noon-day's golden pleasance,
   Little Bice, baby fair,
With a fresh and flowery presence,
   Dances round her nurse's chair,
In the old grey loggia dances, haloed by her golden hair.

Pretty pearl in sober setting,
   Where the arches garner shade!
Cones of maize like golden netting,
   Fringe the sturdy colonnade,
And the lizards pertly pausing glance across the balustrade.

Old Mrs Trollope's weekly evening receptions were 'attended
by some of the pleasantest of the English residents in Florence',
and she always had her own whist table. She made much of her

daughter-in-law Rose, and gave ample return for her own rather scary visit to Mallow in 1849. She took Rose about the sights of Florence, explaining everything to her. She bought her a dress of Italian silk and gave her a mosaic brooch which had been given to herself by Princess Metternich in Vienna many years before. Altogether it would seem to have been a very successful holiday in springtime Tuscany. Yet, though we may rejoice that the visit produced Madeline Vesey-Neroni, Longmans' squeamish reader did not. He informed Longmans that 'prebendary doctor Stanhope's lovely daughter ... is a repulsive, exaggerated and unnatural character'. He also described the seductive Signora as 'a great blot on the work'. The whole of this reader's report on *Barchester Towers* leaves us fully as amazed as was that same gentleman by Anthony's *New Zealander*. As an example of what fiction writers of the 1850s were forced to undergo, this pig-headed man's assessment of the manuscript of *Barchester Towers* deserves our attention.

(iv)

Begun in April 1855, it took Anthony Trollope nineteen months to write *Barchester Towers*, a novel three times the length of *The Warden*. This was the first of his books to be mainly written in railway carriages. His official work no longer required him to go about on horseback, but it still involved an enormous amount of travelling. He therefore made for himself what he called 'a tablet', and after a few days of experimentation found that he could write as easily on it in a moving railway carriage as on his static desk at home. He wrote his pages in pencil, and these the co-operative Rose later copied out in her own fair hand. At first he was embarrassed at writing a novel in front of four or five fellow passengers, feeling that it gave an 'appearance of literary ostentation' from which he shrank. Soon, however, he became accustomed to it. A young journalist whose parents he knew in Devonshire, has recorded that on a November day in the 1870s Trollope happened, at the Euston Station, to enter the compartment of a north-bound train in which the lad was already seated. 'Just recognizing me, he began to talk cheerfully enough for some little time; then, putting on a huge fur cap, part of which fell down over his shoulders, he suddenly asked: "Do you ever sleep when you are travelling? I always do"; and forthwith sank into that kind of snore compared by Carlyle to a Chaldean trumpet in the new moon.' Trollope awoke again at either Grantham or Preston, and then asked another question:

'Do you ever write when you are travelling?' 'No,' said the young man. 'I always do,' asserted Trollope. 'Quick as thought out came the tablet and the pencil, and the process of putting words on paper continued without a break till the point was reached at which, his journey done, he left the carriage.' Meeting him some years later, Trollope told his former travelling-companion that on that particular journey he had written two whole chapters of a novel for serialization.

Barchester Towers completed, Anthony sent it to William Longman, who, in his turn, gave it to a publisher's reader whose identity the novel's author could never discover. This person found the Signora Vesey-Neroni insupportable, as we already know. He called the book 'inferior to *The Warden*' and declared that *Barchester Towers* had no plot. He continued by denouncing the book's vulgarity:

'... The grand defect of the work, I think, as a work of art, is the low-mindedness and vulgarity of the chief actors. There is hardly a 'lady' or 'gentleman' among them. Such a bishop and his wife as Dr and Mrs Proudie have certainly not appeared in our time ... But in noticing these defects I am far from saying that it is uninteresting. On the contrary, there is a fatal facility in the execution that makes you fancy that the author is playing with his reader, showing how easy it is for him to write a novel in three volumes ... It would be quite impossible to compress the three volumes into one without much detriment to the whole.'

William Longman accordingly wrote to Trollope, who replied in a worried letter from Derry assuring his publisher that 'nothing would be more painful' to him 'than to be considered as an indecent writer'. He had asked Longmans for a hundred pounds advance on the book, and when they demurred he sent his brother-in-law John Tilley to see them, and himself suggested going to another firm. On the matter of the money advance, the publishers ended by giving way. They then sent the author a complete list of their reader's suggested deletions. In this case Trollope, ordinarily an impatient man, behaved with modesty and discretion—and that in a situation which all writers must always find maddening: 'I have *de bon cœur* changed all the passages marked as being too warm.' He did, however, refuse to delete and rewrite two complete chapters, and he also refused to reduce the book, as Longmans reader demanded, by at least one-third. 'I am at a loss to know how such a task could be performed,' he tells us in his autobiography. 'I could burn the MS, no doubt, and write another book on the same story; but how two words out of six are to be withdrawn from a written novel I cannot conceive.' The manuscript was then dispatched to the printer, but further sacrifices to Podsnappery were even at this stage required. In March 1857, Trollope wrote to his publishers:

'At page 93 by all means put out "foul breathing"; and page 97 alter "fat stomach" to "deep chest" if the printing will now allow it. I do not like a second title nor the one you name ... I was puzzled for a title, but the one I took at last is at least inoffensive and easy of pronunciation ... I am very thankful to Longmans for the interest they feel in the book.'

Trollope says that *Barchester Towers* was about as moderately successful as its predecessor, 'but it was one of the novels which novel readers were called upon to read'. He also hoped that it would not be thought presumptious of him to believe that *Barchester Towers* 'has become one of those novels which do not die quite at once, which live and are read for perhaps a quarter of a century'. How startled and how gratified would he have been had some seer foretold that *Barchester Towers* still commands a wide and international readership after more than one hundred years.

The tussle with Longmans over, Anthony settled down in various railway carriages to write a new—and today most wrongly neglected—novel, *The Three Clerks*. For this work he drew on memories of his early days as a drudge in the General Post Office at St-Martins-le-Grand. The scenes in which this novel are set are geographically more diversified than those in his two published Barsetshire books, for the action takes place in the Internal Navigation Office, in the Weights and Measures Office, in a grubby yet cosy London public house, and in a pretty villa on the banks of the Thames at Hampton. The plot of *The Three Clerks* displays a certain tidiness often absent from Trollope's novels. The three clerks—Henry Norman, and the cousins Alaric and Charley Tudor—become emotionally involved with the three daughters of Mrs Woodward, a clergyman's widow living at Surbiton Cottage, Hampton. Henry Norman is in love with the eldest daughter, Gertrude, who, however, marries the worldly Alaric Tudor, stands by him when he is imprisoned for embezzlement, afterwards accompanying him as an emigrant to New Zealand. Norman next falls in love with another Woodward sister, and marries her. Charley Tudor, who leads a purposeless but not unenjoyable evening life in London, and has promised to wed a barmaid in Bloomsbury, is reformed by the third and youngest sister, Kate, who manages to survive a lingering illness in order to marry him.

It has been suggested that Charley Tudor is a self-portrait of Anthony Trollope in his youth, a theory which may or may not be valid. It is distinctly known that the chief clerk in the Weights and Measures Office, named in the novel 'Sir Gregory Hardlines', was intended as a caricature of Sir Charles Trevelyan, of Irish Famine ill-name. 'We always call him Sir Gregory,' Lady Trevelyan told Trollope in later years, when the Trevelyans had become friends of Anthony and his wife. The important question of whether Trollope always used, or seldom used, living people for the characters in his novels is an extremely difficult one to answer at this distance of time. His biographer Escott says that 'everyone' knows who was the prototype for Madame Max Goesler—and therefore he did not think it worth putting down on paper. Escott forgot that even the most knowing of 'everyones' follows the general human tendency to die—and, mostly, be forgotten at that.

The long-drawn-out illness of Kate Woodward, the youngest of the three daughters, has been deemed to be derived from Trollope's own unhappy memories of his little sister Emily's death from consumption, at Hadley in 1836. But, unlike Emily Trollope, Kate Woodward recovers. It was this part of the novel which made even the novelist cry. 'The passage,' he tells us, 'in which Kate Woodward, thinking that she will die, tries to take leave of the lad she loves, still brings tears to my eyes when I read it. I had not the heart to kill her. I never could do that. And I do not doubt but that they are living happily together to this day.' Over in Florence, Theodosia Trollope lent her copy of *The Three Clerks* to Mrs Browning. Gone were the days in which Robert Browning (referring to Anthony and Tom's mother) had warned his wife against 'that coarse, vulgar Mrs Trollope'. Presumably it was Theodosia who forged the initial link between the Villino Trollope and the Casa Guidi, for, as a young girl in Torquay, she had been one of the earliest worshippers before Elizabeth Barrett's sofa shrine, had lent her one of Lady Blessington's *Books of Beauty* and, one may suppose, took her own poems to be judged by that fastidious laudanum addict in Beacon Terrace. Tom Trollope, although Robert Browning called him 'a goose' and disliked his mercenary, ungentlemanly ways, was always welcome at the Casa Guidi, and felt, he tells us in his memoirs, that each time he left that hallowed house he was

'a better man, with higher views and aims ... such effect was not produced by any talk or look or word of the nature of preaching ... but simply by the perception and appreciation of what Elizabeth Barrett Browning was; of the immaculate purity of every thought that passed through her pellucid mind, and the indefeasible nobility of her every idea, sentiment, and opinion ... In mind and heart she was *white*—stainless. That is what I mean by purity.'

When Theodosia Trollope pattered up the shadowy staircase of the Casa Guidi, her brother-in-law's new novel in her basket, she must with anxiety have awaited the verdict on it of the two great poets whom she was about to see. She need not have worried, for Mrs Browning, like the novel's author himself, was 'wrung to tears by the third volume'. 'We both quite agree with you in considering it the best of the three clever novels before the public. My husband, who can seldom get a novel to hold him, has been held by all three and by this the strongest. Also it has qualities which the others gave no sign of ... What a thoroughly *man's* book it is!'

It had been Anthony Trollope's intention to sell *The Three Clerks* to Longmans who, however, declined it. The book was finally bought by old Bentley, the founder of *Bentley's Miscellany*, which had been launched in 1837 with Charles Dickens in the editorial chair. Mr Bentley, after his reader had gone through the new novel, agreed to buy it at the price the author named, whereas Longmans had rejected it because it seemed to them that Trollope was asking too much. As countless passages in his *Autobiography* amply prove, Trollope was always ready for a wrangle with his publishers about money. Michael Sadleir, a publisher himself, went into great detail about these transactions and was almost as interested in them as was Anthony. All that we need to know at this distance in time, is that by 1879, the year in which he finished his own memoirs and put them away for posthumous publication, the novelist had earned nearly £70,000, for those days a very big sum indeed. At the height of his fame he could demand up to £3,000 for a novel such as *The Way We Live Now*. Remembering how slow and disappointing were the sales of his first novels, one can forgive him the complacency with which, in the *Autobiography*, he records his subsequent financial success.

In August 1857, the Anthony Trollopes travelled in a leisurely way through Switzerland, and over the Alps to Italy. At the Villino Trollope they found Anthony's mother 'much changed and broken, not caring for her afternoon drive, and indifferent even to her rubber of whist'. Old Fanny Trollope had now withdrawn from the battlefield of authorship, having published no less than one hundred and fifteen volumes. 'She expressed to me,' says Anthony, 'her delight that her labours should be at an end, and that mine should be beginning in the same field.' Three years earlier the old lady had been, for the last time, to London. There she had fallen under the spell of Mr Home the medium, and had been a constant attender of his séances at the house of a Mr and Mrs Rymer at Ealing. In the autumn of 1855 Mr Home and Mr Rymer arrived in Florence, the former as the Trollopes' house-guest. Rose Trollope attributed her mother-in-law's mental and physical decline to the 'excitement' caused by Mr Home's spiritualism. 'It appears very strange,' writes Rose, 'that a woman with so much common sense, should have placed faith in these absurdities. But her imagination and romance got the upper hand.' Mr Home's speciality was to conjure up the spirits of the dead. In Mrs Trollope's case there were a very great many of these: 'the spirits of her father, her mother, and several of her children, were frequently said to be present'. Tom Trollope quickly saw through Home and wrote that the medium was not 'in the ordinary affairs of life an honourable or true man'. Home cannot, at any rate, have been a quiet or soothing guest, for his séances at the Villino Trollope included 'the moving of heavy tables, the twirling round of heavy lamps ... the violent rocking backwards and forwards of a large American rocking-chair with a man or woman seated in it, the tying of mysterious knots without visible agency'. Distinguished women were especially partial to Home. He infuriated Robert Browning by captivating the imagination of Elizabeth Barrett Browning, who proved as credulous as Fanny Trollope herself.

This late summer and autumn of 1857 were almost the last time that Anthony ever saw his mother. He and his wife were once more in Florence, in 1860, but by then she was losing her memory, and was unable to leave the house. She would wander up and down the loggia of the villino, leaning upon her son Tom's arm. 'I want Tom to trot me out,' she would say; and she could still enjoy listening to her granddaughter Bice singing a Tuscan *stornello* and would then, clasping her hands together, exclaim: 'Dear creature! Dear creature!' The old lady finally became bed-ridden. She died painlessly on October 7th, 1863, at the age of eighty-three. 'My dear mother died full of years, and without any of the suffering of old age ... she ate, & slept & drank till the lamp went altogether out; but there was nothing of the usual struggle of death,' Anthony wrote to a family friend of Harrow days. 'I think no one ever suffered less in dying.'

In the spring of 1857, a month or two before his penultimate visit to Florence, Trollope had begun to write a comic novel entitled *The Struggles of Brown, Jones and Robinson*. Described by its author as 'a hit at the present system of advertising', the title of this heavy-handed satire seems to have been suggested by Richard Doyle's *Foreign Tour of Messrs Brown, Jones and Robinson*. Trollope's book was refused by Longmans and then by Mr Chapman of Chapman and Hall, who wrote tactfully:

'I think on the whole that I had better hold to my resolve to decline *B. J. and R.* I should not like to do it without your name, and at the same time I feel convinced that it is better that your name should be withheld, for there is a strong impression abroad that you are writing too rapidly for your permanent fame.'

In 1861 George Smith, of Smith, Elder, agreed to serialize the tale in the *Cornhill*, a shrewd move since it secured for him, in later years, *The Small House at Allington*, *The Claverings* and *The Last Chronicle of Barset*. The serialized satire evoked bad notices: 'Mr Trollope's newly devised comic epic gives but modified satisfaction to the readers of the *Cornhill*,' wrote a reviewer in the *Illustrated London News*. 'The complaint is that nobody can understand what Mr Trollope means.' Smith, Elder, kept on refusing Trollope's demand that *The Struggles* should be issued in book form—but they gave way at last and published the novel in 1870. Here again we have an example of Anthony Trollope's blinding obtuseness where his own work was concerned: 'It was meant to be funny,' he tells us, 'was full of slang, and was intended as a satire on the ways of trade ... I think that there is some good fun in it, but I have heard no one else express such an opinion.'

Probably from discouragement, Anthony put his manuscript aside and did not complete this trivial work until 1861. Meanwhile, in 1858, he was instructed 'by the great men at the General Post Office' to travel to Egypt and there to make a treaty with Said Pasha authorizing the conveyance of the Indian mails by the new Cairo to Suez railway. The existing treaty had become out of date, since it dealt solely with the carriage of bags and boxes between Alexandria and Suez by camel. To posterity far the most interesting aspect of this journey is the attested fact that, during a singularly rough passage from Marseilles to Alexandria, Trollope was writing the third of his great Barsetshire novels, *Doctor Thorne*. 'I wrote my allotted number of pages every day. On this occasion more than once I left my paper on the cabin table, rushing away to be sick in the privacy of my state room. It was February and the weather was miserable; but I still did my work.' He had now begun counting the number of pages he wrote in a week, and jotting these down in a diary. His average, he states, was some forty, each page containing two hundred and fifty words, a week. In lazy weeks (and they were few and far between) he might write a mere twenty pages, but in fruitful weeks he could get up to one hundred and twelve.

Before leaving London, Trollope had sold *Doctor Thorne* to Chapman and Hall. He completed the book in Egypt and, on the very next day, commenced *The Bertrams*. 'I found it to be expedient,' he writes, 'to bind myself by certain self-imposed laws.' After two months of intricate negotiations with one of the Pasha's officials, Nubar Bey, a postal treaty was arranged. Knowing nothing of Eastern ways—Nubar Bey was an Armenian—Trollope was surprised by the combination of obstinacy and elusiveness shown by the Bey during their talks at Shepheard's Hotel. There Nubar Bey would arrive day after day, bringing with him a train of servants, a number of pipes and an adequate supply of coffee. Having firmly opposed Trollope on the specific point of time it would take the mail-train to go across Egypt, Nubar Bey suddenly gave way and agreed that the mail could be got through in twenty-four hours and not, as he had previously asserted, forty-eight. In later years Nubar Bey, by then transmogrified into Nubar Pasha, would relate how bullying Anthony Trollope had been. The Pasha used to say that he had been treated as a peccant publisher might be treated by an expensive author.

Although Anthony had never been out of Europe before, he continued steadily writing *Doctor Thorne* amidst the minarets and ancient tombs of Egypt. Neither this book, nor *The Bertrams* which trod upon its heels, were particular favourites with their author, who persisted in believing *The Three Clerks* to be a much superior work. The judgment of his own contemporaries and that of subsequent generations of readers has not accepted this verdict as true. Possibly because scenes in *The Three Clerks* recalled to him his life as a Post Office clerk in London he would reread it with, as we know, tears coursing down his bearded cheeks; yet, since he had been so notoriously miserable at that early period of his life it is hard to understand why he should wish to recapture its aroma.

Doctor Thorne, one of Trollope's best books, is unlike any of his others in that the plot, turning on the illegitimacy of the Doctor's niece Mary, was not devised by himself but by his brother Tom, during those autumnal weeks in Tuscany. Stranger still, I think, is Anthony Trollope's amazing ability to abstract himself from his surroundings and be lifted by his imagination back into Barsetshire. He visited the catacombs of Sakkara, the tombs of the Caliphs, the pyramids of Giza, the mosque of Sultan Hassan, and Heliopolis, which last he declared to be 'a humbug'. He then returned home by way of the Holy Land, inspecting the post offices at Malta and Gibraltar on his route. Some of his little adventures are recounted in short stories— *Tales of All Countries*, for instance. Despite his bulk and girth he managed to crawl up the sloping passage inside the Pyramid of Cheops and to stoop down to enter the burial chamber, which smelled then as pungent as it does today. Yet all this time, as he went sight-seeing or battled with Nubar Bey about mail-trains, Greshamsbury Park and Courcy Castle, Dr Thorne's little house in the village and Sir Roger Scatcherd's bedroom (where that old reprobate lay dying, propped up with a bottle of brandy under his pillow), were as real to him as Alexandria. He went to hear the dervishes of Cairo, who howled on Fridays, but nothing external ever affected his clear and limpid insight into the loves of Mary Thorne and Frank Gresham, or into the machinations of Lady Arabella Gresham and her sister-in-law Lady de Courcy. The day after he completed *Doctor Thorne* he began, as we have seen, to write *The Bertrams*, which opens with a scene between two Oxford graduates and soon moves swiftly to a hotel in Jerusalem, at the *table d'hôte* of which George Bertram first sees Caroline Waddington—with fatal results. When he began writing *The Bertrams* Trollope came to a questionable decision:

'I was moved now by a decision to excel, if not in quality, at any rate in quantity. An ignoble ambition for an author, my readers will no doubt say. But not, I think, altogether ignoble if an author can bring himself to look at his work as does any other workman ... It is not on my conscience that I have ever scamped my work. My novels, whether good or bad, have been as good as I could make them. Had I taken three months of idleness between each they would have been no better. Feeling convinced of that, I finished *Doctor Thorne* on one day, and began *The Bertrams* on the next.'

Doctor Thorne opens in a slow and apologetic narrative way:

'I quite feel that an apology is due for beginning a novel with two long, dull chapters full of description. I am perfectly aware of the danger of such a course ... It can hardly be expected that any one will consent to go through with a fiction that offers so little of allurement in its first pages; but twist it as I will I cannot do otherwise.'

It was such paragraphs as these which Henry James, admirer though he was, found 'pernicious' in Trollope's work. 'He took a suicidal satisfaction in reminding the reader that the story he was telling was only, after all, a make-believe,' James writes. '... These little slaps at credulity are very discouraging, but they are even more inexplicable.' Referring to 'the magnificent historical tone of Balzac', Henry James remarks that Balzac 'would as soon have thought of admitting to the reader that he was deceiving him as Garrick or John Kemble would have thought of pulling off his disguise in front of the footlights. Therefore, when Trollope suddenly winks at us and reminds us that he is telling us an arbitrary thing, we are startled and shocked in quite the same way as if Macaulay or Motley were to drop the historical mask and intimate that William of Orange was a myth or the Duke of Alba an invention.'

There are a good many examples of such 'suicidal satisfaction' in Anthony Trollope's novels—examples in which he seems to treat both the reader and himself with scorn. But what he really scorned was the very idea that novel-writing was an art and not a craft and this conviction, presumably, inspired these exasperating asides. Had he ever discovered that posterity would consider him as a great artist he would have turned in his grave at Kensal Green.

While he was abroad, Trollope continued to send bundles of manuscript to his wife Rose, and she would copy them out for the publisher. She sometimes had difficulty in deciphering her husband's handwriting and was obliged to ask him what, in certain sentences, he had meant; but she was granted the privilege of altering, where need be, his text. 'You must of course be careful about the reading,' he wrote to her from Paris on the way to Marseilles, 'and also alter any words which seem to be too often repeated ... I have not been inside the Louvre—It is now one, and I have been writing all day—I must do 5 of my pages daily—or I cannot accomplish my task—Do not be dismal if you can help it—I feel a little that way inclined but hard work will I know keep it off.' Tom Trollope, who had come up to Paris to see Anthony before his brother sailed from Marseilles to Alexandria, tells us in his own memoirs that he believed over-working shortened Anthony's life: '... I have a very pretty turn for idleness ... Anthony had no such turn. Work to him was a necessity and a satisfaction. He used often to say that he envied me the capacity for being idle.' To Anthony, indeed, the two words 'spare moment' meant nothing at all; we have seen that he wrote in railway carriages and, during the rough cross-ing to Alexandria, in the public saloon of the ship. He even told Frederick Locker that he had written some of the chapters of *Barchester Towers* 'on the "knife-board" of a bus'. As he gradu-ally became famous, and was lionized in country houses, An-thony would boast, at breakfast time, that he had been awake and writing at a very early hour while fellow guests were slumb-ering. Sir Frederick Pollock, the translator of Dante, records in his diary for January 1867 that 'when Trollope came down to breakfast, after having been writing the novel then on hand, as usual, he rather astonished us by saying: "I have just been mak-ing my twenty-seventh proposal of marriage."'

In May 1858 Anthony Trollope was back in London, but not for long. The Post Office authorities had by now recognized his professional qualities and his gift for reorganization; they, therefore, dispatched him to Glasgow 'to revise' (as he put it) the postal arrangements of that blackened, teeming city. It was summertime, and, we may suppose, dusty and hot—yet he toiled and trudged all over Glasgow with the letter-carriers, go-ing to the top flats of dark tenements and sparing neither him-self nor the postmen whose working hours he was trying to assess. 'It was midsummer, and wearier work I never per-formed,' he tells us. 'The men would grumble, and then I would think how it would be with them if they had to go home after-wards and write a love-scene. But the love-scenes written in Glasgow, all belonging to *The Bertrams*, are not good.' In the autumn he was suddenly asked to go out to the West Indies 'to cleanse the Augean stables of our Post Office system there'. This journey provided him with his first glimpse of the tropics, and resulted in a book which he himself always considered the best of all that he had ever written. This book, *The West Indies and the Spanish Main*, was Anthony's first experiment at travel-writing, a loose and casual form at which both his mother and

161

his brother Tom had long excelled. It was to this volume, and to Anthony's subsequent books on North America, Australia and New Zealand, and South Africa, that the historian J. A. Froude sourly referred as showing 'old Trollope banging about the world'.

(ii)

Apart from its intrinsic merits of liveliness and of genuine, unforced humour, *The West Indies and the Spanish Main* gives us the only account of his own physical appearance that Anthony Trollope ever wrote. Begun in the stuffy cabin of a little sailing brig in which he had impetuously booked a passage from Kingston, Jamaica, to Cienfuegos in Cuba, the book opens with complaints of this boat's lack of victuals and of alcohol, and of its captain's incompetence as they lay becalmed off Kingston harbour. Writing, as it were, to himself, the author then begins to brood upon the description of his looks written at the Spanish consulate in Jamaica when he had applied there for a Spanish passport. He had, in this document, been described as '*alta*' or tall : 'Never before this have I obtained in a passport any more dignified description of my body than robust ... Then my eyes are azure. This he did not find out by the unassisted guidance of personal inspection. "Ojos, blue," he suggested to me, trying to look through my spectacles.' Hair and eyebrows were written down as chestnut :

'Now any but a Spaniard would have declared that as to hair, I was bald; and as to eyebrows, nothing in particular ... But then comes the mystery. If I have any personal vanity, it is wrapped up in my beard. It is a fine, manly article of dandyism, that wears well in all climates, and does not cost much, even when new. Well, what has the Don said of my beard? It is *poblada*. I would give five shillings for the loan of a Spanish dictionary at this moment. *Poblada!* Well, my first effort, if ever I do reach Cuba, shall be made with reference to that word.*

He was now forty-four years old, keenly observing life through his gold-rimmed spectacles, and sheltered against the world by the thicket of a long, wide and luxuriant spade-beard. He tells us that at this time he weighed fifteen stone.

The consciousness of his own weight was becoming an obsession with Anthony Trollope. He was now increasingly attacked

* *Poblada*, translated literally, means peopled or populated. In this case it would have meant a thick, flowing beard.

by moods of dejection and of gloom and, according to an intimate of his, 'these seizures of despondency generally overtook him as he was riding home from a day with the hounds. They began with the reflection that he rode heavier in each successive season, that in the course of nature the hunting ... would have to be given up.' He was often subject to a 'vague presentiment of impending calamity'. Lacking Charles Dickens's perennially boyish zest, and likewise the intellectual weapons with which Thackeray fought off despair, Trollope was not equipped to combat his own fits of melancholia. 'It is, I suppose,' he remarked one day to his friend John Millais, 'some weakness of temperament that makes me, without intelligible cause, such a pessimist at heart.' His biographer Escott connects these black moods with Trollope's 'almost feminine sensibility to the opinions of others, a self-consciousness altogether abnormal in a seasoned and practical man of the world, as well as a strong love of approbation, whether from stranger or friend'. This backlash from his despised and lonely childhood meant that any slight, real or assumed, 'pained and ruffled him beyond his power to conceal'. His physician, Sir Richard Quain, summed up the effects of this extreme sensibility as 'Trollope's genial air of grievance against the world in general, and those who personally valued him in particular'.

Yet, during his journey to the West Indies, and in his junketings from island to island, these dark moments seem to have occurred scarcely at all. From the moment that the steamboat *Atrato* left Southampton bound for the island of St Thomas (then still owned by the Danes) Anthony Trollope surrendered himself heart and soul to a central passion the strength of which, though unrecognized, surpassed and defied those for hunting, writing, revising postal services and playing whist. This was the passion for observation. In this first of his long journeys there was, indeed, a good deal to observe, ranging from tropical forests to steaming shanty towns, from the colour-consciousness of the British colonials to the winning, baroque behaviour of the laughing, chattering Negroes and the quiet, steady ambition of those of Queen Victoria's subjects who were of mixed blood. These latter, as Trollope most accurately predicted, were destined to gain and to hold political power in that Caribbean world to which the French so simply and so charmingly refer as 'les Iles'.

The small, self-contained world of such an ocean liner as the *Atrato* was altogether new to Anthony Trollope. In a touching

163

and admirable short story, *The Journey to Panama*, he has described the life aboard this ship, merely inventing another name, the *Serrapiqui*. He found a particular interest in the way in which, after the fourth day at sea, small cliques were formed amongst the passengers. Until the second day out, sea-sickness ruled the ship. The passengers looked at each other with mutual suspicion and hostility. By the fourth day, however, fervent friendships were being forged between total strangers, flirtations had started and the men began 'to think that the women [were] not so ugly, vulgar and insipid'. The women became less monosyllabic and positively affable—'perhaps beyond their wont on shore'. The upper range of state-rooms on the ship opened on to a gallery, which ran along the top of the dining-saloon, so that you could look down and see what the stewards were giving you for dinner. At first it was generally recognized that the ladies would, before the evening meal, assemble in one gallery, while the men would stand waiting for the bell in the gallery opposite. But soon defections began, and the men would cross to the ladies' side 'and so at last a kind of little drawing-room was formed'. The *Atrato* carried French and Spanish passengers as well as British colonials, but there seems to have been little fraternizing between these national groups. At St Thomas, Trollope disembarked, going on to Jamaica in a British ship, the *Derwent*. The island of St Thomas Trollope found detestable: 'a Niggery-Hispano-Dano-Yankee-Doodle place', where the merchant gentry talked with a nasal twang and drank very strong sherry-cobblers. The *Derwent* proved a more delightful ship than the *Atrato*:

'We had no Spaniards in the *Derwent*, but a happy jovial little crew of Englishmen and Englishwomen—or of English subjects rather, for the majority of them belonged to Jamaica ... We ate and drank and smoked and danced and swore mutual friendship, till the officer of the Board of Health visited us as we rounded the point at Port Royal, and again ruffled our tempers by delaying us for some thirty minutes under a broiling sun.'

Anthony Trollope was not much moved by either the relics or the sorrows of West Indian history. His assignment was to send to the Secretary of the General Post Office in London recommendations for improving the postal services of the Caribbean Crown Colonies. He suggested to Colonel Maberley's successor, Rowland Hill, that the headquarters for colonial mail work should be shifted from St Thomas to Jamaica, and the transfer of postal control to the Crown Colonies themselves. He also had been deputed to make two postal treaties with the colonial representatives of Spain. This work entailed mental preparation, which he would have been making during the voyage of the *Atrato* from Southampton to St Thomas. Moreover he was never alone in his state-room, for sharing the journey with him were Sir Lionel Bertram, his miserly brother George, his only son and Miss Caroline Waddington, by then Lady Harcourt. Her husband, Sir Henry, shot himself in his palatial house in Eaton Square shortly after Trollope landed in Jamaica. While his fellow passengers were trying to continue sleeping in the white, muggy dawn of a tropical day, or were pacing the deck to watch the early-morning dolphins, Anthony was leaning cumbrously over a travelling desk in his cabin. His thoughts were in the churchyard of Hadley, near Enfield Chase, where he was burying old Mr Bertram, who had died without bequeathing to his closest relatives his cool half-million pounds:

'There were not ten people in the church or in the churchyard during the whole of the funeral. To think that a man with half a million of money could die and be got rid of with so little parade! What money could do—in a moderate way—was done. The coffin was as heavy as lead could make it. The cloth of the best. The plate on it was silver, or looked like it. There was no room for an equipage of hearses and black coaches, the house was so unfortunately near to the churchyard. It was all done in a decent, sombre, useful, money-making way, as beseemed the remains of such a man.'

From Kingston, Jamaica, Trollope dispatched a parcel to his publishers, Chapman and Hall. It contained the corrected proof sheets of the first two volumes of *The Bertrams* and a part of the third volume in manuscript. 'There will be 35—or 40 [pages] more—which will give it ample length,' he wrote. '...And now, as I have always a prudent eye to the future, I shall be glad to know whether you will think well of a volume of travels on these parts ... My idea is about 450 pages of the Dr Thorne size ... to come out before Xmas.' He asked, and was given, £250 for the rights in the projected book for three years.

As we should have expected, Anthony Trollope's first travel-book lays more emphasis on the behaviour of his fellow passengers, or the guileless idiosyncrasies of the West Indian Negro or the social and political ambitions of the mulattoes, than on scenic description. He describes the gluttony of some of the passengers on the *Atrato* (Spanish people, of course), but seems to have been unmoved by that most marvellous of experiences available to a Caribbean-bound traveller in the days before air travel foreshortened the pleasures of a slow approach to the West Indian islands aboard a ship leaving Bristol or Southampton in a wet winter. You notice that once past the Azores the air each day becomes more perceptibly balmy. The Southern Cross appears, set slightly crooked in the velvet sky. All other stars take on a new and bewildering brilliance. The phosphorescence at the ship's stern leaves a sparkling trail upon the black surface of the sea. Deck awnings are rigged up, the ship's officers change into white uniforms. Soon porpoises may be seen gambolling by the ship's side, and flying fish dart across the sea and sometimes, unfortunately for them, land on deck. The ship does not look remotely like the one you boarded at an English port, while the passengers most noticeably undergo a sea-change. Everyone is more pleasant and more carefree, as well as more flirtatious in the face of their imminent separation from their new shipboard friends, whom, presumably, they will never see again in their lives. And then you come into sight of the West Indies themselves, so densely green and forested, which seem to be floating on the sea, moving steadily towards you despite the patent fact that it is your ship which is moving towards the islands. These West Indian islands are often melancholy places. They have the power alternately to attract and to repel a stranger, and seem saturated in their own evil histories of old, forgotten slaving days. Outside the so-called cities—Kingston or Port of Spain or Bridgetown, Barbados—there are shack villages and peeling shanty-towns, a wild tropical abundance of fruit and the festoons of parasite orchids, frangipani over which minute humming-birds hover and everywhere the brash colours of bougainvillaea. In all the islands colonial relics linger—old plantation houses and the relentless little tropical graveyards, in which, shaded by silk-cotton trees, the young wives and children of forgotten British soldiers or officials lie buried in simple graves beneath the coarse, wiry emerald weed which, in the West Indies, masquerades as grass.

(iii)

The *Atrato*, which had left Southampton on November 17th, 1858, reached St Thomas on December 2nd. As Trollope's bulky, bearded figure stumped down the ship's gangway, and as he was in the very act of putting his foot for the first time in his life upon tropical soil, an elegant Negress wearing a tight-waisted muslin frock, complete with crinoline and a graceful broad-brimmed hat, gave him a rose. 'That's for love, dear,' she inconsequently explained as she pressed the flower upon him with her pink-gloved hands. He took the rose, and assured her that it should be for love indeed. 'What was it to me,' he writes, 'that she was as black as my boot, or that she had come to look after the ship's washing?' This little incident, in itself, so characteristically and winningly West Indian, must have seemed to him to presage an amiable odyssey through that novel island world.

Part of the insular territories known as the Virgin Islands, St Thomas was in those days 'the meeting-place and central depot of the West Indian steam-packets'. Although a possession of the Crown of Denmark, St Thomas was a Spanish-speaking place. It was a coaling station and a hotbed of yellow fever, of which most of the young officers fresh out from Europe died. The inhabitants seemed to Trollope to make a profession of voracious eating—an activity which so absorbed them that they never spoke at meals. To test out this theory he decided to wait, at meal-times, until he was spoken to: 'For a week I sat, twice daily, between the same persons without receiving or speaking a single word.' He found that on his inter-island or even his mainland journeys he invariably ended up in St Thomas: 'I was compelled to remain there a longer time, putting all my visits together, than in any other of the islands except Jamaica.' The only aspect of St Thomas life which intrigued Trollope was the way in which people in hotels and restaurants ate cheese with guava jelly: 'Some men dipped their cheese in jelly; some ate a bit of jelly and then a bit of cheese; some topped up with jelly and some topped up with cheese, all having it on their plates together.'

When he reached Kingston, Jamaica, and put up at an hotel kept by a Mrs Blundle and named Blundle Hall, Anthony was even more amazed by Jamaican meals than by the guava jelly and cheese in St Thomas. It is a very curious fact that, in old colonial days, the British planters closely connected cooking with patriotism—that is to say that on the most scorching day in Kingston they would eat tinned oxtail soup instead of a fresh soup made from the ubiquitous Jamaican turtle. Roast beef steaks were, as Trollope remarks, 'found at every meal'. The twenty or so excellent vegetables—yams, mountain cabbage, plaintains amongst them—were totally ignored in favour of bad potatoes sent out from Great Britain.

On a damp and disagreeable expedition to see the sun rise from the Blue Mountain peak, eight thousand feet up, Trollope and his companion stopped for breakfast at the highest inhabited house on the island of Jamaica. Here, again, he encountered English potatoes and English pickles. All the host's food had to be carried up on mule-back over the mountains and travelled twenty or thirty miles on the way, so Trollope was a little surprised when his host yelled out: 'What, no Worcester sauce! Gammon! Make the fellow go and look for it.' Nor has Trollope been the only writer to notice this singular phenomenon. It has not died out with the political liberation of the countries which used to be components of the old British Empire. You find it in hotels in Ghana or in Singapore just as constantly as you still find it in the West Indian islands. Trollope writes that he wished he could have explained to Mrs Blundle of Blundle Hall that roast beef and onions, bread and cheese and beer did not compose 'the only diet proper for an Englishman'. Stodgy British cooking indeed is one of the most enduring legacies bequeathed by the defunct British Empire to the countries which it used to rule. It is also one of the most exasperating and comfortless aspects of travelling around these former outposts of Empire.

In his commonsensical, inquiring way, Trollope used his sojourn in the West Indies to examine thoroughly every side of British colonial life. He discovered that the planters and the white creole families looked down upon and socially avoided persons of mixed blood, and that these in turn looked down on the Negroes, who in their turn detested them. Then there was the problem of the indentured labourers—Indian or Chinese—then being imported to replace the Negro labourers who, since emancipation, did not much mind whether they themselves worked or not. His book contains many entertaining vignettes of persons of every colour who crossed his path in the islands, and he observed and described elegant mulatto girls with the same minute precision with which he dealt in his novels with parsons' daughters or with girls of the English aristocracy. His researches convinced him that the political future of the West Indies would one day fall into the hands of the coloured population, which, he believed, combined the twin advantages of European intelligence with the Africans' physical resistance to an enervating climate which few Europeans could maintain. These conclusions may seem trite today, but in 1859 they were as unwelcome to white West Indian planters as Mrs Fanny Trollope's

Domestic Manners had been to Americans twenty-five years before. By sheer good luck the publication of the West Indian travel-book happened to coincide with the current colonial policy of *The Times*, which published three successive laudatory articles. These, Trollope was persuaded, had 'made the fortune of the book'. Some time later he met the writer of these articles, who hoped to gratify his touchy new acquaintance by admitting to their authorship. Gracious as always, Trollope told his interlocutor how great a service he had done the book, adding, of course, that he felt 'under no obligation to him. I do not think that he saw the matter in quite the same light.' Here we have a typical confirmation of his physician's remarks on Trollope's 'genial air of grievance against the world in general, and those who personally valued him in particular'. In his self-tormenting way, Anthony Trollope ached for the good opinion of his contemporaries, yet often administered a slap in the face to those who admired his work or liked him personally.

Trollope's convictions about the future of the West Indian mulattoes were, thus, intelligent and sane. But when he gets down to discussing the state of the former Negro slaves and their numerous progeny, he becomes as sententious as when writing about the native Irish. He is also as wrongheaded. He detested philanthropists, as we have seen; and at the moment when he was stumping around Jamaica and Trinidad, the Exeter Hall enthusiasts had come once more to the fore—not to have slavery abolished, for that had already been done in 1833, but to protect the freed Negroes of the islands from the competition of indentured Chinese and Indian labour. This was more than Trollope could bear, for he thought, probably rightly, that the will to work of the West Indian Negro had steeply declined since liberation. Having no masters, the former slaves and their families found that they could live happily on the wages of three days in the week, and wisely refrained from doing more. The sight of them lying lackadaisically about beneath the banyans and the breadfruit trees riled him more than he could express. He pronounced the West Indian Negro to be 'a servile race, fitted by nature for the hardest physical work and apparently at present fitted for little else'.

Overt references to God are almost as rare in Anthony Trollope's books as references to his contemporaries' fad for *carte-de-visite* photographs. We might go much further and assert that those Trollope characters, lay or clerical, who appeal to the

Deity or admonish someone else to do so are, in the main, presented to us as arch-hypocrites. When broken-hearted over the apparent shipwreck of a love-affair, Trollope's heroines—or more correctly his heroines' confidantes—do remember that there is 'One above who knows all'; but that is about as far as Trollope's public recognition of the Deity goes. In every sense the Barchester series of novels is totally mundane—that is to say that they deal with the social and political position of the Church of England while ignoring the religious truths upon which any Christian community is supposedly to be based. God, under the disguise of 'Providence', would seem to have been Trollope's unrewarding stand-by; so that it is with distinct curiosity that we find him proclaiming, in *The West Indies and the Spanish Main*, that Providence had more or less planned the transatlantic slave-trade: 'Few, probably, will think that Providence has permitted so great an exodus as that which has taken place from Africa to the West without having wise results in view. We may fairly believe that it has been a part of the Creator's scheme for the population and cultivation of the earth.'

The condescending humour with which he had treated many of his Irish peasant characters Anthony now applied to the freed Negroes of the West. We have earlier noted the similarity between the behaviour of Negro slaves to their masters and that of the Irish peasantry towards British soldiers and officials. In each case evasive tactics had been perfected over several centuries. In Trollope's mind, once slavery was abolished, the West Indian Negroes should, by some novel form of tyranny, have been obliged to work.

'What are we to do with our friend, lying as he now is at his ease under the cotton-tree, and declining to work after ten o'clock in the morning? "No tankee, massa, me tired now; me no want more money." Or perhaps it is "No; workee no more; money no 'nuff; workee no pay ... No, massa; no starve now; God send plenty yam." '

In common with many people who work to excess themselves, Anthony Trollope, with his incapacity for being idle, could not bear to think that anyone else 'should be exempted from the general lot of Adam's children ... The fact I take it is, that there are too many good things in Jamaica for the number who have to enjoy them. If the competitors were more in number, more trouble would be necessary in their acquirement.' This personal theory that nothing but a population explosion would coerce the West Indian Negroes into a lifetime of heavy toil, Anthony supports by a comparison with working conditions in the United Kingdom: 'In our happy England, men are not slaves; but the competition of the labour market forces upon them long days of continual labour.' Here we may observe that the horrors of labour conditions during the Industrial Revolution left Anthony Trollope unmoved. In her radical novel *The Life and Adventures of Michael Armstrong the Factory Boy*, written under Lord Shaftesbury's influence and published in 1840, Anthony's mother had written of factory life with all the fiery sincerity of Mrs Gaskell herself. For Anthony, however, these were unpleasant subjects which he did not choose to impose upon his genteel public. Indeed, the smoky caverns of human misery and despair into which both the landlords and the ironmasters of the Midlands and the North were herding a people until recently pastoral seem not to have impinged on Anthony's consciousness at all. His only references to the industrial scene in Britain were to use these as explaining why some of his characters were so enviably rich. In the opening pages of *Mr Scarborough's Family*, for example, a new industrial potteries development is mentioned simply as explaining why the annual income of the pagan old Squire of Tretton Park had increased from £4,000 a year to £20,000:

'Some marvellous stories were told as to his income, which arose chiefly from the Tretton delf-works and from the town of Tretton, which had been built chiefly in his very park, in consequence of the very nature of the clay and the quality of the water.'

Charles Dickens, for whom Anthony affected contempt, would have taken us by the hand and led us in amongst the white-faced, cursing factory girls and the stunted children working at the furnaces of the Tretton delf factory. Emile Zola and Maxence van der Meersch would have spared us no grim detail. But then none of these novelists were bound by a self-imposed limitation to write for well-brought-up English girls and for them alone. The Tretton Potteries are, for Trollope, no more than the derivation of Mr Scarborough's fortune. Their existence makes plausible the vital importance to his near relatives of the squire's mysterious will—a will around which this fine novel revolves.

In Anthony Trollope's credo very hard work is the natural state to which a beneficent Providence has summoned the whole human race. Nor was it just the lazy Negroes lying in the shade or the good-for-nothing Irish peasants brewing up poteen that he condemned. He had it in for the British aristocracy as well. Most of the members of this hierarchy appearing in Trollope's novels have either inherited more money than is good for them, or by squandering their fortunes have ended up proud, impoverished and prepared to stoop to any practical means of regaining their wealth, bar one: working for it. Almost the only exception amongst his aristocratic portraits is Plantagenet Palliser, later Duke of Omnium, and he was considered eccentric by his wife and her circle for the sole reason that he worked hard as a statesman and ended up Prime Minister. His uncle, the previous Duke, is presented as an old nobleman of an immense renown which he himself has done absolutely nothing to achieve. It all comes to him by dint of his untold wealth and of his ancient title. Speaking eight days before his death to Madame Max Goesler, whom he loves and who has come down to Matching Priory to be with him at the end, he asks her why he 'should have been a Duke and another man a servant?' 'God Almighty ordained such difference' is the conventional but insincere rejoinder of Marie Goesler:

' "I'm afraid I have not done it well; but I have tried; indeed I have tried."

Then she told him that he had ever lived as a great nobleman ought to live. And, after a fashion, she herself believed what she was saying. Nevertheless, her nature was much nobler than his; and she knew that no man should dare to live idly as the Duke had lived.'

The old Duke of Omnium got away with it because of his distant manner and his vast estates; even Anthony Trollope was himself sneakingly impressed by this aged nobleman. To the rest of his aristocratic characters he was much less lenient. His British aristocracy consists chiefly of pompous old gentlemen, of scheming mothers, of ladies over-conscious of their rank, and, in a younger generation, of moronic eldest sons who gamble all night and bet all day and of Earls' plain daughters who know that their title enhances their value on the marriage market and therefore hunt down Croesus bachelors no matter how obscure or even Jewish be their birth. *The Way We Live Now* (1875) contains Trollope's final verdict on the English aristocracy. In form a satire, it is in fact a bitter indictment of an hereditary upper class corrupted by the pursuit of money. Trollope himself thought (or says that he thought) that the accusations in the book were 'exaggerated'. 'The vices are coloured,' he writes in his *Autobiography*, 'so as to make an effect rather than to tell the truth.' This hindsight judgment we may dismiss as easily as many other of his own verdicts on his own novels. He himself was obviously unaware of the moral equation between his descriptions of muddy-booted Irish peasants, of black West Indian layabouts and those of such high-born personages as Lady Pomona Longestaffe, wife of the Squire of Caversham, of the dissolute Earl of Ongar, of the snobbish Countess de Courcy of Courcy Castle in West Barsetshire, of the Marquess of Brotherton at Manor Cross, or of the Marquess of Stapledean, an autocratic and miserly misanthrope resident in the wilds of Westmorland. Yet these three disparate groups—Irish peasantry, West Indian Negroes, British aristocracy—have in common one powerful motive for staying alive: an iron-clad prejudice against obtaining money by honest work. It seems as though these idlers had blown in from his 'world outside the world' especially to exasperate Anthony Trollope with their carefree philosophy and *fainéant* ways. As I have indicated in the second chapter of this book, it is just those characters whom he himself held up to universal scorn who get the better of him in the end. They cast around themselves a literally bewitching aura. By their schemes and subterfuges they defeat the bourgeois morality of their begetter. Having successfully prised open the lid of his Pandora's box they fly over the hills and far away, dragging demure vicarage heroines and honest, stupid eldest sons, nice maiden aunts and impeccable parents, reliable family lawyers and sensible clergymen in their shimmering wake.

(iv)

After trundling on horseback along every viable road in the large British island of Jamaica, Anthony Trollope took a passage in a small sailing brig which, long becalmed, finally deposited him at the newly built, gas-lit port of Cienfuegos on the southern coast of Cuba. The voyage had taken nine days instead of three. His cabin was filthy and still stank of a cargo of saltfish which the little ship had taken on board in Newfoundland and unloaded in Jamaica. There was nothing to eat save saltpork, yams and biscuits. This meagre fare Anthony supplemented with a small ham which he had prudently bought in a Kingston store, one box of sardines given him as a parting present by a Jamaican friend, and a bottle of brandy. He tells us that his first object upon landing in Cuba was to see a slave-run sugar estate. In Jamaica he had been warned that this would prove difficult, as Cuban slave-owners did not encourage critical foreign visitors. However, through an English merchant in Cienfuegos, an expedition was speedily arranged, and Anthony set off for a plantation fifteen miles out of town.

Since it was the period for cutting and boiling the sugar crop, he found that the one hundred and fifty men slaves were working hours which even he, at first, thought inordinate. During croptime, which lasted from May to November, the slaves were allowed six hours for sleep, two hours for their meals, and worked for the remaining sixteen. There was no free day at all, and Sunday was treated as a weekday. For the other months of the year the men and women worked twelve hours a day, and were 'usually allowed' a weekly day of rest. These desperately lengthy hours of unremitting and back-breaking labour made even Trollope ponder; but when he began to look more closely at the well-fed, fat and sleek Cuban Negroes, he began to accept their state of serfdom as the equivalent of the cosseted lives of brewer's dray horses back in London. He looked for marks of the lash on their bodies but found none, and did not have the temerity to ask the gentleman who owned the estate when and why and how frequently he used the whip. Anthony clearly saw that it was in their owner's interest to keep his slaves in good fettle so that he could extract the last ounce of work from each. Under this Cuban system the slaves became prematurely old and died early, but this did not trouble a plantation owner. When one old slave was discarded or a young one used to death, replacements could be purchased in the slave-market of Havana. To work the slaves less hard might indeed have prolonged their lives, but since haste was essential at croptime it would have been quite uneconomic.

In connection with the slaves in Cuba, Anthony does not, for once, mention that benevolent Providence which had planned the old slave-trade and was, he must assume, keeping a watchful eye on all the canefields, the Negroes and the overseers of Cuba. Yet he admits that what worried him about the situation of the slaves in Cuba was not so much their long hours—'so long as to appear almost impossible to a European workman'—but the fact that, baptized at birth, they never went to church. 'When all had been said that can be said in favour of the slave-owner in Cuba, it comes to this—that he treats his slaves as beasts of burden, and so treating them, does it skilfully and with prudence. The point which most shocks an Englishman is the absence of all religion, the ignoring of the black man's soul.'

From Cuba, Trollope travelled down the Windward Islands, making those comparisons between the French colonies and those ruled by Great Britian which any traveller could make today. The well-planned shady streets, the classical buildings, the avenues of palmitos in Martinique and Guadeloupe may still be contrasted with such shanty towns as Roseau, capital of Dominica, which in 1859 did not even have a pier, so that you were forced to wade on to the beach. He found it 'impossible to conceive a more distressing sight' than Roseau: 'There are no shops that can properly be so-called; the people wander about chattering, idle and listless; the streets are covered with thick, rank grass ... Everything seems to speak of desolation, apathy and ruin.' Dominica, steeply mountainous and clothed in vivid tropical jungle, is perhaps the most beautiful of the smaller islands—only it has no roads. When it was colonized by the French, who ceded it to the British in 1783, Roseau had an elegant slave-owning society, paved roads leading from the capital along the coast and through gaps in the hills. Under British rule the roads and the very streets of the capital have been neglected, and the whole intelligent structure of French colonial life has long withered away.

The Windward Islands investigated, Trollope went on to Trinidad by a highly circuitous route which took him first to Barbados, 'little England' as its inhabitants liked to call it. This most endemically suburban of all the British West Indian islands might, as a matter of fact, be better called 'little Surbiton'. Anthony approved of this 'very respectable little island', for, having no mountains, waterfalls or forests, every acre of it was cultivated. This cultivation had, in his eyes, a salutary effect on the freed Negroes. In the wilds of Jamaica, Dominica, St Lucia and Grenada, the liberated slave 'could squat and make himself happy'; there was not, in Barbados, 'an inch for him'. The Barbadian Negro thus had 'to work and make sugar—work quite as hard as he had done while yet a slave. He had to do that or to starve.' This was a most healthy state of affairs, even better than that of the stall-beast Negroes in Cuba. In Barbados he found a white ruling class, the 'Bims', almost hysterically loyalist and patriotic, but, like other visitors both before and since his journey, he found these Bims boastful and intoxicated by their own prosperity, and, as they themselves considered it, their political acumen and social sophistication. He gave his accolade to the Barbadians for their agricultural economy and especially for the adroit way in which they got as much work out of the freed Negroes as they had, in days past, exacted by thrashing their slaves. Yet he did not really like this busy, tropical mini-England. With his next port of call, the former French possession of Trinidad, he almost fell in love.

The entrance to the Gulf of Paria lies through a series of Bocas, as they were called in Spanish colonial days before the French obtained control of Trinidad. These mouths—the Dragon's Mouths, the Serpent's Mouth, the Monkey's Mouth—form the channels by which shipping can approach the capital, Port of Spain, which is splendidly situated between a range of high hills and the gulf, which forms a kind of inland sea. From the hills at the back of the city you can, on clear days, gaze out at the estuary of the Orinoco River, which stains the Gulf of Paria with orange mud and provides an ideal stalking ground for gregarious, high-stepping pink flamingos and for the solitary pelicans which, seen from a small boat in the Gulf, seem to rock like large celluloid toys on the water's swell.

Since Anthony Trollope spent less than forty-eight hours in Trinidad he did not go through the High Woods, which at that time can only have been traversed by gloomy bridle paths. He did fit in an early morning ride out into the countryside with a female acquaintance as guide—this expedition had for him the added charm that it obliged him to be up and dressed by half-past four, so as to avoid the gruelling midday sun which makes Port of Spain seethe and bubble in a cauldron of heat. He hired a buggy to drive the three miles round the great savannah, then as now the centre of an affluent residential area. The savannah is lined on two sides by roomy, cool private houses of considerable size. On their deep and high verandahs, protected by slatted jalousies, grow tamed tropical plants in tubs. Orchids hang in wire or wicker baskets from the ceilings of these verandahs. Everything about the Port of Spain savannah is spacious and bears a Latin rather than an Anglo-Saxon air.

At the time of Trollope's whirlwind visit, the Governor of the Crown Colony had vacated Government House, a building which resembles an iron egg-box, and had withdrawn to a half-timbered cottage on the edge of Nutmeg Ravine in the Botanical Gardens. This little house rightly seemed to Anthony a 'perfect specimen' of cottage architecture. The cottage still stands today and has four doors and a great many latticed windows. It looks as though it had been wafted out to the tropics from some German forest—the residence, most probably, of the witch who beguiles Hänsel and Gretel in Humperdinck's operetta. After midnight the cottage re-echoes to uncanny sounds—the thumping fall of a cannon-ball fruit from its tree, the creaking and snapping of bamboos, voices laughing and crying in the hibiscus-fringed lane behind the little building, and that mournful, synchronized wailing of skinny pie-dogs with which all West Indian towns reverberate in the small hours.

Had Anthony Trollope spent longer in Trinidad he might have begun to find it uncomfortably dank and hot. As it was he pushed on from there into Central America, ending up with a voyage by canoe down the fast-flowing Serapiqui River to the port of Greytown on the Caribbean. In this canoe, Trollope tells us, he found for the first time in his life that his bulk and size were of advantage to him, for his heavy person was placed sitting on the middle thwart, leaning back against the luggage so as to keep the canoe in equilibrium. His two companions had to share a single seat between them and could not lean against anything. 'I sincerely pitied my friend,' Trollope relates, 'but what could I do? Any change in our arrangements would have upset the canoe.' He contented himself with smoking cigars and sipping 'weak brandy and water' during the two-day journey down river. From Greytown he proceeded to the Bermudas, where he found the convicts to be ridiculously well treated, and then on to New York, Niagara and Montreal. Returning to New York again he took a passage to Liverpool, completing his travel-book as he went. He claims that he had made no notes at all during his travels:

'Preparation, indeed, there was none. The descriptions and opinions came hot on to the paper from their causes. I will not say that this is the best way of writing a book intended to give accurate information. But it is the best way of producing to the eye of the reader, and to his ear, that which the eye of the writer has seen and his ear heard.'

Anthony was back in Ireland and reunited with Rose in the summer of 1859. On August 4th he was at work again upon a new novel, *Castle Richmond*. This, as we have seen, was set back in the famine days of the 1840s and would seem to have been designed as a valediction to Ireland. Although he himself, his wife and their two boys did not leave Dublin for good and all until December 1859, Trollope knew soon after his return from the West Indies that his superiors in the Post Office had reluctantly granted his petition for a job in England. He was now appointed Surveyor of the Eastern District—which contained the counties of Essex, Suffolk, Norfolk, Cambridgeshire,

Huntingdonshire and the greater part of Hertfordshire. He had long felt that an industrious novelist like himself should not be isolated from the literary world of London, from the publishers, from the clubs and from the dinner-parties. It was this belief that had led him to petition the General Post Office authorities for a transfer. In July he looked over a commodious Georgian house, Waltham House, which stood in its own grounds at Waltham Cross in Hertfordshire. The house was only twelve miles from London, and had a large garden and good stabling. On August 1st, 1859, he signed the lease for Waltham House. It was here that he lived contentedly for the next eleven years, which, so far as his own novels and hs spiralling fame were concerned, were the most productive and important of his writing life. In 1860 he began producing *Framley Parsonage* in serial form for the new magazine which Thackeray was editing, the *Cornhill*. When Smith, Elder, the publishers of the *Cornhill*, had asked him for a novel, he would have liked to have suggested *Castle Richmond*, but this famine book was already sold to Chapman and Hall, and would, anyway, not have filled the bill. What was wanted from him for the *Cornhill* was 'an English tale, on English life, with a clerical flavour'. He therefore temporarily left off working at *Castle Richmond*, and started upon a new novel. With his customary determination to show how mechanical his own novel writing had become he takes pains to tell us, in his *Autobiography*, that he wrote the first pages of *Framley Parsonage* in a railway carriage on his way back to Dublin after seeing his publishers in London. He called it

'fabricating a hodge-podge ... Nothing could be less efficient or artistic. But the characters were so well handled that the work from the first to the last was popular ... I think myself that Lucy Robarts is perhaps the most natural English girl I ever drew—the most natural, at any rate, of those who have been good girls ... Indeed I doubt whether such a character could be made more lifelike than Lucy Robarts.'

Just as it was an immense relief to the Anthony Trollopes to leave Ireland for good and to join in the wholesome, well-ordered country life of East Anglia, so must Anthony have found his return to the dear county of Barsetshire a pleasant change from the starving crones and soup-kitchens of County Cork. All the same, he had been paid £600 by Chapman for *Castle Richmond* and the book had to be finished. For a few months he left pale Lady Clara Desmond, transfixed like some still from an early film, poking her delicate finger into the uncooked yellow mess of Indian corn. When *Framley Parsonage* was half finished, Trollope released Lady Clara from her trance and, after many complications, got her safely married off to the placid Herbert FitzGerald instead of to Herbert's cousin, Owen FitzGerald, the scamp of Hap Hall. In this novel Owen FitzGerald is himself hopelessly in love with Lady Clara. Her mother, the widowed Lady Desmond, is hopelessly in love with Owen, whom she wishes to marry, and is jealous of her own daughter. The book's initial description of Owen FitzGerald, like those of young Sir Felix Carbury in *The Way We Live Now* or of Lucius Mason in *Orley Farm*, shows how well aware Trollope was of the snares and dangers of masculine as well as of feminine beauty. In his preliminary notes for *The Way We Live Now* he jotted down his first notions of Sir Felix Carbury's appearance: '25. Been in the Guards ... Magnificently beautiful, dark with perfect features, brown eyes.' In *Castle Richmond*, Owen FitzGerald is introduced to the reader as 'a very handsome man—tall, being somewhat over six feet in height—athletic, almost more than in proportion—with short, light, chestnut-tinted hair, blue eyes and a mouth as perfect as that of Phoebus'. The dazzling and Byronic monomaniac enthralls not only Lady Desmond but her son, the boy Earl, who when the book opens is still at Eton. It has been suggested by a transatlantic critic that Owen FitzGerald regards the boy as 'a surrogate' for his sister Clara. However that may be, Owen and the boy have several passages which can only be classified as love-scenes:

'"I think you are the dearest, finest, best fellow that ever lived," said FitzGerald, pressing him with his arm ...

'"Owen!" said the boy again ... and throwing himself on FitzGerald's breast, he burst out into a passion of tears.

'"... By heaven! if I were her [his sister Clara] I know whom I should love," said her brother.'

The implications of this relationship may well have escaped Trollope. It would seem, in fact, to be yet another case of his characters getting the upper hand and behaving as they, rather than their creator, wished. At the end of the book the young Earl and his Phoebus Apollo set off abroad together for an unlimited length of time. The Countess of Desmond loses her daughter, her only son and the man whom she adores at one neat stroke of Trollope's pen. Clara and her future husband Herbert FitzGerald are bound together by love. So are the young Earl and Owen FitzGerald. Only the selfish and cold-blooded Lady Desmond is left to eke out a lonely and impoverished life in the great barrack of Desmond Court.

Anthony tells us that the simultaneous construction of *Castle Richmond* and *Framley Parsonage* formed the single occasion on which he handled two novels at the same time: 'This, however, did not create either difficulty or confusion.' He declares that, once the art of fiction has been acquired, there is no reason why 'two or three [novels] should not be well-written at the same time'. This was an experiment upon which, fortunately, even he never tried to embark.

The move to Waltham House in the late autumn of 1859 effected a radical and happy change in Anthony Trollope's pattern of life. For twenty-six years he had had no home that he could correctly call his own. As an ungainly youth in the General Post Office at St Martins-le-Grand he had, for seven long years, lived in cheap and dreary London lodgings such as he provided for Johnnie Eames in *The Small House at Allington*. His memories of that period in his life were pre-eminently memories of darkness: 'lodgings in London are always gloomy', he writes in *The Last Chronicle of Barset*:

'Gloomy colours wear better than bright ones for curtains and carpets, and the keepers of lodgings in London seem to think that a certain dinginess of appearance is respectable ... I doubt whether any well-conditioned lodging-house matron could be induced to show rooms that were prettily draped or pleasantly coloured.'

When, in *The Last Chronicle*, Lily Dale and her uncle come up to London for a month, they take rooms in Sackville Street, but even this good West End address does not ensure them cosy or luxurious surroundings: the rooms are 'as brown, and as gloomy, and as ill-suited for the comforts of ordinary life as though they had been prepared for two prisoners'. At Banagher Anthony had lived in a starkly provincial Irish hotel, at Clonmel in furnished rooms and at Mallow in a furnished house. At 5 Seaview Terrace, Donnybrook, Dublin, he and his family had inhabited a high, repellent, semi-detached mansion built of staring orange brick. During his two-year stint in the West of England, from 1851 to 1853, he was constantly on the move, accompanied by Rose and their two boys who led a rootless, nomad life. These days were now over. He first leased and then bought Waltham House, and later added a large new room to an already capacious dwelling.

Waltham House was dignified, solid and reassuring, and there Trollope wrote several of his finest novels. At the front of this large, early-eighteenth-century house of four stories, a flight of ten stone steps led up to the main door, which had a porch, pilasters and a fanlight. Abutting from the *corps de logis* were two wings. In one of these Trollope kept his hunters and in the other he installed offices in which his staff of postal clerks worked. Everything about Waltham House was just what you expected. There were cows in the meadows and pigs in the sty, apples in the orchard, and umbrageous cedar trees upon the lawn. The old walled garden, which you entered by opening a wooden door, was as private and as secluded as you could have wished. A sundial stood in the centre of this walled garden, and there was a small stone-margined pool in one corner. There was also a summer-house in which visitors and guests liked to sit and chat. One of the charms of the walled garden was the fact that, in summertime, you could pick strawberries while looking at the roses, for flower-beds and strawberry beds were intermingled; the garden also yielded asparagus, peaches, plums and green peas in their season, as well as varieties of potato, and cabbages and cauliflower. On warm summer evenings guests would be invited to stroll out on to the lawn after dinner, where they would find a table laden with fruit and wine set out beneath the cedar trees. 'And good stories were told,' wrote one of the Trollopes' friends reminiscently, 'while the tobacco went curling up into the twilight.' In winter Waltham House would be 'wrapped in snow', as one of Thackeray's daughters noted in her diary; 'a sweet prim chill house wrapped in snow'.

Although he wrote of Waltham House as 'a rickety old place requiring much repair and occasionally not as weather-tight as it should be', Anthony Trollope loved the house and detested selling it, which he decided to do in 1871. In 1936 Waltham House was totally demolished. No vestige of the fine old building remains.

Apart from its pleasant architecture and rural atmosphere, Waltham House had further positive merits in Trollope's eyes. It was but twelve miles from London by railway, the only drawback to this being that you were deposited at Shoreditch Station, a fog-infested region of the City of London from which it was a long haul to the West End in a hansom cab. The little town of Waltham Cross itself, centred on the magnificent romanesque abbey built by King Harold, lay well inside Trollope's new, important postal district. It was also within the Roothing country in which he liked to hunt, and only twenty miles from the Essex meets. The possession of Waltham House had a yet more fundamental appeal to Anthony, for by living in it he was consciously joining that class with which he sympathized most – the old-fashioned landed gentry. He had become a country gentleman at last.

When his two sons were christened in the Protestant church of St Mary in Clonmel, County Tipperary, the sacristan had naturally been obliged to ascertain the father's profession. On both baptismal certificates Anthony Trollope described himself not as a postal surveyor but as a 'Gentleman'. The writing-paper at Waltham House bore the address in crimson Gothic lettering, but it also bore his cousin Sir John Trollope's crest, a leaping stag. In his novels, his autobiography and his brief life of Thackeray, Trollope is always emphatic about the supreme, the transcendent importance of the English gentleman. We are told that there are 'places in life which can hardly be well-filled except by gentlemen'. This conviction led to his vociferous opposition to the new system of competitive examinations for the Civil Service and for commissions in the Army or Navy. In a laudable anxiety to be fair he once conceived a hypothetical case in which a butcher's son who has managed to acquire 'gentle culture' might be thought more suited for some worldly position than the son of a parson. In this unlikely example he asserts that he hopes that he might himself have been the first to welcome some erudite whippersnapper fresh from the slaughter-house but would have thought it preferable to allot the job to the gentleman-parson's son.

By the time Trollope was middle-aged the terms 'gentleman' and 'lady' were losing their coinage. In 1873, the weekly *Vanity Fair*—ordinarily an irreverent enough periodical—solemnly posed the question: 'What constitutes a lady or a gentleman?' It suggested that for the last hundred years 'the term has been granted by courtesy to every person not engaged in the retail trade, who has received a decent education, and lives in a certain style'. The article went on to assert that the terms had lost all meaning in the modern world, and blamed this on 'well-born people' who had been 'a great deal too kind and too familiar with their inferiors'. *Vanity Fair*'s contributor deplored the fact that all the class barriers were being demolished, and that sales-girls and barmaids were called 'young ladies'. In recording the fate of a village girl raped by two soldiers during the Autumn Manoeuvres of 1872 some newspapers had actually headed their reports: 'Outrage by soldiers on young lady'. Costermongers called each other gentlemen, and so did clerks and other lesser breeds without the law. 'The distinguished thing soon will be to be spoken of as man or woman,' the *Vanity Fair* article concludes.

Anthony Trollope was perhaps abnormally conscious of the value, the duties and the status of the English gentleman. The phrase 'you are no gentleman' is not infrequent in his novels, and is usually applied to persons who, though gently bred, behave in an ungentlemanly, dishonest or unattractive way. This phrase is in fact the very worst punishment that can be inflicted on an offender against the accepted social code; the use of a horse-whip in *Doctor Thorne* being a rare occasion of resort to physical violence in the Trollope novels, for his characters mostly rely on verbal abuse, as in *Sir Harry Hotspur of Humblethwaite*. Sir Harry is enraged by his dissolute nephew's attempt to marry the daughter and sole heiress of Humblethwaite Hall:

' "What right had you, sir, to speak to her without coming to me?"

' "One always does, I think, go to the girl first," said George.

' "You have disgraced yourself, sir, and outraged my hospitality. You are no gentleman!"

' "Sir Harry, that is strong language."

' "Strong? Of course it is strong. I mean it to be strong."

' "... Sir Harry, you have told me that I am not a gentleman." '

The deliberate insult to George Hotspur is the more wounding because he is, by birth, a gentleman. Anti-heroes, like Ferdinand Lopez in *The Prime Minister*, who are not of gentle birth, are never expected to behave prettily and are not considered to be worth insulting.

'He is not worth your notice,' says Frank Gresham of Lopez. 'He is simply not a gentleman and does not know how to behave himself.' Sir Harry Hotspur and all the many other maddened parents in the novels are quickly alarmed by any sign that a son or a daughter may be diverging from the stiff class code which they have learned from nursery and schoolroom upwards. But, in the bulk of Trollope's fiction, country gentry are subliminally presented to us as beings to be admired in themselves and not merely for their social tenets.

It would seem unquestionable that Anthony's views on the gentry were inflated by the recollections of his miserable boyhood and wretched lonely London youth. In a memorable phrase already quoted he attributed his father's troubles to a combination of 'poverty and gentle standing'. The only other people of gentle standing whom he had then encountered were Harrow neighbours in his childhood and, later, the hard-riding tippling Irish squireens in County Galway. As we have seen, in his seven years as a young man in London he was emphatically not a young man about town. But now at Waltham House he could forget about his boyhood and youth. His salary from the Post

Office increased, the contracts for his novels were better and better; he could now afford to live very comfortably and to entertain whenever he wished. He calls the work he did at Waltham House during his twelve-year tenancy 'certainly very great. I feel confident that in amount no other writer contributed so much during that time to English literature. Over and above my novels I wrote political articles, critical, social and sporting articles, for periodicals without number.'

As the money flowed in Anthony enjoyed it, but in a prudent, watchful manner. Where his father had utterly failed to achieve anything in his life, Anthony had succeeded. Bailiffs would never darken the threshold of Waltham House, nor would there ever be any question of his having to lug Rose and Harry and Freddie off to cold lodgings in Bruges. At Waltham, in July 1860, he tried to exorcize the black memories of his lonely boyhood and his mad father by choosing the old Harrow farmhouse as the setting for his next novel, *Orley Farm*. At his special request his new friend John Everett Millais made a sketch of the farmhouse for the shilling-number serialization of Lady Mason's ordeal.

(ii)

These, then, were the benefits of the vital move to Waltham Cross—a comfortable, spacious country life, a firm base for hospitalities, available hunting nearby and London within very easy reach. We should now consider the last of these—Anthony Trollope's exciting bound into the metropolitan whirlpool. He was soon on terms of close friendship with Thackeray, who seconded him as a candidate for membership of the Garrick Club in April 1862. He had been proposed for the club by an old friend, the Irish-born journalist Robert Bell.

Trollope had long admired Thackeray, and had even at one time sought to imitate his style in the silly novelette *Brown, Jones and Robinson*. In the autumn of 1859 he had heard about the brand-new monthly, the *Cornhill*, which Smith, Elder and Co. were launching, with Thackeray in the editorial chair. From his Dublin suburb that October Trollope had written to Thackeray, whom he had never met, offering to supply the *Cornhill* with some short stories he was then concocting under the general title *Tales of All Countries*. Thackeray replied at once and so did George Smith of Smith, Elder. The latter asked, as we have seen, for a full-length novel of clerical and country life, to begin serialization in the first number of the new

185

magazine. This honour had previously been reserved by the publishers for Thackeray, since they knew that a fresh work of fiction from his pen would guarantee extensive sales. Thackeray, however, was in one of his ailing and indolent moods, and had scarcely begun to write the novel at all. Industrious Anthony Trollope could and did provide a novel—*Framley Parsonage*—which thus reached a large new public and marked the beginning of his wide popularity and fame.

Anxious to get his authors and illustrators to know each other, Mr George Smith, that most liberal of Victorian publishers, proposed to invite them to a monthly dinner-party at his house in Gloucester Square. The first dinner was given there in January 1861. Amongst others Anthony Trollope was invited to what he termed both 'a sumptuous dinner' and 'a memorable banquet'. Here for the first time he met Thackeray, G. H. Lewes, the young and handsome painter John Millais, George Augustus Sala, Richard Monckton Milnes and several other contemporary celebrities. Above all, Trollope was pining to make friends with Thackeray whom he judged to be far and away the best novelist of the day; but when George Smith led the burly neophyte up to Thackeray before dinner, Trollope's hero muttered 'How do?' and turned on his heel. This apparent snub, which was in reality due to one of Thackeray's recurrent spasms of agonizing physical pain, made Trollope so angry that he told their host at his publishing office next morning that he had nearly left the house and would never, never speak to Thackeray again. George Smith smoothed him down, and Trollope left Smith Elder's establishment 'in a happier frame of mind than when he entered it'.

Anthony Trollope's first experience of the London literary world at this dinner was somewhat amazing to the other guests, for he proved boisterous and self-assertive, contradicting everybody, then trying to mend the damage he had done by friendly words. He also kept dropping off to sleep. Sala, who wrote an account of this first *Cornhill* dinner-party, describes Trollope as 'going to sleep on sofas, chairs, or leaning against sideboards, and even somnolent while standing erect on the hearthrug'. Sala had never before met anyone 'who could take so many spells of "forty winks" at unexpected moments, and then turn up quite wakeful, alert, and pugnacious, as the author of *Barchester Towers* who had nothing of the bear but his skin, but whose ursine envelope was assuredly of the most grisly nature'.

Despite his quaint and giddy conduct at George Smith's dinner-party, where for the first time he met his intellectual peers, Trollope was soon at home in such circles as he aspired to join, being elected to the Garrick Club, the Athenaeum and the Cosmopolitan, as well as to a club he did not much frequent—the Arts Club in Hanover Square. His own impression of his London debut was satisfying: 'I think that I became popular with those with whom I associated ... It was not till we had settled ourselves at Waltham that I really began to live much with others. The Garrick Club was the first assemblage of men at which I felt myself to be popular.'

The Trollopes were now invited to country houses, in particular to one or other of the two estates of a great new friend, Sir Henry James, the lawyer and liberal statesman, later Lord James of Hereford. All this was grist to the novelist's mill, for Sir Henry entertained 'representatives of the polite world in all its aspects', ranging from the Prince and Princess of Wales to Junior Lords of the Treasury, from notable sportsmen to the latest twanging transatlantic beauty. Trollope soon became a distinguished if splenetic figure in his clubs and in what was then known as 'good society'. His prominent forehead and domed bald head, his sharp blue eyes behind the gilt-framed glasses and his flowing beard—recorded by one London crony as 'blonde'—all gave him the air of an eminent German professor. He was now forty-five.

The serialization of *Framley Parsonage* in the *Cornhill* threw open the toll-gates of East and West Barsetshire to admit a new and very numerous flock of readers, who probably applied to Mudie's Lending Library for the previous Barsetshire volumes they had missed—*The Warden, Barchester Towers* and *Doctor Thorne*. An enticing new feature of the *Framley* serial was the set of illustrations by John Millais, who now became one of Anthony's closest friends and at whose lodge in the Highlands the Trollopes would often go to stay in the late summertime. In February 1860, Trollope had written to George Smith, sending more of his current novel for the printer, and had added: 'Should I live to see my story illustrated by Millais nobody would be able to hold me.' Smith, who prided himself on never haggling over contracts and on cosseting his best authors, at once arranged that Millais should begin illustrating the third instalment of *Framley Parsonage*, for the first two were already out. Readers all over the country could now see as well as imagine the appearance of Lucy Robarts, or of the Crawley family or of old Lady Lufton. The collaboration between Trollope and

Millais over these and subsequent sets of engravings for other books was, on the whole, intimate and fruitful. John Millais did his scrupulous homework by acquainting himself with the characters in the earlier Barsetshire novels. Trollope's biographer Escott asserts that 'this fortunate conjunction of pen and pencil' gave the world a 'real revelation' of English country life and 'completed for multitudes the lessons in provincial existence and character which Maria Edgeworth and Jane Austen had begun'. Millais had told Escott that his rare success in illustrating the Trollope novels stemmed from the fact that the writer and the painter set about their different work in an identical way, while Trollope himself told the same friend that

'a right judgment in selection of personal traits or physical features will ensure life likeness in representation. Horace, as Englished by Conington, talks of "searching for wreaths in olive's rifled bower". The art practised by Millais and myself is the effective combination of the details, which observation has collected for us from every quarter, and their fusion into an harmonious unity.'

Anthony Trollope, as we should by now long have realized, was a touchy and a difficult man, and even the harmonious unity of collaboration with Jonn Millais was subject to stress, complaint and sudden frenzy. Although it was often the novelist himself who suggested possible scenes in his work most liable to blossom into illustrations, he and Millais did not invariably agree. In May 1860, for example, Trollope wrote frantically to George Smith about an illustration showing Lucy Robarts after she had refused Lord Lufton's offer of marriage: 'The picture is simply ludicrous, and will be thought by most people to have been made so intentionally.' It was a 'burlesque' suited to *Punch*, except that the drawing was too bad 'to have passed muster for that publication'. Could not the picture be altogether omitted or was it entirely too late? He supposed that 'Mr Millais' had no more time to devote to *Framley Parsonage*. If this were so, should not the remainder of the sketches be cancelled? 'In the present instance I certainly think that you & Mr Thackeray & I have ground for complaint.' The regrettable engraving shows Lucy Robarts lying on her bed weeping, 'with an enormous bustle and spreading flounces that makes her look very like a peacock'.

Smith and Millais seem to have calmed their explosive author down, for in July he was writing to the publisher: 'The Crawley family is very good, and I will now consent to forget the flounced dress. I saw the *very pattern of that dress* some time after the picture came out.' Trollope and Millais continued searching for wreaths the olive's rifled bower for another three novels: *Orley Farm*, *The Small House at Allington* and *Phineas Finn*. Millais also contributed a frontispiece for *Kept in the Dark* but more or less refused to do further illustrations—because, no doubt, he was becoming more and more well-paid and fashionable as a portrait painter. In August 1866, however, he did half promise to do another set of engravings. 'Do *do* them!' Trollope wrote to him. 'They won't take you above half an hour each.' But in the end Millais declined. In his autobiography Trollope writes of John Everett Millais in the highest terms, declaring that unlike some opinionated illustrators 'he was neither proud nor idle' and simply wished 'to promote the views of the writer'. He also tells us that in the fifteen years since he had first met Millais (who was at that time thirty-one years old) his affection for the painter had ever increased. 'To see him has always been a pleasure. His voice has been a sweet sound in my ears ... These words, should he ever see them, will come to him from the grave, and will tell him of my regard,—as one living man never tells another.'

When Millais remained either overworked or obdurate, Smith, Elder, enlisted fresh illustrators for successive novels. Prime amongst these was Hablot Browne, who had illustrated *The Pickwick Papers* and other Dickens novels under the pseudonym of 'Phiz'. Browne was now invited to deal with Anthony Trollope's *Can You Forgive Her?* which appeared in monthly instalments in 1864 and was subsequently published by Chapman and Hall in two volumes. Only the first of these volumes carried Phiz's illustrations, to which Trollope had taken great exception. He wrote to his publishers:

'I think you would possibly find no worse illustrator than H. Browne, and I think he is almost as bad in one kind as in another ... I cannot think that his work can add any value at all to any book ... But of course the question is one for you to settle yourself. As for myself I can never express satisfaction at being illustrated in any way by H. Browne.'

An obscure and spiteful hack-writer named Hain Friswell, who in 1870 published a book entitled *Modern Men of Letters Honestly Criticised*, while including in it a vituperative chapter on Anthony Trollope, did not omit to mention the illustrations of Millais and of Phiz. He suggested that 'Trollope's pictures of an age very poor and weak in its nature' had suited Millais well, but that when Phiz tried to illustrate *Can You Forgive Her?* he had miserably failed because he 'actually put life and humour into some of the figures under which Trollope had written descriptions dry as old nuts, but singularly descriptive of the author and his mind'. At Trollope's behest another illustrator was called in, a Miss Taylor, a lady resident in St Leonards, whose 'drawings on wood' the Trollopes personally admired. In the end Marcus Stone was commissioned to illustrate the second volume of the novel. He created a series of chunky engravings in which he made little effort to match his personages either with those in the first volume by Phiz or with Trollope's own descriptions in the text. The rejection of Phiz's drawings was comprehensible, for he was so closely connected in the public mind with comic illustrations to the books of Charles Dickens and of Charles Lever that the spindly people he drew for *Can You Forgive Her?* looked as though they had strayed out of some new novel by either of these authors, and bore no resemblance to Trollope's characters at all. For *The Last Chronicle of Barset* the artist George Thomas was selected; he had painted pictures for the Queen and had done engravings for *Uncle Tom's Cabin* and for *Hiawatha*. Although examples of Millais's drawings for earlier Barchester novels were supplied to Thomas, the result did not much satisfy Anthony Trollope: 'Grace is not good. She has fat cheeks and is not Grace Crawley ... Mrs Proudie is not quite my Mrs Proudie.'

The friendly defection of John Everett Millais continued to be felt by author and publishers alike. To *He Knew He Was Right* Marcus Stone contributed some unusually lively and pleasing illustrations. When *The Way We Live Now* appeared in 1873 it included plates by Luke Fildes, then a young portrait painter who lived to execute state portraits of King Edward VII and Queen Alexandra, was made a knight and died in 1927 at the age of eighty-three.

As time went on, Anthony Trollope ceased to be much interested in any illustrator but his beloved Millais. He had never had much of an eye for pictorial art, although he would go with his wife to art galleries abroad, and could appreciate the stained glass windows at Chartres. That he failed to understand contemporary painters' methods and feelings is blatantly shown in some of the London chapters in *The Last Chronicle of Barset* when we come across the foolish, intrusive figure of the painter Conway Dalrymple. Anthony had originally been uncertain about the Pre-Raphaelites and in particular the Pre-Raphaelite phase of John Everett Millais, whom he did not then know. In one of the scenes in *The Warden* taking place in the sybaritic chambers of the powerful journalist Tom Towers, his *garçonnière* is described as being furnished more comfortably than Stafford House. We are further informed that the book-lined study contained one painting only—'a singularly long figure of a female devotee by Millais ... The picture was not hung, as pictures usually are, against the wall ... it had a stand or desk erected for its own accommodation; and there on her pedestal, framed and glazed, stood the devotional lady looking intently at a lily as no lady ever looked before.' Such Pre-Raphaelite women, and their improbable postures, gave Trollope 'an idea of pain without grace, and abstraction without a cause'. His close friendship with Millais and the development of the painter's maturer style turned Trollope's ridicule into sincere and lasting admiration. He likewise respected Sir Frederick Leighton who illustrated *Romola* for George Eliot's publishers in 1862. Writing to congratulate the authoress on the perfection of her 'pen painting' in this novel Trollope added: 'You have been nobly aided by your artist. I take it for granted that it is Leighton.'

The vogue for illustrated novels has been long, long dead. Whether the drawings aided or hampered the enjoyment of the reader is, I think, very much open to question—and particularly so in some of Trollope's work illustrated by frankly inferior draughtsmen. These merely interfere with the mental image of characters he himself had created in signal depth and detail.

(iii)

At much the same time that his speedy friendship with young Millais was developing, Anthony had made a literary conquest in no less a personage than George Eliot. He had first met Marian Evan's titular husband at that *Cornhill* dinner at which he himself had alternately slept and barked out his opinions; and through Lewes he became acquainted with George Eliot. Very soon he was a recognized favourite with that austere authoress, who declared that she found him 'the heartiest, most genuine, moral and generous of men'. At the small, eclectic gatherings of friends and admirers over which George Eliot solemnly presided at The Priory, North Bank, Regents Park, on Sunday afternoons, Anthony was often allowed to take the privileged seat next to George Eliot's armchair on the left of the fireplace in the double drawing room, the walls of which were hung with Leighton's original sketches for *Romola*. Here, too, he would meet Leighton himself, Robert Browning (whom he had first known in Florence), Alfred Tennyson, such philosophers as Herbert Spencer, Tyndall and Piggott, Professor Beesley of London University and other intellectual celebrities of the day. At times the double drawing room was lent a cosmopolitan air by the awed presence of 'foreigners of distinction in letters, science and art'. But to Anthony it was George Eliot herself whom he had come to see, and he grew to 'love her very dearly'. Her particular cast of mind, her ponderous sibylline epigrams, even her lack of humour, stimulated and yet soothed him. His pronounced admiration for *Adam Bede, Silas Marner, Felix Holt* and *Romola* gratified her, and he is said to have relished 'those qualities in her work that secured her the compliment of comparison with Shakespeare'. She, on her side, readily acknowledged the influence of his novels on the writing of *Middlemarch.* 'I am not at all sure,' she remarked thoughtfully to a dangerous literary gossip, Mrs Lynn Lynton, 'that, but for Anthony Trollope, I should never have planned my studies on so extensive a scale for *Middlemarch*, or that I should, through all its episodes, have persevered with it to the close.'

Trollope and his hostess never discussed their own work on these productive Sunday afternoons, although on other days when he lunched quietly with her and Lewes they may have done so. George Eliot had in any case the secretiveness common to almost all female writers before and since, to whom talking about a book in the process of being written has been as taboo as talking about the early stages of a secret love affair. George Eliot's 'love of approbation', which a mutual friend of herself and Trollope suggested to be 'with her a phrenological organ strongly developed', corresponded well with Anthony's own yearning for constant approval. He did not tell George Eliot *viva voce* how much he admired her books, but confined himself to writing her letters on the subject. One such letter about *Romola* (from which I have already quoted above) she thought 'delightful' and 'generous', even though he had warned her not to 'fire over the heads of the crowd' and to 'make your full purpose compatible with their taste'. He was not at all blind to her literary faults, for he wrote to another correspondent, a spinster pen-friend named Mary Holmes, whom he had some-how inherited after Thackeray's death: 'She is sometimes heavy —sometimes abstruse, sometimes almost dull,—but always, like an egg, full of meat.' This was a note about *Daniel Deronda* which he admitted to be 'a trying book ... all wrong in art ... She is always striving for effects which she does not produce ...

Cartoon of Trollope by Frederick Waddy
for *Once a Week*, 1872

Mrs Fanny Trollope:
from a portrait by Auguste Hervieu, 1832

Carte-de-visite photograph of Anthony Trollope at about the age of forty

The yellow-back binding for *The Warden*

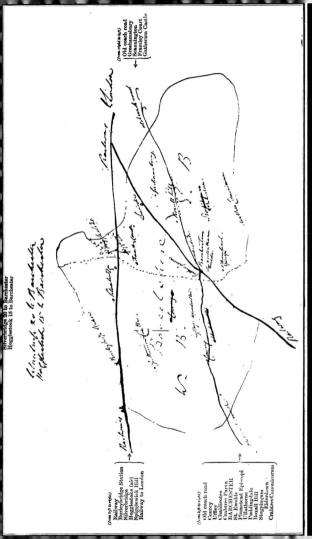

Trollope's Barsetshire. From a sketch map drawn by the novelist himself

RECEIVING LETTERS AT THE E.C. WINDOW

Four sketches of the General Post Office,
St Martins-le-Grand

MAKING-UP AT 7·57

RECEIVING PROVINCIAL BAGS IN THE INLAND LOBBY

FACING LETTERS

The exterior of the General Post Office building, St Martins-le-Grand

The interior of the General Post Office, c. 1835

Was it not a lie?

'Very like a peacock' – The Millais illustration to
Framley Parsonage (1861) which irritated Anthony Trollope.
This presentation of Lucy Robarts in tears he called
'simply ludicrous' and 'a burlesque'.

Posy and her Grandpapa

Posy Arabin and her grandfather, Mr Harding,
at the Deanery, Barchester
(illustration by W. H. Thomas for
The Last Chronicle of Barset, 1867).

'I might as well see whether there is
any sign of violence having been used.'

Illustration by Luke Fildes for
The Way We Live Now (1873).

Dolly Longstaffe, one of the young men-about-town
trying to marry the Melmotte heiress, keeps on his hat.

'She is my niece,' said the doctor,
taking up the tiny infant in his arms.

Dr Thorne deciding to adopt his dead brother's
illegitimate child, Mary
(Illustration by H. L. Shindler for *Dr Thorne*, 1858).

Trevelyan at Casalunga

Louis Trevelyan at the height of his madness, in Tuscany
(Illustration by Marcus Stone for *He Knew He Was Right*, 1869).

Anthony Trollope in old age:
from a photograph by Mrs Cameron

but Homer was allowed to nod once or twice, & why not the author of *Adam Bede* and *Romola*?' There was one point on which Anthony Trollope and George Eliot were constitutionally unable to agree; this was his by then notorious shoe-maker approach to the act of writing fiction.

While always unwilling to discuss work in progress, George Eliot was at times drawn into an argument about writing methods or techniques. In his essay on Trollope Frederick Harrison recalls a small dinner-party at The Priory at which, in his harsh loud voice, Anthony began his customary brag about sitting down to write each morning at five thirty, with his watch upon his desk; in three hours, he said, he regularly produced 250 words every quarter of an hour. This piece of information—which can scarcely have been news to her or to anyone else at the table—shocked George Eliot, who 'positively quivered at the thought'. She then revealed her own predicament—that she could only write when in the vein, that she wrote, rewrote and destroyed her manuscript two or three times, and as often as not sat upright at her table without being able to write at all. 'There are days and days together,' she wailed, 'when I cannot write a line.' Trollope, in the conciliatory mood which usually followed some egocentric outburst, tried to mollify his friend: 'With imaginative work like yours that is quite natural,' he said, 'but with my mechanical stuff it's a sheer matter of industry. It's not the head that does it,—it's the cobbler's wax on the seat and the sticking to my chair.' This was but a moment's incident in a long and affectionate friendship between the two great novelists. For Anthony this was of peculiar value, for he had never before had the opportunity of close friendship with a woman of superior intellect and considerable wisdom. Her sudden death in 1880, just two years before his own demise, inflicted on him, as he has written, a very severe wound. Afternoons or evenings at The Priory also put him on speaking terms with other distinguished *habitués* of the house. Because Marian Evans and Lewes were never legally married the company at The Priory consisted in the main of men; but before G. H. Lewes died their union had, so to speak, received an unexpected royal accolade. Trollope wrote to Kate Field:

'She was asked to dine with Queen Victoria's daughter (Crown Princess of Prussia) when the Princess was in England. I mention this, because the English Royal family are awfully particular as to whom they see and do not see. That at any rate is true, because I saw her there. But in truth, she was one of those whose private life should be left in privacy,—as may be said of all who have achieved fame by literary merits.'

(iv)

In sharp contrast to the inspiring yet sombre atmosphere of The Priory, Regents Park, was the tone of genial good fellowship ordinarily prevalent at the Garrick Club, to which Anthony Trollope was elected in the spring of 1862. He thus missed the notorious row of 1858 between Thackeray and Dickens over a scurrilous article in which Edmund Yates had purported to give an account of Thackeray's manners and demeanour when at the Club. When Trollope was voted a member, with a large and gratifying list of supporters, the Garrick Club was still crammed into its birthplace, a couple of rooms in King Street, Covent Garden, leased for the purpose in the autumn of 1831.

The Garrick had begun life under the auspices of its first patron, the Duke of Sussex, who had the sensible idea of forming a club in which the more liberal members of the aristocracy might meet actors, painters and writers on equal, casual terms. In its earliest years it numbered Macready, Charles Mathews and Charles Kemble amongst its members, as well as John Murray, Byron's publisher, Lockhart, the son-in-law and biographer of Walter Scott, Sergeant Talfourd and the poet Samuel Rogers. The first Marquess of Anglesey, who lost his leg at Waterloo, was one of the Club's Trustees. In July 1864 the Garrick Club entered into possession of its fine new building, designed by the architect Frederick Marrable on a street site created by the sweeping away of a congested block of alley-ways and, at first, named New King Street, but later, at the Club members' petition, given its present name of Garrick Street. In the dining room, on the staircase and indeed all over the Club were assembled a varied collection of theatrical scenes and portraits by Zoffany and other painters. These pictures helped to give the Club its ethos, as they still do to this day. The occupation of the new building took place a year after the death of Thackeray, who during his period of membership had been recognized as the Garrick Club's 'centre ... soul and cynosure'. In a speech at some Club festivity, Thackeray rhetorically once asked his fellow members: 'Do we, its happy inmates, ever speak of it as "The Garrick Club"? No, but "The G.", "the little G.", the dearest place in the world.' He was of course referring to the modest rooms in Covent Garden, for no one could rightly have called Marrable's palatial building 'the little G.'

194

After the failure of his four-year-old marriage in 1836, when his wife had become certifiably insane, Thackeray used his clubs as a substitute for home. The Garrick was his favourite of all, and there this tall, proud, unhappy man, with his bloodless face and fractured nose was to be found in the afternoon and evening. Thackeray was as sensitive and tormented as Anthony Trollope himself, was equally generous but more caustic, and protected his vulnerability by a veneer of cynicism. He had been elected to the Club in 1833, a young man with no literary pretensions who spent his time in drawing caricatures of his companions—he is said to have literally 'drawn' one member out of the Club altogether. As the years rolled by and fame swooped down upon him, he became the pride of the Garrick and found solace there for what Trollope once termed his widowed state. Anthony, on the other hand, scampered into membership of the Garrick when he was already a newly successful author. He did so with an innocent, contagious enthusiasm:

'I enjoyed infinitely the gaiety of the Garrick. It was a festival to me to dine there ... and a great delight to play a rubber in the little room upstairs of an afternoon. This playing of whist before dinner has since become a habit with me ... when I began to play at the Garrick, I did so simply because I liked the society of the men who played.'

On Thackeray's death in 1863, Trollope was already so popular at the Club that he was asked to take his dead friend's place on the Committee, was chairman at the inaugural dinner at the Club's new premises, and ended up as a Club Trustee.

Once Trollope had recovered from the unintentional snub which Thackeray had seemed to have hurled at him on their first meetings in the house of their publisher, the two novelists became intimate friends. Their characters were dissimilar, but they had in common an abnormal sensibility to criticism and a generosity of heart which was as rare then as it is now. A single example of this latter trait will here suffice. In May 1862 William Follett Synge, a professional diplomatist and contributor to *Punch* and to the *Saturday Review*, and 'the dear friend' both of Trollope and of Thackeray, had just been appointed H.M. Consul in Honolulu. Synge was heavily in debt, and needed some two thousand pounds to free himself before he could take ship for his new appointment. He came to Anthony Trollope to ask him for a loan—the sum, of course, then being of far greater value than it would rate in sterling currency today. Ruminating on this problem as he walked that day across Horse Guards'

Parade, Trollope met Thackeray, who was also on foot, by the gate into Whitehall. He stopped him between the two mounted Household Cavalry troopers on guard, and told him the sad tale of Follett Synge. 'Do you mean to say that I am to find two thousand pounds?' Thackeray shouted angrily, cursing as he did so. Trollope explained that this was not what he was asking at all—he merely wished to discuss the matter with Thackeray:

'Then there came over his face a peculiar smile, and he whispered his suggestion, as though half-ashamed of his meanness. "I'll go half," he said, "if anybody will do the rest." And he did go half at a day or two's notice ... I could tell various stories of the same kind, only that I lack space, and that they, if simply added one to the other, would lack interest.'

Trollope was recounting this incident in the monograph on Thackeray which he had been commissioned to write in 1879. He naturally refrained from mentioning that he himself lent Synge the other half of the money, which seems never, somehow, to have been entirely repaid.

The monograph for the *English Men of Letters* series, Trollope found 'a terrible job' to compile: 'There is absolutely nothing to say,—except washed out criticism. But it had to be done, and no one could do it more lovingly.' It was indeed a terrible job to do, since shortly before his death Thackeray had made his two daughters solemnly promise that no biography of himself should ever be attempted, let alone published. Trollope was consequently driven back on to his own views of *Henry Esmond* or of *Barry Lyndon* or of *Vanity Fair*. Of *Vanity Fair* he confessed that he had always been staggered by the brilliant 'audacity' with which Thackeray had introduced the miserly curmudgeon Sir Pitt Crawley eating tripe with his ragged old maid-of-all-work, Mrs Tinker, in the chilly dining room of his London house. Trollope considered it 'quite clear' that, while writing this scene, Thackeray 'had known nothing of what was coming' about the rest of the Crawley family. It is an intestesting comment, for it implies that great novelists generally do know how many characters they will bring into a novel, how these shall behave and why. As we shall see later when considering Anthony Trollope's own writing techniques, he did not begin a new novel until he had drawn up a methodical list of his own *dramatis personae*, with abbreviated notes about the appearance, the life-purpose and the antecedents of each of them. But once he had begun to write, the characters he conjured up would hijack the plot—in the preliminary notes, for example, on *The*

Way We Live Now, Melmotte, the tycoon who dominates that novel is not mentioned at all—or, rather, his name is merely mentioned to explain why his daughter is an heiress: '*Marie Melmotte*. Daughter of Augustus Melmotte, the great French swindler.'

In the course of writing the monograph on Thackeray, Trollope compares his subject with Charles Dickens, 'a firm reliant man' who knew the nature of his own talent and did the best he could with it. Thackeray, on the other hand, seemed to Trollope 'the very opposite of this'. He called him unsteadfast, idle, changeable of purpose, not trusting his own intellect: 'no man ever failed more generally than he to put his best foot foremost ... There is a touch of vagueness which indicates that his pen was not firm while he was using it.' Not very surprisingly, Thackeray's surviving daughter Annie, herself a novelist of repute, seems to have much resented this bald assessment of her father's talents and of his indolence. 'I dined at Smith's last night,' Anthony wrote to his wife in 1882, 'and met Annie Thackeray, and we smiled at each other, and we had a thorough good talk. I am very glad because my memory of her father was wounded by the feeling of a quarrel.'

While *Framley Parsonage* was being serialized in the *Cornhill* because Thackeray's projected novel *Lovel the Widower* was not ready for that periodical, Trollope came to the conclusion that his eminent Garrick Club crony was not an efficient editor. There must have been a certain satisfaction in finding that he himself, for the first and almost the last time in his life, was able to write a whole novel in sections and each month deliver a part punctiliously to the press, while Thackeray's *Lovel the Widower* was still held up and, when serialized in the *Cornhill*, was not found 'substantial as the principal joint at the banquet ... I was the saddle of mutton. My fitness lay in my capacity for quick roasting.' Moreover, the *Cornhill*'s publishers had paid £1,000 for *Framley Parsonage*. In the same frank passage of his monograph, Trollope remarks that 'almost anything would have been then accepted coming under Thackeray's editorship'. Yet in the same year, 1860, one of Trollope's short stories, a tale set in the Roman campagna and entitled *Mrs General Talboys* was rejected by Thackeray as being too immoral for the readers of the *Cornhill*, since the story presents a group of English and American aesthetes and expatriates, one of whom has an Italian mistress and several children by her, while Mrs Arabella Talboys, whose husband lives in England, conducts an esoteric flirtation with a young painter. Trollope was certain that Thackeray had never read the story at all, but had trusted to 'some moral deputy'. Thackeray had, as a matter of fact, found the whole business so painful that he left Trollope's reply to the letter rejecting the tale unopened and finally got one of his daughters to read it for him—'to see whether the thorn had been too sharp, whether I had turned upon him with reproaches. A man so susceptible could not have been a good editor'. Trollope's letter, in fact, was witty and showed no overt ill-feeling. He suggested that his characters were much less immoral than Effie Deans in *The Heart of Midlothian*, or Beatrice in *Henry Esmond*, or a woman in *The Virginians* who is surprised that Warrington will not 'do as others use' with a young girl. Then in *Jane Eyre* the whole story of the birth of the 'illegitimate brat' is retailed at length. 'I could think of no pure English novelist,' he wrote, 'pure up to the *Cornhill* standard, except Dickens, but then I remembered *Oliver Twist* and blushed for what my mother and sisters read into that very fie-fie story.' He stoutly declared that he 'would not allow' that he was an indecent writer, and porfessed that squeamishness 'in so far as it is squeamishness and not delicacy—should be disregarded by the writer'.

As Trollope aged he seems to have jettisoned, or, at any rate, to have modified his exalted conviction of the British novelist's first duty—that of selecting subjects suited to perusal by shy young vicarage girls on the doorstep of life. The plots, for instance, of *Mr Scarborough's Family* and *Is He Popenjoy?* revolve entirely round the question of illegitimate birth, while in *The Way We Live Now*, *Sir Harry Hotspur of Humblethwaite* and that superb detective novel, *John Caldigate*, the novelist is perfectly straightforward about, and unperturbed by, the mistresses with whom the younger characters have, for better or for worse, elected to live. We may even say that only Anthony Trollope's private paradise of Barsetshire is morally unstained, for Dr Thorne's illegitimate niece, Mary, is grown up when the novel opens, and, as we know, her very illegitimacy brings her a fortune which otherwise she would never have inherited.

(v)

Whatever Anthony Trollope may or may not have thought about him as an editor, there is no question that Thackeray's serialization of *Framley Parsonage*, coming on the heels of the success of the West Indian travel-book brought Trollope at last a thorough going fame and shot him up into the sparse ranks of the really prosperous mid-Victorian novelists. Discussing *Framley Parsonage* in his autobiography, he writes of this deathless novel in his customary debunking vein. He had conceived it, he tells us, as

'a morsel of a biography of an English clergyman who should not be a bad man but led into temptation by his own youth and the unclerical accidents of the life of those around him. The love of his sister for the young lord was an adjunct necessary, because there must be love in a novel ... Out of these slight elements I fabricated a hodge-podge in which the real plot consisted at last simply of a girl refusing to marry the man she loved till the man's friends agreed to accept her lovingly. Nothing could be less efficient or artistic. But the characters were so well-handled, that the work from the first to the last was popular ... I think myself that Lucy Robarts is perhaps the most natural English girl that I ever drew ... Indeed I doubt whether such a character could be made more lifelike than Lucy Robarts.'

More interesting is his admission, in this personal verdict on *Framley Parsonage*, that a novel written and published in serial form

'force upon the author the conviction that he should not allow himself to be tedious in any single part ... he cannot afford to have many pages skipped out of the few which are to meet the reader's eye at the same time ... I had realized this when I was writing *Framley Parsonage*; and working on the conviction which had thus come home to me, I fell into no bathos of dullnes.'

He also writes that he is aware of the tedium in many of his other novels: 'That I have been so is a fault that will lie heavy on my tombstone.'

One of the more irritating aspects of Anthony Trollope's mind is that he could frankly recognize the very considerable tedium evoked by a good many of his novels, and could realize the literary advantage of writing in serial parts, but that he never, after *Framley Parsonage,* did anything more about it. He has accused Thackeray of idleness—presumably because he did not begin writing at five thirty of a winter's morning—and of allowing his characters to proliferate in an uncontrolled manner; 'his pen was not firm'. It never occurred to Anthony that he was, as a matter of fact, a very great deal idler than Thackeray had ever been—for Thackery would agree to shorten stories or articles at his editor's request, whereas Trollope, on being asked by Longmans to reduce *Barchester Towers* by one-third had flown into a rage and refused. With the coming of fame, Trollope more and more let himself go in prolixity, in sheer verbiage, in the use of those pseudo-comic surnames which annoyed Henry James—such as Quiverful for the clergyman with fourteen children or Curlydown and Bagwax for a couple of Post Office clerks. One cannot but presume that his literary output would have distinctly benefited had he spent several mornings a month asleep in bed until a human hour for rising. But he himself was perfectly satisfied that his morning's ration of novel-writing, timed to the second by the gold repeater on his desk, was a sign of industrious virtue to which more frivolous or spasmodic writers lacked the courage to aspire. Scribbling two thousand words before breakfast, never rereading them, scarcely correcting the text save in proof-sheets for printers' errors— does not all this essentially smack of a gross and careless form of self-indulgence? Had he disciplined his pen with the same harsh rigour as that with which he disciplined his body to blunder from bed to desk at dawn in response to poor old Barney MacIntyre's early-bird call with a cup of coffee, he could undoubtedly have achieved a concision which he too seldom displays. If he could write a novel as marvellously free from padding or repetition as *Framley Parsonage* because he wrote it in sections, why did he not conclude that he could and should assay this feat again? The answer would seem to be that, not withstanding his lifelong habit of introspection, he could never truly distinguish his good work from his bad.

Trollope finished writing *Framley Parsonage* on June 30th, 1860; he began another of his greatest books, *Orley Farm*, on July 4th. This book he did not give to George Smith and the *Cornhill*, but sold to Chapman and Hall, who cut it up and issued it in shilling parts illustrated by John Millais. Anthony then took a step almost deliberately calculated to lower himself in the reading public's esteem: as I have earlier mentioned, he insisted that the *Cornhill* serialize his dust-laden, eight-year-old burlesque, *The Struggles of Brown, Jones and Robinson*, which the critics ridiculed and the *Cornhill* subscribers could not even understand. 'It was meant to be funny,' Anthony winningly informs us, 'was full of slang, and was intended as a satire on the ways of trade. Still I think that there is some good fun in it, but I have heard no one else express such an opinion. I do not know that I ever heard any opinion expressed of it, except by the publisher, who kindly remarked that he did not think it was equal to my usual work.' It was, of course, very much in George Smith's interests to print this trivial book, since by doing so he further ensured himself the good will of Anthony Trollope, and the publishing rights of certain of his future best-sellers.

In the autumn of 1860, Anthony Trollope and his wife went again to Florence, to see for the last time old Fanny Trollope, who had fallen into a long mental and physical decline. A few days before their departure as he and his wife were 'sitting over the "damp" number of the last—rather next— *Cornhill*' a large parcel arrived for him from the wayside station of Waltham Cross. It was a luxurious gift from George Smith, a lavish token of gratitude for the current success of *Framley Parsonage*. Anthony's letter of thanks is worth quoting because it provides us with a vivid marital conversation piece:

'One attains by experience an intuitive perception whether or no a parcel is or is not agreeable; whether it should be opened on one's study table, or sent down to the butler's pantry. This parcel I myself opened at the moment, & took from it fold after fold of packing paper—varying from the strongest brown to a delicate tissue of silver shade—till I reached—a travelling bag.

' "I never ordered it," said I angrily.

' "It's a present," said my wife.

' "Gammon—It's a commisson to take to Florence for some dandy and I'll be——".

'For a moment I fancy she imagined it was intended for her, but we came at once on a brandy flask & a case of razors, and that illusion was dispelled.

' "It's the lady who said she wrote your book intending to make you some amends," she suggested.*

'And so we went on but never got near the truth.

'No one is more accessible to a present than I am. I gloat over it like a child, and comfort myself in school hours by thinking how nice it will be to go back to it in play time. In that respect I have by no means outgrown my round jacket, & boy's appurtenances.

'Whether or not I shall ever become a proficient in using all those toilet elegancies with which I now find myself supplied,— gold pins, silver soap-dishes, & cut glass, I cannot say. I feel a little like a hog in armour, but will do my best.

'However let me thank you sincerely for your kind remem-

* A neurotic young lady in the provinces had recently created a local stir by claiming the authorship of *Framley Parsonage*.

brance. I argue from your good nature that you are satisfied with all the work I have done for you, & that after all is better than any present. I also feel that I owe you some *cadeau* of worth, seeing that you have brought me in contact with readers to [be] counted by hundreds of thousands instead of by hundreds ... I am just now starting for Italy.'

George Smith, to whom posterity is so much beholden for his bold and costly undertaking *The Dictionary of National Biography*, was a kind and imaginative friend to his authors. In July 1864 he gave the Anthony Trollopes Samuel Laurence's portrait of Thackeray: 'This morning,' wrote Anthony, 'we hung Thackeray up in our library, and we are *very much* obliged to you for the present—not only that it is in itself so valuable, but more especially because it is one so suited to our feelings'. In that same summer of 1864, Smith commissioned Laurence to sketch out a sepia head-and-shoulders of Anthony himself; the painter executed two separate pictures, one of which may be found in this book. After over seven sittings, Laurence demanded a few more. 'He compliments me,' Anthony oddly reported, 'by telling me that I am a subject very difficult to draw. He has taken infinite pains with it. Of course I myself am no judge of what he has done.' In another letter to Smith thanking him for a version of the new portrait, Anthony writes that when he looks at the portrait he finds himself to be 'a wonderfully solid old fellow. The picture is certainly a very good picture & my wife declares it to be very like,—and not a bit more solid than the original ... She seemed to have a fuller respect for me when she had seen it than ever before.'

Owing to his mother's growing senility this last visit to Florence was sad for Anthony; yet it was also fateful. In the romantic setting of the Villino Trollope, Anthony shyly welcomed an experience to which his fictional heroes and anti-heroes were far more prone than he had ever been himself: he fell in love. The object of this perforce platonic yet enduring passion was a beautiful girl from Boston named Kate Field. She was the daughter of a well-known American actor, Joseph Field, who had been a friend of Edgar Allan Poe, and who was, incidentally, the recipient of the letter from Nathaniel Hawthorne in which he compared the Trollope novels to a great lump of earth placed beneath a dome of glass. Anthony Trollope's knowledge of Americans, and particularly of the artless, fervent American girl on her first trip to Europe was, so far, meagre. From now on this knowledge was to be constantly increased.

In a passage of his autobiography which must have aroused some speculation when the book was first published after his death, Anthony Trollope tells us of 'a woman of whom not to speak in a work purporting to be a memoir of my own life would be to omit all allusion to one of the chief pleasures which has graced my later years'. Writing these words in 1876, he explains that for the last fifteen years this woman had been, beyond his own family circle, his 'most chosen friend ... a ray of light to me from which I can always strike a spark by thinking of her'. He declares that to have left her unmentioned in his memoirs would have amounted 'almost to falsehood'. He refrained from giving her name, but hoped that she would live 'to read the words I have now written, and to wipe away a tear as she thinks of my feelings while I write them'. This mysterious lady has always been identified as Miss Mary Katherine Keemle Field, a lovely and vivacious girl from Boston, who was born in 1838 and died in 1896. She was known in her family and to her many friends and admirers as 'Kate'.

When the Anthony Trollopes first met Kate Field in Florence in the autumn of the year 1860, she was an outstandingly independent-minded girl of twenty-one, come to Italy in the care of her uncle and aunt. Back home in Boston her aunt's salon was much respected in the more esoteric spheres of intellectual Boston society. This uncle and aunt had now returned to Beacon Hill, Kate's staid and quiet mother replacing them as her daughter's nominal chaperone. Mother and daughter had taken an apartment near the Palazzo Pitti, where Kate was breathlessly studying Italian *cinquecento* art. Her bright beauty and her eager, candid transatlantic manner had captivated the fastidious and, at times, world-weary expatriates of Florence: the Brownings, Miss Isa Blagden, Walter Savage Landor, Anthony's own relatives at the Villino Trollope, all readily succumbed to the American girl's fresh charm and welcomed her relentless thirst for Renaissance painting, sculpture and architecture, as well as her interest in music. In a letter home Kate compared Old Tom Trollope (now excessively deaf) both to Socrates and to Galileo, and she wrote of his wife Theodosia as 'promiscuously talented, writes for the *Athenaeum*, composes music, translates but does not go very far in any one thing'. Her last phrase could, in the long after years, have been applied to Kate Field herself; for, from an enthusiastic girl who wished to paint, to write novels and stories and poetry, to play the piano and to sing, she developed into a Boston blue-stocking and finally into a fervent and famous lecturer on Women's Rights. After her death her activities were listed as: 'American journalist, actress, author, lecturer and singer'. Kate, inevitably was also fascinated by the Spiritualism of Home, by mediumistic séances and by the ouija-board, otherwise known as a planchette. She published, in 1868, a little book under the title of *Planchette's Diary*. She remained a spinster all her life, having, in her own opinion, a rare and self-reliant personality likely to be held captive in the married state.

When she first frequented the Villino Trollope, Kate Field was overwhelmed by the beauty of the objects accumulated by Tom Trollope, who was a dealer as well as a connoisseur. She gushed when writing about the whole house so 'quaintly fascinating', with its collections of bronzes and terracottas, its bridal chests and Renaissance furniture and its marble pillars. She adored the late spring evenings spent at the Villino Trollope: 'Soft winds kiss the budding foliage and warm it into bloom; the beautiful terrace of Villino Trollope is transformed into a reception-room ... No lights but the stars are burning, and men and women, talking in almost every civilized tongue, are sipping iced lemonade—one of the specialities of the Villino Trollope.' It is easy to understand how Tuscany would have been a revelation to a clever young girl brought up on Beacon Hill.

It was at one of such parties at the Villino Trollope that Kate first encountered Anthony and his wife. In the weeks that followed she found Anthony Trollope 'a very delightful companion'. She wrote home to Boston that she was seeing 'a great deal of him' and that, learning that she had never read the *Arabian Nights* he had promised to send her a copy from London with an inscription on the fly-leaf: 'Kate Field from the Author'. He said that he would also write her a four-page letter if she undertook to answer this. Back home at Waltham Cross in November, Anthony did indeed write her what was for him an unusually long letter, telling her that the volumes of *Arabian Nights* were on the way but cautioning her not to read them straight through 'at a burst, but take them slowly and with deliberation and you will find them salutary'. Almost from the beginning of their romantic friendship, he evidently realized that the American girl's undisciplined zest for the arts, combined with a later one for lecturing on women's suffrage, might capsize her frail and overloaded craft. When in the winter of 1861 she sent her new friend the first of the many poems about which she consulted him, he replied with a letter which he said he knew would pain her. His verdict was simple: the poem was sloppily written and insufficiently worked over. Although she might flower into a poetess in the course of time, Kate was certainly not, in his view, at all like one as yet. 'Poetry should be very slow work—slow, patient and careless of quick result. That is not your character ... As you grow older and calmer, and as you learn to think slower and with less individual blood in your thought, the gift of poetry may come to you. But I doubt that it is to be desired.' In others of his twenty-three long letters to Kate Field which are still extant, he would take pains to analyse and kindly to condemn her literary efforts. A typical example of his editorial method may be taken from a letter he sent her in May 1868. She had posted him a printed short story by herself. Trollope replied:

'I have read [it]. It has two faults. It wants a plot, and is too egoistic ... it is always dangerous to write from the view of "I" ... The old way, "Once upon a time," with slight modifications, is the best way of telling a story. Now as to the plot:—it is there that you fail and are like to fail. In "Love and War" there is absolutely no plot ... The end of your story should have been the beginning.'

It is tempting to make either too much or too little of Anthony Trollope's profound and lasting affection for Kate Field. One of the most remarkable gifts bestowed by fate upon witty and intelligent American women is that of rendering shy and emotionally insecure Englishmen happy. In our own lifetime we have, in the Abdication of 1936, seen this flair operating on a magnificent and positively international scale—although this particular notable example may seem to bear scant relevance to Anthony Trollope's love for Kate Field. Yet it was surely just that transatlantic tang of lively, easy-going and novel candour which must have won Anthony's heart. Save for George Eliot—who anyway seems almost to rank as a man—he had had no intimate friendships with women, and was happiest in the hunting field or in the totally masculine ambience of the Garrick Club. When, in those golden October weeks in Tuscany, he first saw Kate Field, he must have been taken suddenly unawares. We can imagine that she flashed into his nerve-ridden and often melancholy life in much the same way in which Hilda

Wangel, the embodiment of flaming youth, invades the life of Ibsen's Master Builder. Since Anthony bore no resemblance to Halvard Solness, the invasion of his heart and mind by the sparkling girl from Beacon Hill had singularly happy, not dire, results. His letters to her show an anxiety for her welfare such as a devoted uncle might foster for a beloved niece; yet they are longer, more amusing and more affectionate than any other of his letters that survive. From five of these letters she has snipped out passages with her nail scissors, but her motive can hardly have been to deprive posterity of an English celebrity's passionate declarations; it is far more likely that the offending sentences contained severe criticism of her own work. From his first letter to her on his return from Florence to Waltham Cross and beginning 'Dear Miss Field', he graduates in his next to 'My dear Kate', pleading his bald head and the geographical distance between them for taking that liberty. Very soon she has become 'Dearest Kate' and he signs 'yours as always affectionately'.

There is in reality nothing arcane or perplexing about Anthony's love for Kate Field. Although his later novels have been subject to a most diligent tooth-combing by Trollopian students, the process has never yielded convincing proof that he used her as a heroine for any of his books. There is, however, in one of his collections of *An Editor's Tales*, a little-known story entitled *Mary Gresley*. Many of the *Tales* are known to have been indirectly taken from real incidents happening to Trollope while he was the editor of a new unsuccessful monthly magazine, *St Paul's*, in the years 1867 to 1870. *Mary Gresley* is an exceptionally delicate and gem-like tale of a middle-aged editor who, against his will, falls in love with an eighteen-year-old girl who has come to London with her provincial mother in order to make her name in literature. She is engaged to a consumptive young clergyman in Dorsetshire, who dies; as, indeed, does Mary Gresley herself at the end of the story. Now there is nothing in common between Mary Gresley, a timid, 'fair-haired little creature' and the loquacious Bostonian Kate Field. What is, however, pertinent and interesting is Anthony's description of the growth and the quality of the editor's disinterested love for Mary Gresley:

'Where is the man of fifty who in the course of his life has not learned to love some woman, because it has come in his way to help her? ... But in thus talking of love we must guard ourselves somewhat from miscomprehension ... In love with Mary Gresley, after the common sense of the word, we never were, nor would it have become us to be so ... We were married and old; she was very young ... Nevertheless we were in love with her, and we think such a state of love to be a wholesome and natural condition ... We thought of her constantly ... We forgave all her faults. We exaggerated her virtues ... We loved her, in short, as we should not have loved her, but that she was young and gentle and could smile.'

When Mary Gresley and her mother are asked by the editor to come out of their Euston Square lodgings to dine on Christmas Day, the middle-aged narrator glosses: 'We had made a clean breast of it at home with regard to our heart-flutterings' and the result had been his wife's suggestion of the Christmas meal. It seems to me that in this very touching story, which it would be criminal to condense, we gain some insight into Anthony's own love for Kate Field. Rose Trollope, like the editor's wife in this story, seems to have wisely accepted this new, unexpected phase in her husband's jolting and inhibited emotional career. Showing both common sense and imagination, she immediately extended her friendship to the transatlantic heroine of her husband's platonic romance. She gave Kater her friendship cordially: 'Dear Kate—Why don't you write to me?' she asked in a letter of December 1862. 'We are both really unhappy —I because I still think you are offended with me—My husband because he does not know why ... Well, at any rate if you are angry with me I am not going to care and shall torment you when the fit comes on.'

This purely temporary breakdown in communications must certainly have been caused by the Anthony Trollopes' belief that Kate should get married. This was Anthony's constant advice. In a letter of February 1862 he tells her that he has been talking to a mutual friend, Dr William Eliot, who became chancellor of Washington University in St Louis. 'Let her marry a husband,' Dr Eliot had urged. 'It is the best career for a woman.' Anthony had agreed with him: '—and therefore bid you in his name as well as my own to go & marry a husband.' This kind of friendly interference was what Kate Field resented. In 1870, when she was in her thirties, she came to London as an established international lecturer on Women's Rights. It was almost a decade since she and Anthony had first met in Florence, but he was still urging her to marry:

'I don't in the least understand why you fly out against me as to matrimony—or as to what I have said on that subject in regard to you [Trollope wrote to her in April 1870]. I have said, and I say again that I wish you would marry ... You tell me I don't know you. I think I do—as to character and mind. As to the details of your life, of course I do not. You may at this moment be violently in love with some impossible hero, and I know nothing about it ... As I think that at any rate in middle life married people have a better time than old bachelors and spinsters, I do not like that tendency in you.'

He warned her not to bind herself to a bold idea of personal independence, to the exclusion of that other idea, marriage. He knew what he was telling her, for as a boy in their house at Harrow he had seen his own mother captivated by Fanny Wright, that hysterical yet handsome specimen of the New American Woman, who had beguiled Mrs Trollope out to the swamps of Ohio on an idealistic mission and had herself moved on from the camp for the freed slaves at Nashoba to lecturing on feminine rights in New York. Whether he quoted Miss Wright as a dangerous example we cannot tell, but in any case Kate Field, in so far as matrimony went, never took his advice.

Anthony Trollope's love for Kate Field did not wane, although he watched with discomfort her career as lecturer, writer and actress—she once appeared disastrously on the New York stage as the heroine in *Peg Woffington*. His constancy to her original image at Florence had a quality not of pathos but of a certain unclouded beauty. Over the speeding years they met whenever they could. While in the United States from 1861 to 1862 he saw her intermittently, sometimes changing his itinerary to do so. He saw her again six years later, when on an official Government mission to Washington. Kate herself was staying in London during the years 1871 to 1873, only leaving it to make hectic flying visits to lecture across the Channel. She was in England again in the spring of 1874, in 1877 and then from 1878 to 1879. During all these London sojourns she saw the Trollopes a great deal. When Anthony Trollope died in 1882, he had not seen Kate for almost three years, but she remained to him 'a ray of light' from which he could 'always strike a spark by thinking of her'.

It is natural that previous writers on Trollope should have poked about in his novels hoping to root out American girls who might be taken as qualifying for the role of Kate Field. Michael Sadleir went even further when he suggested that the plot of *An Old Man's Love*, a good, sharp novel published after its author's death, was inspired by Anthony's love for Kate. In this posthumous work Mr William Whittlestaff, a greybeard of forty-nine, wishes to marry his ward, stately young Mary Lawrie, a thin, tall, dark-complexioned girl who has the peculiarity as against other Trollope heroines of 'blushing black'. With a grudging generosity, Mr Whittlestaff, who is shown to be a sharp-tongued and irascible Hampshire squire, finally allows Miss Lawrie to marry the young man she loves. The tale has clearly nothing to do with Anthony's feeling for Kate Field. In *The Duke's Children*, the transatlantic beauty Isabel Boncassen who ends by marrying Lord Silverbridge, the Duke of Omnium's heir, could, but equally could not, be a portrait of Kate:

'She was slight, without that look of slimness which is common to girls, and especially to American girls ... It was ... the vitality of her countenance,—the way in which she could speak with every other feature, the command which she had of pathos, of humour, of sympathy, of satire, the assurance that she gave by every glance ... that she was alive to all that was going on.'

Another young American candidate is Caroline Spalding, in *He Knew He Was Right*. Miss Spalding, cousin to the United States Minister in Florence, becomes engaged there to the Honourable Charles Glasscock, afterwards Lord Peterborough. Caroline has never been in England, and is comprehensibly shy about how her husband's family will welcome her. This anxiety also pervades the soul of the Boston heroine of a charming tale about a sleighing accident—*Miss Ophelia Gledd*. Miss Gledd asks the narrator how she will be received in London society if she marries a middle-aged English gentleman well known on Beacon Hill. Apart from his description of Miss Gledd's appearance—'slight, thin and even narrow'—which in no way resembles the ampler figure of Kate Field, is it likely that Anthony Trollope, even at his most tactless, would willingly have suffered her to appear in print in the guise of Ophelia Gledd? For neither Kate nor any other girl of good New England stock would have been flattered to find herself presented to English readers as a social conundrum: 'Now I will tell my story and ask my readers to answer this question—was Ophelia Gledd a lady?' In the United States, as we shall soon see, Trollope became even more engrossed by the grades of social standing than he was in his own country. 'In England,' he writes in his travel-book *North America*, 'women become either ladylike or vulgar. In the States they are either charming or odious.' 'For myself,' [he states in a more ferocious passage] 'I have entertained on sundry occasions that sort of feeling for an American woman which the close vicinity of an unclean animal produces.'

We look in vain, then, for an identifiable portrait of Kate Field in any of Anthony Trollope's numerous works. He liked chaffing her feminist ideals, in print as well as in letters or in conversation. In *Is He Popenjoy?* he thrusts upon us a stupid and unfunny scene at the Female Disabilities, a lecture-hall near the Marylebone Road. Here we are forced to meet Miss Dr Olivia Q. Fleabody, an earnest young lecturer who comes from Vermont and wears spectacles, a tunic and trousers. Dr Fleabody's tenets may no doubt have been caricatures of Kate Field's own vehement beliefs, but there the likeness certainly ends.

In that perceptive essay in his *Partial Portraits*, from which several excerpts have already been quoted, Henry James points out that Trollope's American characters were usually sketched in a friendly mood. He thought that in this Trollope had 'hit it off more happily than the attempt to depict American character from the European point of view is accustomed to do'. Trollope's knowledge of the United States had, according to James, 'all the air of being excellent though not intimate. Had he indeed striven to learn the way to the American heart?' James had evidently not read, or else did not remember reading, the heavy two-volume work, *North America*, which Trollope wrote during his nine months of travel there in 1861 to 1862, in the midst of the war between the States. This massive compilation, which we must now consider, was not especially friendly to America, and Trollope to his sudden regret realized that it was not. He did not give a copy to Kate Field; and in his autobiography he rather gingerly dismisses the book as 'not well done, it is tedious and confused'. The closing chapter of this book, which even in Harper's close-typed, pirated edition ran to well over six hundred pages of facts, statistics, impressions and aversions, strikes a guilty and a wistful note. He pictures to us his own sorrowful figure tramping the decks of the Cunarder which is bringing him back home—tramping the decks from uneasy regrets at the many offensive judgments upon Americans that he is about to publish to the world at large:

'I have used language stronger than I intended. O my friends with thin skins [he admonishes his American readers, in a vein not unworthy of Carlyle at his most unlikable], O my friends with thin skins, ye whom I call my cousins and love as brethren, will ye not forgive me these harsh words which I have spoken? They have been spoken in love ... I had my task to do

and I could not take the pleasant and ignore the painful ...
And yet ye will not forgive me; because your skins are thin and
because the praise of others is the breath of your nostrils.'

It was the spring of 1862, and in England most of the book
was already printed. It was too late to make changes, even had
he genuinely wished to do so; he might indeed have been wiser
to suppress the final chapter of cant while there was still time.
One can only say that, as a serious book by a man himself
abnormally thin-skinned and morbidly conscious of the attitude
of others to himself, a man who openly admitted that he would
like to be popular with everyone he met, Anthony Trollope's
North America was emphatically not the way to the American
heart.

The pitiful paradox is that Anthony had for many years
wanted to go to the United States to write a book correcting
what he conceived to be the injustice of his mother's famous
two volumes of *Domestic Manners of the Americans* which, we
may recall, was the best-seller of the London publishing season
back in the year 1832. 'My mother had thirty years previously
written a very popular, but, as I had thought, a somewhat unjust book about our cousins over the water,' he explains to us in
his autobiography. 'She had seen what was distasteful in the
manners of a young people, but had hardly recognized their
energy.' In the event, his mother's sharp and witty yet loftily
genteel criticisms of the American way of life were but a quiverful of elegant arrow-shafts when compared with the thundering
broadsides of her son Anthony. Where she had irritated and
drawn a few drops of blood, her younger son scornfully bom-
barded American institutions, cities, military corruption, big new
hotels, railway systems and manners in public vehicles—in fact
almost every aspect of American life which came under his
sights during his nine months' stay.. We have seen, and we shall
shortly see in more detail, Anthony's opinion of most American
women. Perhaps even more shocking to his transatlantic public
was the ridicule he poured out upon that most sacred of all
American domestic deities—the All-American Child. In the dining saloons of the great new caravanserai which were replacing
older, more friendly hotels, he observed the 'comedy' daily enacted when a 'little precious, full-blown beauty of four signifies
that she .,. is "through" her dinner'. Anthony and his wife
watched dumbfounded as, at a haughty signal from the child,
who had by now unswathed herself from a series of napkins, a
deferential waiter pulled back her chair: 'the young lady glides

to the floor ... Her father and her mother, who are no more than her chief ministers, walk before her out of the salon and then she,—swims after them.' This picture of the behaviour of wealthy children staying at the fag-end of the summer season in the Ocean Hotel at Newport, Rhode Island, is perfected by Anthony's comments on how these tiny girls are taught a special walk. He found that the 'gait of going which American mothers —some American mothers I should say—love to teach their children' was 'a dorsal wriggle' only to be seen in Europe on the Paris boulevards, 'in second rate French towns, and among fourth rate French women'. His mother had been quite frank enough about brash American children in Cincinnati thirty years before, but even she would never have dared to state in print that the fashionable, well-to-do mothers at Newport brought up their infant daughters to walk and wobble like the street prostitutes of France.

(ii)

The outbreak of the American Civil War in the spring of 1861 crystallized Anthony Trollope's long-concealed desire to tour the United States and write a book about that country. The few rushed days he had spent there on his way home from the West Indies in 1859 had merely served to titillate his appetite; and his childhood recollections of the sense of betrayal he had felt when his entire family seemed to have been swallowed up by America must have infected his subconscious mind with a fearful curiosity. He was now earning £4,500 a year, yet even so he exercized his habitual foresight and first got a firm contract from Chapman and Hall for a book on America, drawn up on his own terms. So far, so good; but Anthony Trollope was still in the service of the General Post Office, and had already been granted extensive local leave while on his arduous official journeys to Egypt and to the West Indies and Panama in the recent past. These bonanza assignments had aroused much jealousy within the walls of the big Post Office building at St Martins-le-Grand. It was now fully twenty years since Anthony had slaved and suffered within this metropolitan headquarters in his seedy youth. His habit now was to blow in there nonchalantly from time to time, and he even had a little room assigned to him for interviews just inside the private entrance. These irregular invasions of the General Post Office had not served to endear him to junior officials, for he would, in the words of a colleague, Edmund Yates, 'bluster, rave and roar, blowing and spluttering like a grampus'. His hectoring manner, so much resented in the old Irish days, was now turned full blast on to the London clerks, messengers, letter-carriers and others in menial positions at St Martins. All this went against him; but more important, for his immediate purpose of demanding nine months' leave of absence, was the incandescent hatred that had always blazed between himself and the distinguished Secretary of the Post Office, Sir Rowland Hill.

Anthony Trollope has written with a certain flatulent conceit of his 'delicious feuds' with this most remarkable civil servant, who had invented the adhesive postage stamp, introduced the penny postage and had, indeed, revolutionized the postal system of the United Kingdom and the British Colonies. Trollope, notorious throughout the service for arousing the undying enmity of those forced to work under him, affects, in his *Autobiography*, to have regarded his official superior Sir Rowland as 'entirely unfit to manage men or to arrange labour', and writes of the special pleasure he used to take in contradicting the Secretary at every opportunity. These were many, but Trollope's efforts were noisy rather than successful. Sir Rowland Hill, a small, grey, ageing man whose reptilian eyes looked coldy up at Trollope from under his gold-rimmed pince-nez, would sit back in his chair and remain mum until the shouting stopped. He would then reply with a chill, concise sarcasm which left Trollope floundering. One of Anthony Trollope's defects in office-work was a habit of bursting in upon any round-table discussion and trying to yell everyone else down. On one occasion he roared out at the last speaker: 'I differ from you entirely! What was it you said?' And on another, when he had actually interrupted a brother surveyor in mid-speech, Sir Rowland Hill, crouching in his chair and pointing his pencil at Anthony Trollope, merely said: 'One at a time, Mr Trollope, one at a time, if you please; another gentleman is speaking now.'

It will be readily seen that this powerful enemy would be unlikely to recommend Trollope for a nine months' leave of absence. In fact, as might have been predicted, Sir Rowland did his best to make difficulties. But Trollope had, by now, learned something about the world, and wisely believed that with an outrageous request it is best to go straight to the top. Therefore, ignoring the saurian old Secretary, he asked for an interview with the Postmaster-General, who ranked in the Cabinet as a Secretary of State—at that time the Earl of Elgin. Lord Elgin was well acquainted with the skilful and wily ways of civil servants applying for special leave. Looking up from his desk at the robust and fresh-faced Surveyor standing in front of it, he inquired whether Mr Trollope was pleading ill health. Trollope replied that he was perfectly hale but that, having served the Department so well for so many years, he felt that he had a right to be indulged. The Postmaster-General granted his request. Although Sir Rowland Hill desperately tried, in an official minute on Trollope's personal file, to alter the conditions of the leave granted, he did not succeed. So it was that, in the last week of August 1861, Anthony Trollope was watching the lights of Liverpool recede into the warm dusk on board the Cunard North American steam-packet *Arabia*. By his side, leaning a gloved hand lightly perhaps upon the boat's rail, was the diminutive and fashionable figure of his wife.

This was Rose Trollope's first venture into the non-European portions of the globe. It was understood that she would return to England in November when her husband planned a species of front-line safari into 'a part of the country in which, under the existing circumstances of the war, a lady might not feel herself altogether comfortable'. Anthony himself proposed to stay in the United States for the whole of the winter, not leaving again until the spring of 1862. Kate Field, with her sharp nose for anything that might imply inequality of the sexes, seems to have thought Rose's separate and earlier return home unfair. 'You write about my sending my wife home as tho' she were as free from impediments in this world as your happy self,' he wrote to Kate from New York in November 1861:

'She has a house, and children & cows & horses and dogs & pigs—and all the stern necessities of an English home. Nor could a woman knock about in winter as we have both done during the autumn. But we shall have a fortnight in Boston & I do hope we have a good time of it. I can assure you that in looking forward to it, I do not count a little upon you. I have been real angry with you this week for not turning up.'

As I have suggested earlier, we should be making a grave error if, because we now know so little about her, we were to underestimate Rose Trollope's influence on her husband's work. To Rose—and to Rose only—can we attribute Anthony's minute knowledge of fashions in dress, of the immense variety of materials, of the difference between dresses for the morning at Framley Court or the Small House at Allington and morning dresses for Eaton Square or Carlton House Terrace. It is also fairly apparent that that expert knowledge of what ladies talked about between themselves when, after dinner, they had left the gentlemen over their claret can only have been derived from Rose, serving as a clever social spy. It was she who did the fair copies of the bulk of the novels, until her niece Florence Bland took over this essential task—for Anthony's hand these days was so hurried as to be scarcely legible. On this American expedition the quality of Rose Trollope's aid to her husband can be judged by a very simple yardstick—the uneven quality of the two big volumes the journey engendered. *North America* is, in a sense, two books, not one—a travel book as delightful as Anthony's *West Indies*, and a heavy and (as he himself says) tedious and confused compilation on the American Constitution, Government, Laws, Institutions, Women's Rights Movement, Municipal Public Services and so on. With three cumbersome exceptions—sections dealing with the political future of Canada, the constitution of New York State and the Rights of Women movement—the first nineteen chapters of *North America* are spontaneous and engaging. In point of fact they surely represent the impressions not of one perceptive traveller, but of two. We have only to read the opening sentence of Chapter Twenty to realize why so much of the remaining sixteen chapters are so deadly dull: 'From Boston, on the 27th of November, my wife returned to England, leaving me to prosecute my journey southward to Washington by myself.' The spoiled brats at the Ocean Hotel, Newport, had been watched by both the Trollopes and it is not unsafe to ascribe some of Anthony's feline comments on these, as well as on American women, to the scathing whispered verdicts, the little secret nudges, of that astute English lady, his wife.

Rose Trollope, alas, remains for us as shadowy as some badly focused figure on an out-of-date television screen. All we really know of her appearance is that her hair went white early and that she had a passion for beautiful clothes. On the American journey this passion involved Anthony and the porters of the Great Western and kindred railroad cars in difficulties. Anthony travelled with his small desk, in which he kept his money, his new dressing-case from George Smith and probably no more than one portmanteau. The rest of the ten heavy trunks, hold-alls and boxes which were hurried from platform to platform when the Trollopes changed trains (which they seem to have done quite ceaselessly) belonged to Rose. On two or three occasions Anthony heard the baggage-check men grumbling at the quantity of the English people's luggage, and even suggesting 'that some of these "light fixings" might have been made up into one'. When Anthony learned that the number of every metal check on every piece was entered in a book and re-entered at every change he whispered to Rose that she 'ought to do without a bonnet-box'. Possibly the use of the word 'ought' annoyed his wife, as well as his masculine ignorance of the fact that smart new bonnets could not be bundled up with 'light fixings'. 'The ten,' Anthony adds resignedly, 'went on, and were always duly protected.' This was not the only embarrassment caused by Rose's personal baggage. She once related to her sister-in-law, Tom Trollope's second wife, that soon after she had landed at Boston, she had been approached 'by an inquiring female' who asked her whether she had altered her opinion on the United States. Rose replied that she had been too short a time in the country to venture to form any opinion and that she had certainly never expressed any. After a few minutes of confusion, she discovered that the American lady had seen the label *Mrs Trollope* on her dressing-bag and had jumped to the conclusion that she was the authoress of her mother-in-law's unpopular book *Domestic Manners of the Americans*. Rose, who was only thirty-eight, tried to explain that she was not the culprit—that she had indeed but 'reached the mature age of ten' when the book had first come out. She could not convince her interlocutrix, who went away murmuring with a quiet, steady persistence: 'I guess you wrote that book.'

(iii)

The Trollopes' first sight of Boston Harbour, as their Cunarder nosed its way towards the wharf, disappointed them. They had heard it so greatly praised by American fellow passengers that they had perhaps pitched their expectations too high. Anthony anyway held a private belief that all famous views look their best by the light of evening, and now they were landing at Boston on the sparkling morning of a clear and brisk New England autumn day. On later visits to Boston he came to recognize how incomparable are the sunsets along the Massachusetts coastline. He grew as fond of Beacon Hill as any born Bostonian. He likewise loved Boston Common, which had become, as he termed it, dear to his eyes. On his initial contact with the Athens of the West, however, he was more concerned to realize that this was the actual harbour into which the colonists had tossed the chests of tea at the 'Boston tea-party', than to consider its visual effects. As he landed at Boston he was extremely conscious of Anglo-American politics, both past and present. He knew that the city was a traditional stronghold of anti-British feeling, far more deeply so than Philadelphia or Washington or New York; he realized that Lord John Russell's recent declaration of Great Britain's official neutrality in the War between the States had been especially resented in New England. With that 'presentiment of impending calamity' with which he approached most new experiences, Anthony stepped ashore 'burdened with much nervous anxiety' as to how he and his wife, as English people, would be received. He need not have troubled himself, for they were welcomed with open arms by Bostonian friends—friends to whom he had letters, friends who admired his novels and who wanted to show off to himself and his wife the supreme advantages of living in Boston. That they were friends upon whom they had not previously set eyes turned out to be the least of the Trollopes' worries. Indeed Anthony's final verdict on Boston holds good to this day: 'I know no place,' he wrote in *North America*, 'at which an Englishman may drop down suddenly among a pleasanter circle of acquaintance, or find himself with a more clever set of men, than he could do at Boston.' He was thinking in particular of New England when he wrote, more generally, of the United States as a country in which 'social intercourse will ripen into friendship, and how full of love that friendship may become'.

From what they had learned in London of Boston habits, Anthony and his wife did not expect to find many of the leading families of Boston already back in town so early in the Fall, for then as now Bostonians left their city in the summer and only returned in October. They would withdraw to their large, plain, airy, old clapboard houses near villages in the hinterland of Boston, or on the North Shore where, for instance, Trollope's friend the publisher James T. Fields had a gabled, crimson-painted house called Thunderbolt Hill with a a very good library at Manchester-by-the-Sea. But this summer and autumn of 1861, the first year of the Civil War had brought with it changes even in the smooth and regulated migratory habits of Boston society. Everyone seemed to be on the alert in the hot streets and squares hoping for news of some positive Northern victory against the South. As Trollope had supposed, the war was at the moment almost the sole topic of conversation in Boston, for in the first months before disillusionment and boredom set in, all wars are news. People were polite to Trollope about British neutrality, which they themselves found incomprehensible. They listened attentively to his explanations, but remained sceptical and unconvinced. He was constantly asked what the British public thought of the war, and sensibly replied that there were so many varied opinions upon the subject that he could not really say. He himself had been convinced from the beginning that the North would win, but somewhat irrationally supposed that after such a victory the North would permit the Southern states to secede and form a separate country. 'We shall never give it up,' one of his new friends declared, 'till the whole territory is again united from the Bay to the Gulf!' The fact that Britain had specifically declared herself neutral, with its implication that this civil conflict was virtually a war between two independent countries, both puzzled and annoyed New Englanders. In Boston they teased their distinguished visitor by conjuring up hypothetical cases out of the past: what, for instance, would have been Trollope's opinion of the States if they had announced their neutrality between Great Britain and India at the time of the Indian mutiny? He answered such inquiries as best he could; and he discovered during his subsequent travels to the mid-West that the further he got from Boston the fewer anti-British sentiments were voiced.

In Boston itself, which he visited three or four times during his tour, his friends and acquaintances were far too courteous to make him feel uncomfortable about the British Government's attitude to the war; they merely asked him questions, seeking for information in their precise, polite Bostonian way. He was unfortunate enough to be back in Boston at the moment of the *Trent* incident, when the Confederate envoys, Slidell and Mason, had been forcibly taken off a British ship in mid-ocean by the captain of a Northern frigate in November 1861. In Great Britain this illegal seizure seemed an excellent pretext for declaring war upon the Northern states. Many of Trollope's Boston friends were also in a warlike and foolhardy mood, ready to fight the British as well as the Confederate South. Trollope himself expected such a war: 'There will be war if those two horrid men are not given up,' he wrote to Kate Field. '...I am no lawyer but I felt from the first that England would not submit to have her ships stopped and her passengers hauled about and taken off. The common sense of the thing is plain.' He went down to Washington during this scare, and found some of the senators he met very belligerent. 'So we are to have no war,' he wrote to Frederick Chapman when the *Trent* incident had been diplomatically settled. 'I for one am very glad—

The Americans just at present are rather quiet on the subject; but they will not forget to tell us all about it, when their present troubles are over.'

Anthony Trollope and his wife spent no more than a week in Boston on their first visit. They wanted to see as much of the country as was possible, and thought it would be fun to begin with one of the fashionable watering-places on the east coast. The custom of going to stay by the sea, or beside a lake for holidays, was then little practised in England but was very popular in Ireland—it was indeed at Kingston that Anthony had first met his wife nearly twenty years ago. They were strongly advised to go to Newport, 'of all such summer haunts ... the most captivating'. The advice was good, but the timing was bad, for when on arrival at the Ocean Hotel at Newport Anthony asked for rooms, he was told that there were guest-rooms for six hundred but that only fifty people, late summer left-overs, were still in the hotel. These fifty dwindled while the Trollopes were there to twenty-five. The depression of the management made the servants sad-faced and the few remaining guests listless. Drifting down the long, echoing passages and upon the deserted balconies these twenty-five guests seemed to the Trollopes 'like the ghosts of those of the summer visitors who cannot rest quietly in their graves at home'. At evening the great 'ladies' drawing-room' seemed to Anthony to be 'a huge furnished cavern' inhabited by six or seven ladies 'located on various sofas at terrible distances'. One evening in this drawing-room was more than enough for Anthony, who deserted Rose for the smoky companionship of the bar, where the husbands or brothers of the other ladies would be 'liquoring up' as they discussed the war. Even engaged couples were completely van-quished by the vacancy of the hotel drawing-rooms: 'I have seen lovers, whom I have known to be lovers, unable to remain five minutes in the same cavern with their beloved ones.' As Trollope travelled through the larger, more sophisticated cities of the United States he was always faced with these drawing-rooms, most of which, to make matters worse, contained a piano, thus offering a temptation to play and sing no American lady could resist: 'Then the ladies, or probably some one par-ticular lady will sing, and as she hears her own voice ring and echo through the lofty corners and round the empty walls, she is surprised at her own force ... and filled with the glory of her own performance shouts till the whole house rings.'

It was during their 'rather melancholy week at Newport' that

Anthony and his wife observed the adult manner and affected walk of rich American children. In these earliest weeks of his American sojourn, an account of which he recorded day after day, Anthony showed a certain leniency towards American women, saying that they were as lovely as Englishwomen, and better instructed, 'though perhaps not better educated'. But as he travelled onwards, further and further away from the trim ladies of Boston whom he had admired, his verdict on American women as a whole was altered—or perhaps we should say his verdict on those American women whom he encountered in railroad cars, on street-cars, or in the cheaper Western hotels: he was forced to take a far less rosy view. He thought that most American men treated women with a suitable, chivalrous deference; but that this treatment was taken for granted by the ordinary woman, who would never acknowledge with so much as a smile the kindness of a man who stood up in an omnibus or a crowded railroad car to give her his seat.

Worst of all, he found, was New York. A woman elbowing her way on to a street car would drag after her 'a misshapen, dirty mass of battered wirework, which she calls her crinoline, and which adds as much to her grace and comfort as a log of wood does to a donkey when tied to the animal's leg in a paddock'. As she struggled through the car to find a gentleman who could be stared into giving her his seat, such a woman would bang the other passengers' shins and knee-caps with this would-be crinoline, using a jostling, thrusting movement which Trollope likened to 'blows from a harpy's fin'. In the city streets you met such women daily, hourly; 'now and again you find them in society making themselves even more odious there than elsewhere'. This was the most boorish and, Trollope found, the most ubiquitous female American type. Almost worse, though, were the better-dressed, indeed well-off and fashionable New York women. The machinery of these ladies' hoops was not battered; each lady had an air of wealth as she crossed the pavement, and she seemed 'a personage much more distinguished in all her expenditures' than the woman on the street-cars. Yet all the same she proved but a more expensive version of the same, for she dragged a silken train behind her over the dirty pavement—'where the dogs have been, and chewers of tobacco, and everything concerned with filth except a scavenger'. Every few hundred yards some clumsy, hurrying man would accidentally tread upon this silken train—and the demeanour with which his humble apology was acknowledged was not pleasant to see.

It is instructive to note that the social and domestic dominance of the American woman, so essentially a part of modern American life, had already been achieved more than a century ago. Trollope writes that he had heard young Americans complain of the arrogance that their women had so quickly learned, and heard them swear that they would change 'the whole tenour of their habits towards women'; he had also heard 'American ladies speak of it with loathing and disgust'. It seemed to him to form a parallel with the conceit and the pretentiousness with which even intelligent, Europeanized American men would praise their own country, its institutions, its achievements and its laws. Attending a lecture in Boston, that citadel of lectures, he was grateful to hear Ralph Waldo Emerson denounce this bragging habit: 'Your American eagle is very well,' said Mr Emerson from the dais in Tremont Hall. 'Protect it here and abroad. But beware of the American peacock.'

It was the raucous screech of this peacock which came near to deafening Anthony Trollope as he bravely headed for St Louis, Cairo and the Middle West.

(iv)

From Newport the Anthony Trollopes went back to Boston and then set off with all their luggage through Vermont and Maine for the Niagara Falls and a glimpse of Lower Canada. They crossed back into American territory and took the ferry on Lake Michigan which deposited them in the small city of Milwaukee, and went by train through a land of virgin forest to a port on the Upper Mississippi where they boarded a large river-boat; the wild bluffs along this portion of the Mississippi seemed to them fully as beautiful as the landscape of the Rhine. They then took to the railroad again and saw a number of thriving cities, including Chicago, Cleveland and St Paul, Illinois. Anthony's reactions to this intermittent tour, now by rail, now by river, were those of most contemporary Britishers: the tedious absence of first-class carriages on the railroad, the amazing size of the hotels and, above all, the stifling central heating with which Americans preferred to live. Looping back via Buffalo, they finally reached New York, a city which Anthony found 'infinitely more American than Boston or Chicago' or any other big town he had so far seen.

New York had become a major commercial centre only in the past fifty or sixty years, but it was already dedicated to the making of money. Trollope was stupefied by the local worship of the dollar:

'Every man worships the dollar, and is down before his shrine from morning till night ... Other men, the world over, worship regularly at the shrine with matins and vespers, nones and complines and whatever other daily services may be known to the religious houses; but the New Yorker is always on his knees.'

Conversation in New York seemed to concern nothing but money—and Anthony writes that, after a very few days there, he would find, if he was walking along Fifth Avenue alone, that he would be thinking about money, and if walking with a companion that he would be talking about it. He advised any foreigner who could no longer bear to hear about the state of the market to flee from New York as soon as possible. When he would mildly inquire at his New York bank what was the price of the gold sovereign today, he was conscious that the teller behind the counter regarded him as an absurdity: he said he felt like a man who goes out hunting for the first time at forty years of age.

Whenever he found himself back in New York he was possessed by a desire to get out of it. Yet, to an English novelist, New York offered a tantalizing example, in quantity, of that enigma, the all-American face—or as he called it 'the characteristic physiognomy' of the white American. Anthony's attitude to Americans was more judicious and less plaintive than his mother's had been, thirty years before. He had an unblinking photographic eye for detail, but he was, at the same time, for ever anxious to know the reasons behind what he saw. In his day the city of Boston prided itself on having preserved the original type of the white American, as it were, in amber—but Trollope found that New York offered a considerably richer crop. The pristine, New England Yankees did indeed display 'the lantern jaws, the thin and the lithe body, the dry face on which there had been no tint of rose since the baby's long clothes were first abandoned, the harsh thick hair, the thin lips, the intelligent eyes, the sharp voice with nasal twang'—but it was in New York City that Trollope could survey a myriad variations on this national type. Was it blood, he wondered, or food, early habits or subsequent education which had produced this recognizable American pattern of a human being? Why should the Americans so quickly have evolved a national figure and a national face? The chief racial strain in the United States was still, in those days, Anglo-Saxon, although Irish, Dutch,

German, French and Swedish blood was diluting it. This genetic confusion, Trollope thought, should have given Americans 'no claim to any national type of face. Nevertheless, no man has a type of face so clearly national as the American'. On the assumption that obsessive interests tend to contribute to a man's physiognomy—he took as an example the Jesuit face which all Jesuit priests seemed to possess—Trollope came to the conclusion that American faces reflected the dominant American interest—the making of money.

Anthony Trollope's theory about the lean and the lank transatlantic face and body was altogether less obstruse. These were due to the hot-air pipes which he held responsible for 'the murder of all rosy cheeks throughout the States'. Had this dehydrated look been confined to Wall Street bankers his theory would not have proved valid, but he perceived with regret that 'the young ladies of Fifth Avenue' looked equally washed-out: 'The very pith and marrow of life is baked out of their young bones by the hot-air chambers to which they are accustomed.' A visit to a girls' school in New York with five or six hundred pupils, many of them very pretty, pained him because 'among them all there was not a pair of rosy cheeks. How should there be when every room in the building was heated up to the condition of an oven by those damnable hot-air pipes?'

Throughout his travels in the States, Trollope was more and more impressed by the superior standard of free-school education compared to that of his own country. There were more such schools in New York than in the whole of London. All the same he wished that working-class girls and young women in New York were taught good manners and a decent deportment. 'Seeing how high the girls have been raised, one is anxious that they should be raised higher. One is surprised at their pert vulgarity and hideous airs.' He was, however, just enough to admit that even their 'impudent, unattractive self-composure' was morally more healthy than the 'crouching and crawling' of British working women, with their lowly, humble gestures, their habit of apologizing for their very presence, and who, in public transport vehicles, 'show ... that they hardly think themselves good enough to sit by us'. As we have seen, the New York ladies did not cringe in the street-cars—indeed, when Anthony happened to be at the driver's end of the car, women passengers would thrust a fistful of small change at him so that he could pay the driver in their stead. Later, when he spent some time in Washington, Trollope was immensely touched by the solicitude and sincerity of the coloured landlord of his lodging-house. This had made so pleasant a contrast to the behaviour of other Americans whose job it was to serve you—the clerks and managers of hotels, the railroad station officials, the bank cashiers, all these treated you with a kind of scorn. The women in shops he found to be the worst of all: 'An American woman who is bound by her position to serve—who is paid in some shape to supply your wants, whether to sell you a bit of soap or bring you a towel in your bedroom at an hotel—is, I think, of all human creatures the most insolent.'

When he had seen his wife aboard a homeward bound Cunarder at Boston, Anthony Trollope set off for Washington and Baltimore and hoped to be able, in time, to penetrate the lines of the Northern Army so as to get into the Confederate South—an aim which proved impossible as he was told he would be shot by one side or the other in the attempt. Washington he found primitive and muddy—the square in front of the White House, and indeed the White House gardens themselves, were simply one sea of mud. The capital seemed to be less a city than an aspiration—you could walk a few blocks up Massachusetts Avenue to find yourself in the middle of fields, and, soon after that, in 'an uncultivated, undrained wilderness'. Half of Washington society had left town for the South whence they had come; Anthony was told that their absence had 'almost destroyed' the social life of the capital. In Washington at that period there was no civic sentiment nor local patriotism. The people Trollope met seemed to him to 'turn up their noses' at Washington altogether: 'They feel that they live surrounded by a failure.' Save for the White House and the Capitol, Washington then consisted of long, named avenues which looked fine on a street-map, but in fact contained more weed-grown vacant lots than houses. The people were at least hospitable to their visitor: 'I do not dislike the people at Washington,' he wrote to Kate Field, 'tho' the town itself is bad.' But the place that worried him most deeply on this leg of his journey was the capital of Maryland—Baltimore.

When the Civil War broke out, Maryland could not secede for geographical reasons, but had been anxious to stay neutral. In May 1861 the state legislature had passed a motion declaring the war to be 'unconstitutional and repugnant to civilization', emphasizing their sympathy with the Southern cause, imploring the President to 'cease this unholy war' and protesting against the presence of Northern troops in their state. This declaration resulted in the Yankee arrest of thirteen members of the legislature, two newspaper editors and the chief of the Baltimore police. By the time that Trollope reached it, Baltimore was living under the tyranny of General Dix and his Federal force, who ruled this city of 200,000 inhabitants by martial law. General Dix personally conducted Anthony Trollope over Federal Hill, on the summit of which the General had had earthworks thrown up and heavy guns installed. To Trollope's dismay, all these guns were pointing into the city of Baltimore. 'This hill was made for the very purpose,' the General commented, as he shocked Trollope by explaining how instantaneously the whole city could be destroyed: 'Though I regarded General Dix as energetic ... I could not sympathize with his exaltation.'

Anthony Trollope, who had been born in the year of the Battle of Waterloo, had grown up in that wonderful interlude of forty years of peace, when Great Britain took part in no major war, and a belief in human progress prevailed. Looking over General Dix's gun batteries in Baltimore depressed Anthony, for he thought the idea of any war 'terrible':

'It seemed in those days all the hopes of our youth were being shattered. That poetic turning of the sword into a sickle, which gladdened our hearts ten or twelve years since, had been clean banished from men's minds. To belong to a peace-party was to be either a fanatic, an idiot, or a driveller ... Armstrong guns ... were the only recognized results of man's inventive faculties.'

This new martial spirit he attributed to the Crimean War; it had come upon the British 'with very quick steps, since the beginning of the Russian war'. In Trollope's novels it is interesting to note that there are hardly any military characters or any references to the Crimea—perhaps because that war, despite its horrors, had impinged little on the national consciousness of Britons. When Anthony had reached Washington from Boston the notion of war with Great Britain was, as a result of the *Trent* incident, still a distinct possibility, and at one moment he was warned by the British Legation to be ready to pack and leave the United States at once. When the North surrendered Mason and Slidell, this war scare ended—but Anthony was still haunted by the spectre of 'a fratricidal war' between Great Britain and the States.

(v)

In Washington and now in Baltimore, Trollope had become used to the sight of soldiers on leave, recruits being trained, guns being sent south. He thought both the professional soldiers and the raw recruits to be fine physical specimens of American manhood. Accustomed to the beauty and precision of Household Cavalry manoeuvres even in the changing of the guard in Whitehall, he was amazed at the slackness and dirt of the mounted sentries outside the White House and elsewhere in Washington; their hair was long, their untidy packs were usually topped by a tin mug—in fact he could only describe these sentries as looking like mud-bespattered gypsies. At least these wretched youths were visibly suited to the American capital, with its unfinished streets awash in rain and mud. The element of thick, cloying mud now became a predominant feature of this part of Anthony's journey—for he went south-westwards to St Louis and then on to Cairo, a garrison shanty town in Southern Illinois. 'Till I came here,' he wrote to Kate from Cairo, 'I thought St Louis the dirtiest place in the world; but this place certainly bears the palm.'

At some stage of his travels, Anthony had joined forces with an Englishman whose name he does not reveal. All that we know of this anonymous character is that he wore an immensely heavy and unpractical fur-lined cloak by which he was stuck in the mud in Rolla, when he and Anthony found that they had to carry their portmanteaux themselves. He got stuck, but Anthony fared worse, for he fell flat on his face in freezing slush: 'Why is it,' he wrote, 'that a stout Englishman bordering on fifty finds himself in such a predicament as that?' Rolla, where they went to see the Federal soldiers in camp, was an excessively primitive little place; they were glad, however, to meet two brigadier-generals, one of whom, Siegel, was a German and the other, General Ashboth, a highly civilized Magyar who had been an intimate friend of Kossuth. At Rolla they became accidentally involved with a group of Northern pressmen, who mistook Anthony and his friend for journalists. One of these newspaper correspondents recognized Anthony Trollope's surname. 'Are you a son of Mrs Trollope?' he asked. 'Then, sir, you are an accession to Rolla.'

Rolla was bad, but Cairo proved worse. One train entered Cairo per day—or rather per night, arriving at four-thirty a.m.: 'To whatever period my days may be prolonged, I do not think that I shall ever forget Cairo.' This Illinois township was the centre of a district named Egypt, and had first been created because the Illinois central railroad came to its end there. The terminus town was even more muddy than any place that Anthony and his acquaintance had yet found; nobody moved about the streets, which were knee-deep in slush; in front of the grog shops boards had been laid on top of the mud as an effort at paving. A thousand troops were stationed in rotting sheds. Fever and ague were rampant, the townspeople looked like ghosts and the children were prematurely old. With difficulty and by dint of waiting, the two Englishmen got a small double room with two beds. Anthony's companion, at whose absolute insistence they had come to Cairo at all, tried to be philosophical about their plight. 'It is,' he would repeat, 'a new phase of life,' and Anthony had to confess that that, at any rate, was true. As well as the questionable luxury of the fur-lined cloak this gentleman had luckily brought with him a quantity of tinned food from Fortnum and Mason. Later, to their surprise, they were given good meals in an eating-house frequented by the officers, and were also plied with brandy and champagne. Getting away from Cairo as soon as they could they nearly missed the five-thirty train one morning, and had to run and slither along the sleepers through the mud and melting snow, amidst the jeers of bystanders, while deafened by that 'melancholy wailing sound, as though as of a huge polar she-bear in the pangs of travail upon an iceberg', which Anthony had learned to connect with every 'American railway engine before it commences its work.'

Both in St Louis, which like Baltimore was under martial law, and in Cairo, Trollope had been greatly shocked by the sickness and the squalor within army barracks, sheds and tents. At Benton Barracks, near the old St Louis fairground, two hundred soldiers slept in each dormitory; the wooden walls had three rows of projecting trays, and four soldiers, slept together on each tray. The stench of these barracks, which formed units of a huge encampment, was 'foul beyond description', and Anthony and his friend quickly retreated from those which were full of sweaty, unwashed men when they peered in. Wherever they went in the Northern lines the English tourists found evidence of disease and of a complete ignorance of normal hygiene. There were grim tales of the execution of suspected secessionists or saboteurs who were shot 'quietly', as one officer put it when talking to his English visitors. 'But will they be shot?' Anthony Trollope had asked about eight men condemned for destroying

227

railway bridges. 'Oh yes,' was the reply. 'It will be done quietly and no one will know anything about it. We shall get used to that kind of thing presently.' The stories of dishonesty and misappropriation of army funds were legion. From Cairo Anthony found time to write another letter to Kate Field:

'I do not love the Westerns. They are dirty, dry and unamusing ... I am great in guns, bombs, shells, mortars and questions of gunpowder generally. Oh, what thieving, swindling, and lying there has been in the management of this war! How your unfortunate country has been plundered! Gunpowder that won't explode. Shells that won't burst. Blankets rotten as tinder. Water put up in oil casks. Ships sent to sea that can hardly hold their planks together.'

Kate had, seemingly, wanted to follow him to St Louis but could not raise the fare. 'If you only want money to go to St Louis,' Anthony wrote to her, 'I will not pity your poverty. You are better at Boston. But if it was wanted to carry you to England, I would negotiate a loan for you under Mr Chase's wing among the Croesus's of Wall Street.'

On his way to St Louis and on his way back East, Anthony passed through Cincinnati. When first there, he visited that ill-fated bazaar which his mother had built and then relinquished when she found she could not pay the builders. This oriental monument to Fanny Trollope's optimism was now dwarfed by great blocks of buildings alongside it. At the time of Anthony's visit the bazaar had been taken over by quack doctors, male and female. 'I believe, sir,' the proprietor told his visitor, 'no man or woman ever yet made a dollar in that building—and as for rent, I don't even expect it.'

Anthony Trollope was due to sail from New York in mid-March, but he could not bear to leave the United States without once more visiting his friends in Boston. He believed that he would never see Boston again, and that, were he to do so, the judgments published in his *North America* would make him a most unwelcome guest. In point of fact he did pay one more visit to America, to negotiate an Anglo-American postal treaty in Washington in the summer of 1868. Although he saw Kate Field and even posed with her for a photograph, he very much disliked this time in Washington, what with the heat and the mosquitoes; and he hated the political atmosphere of post-war Washington. Writing to his brother Tom he dismissed this episode as 'a most disagreeable trip to America'.

The earlier, longer trip from August 1861 to March 1862

had, however, proved far from disagreeable. Even Cairo might be written down to experience, or, in the words of his former travelling-companion, as 'a new phase of life'. Back in Boston to say farewell to his many friends there, he was saddened. There were houses to which he thought that he could find his way blindfolded, 'doors of which the latches were familiar to [his] hands; and faces which [he] knew so well that they had ceased to put on ... the fictitious smiles of courtesy'. Although the thaw was imminent, 'the world of Boston was moving itself on sleighs. There was not a wheel to be seen in the town.' Omnibuses had had their wheels removed and had been put upon snow runners. To show himself and others that Englishmen also knew how to drive a sleigh, Anthony hired one, asked a fur-wrapped lady to drive out with him along the Brighton Road and ended up with runaway horses which smashed the sleigh into a ditch. The men of Boston spoke of the coming thaw as 'we all, in short, speak of death'. The thaw began just before he left. On his last evening he watched men carting away 'dirty uncouth blocks' of icy snow which had been broken up with pick-axes, and he reflected that he, too, like the snow, would no more be known in Boston's streets: 'And when the snow went in Boston I went away with it,' he wrote.

Anthony Trollope's North American volumes were almost ready for the printers; there were only two more chapters to compose, and these he did in his cabin aboard ship. His mind was now busy with ideas for a new novel. In his absence *Orley Farm* had been published in two volumes, priced at eleven shillings each instead of the more usual ten shillings. Rose had written to him at Cincinnati with a message from Frederic Chapman, of Chapman and Hall. 'Mrs Trollope,' Anthony wrote to Chapman, 'says you are disappointed about the 1st vol of Orley Farm. Who the deuce buys the first volume of a book? As far as I can hear, the novel is as well spoken of as any I ever wrote. I fear we made a mistake about the shilling.' His transatlantic adventures had not, at any rate, blunted his native pugnacity. The novel which he was planning to write so soon as *North America* and its proof-sheets were out of the way, was to be called *The Two Pearls of Allington*. George Smith, of Smith, Elder, told him that this title would not do, since a novel by Mrs Beecher Stowe, *The Pearl of Orr's Island*, was then being serialized in England. Trollope wrote back to Smith:

'I will change the name, though I cannot as yet say what the name shall be. I will change it as you don't like it, as I myself do not feel strongly in its favour. But I must say your reasons against it as touching Mrs B. Stowe's novel would not have much weight with me. Am I to eschew pearls because she has got one? Not if I know it.'

This fine novel was ultimately published as *The Small House at Allington*. Its flawless plot and its vivid characterization may well be due to the fact that its industrious author had taken time off from novel-writing for the best part of eight months.

During his long absence in the United States, and in the years immediately following his return, the reading public were not for one minute allowed to forget the name of Anthony Trollope. *Orley Farm*, prettily illustrated by Millais, had begun to appear in monthly shilling parts in the spring of 1861 and came out as a book early in 1862. In the meantime, at Anthony's unwise insistence, his disastrous old skit, *The Struggles of Brown, Jones and Robinson* now completed, was being serialized in the *Cornhill*. Month after month, this serial was undermining the faith of both readers and the critics in his great gifts. The *Saturday Review* condemned it as

'a dreadful story ... so odiously vulgar and stupid that the staunchest champions of realism were forced to give it up in disgust. It may be questioned whether any living being ever got to the end of *Brown, Jones and Robinson,* or had any other sentiment than mingled loathing and despair towards that weary tribe of butchers and drapers, and their still more wearisome wives.'

As we have already observed, the pages of the *Cornhill* gave Trollope access to a serried host of new readers. In its first year, 1860, the magazine could count on no less than 120,000 subscribers; in subsequent years this figure was stabilized at a still handsome 84,000. Such figures do not, of course, indicate how many more persons were actually reading the *Cornhill*, for Victorian families were large, and copies of the magazine would have been lent around to country neighbours. So successful was George Smith's venture that writers for other sober-minded periodicals believed that the magazine had a circulation of 'millions':

'Mr Trollope has become almost a national institution [we are informed in an essay on *Orley Farm* included in a copy of the *National Review* for January 1862]. The *Cornhill* counts its readers by millions, and it is to his contributions, in ninety-nine cases out of a hundred, that the reader first betakes himself ... If there are some men in real life whom not to know argues oneself unknown, there are certainly imaginary personages in Mr Trollope's canvas with whom every well-informed member of the community is expected to have at least speaking acquaintance.'

That Trollope's foolhardy, wayward conduct in foisting *Brown, Jones and Robinson* on to the proprietor and the editor of the *Cornhill* did not do permanent damage to his reputation was proved by the triumphant success of the first instalments of *The Small House at Allington*. His readers breathed sighs of relief to find themselves back again amongst country gentlefolk and modest, well-brought-up girls, and to be taken behind the scenes at the West Barsetshire seat of the Earl and the Countess de Courcy at Courcy Castle. Allington itself is not in Barsetshire, but the county town, Guestwick, lies on the direct rail-route to London, the train stopping at Barchester Junction to take on passengers from the Barset branch line—which always loses time to the Junction so that the up train has to wait. Many Barsetshire characters appear in the *Small House*, and only the scenes in Johnnie Eames's London boarding-house are reminiscent of those offensive butchers and drapers in *Brown, Jones and Robinson*. Trollope's *North America* also came out in 1862. These two ponderous tomes were directed at a serious, thoughtful, masculine public, and were justly criticized in the Press as being 'to a great extent book-making'.

In August 1863 *Can You Forgive Her?* came on the market in monthly parts, which ran on into 1864, when the novel was published in book form. In October 1863 Trollope's tirade against the West Country evangelical clergy, *Rachel Ray*, came out as a book, having been rejected on religious grounds by the clerical editor of *Good Words*, who had contracted to give Trollope £1,000 for an original short novel. In 1864 Anthony wrote both *Miss Mackenzie* and *The Claverings*—*Miss Mackenzie* being published in 1865, and *The Claverings* beginning serialization in the *Cornhill* in February 1866. In May 1865 *The Belton Estate* was released in segments as the prime attraction of the first issues of the new *Fortnightly Review*. Two volumes of short stories, *Tales of All Countries*, the produce of Anthony's foreign travels, came out in 1861 and in 1862 respectively. He was also contributing hunting, clerical and travel 'sketches' for yet another embryonic periodical, the *Pall Mall Gazette*, which made its début in February 1865. On the last day of 1865 Trollope completed *Nina Balatka, The Story of a Maiden of Prague*. The only interest in this dreary tale of bankruptcy and anti-Semitism is to be found in the fact that it was published anonymously. Its author had begun to feel that his sales might now have become dependent on his mere name rather than on the quality of his books; so he wanted to launch *Nina Balatka* on its own merits and without any adventitious aid. This honest fad was not rewarded, as nobody was particularly interested in Nina and her Jewish lover. The Bohemian novelette, as Anthony in his autobiography sadly admits, 'never rose sufficiently high in reputation to make its detection a matter of any importance'. With *Nina* completed on December 31st, 1865, Anthony Trollope seems to have taken three weeks' unusual respite from his desk, for he did not set out to write the monumental *Last Chronicle of Barset* until January 20th, 1866. This long, rich novel was his final farewell to Barsetshire—the 'dear county'. In mid-September 1866 he set off on a totally new tack—politics.

Debarred from Barchester Close and no longer permitted to wander in the woods and meadowlands of the dear county, Trollope's reading public were now invited to explore the social and political stratosphere of mid-Victorian London. This great saga, generally known as the 'Palliser Novels', comprises six separate books, all of which are subject, as the Barsetshire novels had been, to a recurrence of characters reminiscent of Balzac. The first of these, *Can You Forgive Her?*—which had come out in serial form from 1863 into 1864—had really introduced readers to Mr Plantagenet and Lady Glencora Palliser, although Palliser, then a bachelor, had made a brief appearance in *The Small House* as a guest at Courcy Castle. Like the chronicles of Barset, the Palliser novels are six in number: *Can You Forgive Her?* (1864), *Phineas Finn: the Irish Member* (1869, after serialization 1867–69), *The Eustace Diamonds* (1873), *Phineas Redux* (1876), *The Prime Minister* (1876) and *The Duke's Children* (1880). In the time-gap between each of these novels, and over the sixteen years 1864 to 1880, Anthony wrote and published another eighteen full-length novels, as well as books of short stores and heterogeneous articles for a number of the monthly magazines.

(ii)

Anthony Trollope was himself aware that this spate of novels and stories might harm his reputation. He called it crowding his wares into the market, and he suspected that the reading public 'could not want such a quantity of matter from the hands of one author in so short a space of time ... I had probably done enough to make both publishers and readers think that I was coming too often beneath their notice.' An undated letter to George Smith makes it clear that Trollope had been asked by the proprietor of the *Cornhill* to promise that he would not have another novel serialized anywhere until six or eight months after the completion of *The Small House at Allington*. Although ready to confess that he was, in all probability, crowding the market, Anthony continued to write novels early every morning and at breakneck speed, although he assures us that no book of his was ever published until he had reread it four times in manuscript and at least once in proof form. He was, as usual, convinced that he was right to go on and on and on fabricating novels. He had, moreover, managed to convince himself that the faster he wrote the more perfect in form were his stories and his style: 'I believe that the work which has been done quickest has been done the best.'

In the early 1860s literary critics began to apply distasteful adjectives such as 'voluminous' to Anthony Trollope's work; one of them called *Orley Farm* 'a masterpiece of easy writing'. Another critic, in the *London Review*, compared Anthony Trollope to the contemporary *genre* painter W. P. Frith: 'both artists have achieved the very best of second-rate reputations ... Everybody has read *Framley Parsonage*, just as everybody has been to see the "Derby Day" or the "Railway Station".' The same reviewer suggested that no diner-out in London 'would imperil his reputation' by venturing into society without being thoroughly up to date on the details of Sir Peregrine Orme's courtship of Lady Mason, or 'the transcendental inefficiency' of her son Lucius. Besides being slovenly written, *Orley Farm* was peopled by 'commonplace individuals'. The book's only merit, in this critic's eyes, was 'its close and studied similarity to the domestic life of the nineteenth century'.

Even the sternest critics were obliged to admit that most of Trollope's characters were astoundingly lifelike. Indeed, the comparison of a Trollope novel with one of Charles Dickens's still bears this out. Anthony himself thought his own fictional people much superior to what he called the puppets of Dickens, which bore, in his considered opinion, no relation whatsoever to real flesh-and-blood human beings. Writing an essay in 1894, twelve years after Anthony Trollope's death, his intimate friend Frederick Harrison confirmed the accuracy with which the persons and the scenes in Trollope's novels were drawn. Harrison well knew the world in which Trollope had lived. They had used the same clubs and had met one another at luncheon- or dinner-parties in familiar dining-rooms. In old age, Harrison would reread the best of the Trollope novels, and so seemed to himself to be leafing through the stiff pages of a photograph album of his acquaintances and companions of thirty years before.

Anthony Trollope's choice of the Harrow farmhouse of his miserable boyhood for the setting of *Orley Farm* may have been, as I have already suggested, a form of exorcism of those hideous years of loneliness. On the other hand the selection of a place in which he had been unhappy was, in a sense, well suited to the sufferings of Lady Mason, a widow who lived in Orley Farm for twenty years, suffering from the knowledge that, to save the house for her only son, she had forged a codicil to her husband's will. She had sat up all night forging with admirable sangfroid her husband's signature and those of its alleged witnesses, while Sir Joseph Mason lay dying in the adjacent room. Prosecuted for forgery by the son of Sir Joseph's first marriage, Lady Mason, by adding perjury in the dock to her previous crime, had been found not guilty. For twenty years this young widow had developed a candid but cold facial expression and had been haunted by the fear of discovery. As in the case of Lady Eustace and her diamonds, Anthony Trollope presents the swindling Lady Mason as a far more interesting and more sympathetic character than the nominal heroine of *Orley Farm*, Madeline Staveley, a judge's daughter living in a neighbouring country house. In Miss Staveley's case her love runs smoothly and is crowned by marriage to her ugly young barrister, Felix Graham; but Lady Mason, tormented by guilt and now forced to stand another legal trial, is, in truth the heroine of the book.

Many of Anthony's friends kept on telling him that *Orley Farm* was his best book. He himself thought it the best plot he had ever contrived and that he had, on the whole, handled his characters well. 'There is not,' he claims in his autobiography, 'a dull page in the book.' He suspected, however, that he had committed a major mistake in letting Lady Mason confess to her crime midway through the book, as she kneels at the feet of Sir Peregrine Orme in his library at The Cleve. 'When Lady Mason tells her ancient lover that she did forge the will,' he writes, 'the plot of *Orley Farm* unravelled itself;—and this it does in the middle of the tale.' There are no less than eighty chapters of *Orley Farm*; Lady Mason's confession comes suddenly in Chapter 44. Yet the interest of the novel does not evaporate, and that it does not do so is a high tribute to its author's skilful exploration of the reactions of such honourable gentlefolk as Sir Peregrine Orme and his widowed daughter-in-law on finding that they have become intimate with a woman guilty of both forgery and perjury. The way in which the Ormes pardon her crime, and continue to give her moral support during her second trial, is unexpected, and is yet another proof of Anthony Trollope's compassion and belief in human nature. Lady Mason's future plans—a voluntary exile with her son in a small German town, possibly to be followed by emigration to Australia—are not, in the circumstances, too sad. It is to old Sir Peregrine Orme, who had wished to marry her, and who had tried his best to help her, that Lady Mason's friendship has proved fatal: 'The old baronet ... lived but he never returned to that living life that had been his before he had taken up the battle for Lady Mason. He was waiting patiently, as he said, till death should come to him.'

In this case Trollope, moralist though he strove to be, could not conceal the fact that it was upon her son Lucius, and on the fine old squire Sir Peregrine, that Lady Mason's illegal actions fell most brutally. Her motive for forging her husband's will is shown as perfectly explicable, as is the fact that to sustain the validity of the forgery she had to perjure herself about it in a court of law. By trying to secure Orley Farm for Lucius, his mother had in effect led him into the shifting sands of life. When he is told the truth, he immediately decides to hand Orley Farm over to his half-brother, to whom it should have belonged by right. Lucius Mason is tall and handsome. Not having been sent to public school he is swollen-headed and unstable. But, on understanding what his mother had, by her crime, hoped to do for him, he has the courage and, in a way, the gratitude to tell her that she must always count on him and live with him: 'Mother,' he tells her, 'were I to say that I forgave you my words would be a mockery. I have no right either to condemn or to forgive. I accept my position as it has been made for me ... There is my hand. I shall stand by you through it all.'

(iii)

The issue from March 1861 to October 1862 of *Orley Farm* in monthly parts, with illustrations by Millais, marked Trollope's first venture into the world of shilling numbers. *The Pickwick Papers, Nicholas Nickleby* and other contemporary best-sellers had proved this method of publication popular—although it is improbable that these isolated chapters gained Trollope anything comparable in size to the number of educated subscribers to the *Cornhill*. When it appeared in volume form, the book had good and serious press notices, including that unfriendly one in the *London Review* in which Anthony Trollope had been compared to W. P. Frith. Another, more enthusiastic critic praised

Orley Farm as 'not only Mr Anthony Trollope's best novel', but 'one of the best novels of the day'; the only complaint he made was that such flabby adjectives as 'nice' and the phrase 'all the same' came too frequently into the characters' colloquial speech. In 1868 the book reappeared as a two-volume 'yellow back' at six shillings a volume. These shiny, cheap reprints, bound in buttercup-yellow boards with a picture from the story on the front cover, were the property of Mr W. H. Smith, who, besides being a statesman of distinction, covertly guided the mid-Victorian reading public's taste in fiction by having in 1858 established a monopoly of all railway-station bookstalls and their wares. He had likewise developed a new circulating library to compete with Mudie's. Mr Smith's system was to buy the copyrights of popular authors' published works, and then to permit Chapman and Hall to use on these books their own imprint— 'Chapman and Hall's Select Library of Fiction'. On the cover of *Orley Farm* is a reproduction of a Millais drawing in which Lady Mason, wearing a black crinoline, a black bonnet, a thick black veil and holding a muff, faces us with an air of mystery, while stooping at her side stands Sir Peregrine Orme; a younger gentleman, presumably Lucius Mason, is to be seen in the background, over her shoulder.

The cautionary tale of Lady Mason and her husband's will was enjoyed both by the general British reader and by more eclectic circles such as that of Anglo-Florentine society. The Brownings, and presumably other expatriates in their vicinity, took in the monthly parts: 'How admirably this last [*Orley Farm*] opens!' Elizabeth Barrett Browning wrote to her friend Isa Blagden in the spring of 1861. 'We are both delighted with it. What a pity it is that so powerful and idiomatic a writer should be so incorrect grammatically and scholastically speaking! Robert insists on my putting down such phrases as these.' Here the poetess jots down a handful of grammatical errors, reassuring Miss Blagden, however, that the very 'pedantry' of their remarks only goes to show how 'full of admiration' for *Orley Farm* they both were. 'The movement is so excellent and straightforward—walking like a man ... and not going round and round, as Thackeray has taken to do lately. He's clever always, but he goes round and round till I'm dizzy, for one, and don't know where I am. I think somebody has tied him to a post, leaving a tether.'

The heroine of *Orley Farm* was, then, but a moderately penitent criminal: on the second day of her trial at the County

Assizes, as the people of Hamworth 'began to believe that Lady Mason had in truth forged a will, so did they more regard her in the light of a heroine. Had she murdered her husband after forging his will, men would have paid ... a guinea for the privilege of shaking hands with her.' Lady Mason owed her acquittal to a combination of factors: the beauty of her resolute features when she sat in the well of the Court with her black veil up, the 'clear silver tone' in which she pleaded Not Guilty, her calm demeanour and the brilliance of her attorney, the redoubtable Mr Chaffanbrass, who did his wily best to discredit the witnesses for the prosecution. In his next novel, that supreme work of his art *The Small House at Allington*, Anthony Trollope gave the *Cornhill* public a heroine who was not a criminal but a victim—pretty, romantic, tormented Lilian Dale. The hero of the book was intended to be the shy, weak-willed 'hobbledehoy', Johnnie Eames, thought by some modern admirers to be a self-portrait of the author in his clumsy, tongue-tied youth. In fact it is the villain of *The Small House*, Adolphus Crosbie, who assumes the major role; and, though categorized by his creator as a 'reptile' and as 'vermin' for jilting Lily Dale, Crosbie (in the words of a critic reviewing the novel when it first came out) 'is the life and soul of the book'. Another reviewer wrote that it was 'not so much a story ... as a fragment of complicated social strategy'.

One of the many innovations in *The Small House* is that the heroine is abruptly jilted by Adolphus Crosbie, the man who had won her heart and to whom she is engaged. Other of the Trollope novels display as jilts not young men but girls: *Can You Forgive Her?* (based upon Anthony's appalling blank verse play, *The Noble Jilt*), *The Bertrams*, *The Vicar of Bullhampton*, *The American Senator* and *Kept in the Dark* provided examples. His heroines, good and true-hearted young ladies though they be, tend to find themselves in a dilemma—an uncertainty of choice between two suitors. Henry James called this feminine predicament Trollope's 'inveterate system', and remarked that such plots did not confront the reader with 'a very tangled skein'. He appreciated these love stories: '[Trollope] had described again and again the ravages of love, and it is wonderful to see how well, in these delicate matters, his plain good sense and good taste serve him.'

The Small House at Allington is a paean to thankless, unrequited love. There is Johnnie Eames's love for Lilian Dale, who in her turn cannot, naturally enough, cure herself suddenly of her passion for Adolphus Crosbie, who has jilted her to make a wintry, snobbish marriage to Lady Alexandrina de Courcy—a marriage which breaks up after exactly ten weeks. In a powerful and ruthless way Trollope invokes the clawing misery of unreciprocated love. He is no more surprised than her own mother to find that Lily cannot expel Adolphus Crosbie from her heart; in this long and beautiful book he proves once and for all that he did indeed know what it was to be in love. We could surmise that his middle-aged love for Kate Field was in some way worked out in *The Small House*. On the blindness of real love he can write with a kind of tender forbearance: 'Love does not follow worth,' we read in this novel, 'and is not given to excellence; nor is it destroyed by ill-usage.' Another view of love is expressed by old Lady Julia de Guest, whose bachelor brother owns Guestwick Manor. Lady Julia happens to find Johnnie Eames standing upon a rustic bridge in Guestwick woods. He has just erased in despair the name of Lily Dale which he had, in years gone by, cut into the wooden railing. He is watching the chips of wood as they bob down stream; Lady Julia asks him whether he intends also to cut the name out of his heart. She speaks to him of love:

' "To have loved truly [she says], even though you have loved in vain, will be a consolation to you when you are as old as I am. It is something to have had a heart."

' "I don't know [Johnnie replies], I wish that I had none." '

The sub-plot of this novel is staged in the seamy London boarding-house in which young Eames is living. These rowdy, intermittent chapters offended even the most flattering reviewers, who held to that mid-Victorian myth that the poor did not exist, and if they did intrude into novels they should be merely made as comical as Dicken's cockney characters. 'The scenes at the boarding-house are vulgar and absolutely unpleasant,' wrote the *Athenaeum's* critic. As a matter of fact, the scenes in Mrs Roper's boarding-house in Burton Crescent are poignant rather than 'vulgar'. They act as a species of counterpoint to the main theme of the book, for here we have unrequited love at its most pathetic. Lovelorn Johnnie Eames has no compunction at flirting with Mrs Roper's daughter Amelia, who had come to London from Manchester, where she had worked in a milliner's shop. Officially absorbed in his love for Lily Dale, Johnnie proves himself amiably vulnerable, and even, in a rash moment, writes Amelia a pencilled note proposing marriage. This note, of much value in a possible breach of promise case, Amelia retains. When Johnnie's position in the Income Tax Office improves and he gets a better salary, he peremptorily changes his London abode. In a last interview with poor Amelia—whom he has, in a sense, treated nearly as badly as Crosbie treated Lily Dale, he tries to comfort her with a promise to come to see her when she is married. This suggestion she rejects with disdain, and then speaks eloquently of her own love:

'"John Eames, I wish I'd never seen you. I wish we might have both fallen dead when we first met. I didn't think ever to have cared for a man as I have cared for you. It's all trash and nonsense and foolery; I know that. It's all very well for young ladies as can sit in drawing-rooms all their lives, but when a woman has her way to make in the world it's all foolery."'

She also declares how harmful and useless is emotion: 'Indeed I don't know what's the good of feelings. They never did me any good.'

The Small House at Allington seems to offer yet another instance of Trollope's characters taking over the plot. He clearly did not intend that Adolphus Crosbie—jilt, snob and coward—should emerge as far the most arresting male character in the book. He seems also to have meant Lily Dale to be an enchanting creation: 'Lilian Dale, dear Lily Dale,' he writes, when we first meet her in *The Small House*, 'for my reader must know that she is to be very dear, and that my story will be nothing to him if he do not love Lily Dale.' But as Lily's masochistic passion for Crosbie began to infect the whole book, her creator slowly became annoyed with her. In his *Autobiography* he writes of Lily as 'one of the characters which readers of my novels have liked the best. In the love with which she has been greeted I have hardly joined with much enthusiasm, feeling that she is somewhat of a female prig.' Year by year Anthony was pestered by correspondents who insisted that Lily should marry John Eames. This advice he resented, cynically concluding that 'it was because she could not get over her troubles that they loved her'.

Reading or rereading this great book is like entering some magic house with many rooms and many windows. It is one of the Trollope novels which can never pall, and which, apart from the story and the people, contains an unusual quantity of examples of the felicitous phrase. The description of a whisper in a London ballroom for instance. 'His words sank softly into her ear, like small rain upon moss.' Or a passage in which the author reflects upon the fate of superannuated landladies no longer able to find lodgers:

'One fancies that one sees them from time to time at the corners of the streets in battered bonnets and thin gowns, with the tattered remnants of old shawls upon their shoulders, still looking as if they had with them a faint remembrance of long-distant respectability. With anxious eyes they peer about, as though searching in the streets for other lodgers. Where do they get their daily morsels of bread, and their cups of thin tea—their cups of thin tea, with perhaps a pennyworth of gin added to it, if Providence be good!'

The London chapters of the book, in one of which this quotation occurs, are unquestionably based upon Anthony's impoverished years in boarding-houses, before he left for Ireland at the age of twenty-seven. In *The Small House* he applies an old English phrase to young John Eames: 'He had not grown up on the sunny side of the wall.' It was equally relevant to his own London youth.

(iv)

Can You Forgive Her?—the first of the six Palliser novels—was published in the same year as *The Small House at Allington*. In Alice Vavasor, the reading public were presented with an official heroine yet more stubborn and self-willed than Lilian Dale. Miss Vavasor—of whom the young Henry James wrote that we could certainly forgive her 'and forget her too, for that matter' —cannot decide whether to marry her evil cousin, George Vavasor, to whom in a romantic moment of her extreme youth she had given her heart, or the placid yet determined John Grey, a gentleman with a country house in Cambridgeshire, whom she has now learned to love. Alice in fact jilts both her admirers twice, but ends up by marrying Grey. A discriminating devotee of Trollope's novels, the late Sir Edward Marsh, once pointed out that Alice Vavasor, Lilian Dale, Emily Wharton (in *The Prime Minister*) and other heroines seem guided by a complex personal creed in love matters, which Sir Edward declared to be to his knowledge unique in Victorian literature, not only rendering these girls unhappy themselves but making them almost unendurable nuisances to their families and friends. This was a simple, strange conviction that, once a girl has given her heart to a man, however unworthy he turns out to be, she has neither power nor right to retrieve or recapture it in order to hand it to somebody else. These heroines are for ever blaming themselves—

Lily Dale because she gave her love to Crosbie too quickly, Alice Vavasor because she thinks her original love for her wicked cousin George makes her unworthy to be the wife of John Grey or indeed of anybody else. Alice, whom Trollope himself thought a strong but not attractive character, is obsessed with a sense of social sin: she had 'made a fool of herself in her vain attempt to be greater or grander than other girls, and it was only fair that her folly should in some sort be punished before it was fully pardoned.' The most sensible comment on Alice Vavasor's obstinacy is made by her cousin Lady Glencora Palliser: 'You want someone to break your heart for you, that's what you want.'

While we can feel but a very lukewarm interest in the fate of Alice Vavasor, the pages of *Can You Forgive Her?* are made lively and luminous whenever Lady Glencora Palliser enters a room, whether to speak her mind, to tease or to sulk. Plantagenet Palliser, her husband, does actually peep into *The Small House at Allington*, but he plays no important part in that earlier novel, being just a tongue-tied young politician, heir to his uncle the Duke of Omnium. In the last of the few references to Palliser in *The Small House* we are told that it had been arranged for him to marry the greatest heiress of the day, Lady Glencora McCluskie, an eighteen-year-old orphan, who owned many Scottish estates as well as a large part of industrial Glasgow. In her first London season, Lady Glencora had made her relatives uneasy by her blatant attachment to a young society scamp, Burgo Fitzgerald, whom Sir Edward Marsh called 'beyond a doubt the most convincingly beautiful man in fiction'. All this information is condensed into two seedling paragraphs at the end of *The Small House*; but from these scraps of knowledge there flowered the most fascinating and original of all Trollope's married women—Lady Glencora Palliser, afterwards Duchess of Omnium.

It is impossible to know, and thus idle to speculate, just when Trollope realized that the orphan daughter of the Lord of the Isles, her husband and Fitzgerald, the love of Lady Glencora's life, were going to invade the world of *Can You Forgive Her?* and, having done so, to monopolize the centre of the stage. The plot of that novel was what Trollope called 'formed chiefly on' that of his jejune, rejected play *The Noble Jilt*. He even wanted to use this cherished title for the book, but changed it for fear that critics would say that Miss Vavasor, granddaughter to a crusty old squire, a recluse living in the fell country of Westmorland, was not sufficiently noble, even though she had 'great relations'. The Pallisers have no counterparts in the theatrical piece written and stuck away in some desk or cupboard fourteen years before. Alice herself was, in a sense, extracted from *The Noble Jilt*, brought up to date and made English instead of Flemish. So, alas, are the three regrettable figures of farce, the widow Greenow and her 'comic' suitors. Lady Glencora, her husband and Burgo Fitzgerald enter *Can You Forgive Her?* rather late in the first volume. So absorbed with these three characters and their predicaments do you become that you resent not only the widow Greenow's frolics, but even Alice Vavasor herself—with whom, we may notice, Mr Palliser, the very mildest and most courteous of men, twice loses his temper and to whom he is very rude. You feel as deprived when Lady Glencora steps aside from time to time so as to give Alice the reader's whole attention as you might feel disappointed when placed between two bores at some dinner-party when you see that clever friends with whom you long to chatter are at the other end of the table.

Although Trollope had invented Alice Vavasor, with her *retroussé* nose, her dark hair worn fashionably low over her forehead and her dark, deep eyes, and although he shows her sharing with her father a respectable little house in Queen Anne Street, he did not like her, any more than she and her father liked the green drawing-room they had mistakenly created in their home: 'It's the ugliest room I ever saw in my life,' Mr Vavasor would say to his daughter, suggesting that they club together to change it entirely. As so often happens in Trollope's preliminary conversations, their brief dialogue about the room places father and daughter neatly, Mr Vavasor extravagant, Alice prudent:

' "It's the ugliest room I ever saw in my life," her father once said to her.

' "It is not very pretty," Alice replied.

' "I'll go halves with you in the expense of redoing it," said Mr Vavasor.

' "Wouldn't that be extravagant, papa? The things have not been here quite four years yet." Then Mr Vavasor had shrugged his shoulders and said nothing more about it.'

The use that Trollope makes of his people's own drawing-rooms, or dining-rooms or boudoirs, bedrooms or dressing-rooms, was deliberately intended to reflect upon or to reveal their inmates' characters. Alice's gloomy green drawing-room, with its green wallpaper, green carpet, green curtains, and green damask sofa and chairs—which must altogether have made a subaqueous or tank-like effect—is typical of Alice Vavasor, who had not chosen anything in the little house, but had left it all to her indolent father, who had himself left the decorating to a tradesman. Lady Glencora's dressing-room at Matching Priory, their house in the north of England, is, on the other hand, rare, luxurious and ravishingly pretty.

Trollope's own opinion of *Can You Forgive Her?* was altogether influenced by his love for the Pallisers. He writes that he 'cannot speak [of it] with too great affection', and explains:

'By no amount of description or asseveration could I succeed in making any reader understand how much these characters with their belongings have been to me in my latter life; or how frequently I have used them for the expression of my political and social convictions. They have been as real to me as free trade was to Mr Cobden or the dominion of a party to Mr Disraeli ... they have served me as safety-valves to deliver my soul.'

He considered the string of Pallisers, their relations and their friends as the best productions of his literary life: 'Take him altogether I think that Plantagenet Palliser stands more firmly on the ground than any other personage I have created.' I do not think many Trollope readers would disagree. Lady Glencora, though she can hardly be described as standing firmly on the ground, is the most winning and entertaining of any of Trollope's women—with the possible exception of Madame Max Goesler. The quality of Lady Glencora's forbidden love for Burgo Fitzgerald is described with that compassion which Trollope often shows—but with realism too: 'She knew Burgo to be a scapegrace, and she liked him the better on that account. She despised her husband because he had no vices.' When, after her marriage, Fitzgerald schemes to persuade her to run away with him, she nearly succumbs to the temptation. Her final waverings are recorded with the greatest delicacy and sympathy. Henry James thought that should such a headlong girl have been encountered in actual life she would have 'made a fool of herself to the end with Burgo Fitzgerald'.

Like his aunt, Lady Monk of Monksdale, who gives him money to finance the elopement, Burgo is 'one of the Worcestershire Fitzgeralds, of whom it used to be said that there never was one who was not beautiful and worthless'. We are told that Burgo has brilliant blue eyes and dark hair, and that his family were still fond of him in spite of all his debts and dissipation, because he was beautiful and never vain of his beauty ... he seemed to think so little of himself'. Burgo has, however, a fatal gift not unakin to that of Dorian Grey: his dissipations never make him look older. Trollope, as an observer of life, knew a good deal about the effects of alcohol, and condemned a number of his characters to death from *delirium tremens* or, more colloquially, 'the horrors'. He considers it Burgo's misfortune that Providence should not have afforded him the protection of a reddening nose or any other visible outward sign of his drinking habits. 'The first appearance of a carbuncle on the nose, has stopped many a man from drinking,' Anthony wisely reminds us. Burgo sometimes looked 'pale, sallow, worn and haggard'. He grew thin and thinner and he would tell his cronies that his liver 'had become useless to him' and that he had no gastric juices left at all: 'But still his beauty remained. The perfect form of his almost god-like face was the same as ever, and the brightness of his bright blue eye was never quenched.' It almost seems at times as though Anthony Trollope, ursine and plain as we know him to have been, took it out on the beautiful young men of his novels, for practically every one of them is a spendthrift, a liar or a scamp. He evidently felt the supreme gift of beauty to be fatal to young men.

It is in *Can You Forgive Her?* that Anthony Trollope begins to describe his personages through the eyes of others, and most successfully he does it. Alice Vavasor, for instance, conjures up to herself the mental picture of her friend Lady Glencora Paliser: 'What a strange weird woman she was—with her round blue eyes and wavy hair, looking sometimes like a child and sometimes almost like an old woman! And how she talked!' Very late one evening, while Burgo is walking back to his aunt's house in Cavendish Square, he is stopped by a sixteen-year-old street-walker, shivering with cold, who begs him for a shilling. As the girl looks up into his face she exclaims: 'Gracious—how beautiful you are! Such as you are never poor ... O, you are so handsome!' He takes her to a tavern and stands her a meal and a glass of beer. The governor's wife behind the bar, the sleepy pot-boy, the watermen, the working women coming in to fetch gin, all stare at him: ' "He's a good'un," the woman at the public house said as soon as he left it: "but, my! did you ever see a man's face handsome as that fellow's?" ' On another night he is again accosted by the same girl, who asks him to give her a kiss. By this time Lady Glencora has decided not to elope with

Burgo. He knows his luck to be out, and that the money his aunt, Lady Monk, had pressed on him to help him elope with the heiress has, like all the money he has ever had, vanished. As he tramps on in despair through the gas-lit streets he wonders if even the abject poverty and precarious life of the little street-walker is not preferable to his own plight: ' "I'm damned if I wouldn't change with her!" he said to himself.'

The importance which Trollope gave to the Palliser series of novels in his own mind, and the gusto with which he imagined and then wrote them, did not mean that they were composed in close sequence; as we have seen, he spread these books over sixteen years from 1864 to 1880, interspersing them with many other quite unconnected novels. In his *Autobiography* he stresses that the Palliser books were meant to be read sequentially, though he doubted whether any of the public would ever bother to do so, or would comprehend his purpose in writing this clutch of socio-political novels. He had taken particular, indeed Proustian, pains to show how 'these people, as they grew in years should encounter the changes which come upon us all'. 'I think,' he commented, 'that I have succeeded.' This anxiety for chronological consistency may well be the reason for his writing of the Palliser novels at calculated intervals, so as to reveal the ageing process at work, and the manner in which the passing years either modify or exaggerate young people's character traits, but do not ever absolutely change them. 'The Duchess of Omnium, when she is playing the part of Prime Minister's wife,' he explains, 'is the same woman as that Lady Glencora who almost longs to go off with Burgo Fitzgerald, but yet knows that she will never do so.' He says that he had come to doubt 'that the game had been worth the candle', for he had set himself to work on such a wide canvas that he wondered whether anyone 'should trouble himself to look at it as a whole'. I do not think it is ungrateful to recognize that certain chapters of pure political intrigue and of political canvassing do nothing to help lighten five out of six Palliser novels; but these scenes have usually so slight a relevance to the real plot that they can conveniently be skipped by a restless reader.

While he prepared these scenes of English politics, Anthony would spend much time listening to House of Commons debates —and he would, alas, reproduce with his customary verisimilitude that most tedious expression of British ways. When he was a youth in London his mother's brother Henry Milton had once asked him what he most wished to be in life. He replied it was to become a Member of Parliament. Uncle Henry Milton, who was of a sarcastic turn of mind, jeered at young Anthony, saying that as far as he knew, few clerks in the Post Office had ever become Members of Parliament. In November 1868, Anthony Trollope did stand for the constituency of Beverley in Yorkshire, a foolish enterprise which wasted his time and his money, badly tried his temper and ended in fiasco. Yet, to his dying day he 'always thought that to sit in the British Parliament should be the highest object of ambition to every educated Englishman'. At the time of the Beverley election Charles Dickens wrote in a letter to Tom Trollope: 'Anthony's [political] ambition is inscrutable to me. Still it is the ambition of many men; and the honester the man who entertains it, the better for the rest of us, I suppose.'

(v)

While evoking the love of a young, newly-married woman for a man other than her own husband, Trollope had suspected that he was 'walking, no doubt, on ticklish ground'. Since *Can You Forgive Her?* made its first appearance in shilling parts, and since a couple of other plots wove in and out of the novel, his readers were left in the shadows of suspense about Lady Glencora Palliser: would she or would she not run away with Burgo Fitzgerald? To some this state of suspense must have been teasing and agreeable, but to others it seemed that Trollope was merely bent on providing his readers with 'a vicious sensation'. So at any rate thought a distinguished cleric—'a man whom all men honoured'. This gentleman, whose name we do not know, penned a very severe letter to the novelist, complaining that he had been 'deprived of one of the most innocent joys of his life'. This joy had been to listen to his daughters as they read the latest Anthony Trollope aloud; but now Lady Glencora's predicament had stopped all that, and the girls were told to read Mr Trollope no more. Anthony replied to this complaint that he supposed that his correspondent preached against adultery from the pulpit, and so it seemed unfair to rebuke a novelist for writing on the same theme. This lame excuse was found unsatisfactory—and indeed it was pretty specious, for mid-Victorian clergymen would have been most unlikely to choose adultery and abduction as subjects for a rural Sunday morning's sermon.

As we have seen, Anthony Trollope wrote—or thought that he wrote—within a strict framework of British morality. When we reflect that there is hardly a novel by any of his great French contemporaries which does not involve the love affairs of married women with beautiful Parisian or provincial youths, it may make us fancy that Trollope would have written much more freely had no stiff moral code for novelists deformed the landscape of Victorian literature. We have seen how deeply he understood love, happy or unhappy, fulfilled or without hope. His account of Lady Glencora's true passion for Burgo Fitzgerald provides another example of Anthony's real insight; he knows, and we know through him, that Burgo is as much after her money as he is after herself. This supposition had been placed before her while she was still an unmarried girl. As is inevitable with the love-sick, she had been deaf to remonstrance and blind to facts which she did not wish to believe. Immediately after her marriage to Palliser, a union into which she has been bullied by her family connections, she still feels for Burgo with all the intensity and idealism of a romantic girl. Her favourite possession amidst all the ostentatious luxury of her husband's London and country houses, is at that moment a small water-colour sketch, showing Raphael and the Fornarina. Often she sits in contemplation over this little picture, daydreaming about Italy. She sees herself reclining on a marble balcony, a canopy of clustering vines above her head, while Burgo at her knee tells her how much he loves her, by the light of a pale Italian moon. As part of his final attempt to get her to elope with him Burgo has by some surreptitious means managed to smuggle a love-letter into Lady Glencora's writing-case. In this inflammatory note he urges her to come away with him at once. She carries the letter everywhere with her, in the pocket of her dress, stroking it with her fingers during hours of indecision, and wondering whether to show it or not to show it to Alice Vavasor, her greatest friend. In the end, as we all know, Lady Glencora does not elope, confesses her guilty passion to her husband, and he takes her abroad for several months. From this second honeymoon she returns to London happy and, for the first time, pregnant.

This sudden ending to the love story of Lady Glencora Palliser and Burgo Fitzgerald may have been a sop to such members of the reading public as the Church dignitary who had objected; it may have been that Trollope had become so attached to her, and foresaw for her so great a future as wife, hostess and political intriguer that he refused to send her off to Italy as Fitzgerald's mistress. Or else it may have been that Lady Glencora had by then become so lifelike to him that he knew she would refuse to flee. This is by no means a matter of regret—for had she fled to Naples with Fitzgerald we would have lost sight for ever of both her and of that iridescent charm, that dazzling gift for the outrageous with which she makes even the stodgiest chapters of the political novels gleam.

Rachel Ray—a short novel written between *The Small House* and *Can You Forgive Her?*—also gave acute offence in clerical quarters, this time not for immorality but because it exposed and held up to scorn the rigours and the humbug of the Evangelical sect in one of their strongholds which Anthony knew well—Devonshire. Amongst the *dramatis personae* of this vigorous book is one Mr Prong, an Evangelical curate even more vile and hypocritical than Barchester's Mr Slope. Trollope had been approached by the editor of *Good Words*, a magazine devoted to providing the pious with safe family reading for Sunday afternoons. The editor of this worthy periodical was the Reverend Norman Macleod, one of Queen Victoria's favourite royal chaplains, who had, in 1847, founded the Evangelical Alliance. Anthony, who strongly disapproved of the Evangelicals' spoilsport attitude to any kind of pleasure in this vale of tears, sensibly replied that he was not a suitable writer for *Good Words*. Macleod pooh-poohed this objection, so Anthony set to work to satirize the Evangelicals, although, or perhaps because, he was writing for one of their magazines. Once completed, the novel was sent off to Glasgow for Dr Macleod to read. Now Macleod had commissioned the novel because he seriously believed that it would give Anthony Trollope a chance to reveal, indeed to improve, his deeper nature: 'I think you could let out the *best* side of your soul in *Good Words*,—better far than ever in *Cornhill*.' *Good Words* was a popular magazine, and was reputed to have a circulation of 70,000 readers. When he first received the manuscript Macleod had some of it set up in type, then panicked and dispatched the whole novel, holograph and bits in print, back to its author with a letter of rejection: 'A letter more full of wailing and repentance no man wrote,' was Anthony's comment on this embarrassing missive. Macleod's letter was at once patronizing and impudent:

'I thought you would bring out more fully the positive good side of the Christian life than you had hitherto done, or avoid at least saying anything to pinch, fret, annoy or pain those Evangelicals who are *not* Recordites.* Now, my good Trollope, you

* *The Record* was a Sunday rival to *Good Words*, but far more strict. It had been running a campaign against *Good Words* for

have been, in my humble opinion, guilty of committing this fault—or, as you might say, praiseworthy in doing this good— in *Rachel Ray* ... There is nothing, of course, bad or vicious in it—that *could* not be from you—but quite enough to keep *Good Words* and its Editor in boiling water until either were boiled to death.'

One of the very many incidents in *Rachel Ray* against which Dr Macleod protested had been an enthusiastic description of an innocent, amusing little dance given by the brewers of Basleton. Macleod resented Trollope's 'casting a gloom over Dorcas Societies—a glory over balls till four in the morning'. To John Millais, who had originally agreed to illustrate *Rachel Ray*, and who was at present himself drawing sketches from the Parables for *Good Words*, Trollope wote that: 'X (a Sunday magazine) has thrown me over. They write me word that I am too wicked ... It is a pity that they did not find it out before, but I think they are right now. I *am* unfit for the regenerated and trust I may remain so, wishing to preserve a character for honest intentions.'

In *Rachel Ray* we find the slimy Evangelical curate, Mr Prong, trying to marry Rachel's widowed sister Mrs Dorothea Prime, a morose woman who had 'taught herself to believe that cheerfulness was a sin' and held that the sadder you could make your life in this world, the happier you would be in the next. Mr Prong is, of course, after her small income, and they quarrel over Mrs Prime's refusal to give up her money into a husband's control. The hero of the book is an attractive provincial boy, Luke Rowan, who has left his law studies in London to try to take charge of the brewery at Basleton—'a town with a market and hotels and a big brewery and a square and a street'. Luke is, like almost all of Anthony Trollope's characters, interested in money as well as in improving the strength of the beer brewed at Basleton. In the novel which he wrote after *Can You Forgive Her?*, called *Miss Mackenzie*, a sensitive portrait of an old maid who inherits a little money and wishes to enjoy it, the whole plot centres on money. This seems a propitious moment to examine an aspect of Trollope's work which puts him in a position to which no other Victorian novelist could or did aspire— the blunt recognition that it is money as well as hard work and,

---

advertising unsuitable forthcoming attractions – Trollope was attacked in this as 'a secular novelist' – apropos of which *The Record* asked its readers: 'Does this recall the spirit of Apostolic times?'

possibly, love that makes the world go round.

To my knowledge this quality in the Trollope novels has been almost ignored. The only passage written about it comes in a shrewd anonymous review of *Miss Mackenzie* published in the *Saturday Review* for March 1865. Here the critic declared that no other contemporary novelist has made money so prominent a feature of his book as had Anthony Trollope—and that in his novels he approached money from a serious and not from a comic point of view. The money worries of Trollope's characters have nothing in common with the light-hearted buffoonery of Mr Micawber or Mr Skimpole. To Trollope, as this reviewer further remarks, there was nothing either funny or sordid in having a bailiff in your house—it was 'a grave, human care, and a thing, therefore, to be gravely and even tenderly written about'. The miseries of a defrauded old lodging-house keeper or an insolvent tradesman 'are in [Mr Trollope's] eyes neither mean nor amusing, but genuine sorrows which an artist, who is not too grand to be content with human nature, need not be ashamed of handling with sympathy'.

Like the ghosts in *A Christmas Carol*, the spirit of money stalks, clanking its chains, through every one of Anthony Trollope's novels: the melancholy spirit of money spent, stolen or lost; the evil spirit of money used to dominate, to enthral or to tantalize poor relations; the genial, comforting spirit of money secured by theft, by marriage or by fraud. This profound knowledge of the effects of money on character has an eternal relevancy and cannot ever be outmoded. Manners and fashions change, sexual *mores* also. But the wish to become rich, or at any rate richer, has never altered by one iota. In many of Trollope's novels we are today surprised and diverted by Victorian etiquette or ways of living which to his contemporaries were so actual as to verge upon the dull. But his passages on money and its side-effects are as valid today as they were when he wrote them in the heyday of the Widow-Queen, more than a century ago.

(vi)

Lack of means haunts a multitude of Trollope characters of every social class or mental level. Even those who have acquired wealth either by inheritance or in some more questionable manner always want to increase it—the old Duke of Omnium, for instance, one of the millionaires of the United Kingdom, is for ever trying to buy more and more farms so as to round off his vast Barsetshire estates. There is no mid-Victorian literary parallel to Trollope's persistent emphasis on money, and certainly none in the works of his three great contemporaries, Charles Dickens, W. M. Thackeray and George Eliot. Dickens dealt sentimentally with poverty and derisively with wealth. In *David Copperfield* and in *Oliver Twist* the little heroes' penury is turned off like a tap at the appearance on the scene of a fairy godmother and of a fairy godfather. These transformation scenes are pantomimic, delightful and illogical but they have little or nothing to do with reality. There is in Dickens none of the inevitable interplay of character and event, or of cause and result which makes the lives of Trollope's people so convincing. Thackeray, on the other hand, did understand the diamond-bright lures of wealth and of the social position which wealth can bring; but he saw them as targets for irresistibly amoral men and women—Barry Lyndon, that most engaging mid-Victorian forerunner of Thomas Mann's Felix Krull, or the thirstingly ambitious Becky Sharp. In George Eliot we find, as we might expect, very little about money at all. The troubles of Dorothea Casaubon were not mundane; they had nothing to do with her husband's income, but stemmed from a crescent dissatisfaction with her chosen lot. If we raise our heads and glance once more across the English Channel, we are confronted by the steadfast gaze of that titan Honoré de Balzac, in many readers' opinion a greater novelist than any of these English writers, and certainly as concerned with the money syndrome as Trollope himself. Yet Balzac, at times, romanticizes money and at others exposes for us the sharpened, polished claws of avarice. He also portrays money as an inspiration to sublime generosity as in the case of Père Goriot, or to an effort to purchase a young male lover as in the case of Vautrin. There are no Pères Goriot and no Vautrins in the novels of Anthony Trollope.

Trollope's attitude to money was neither romantic nor, on the other hand, was it cynical. In his boyhood and his youth his whole existence had been blighted by genteel poverty—and certainly there was nothing romantic about his memories of his mother, quill-driving into the small hours by the light of a flickering tallow candle, keeping herself awake with green tea, rubbing her aching fingers in a cold room of that grim house in Bruges, while the rest of her family, the dying and delirious Henry included, were dependent on her novels to keep them even nominally alive. Anthony's early years in London had not made him stingy, but they had made him thrifty and penny-wise. He had nothing in common with Balzac and his full-blooded, blustering career of debt, fooling the bailiffs by disguising himself as an old woman, or by withdrawing to a desk inside the double wall of the salon in his house at Plassy. In Trollope's very earliest novels—the Irish ones—money is already a predominant theme, money in the ugly shape of unpaid land-rents, of contested wills or of the unhappiness of Trollope's first heiress-orphan, Miss Fanny Wyndham. When he turned to England for the source-material for his novels, his increasing pessimism about the British upper and middle class began to show itself. Heavy and yet heavier is his emphasis on the material side of life. Religion in its real, spiritual sense, does not bother his clerical characters. Livings are nice things to have, and so are comfortable vicarages in the gift of some friendly landed family such as the Luftons. The stipend of a living is almost more important than the necessity of preaching every Sunday. In Trollope's accounts of all this there is no cynicism, but only humour and sadness. Trollope recorded the behaviour and morality of the English upper classes as he saw it in London and the shires, or as he heard tell of it in the smoking-room of the Garrick Club. His simmering distaste for what he saw is reflected in successive novels until, in the year 1873, it boiled over and goaded him into writing that bitter satire on London society *The Way We Live Now*. It was this novel from which Henry James shrank: 'A more copious record of disagreeable matters could scarcely be imagined ... than *The Way We Live Now*.'

In the world of the Barsetshire novels, as in that of the Palliser series, a rich unmarried woman was a fortune-hunter's legitimate quarry. An excellent example is the predicament of Miss Martha Dunstable, sole heiress to a huge patent medicine fortune, who ends by marrying the only disinterested bachelor she has ever met—old Dr Thorne himself. Miss Dunstable has learned to regard any man who proposes to her as 'a bird of prey'. She senses that he has already counted up her assets in terms of land or of steadying his balance at his banker's. Miss Dunstable, with her red cheeks, large mouth, squat nose and bright little black eyes is surely one of the most agreeable, forthright and amusing women in all the Trollope novels. Lady Glencora's fortune trapped her into a marriage when she was too young. Miss Dunstable is over thirty and possesses a down-to-earth, *nouveau riche* common sense. We are first introduced to her at Courcy Castle, where she has come to stay for a week with the de Courcys, who would like to secure her fortune for their nephew Frank Gresham, only son of the wasteful and indebted squire of Greshambury. Miss Dunstable had arrived at Barchester by train, bringing with her her carriage, her coachman, her footman and her lady's maid, together with ten trunks of clothes: 'But she brought all these things, not in the least because she wanted them herself, but because she had been instructed to do so.' Frank Gresham, a good-looking young man just twenty-one, and already in love with Mary Thorne, demurs at the brain-washing process to which his mother and his aunt persistently subject him: 'Of course you must marry money,' Lady de Courcy drums into him during Miss Dunstable's stay at Courcy Castle. The crudity with which these aristocratic sisters speak of an heiress seems as shocking as it seems true to life. 'What does it signify, whether Miss Dunstable be 28 or 30?' his aunt asks Frank. 'She has got money; and if you marry her, you may then consider that your position in life is made.' Miss Dunstable is miserably aware of this sordid intrigue, but since she was taken up by London Society—by the mothers, sisters and aunts of impecunious sons—she has shown herself quite able to hold her own. When one of her devotees hints that her coiffure of crisp, strong, black ringlets is out of date and that ringlets have long ceased to be fashionable, Miss Dunstable replies: 'They'll always pass muster when they are done up with bank-notes.'

An essential aspect of the hunt for an heiress which we tend to forget is that, before the passing of the first of the Married Women's Property Acts in 1870, a wife's fortune automatically passed to her husband on marriage. Mr Palliser, for instance, is respected for the delicacy with which he spends his young wife's money; it is only when she loses her temper that Lady Glencora refers to the fact that her husband's great wealth is by origin hers. In *Can You Forgive Her?* while Alice Vavasor is visiting her cousin Lady Glencora one evening at the Pallisers' house in Park Lane, a most unwelcome guest, old Mrs Marsham, calls and is shown in. She had been a dear friend of Mr Palliser's dead mother, but is suspected by Lady Glencora of acting as a spy upon her own movements. When it is time for Alice to go home to Queen Anne Street by hackney cab, Lady Glencora announces that she will, of course, send her cousin home by carriage. The interfering old lady suggests that Alice should walk back accompanied by Mrs Marsham's own maid:

' "I was going to offer my servant to walk with her. She is an elderly woman and would not mind it."

' "I'm sure Alice is very much obliged," said Lady Glencora; "but she will have the carriage."

' "You are very good-natured," said Mrs Marsham; "but gentlemen do so dislike having their horses out at night."

' "No gentleman's horses will be out," said Lady Glencora savagely; "and as for mine, it's what they are there for." It was not often that Lady Glencora made any allusion to her own property ... In some things her taste was not delicate as should be that of a woman. But, as regarded her money, no woman could have behaved with greater reticence or a purer delicacy.'

It was not usual for well-bred mid-Victorian girls, whether heiresses or aristocrats' or vicars' daughters, to know much about money. Except for checking the house-books in London or for discussions with the housekeeper in the country, married women were not supposed to bother about money in detail. 'Upon my word, Clara, you surprise me,' says old Mr Amedroz to his daughter in the novel *The Belton Estate*. 'But women never understood delicacy in regard to money. They have so little to do with it, that they can have no occasion for such delicacy.' When her father dies, Calara Amedroz is left alone in the world, as Belton Castle goes by entail to her cousin Will Belton. She becomes engaged to a Captain Aylmer, with whom she supposes herself to be in love. Captain Aylmer proves a tepid wooer, but persuades Clara to make the mistake of going to stay with his parents and his sister at Aylmer Park in Yorkshire. Here she finds that she herself is unwanted and that her engagement goes unrecognized, for she has neither a title nor a suitable jointure—in fact she has no material advantages to offer the Aylmer family at all. Her first arrival at Aylmer Park is inauspicious, since Lady Aylmer does not come forward to greet her:

'Had her son brought Lady Emily to her house as his future bride, Lady Aylmer would probably have been in the hall when the arrival took place; and had Clara possessed ten thousand pounds of her own, she would probably have been met at the drawing-room door; but as she brought neither money nor title ... Lady Aylmer was found stitching a bit of worsted, as though she had expected no-one to come to her. And Belinda Aylmer was stitching also—by special order of her mother.'

It is in the observation of such minute, wounding social subtleties and ill intentions that Trollope excels. The world he shows is a stippled world; even at his clumsiest and most clownish there is nothing in it of black or white. Almost every human action is shown as having a calculation behind it and, for all the moral zeal which he believed himself to apply to the writing of his novels, none of his characters is either wholly to blame or wholly exonerated. Had Lily Dale's betrothed not gone from Allington to Courcy Castle, there to become ensnared from snobbery into engaging himself to Lady Alexandrina, Trollope gives us several slight but most clear indications that he might never have been able to keep his word to Lily Dale. Crosbie is a brilliant portrait of a fashionable young man with good prospects in his government office, but so far without the means to keep a wife or rear a family. He discovers just too late that Lily's crusty uncle, the Squire of Allington, whom Crosbie had assumed would give her a dowry, has no intention of giving her anything of the kind. It is on this discovery that the first small dark doubt flits bat-like across his brain—how can he afford to marry Lily and continue to lead that social life in London of which he is so famous an ornament? Then, also, would not Lily Dale be too unsophisticated to cope with staying in such a country house as that of the de Courcys—in the improbable case that, once they were married, they would ever again be asked to house parties of that calibre? By these lights his jilting of Lily was inevitable—and yet he has enough sensibility to know that he is behaving shamefully. In their last days together at Allington Lily had in her thoughtless, generous behaviour become almost cloying to Crosbie's senses. It is thus Crosbie's romantic promise of marriage, based on a mistaken financial assumption, that almost destroys Lily Dale's life, and subsequently ruins his own. The fact that Lily would come to him as an eager, penniless bride has as much, if not more, to do with Crosbie's treachery as the spurious glamour of the high-stepping inmates of Courcy Castle.

In a short magazine story, *The Adventures of Fred Pickering* (published in 1867 in the same volume as *Ophelia Gledd, Lotta Schmidt* and *Malachi's Cove*), Trollope presents his readers with a sharp, indeed a cruel, cautionary tale about a young man of good education articled by his father to a Manchester attorney. Fred, who has literary ambitions, is restless in this prosaic job of writing 'lawyers' letters full of lies', while the nineteen-year-old girl whom he loves (an orphan but no heiress, she) is going as governess in the household of 'a very vulgar tradesman' named Boullem. Inheriting the tiny sum of £400 from an aunt, Fred throws up his job, marries Mary Crofts, takes her to the Lake District for a honeymoon which they can ill afford, and then settles down with her in lodgings in Museum Street, a region of Bloomsbury 'not cheering by any special merits of its own; but lodgings there were to be found cheap, and it was near the great library by means of which, and the treasures there to be found, young Pickering meant to make himself a famous man.' We need not follow the Pickerings' stumbling downward path, which the usually compassionate Anthony describes with a certain zest. Suffice it to say that Fred is as conceited as he is untalented, that they have a baby and end up half-starving in a single furnished room. They are forced to return to Manchester where Fred fails to placate his hard old father, who offers to pay him thirty shillings a week on condition that he sets to work as a dog's-body in the employ of that very attorney whom he had so grandly and so wilfully despised. Trollope asserted that most of the plots of his short stories were taken from incidents which he had seen in real life. As he delineates it the poor little Pickerings' fate seems, alas, only too authentic.

To revert from this cautionary tale to the novels themselves, it is important to notice that it was not merely Trollope's ambitious young men nor his heirs to impoverished estates who panted over and became hypnotized by the money stakes. Anthony has admitted that he was happiest living mentally with the Pallisers or the Barsetshire gentry or the clergy of Barchester Close; but evidently he was likewise intent on demonstrating how universal the lust for money had become, so that it now cut through classes, educational standards, social conventions and Christian belief. From May to August 1864 he was posing himself a riddle—he would try to write a popular novel which would have no love-story in it at all.

Miss Mackenzie, which came out in 1865, was the result. It concerns a devoted spinster aged between thirty-five and forty, who has valiantly nursed her sick brother for so many years that, when his death frees her at last, her own youth has passed by without her realizing it. The brother has left her the small, but in those days tidy, income of eight hundred pounds a year. She leaves London and settles in comfortable lodgings in Little-bath—Trollope's pseudonym for the actual city of Bath. Naturally enough, as a spinster with a pleasant income she attracts scheming admirers, but she avoids committing herself. As Margaret Mackenzie is neither a fool nor a prude, she does not exactly see why, after all, she should not get married one day. In a finely drawn picture of her as she studies her fading looks in the glass, Trollope invites us to see her as she now begins to see herself:

'She got up and looked at herself in the mirror. She moved up her hair from off her ears, knowing where she would find a few that were grey, and shaking her head, as though owning to herself that she was old; but as her fingers ran almost involuntarily across her locks, her touch told her that they were soft and silken; she looked into her own eyes and saw that they were bright; and her hand touched the outline of her cheek, and she knew that something of the fresh bloom of youth was still there; and her lips parted, and there were her white teeth ... She pulled her scarf tighter across her own bosom, feeling her own form and then she leaned forward and kissed herself in the glass.'

After some worrying adventures, the most seemingly fatal being a lawyer's discovery of a fault in her brother's will so that she loses all her money to an old widower cousin with nine children, Margaret Mackenzie goes clean against her creator's intentions by really falling in love. Her love is reciprocated, and she ends up happily married to this same cousin.

In those passages of his autobiography in which he gives his advice to young novelists and his rather cold-blooded instructions on how to write a novel, Anthony Trollope always insists on the necessity of a love story as one of the ingredients of any work of fiction: 'It is admitted that a novel can hardly be made interesting or successful without love. *Pickwick* has been named as an exception to the rule ... I tried it once,—with *Miss Mackenzie*; but I had to make her fall in love at last.' Any witness of that dressing-table scene could have told him that Miss Margaret Mackenzie intended to fall in love, and intended this autumnal love to be a happy one. Seldom mentioned by Trollope addicts, almost ignored for all her kindness and humility, Margaret Mackenzie can claim a prominent position in a good light in the long and sometimes dark gallery of Trollope's heroines.

There would be neither time nor space to dig out a myriad more examples of the power of money from the works of Anthony Trollope—the gaming salons at Monte Carlo or at Baden, the money-lenders in the City of London, the cupidity of shady jewellers' shops, the avarice of great ladies in London Society, the elder sons who race, and sign bills to be repaid at their fathers' deaths, the lures and snares thrown in the way of wealthy bachelors, the girls who go out year after year into the marriage market and become embittered by their perennial failure and, finally, by their self-contempt. We may now turn to confront that Alp of a novel—*The Last Chronicle of Barset*. The main plot of it is, as it happens, the theft or the loss by a clergyman of a cheque for the sum of twenty pounds.

(vii)

' "I can never bring myself to believe it, John," said Mary Walker, the pretty daughter of Mr George Walker, attorney of Silverbridge.' With these opening words of *The Last Chronicle of Barset*, this very long but most enjoyable novel gets off to a good, clean start. It often seems that, when setting to work on a new book, Anthony Trollope was, in his later life, gravely tempted to devote the first chapter or two (or even three) to labyrinthine explanations of the ancestry, mutual connections and current backgrounds of his major characters. Where the country gentry are concerned, we are in addition treated to an account of a country house standing in its own park. Such taxing openings of a fresh novel may perhaps have been his own way of persuading himself of the reality he was trying to manu-facture. To the leisured reader of his own day this method was probably not at all an irritant, for patience was a virtue very prevalent amongst a lettered generation brought up to relax over a good volume of sermons after Sunday luncheon, who still read Sir Walter Scott for kicks and who could fight their way with a mental machete through the tormented undergrowth of Thomas Carlyle's teutonic prose. Such comfortable readers would not have flinched before the maze-like plot of *Ralph the Heir*, for instance; this depends on the rivalry of Ralph Newton and his illegitimate cousin, also conveniently named Ralph Newton, for the hand of Mary Bonner, a tall, large, fair-haired beauty who 'might have been taken as a model for any female saint or martyr'. The critics who attacked Anthony Trollope's 'facility' can scarcely have read *Ralph the Heir* or the first two chapters of *The American Senator*, which concern Dillsborough and the Morton family; a peculiarity of the Mortons had been to die young, so that the old squire had survived both John Morton his son, and John Morton his grandson, and had finally died leaving the Morton property in entail to John Morton his great-grandson, who has lately been Secretary to H.M.'s Legation in Washington.

Once broached, *The American Senator* is a thoroughly enter-taining novel, with lively hunting scenes. It also introduces us to the good-natured, misguided philanthropist, the Senator from Mikewa himself. The bouts of perseverance which the early chapters of certain Trollope novels demand of the reader are not at all typical of his general method, for he does not customarily leave him fumbling to find his own way out from the musty passageways of genealogy. All the same there are times when he behaves like a genial, informative guide to the Catacombs whose candle has blown out. At any rate we can leave Arabella Trefoil for the moment, returning to pretty Mary Walker of Silverbridge who, like a well-bred girl at a stiff cro-quet party, tries to get things spinning by a smart click with her mallet. '"I can never bring myself to believe it, John" [she repeats]. "... A clergyman—and such a clergyman too!"' At this expostulation her brother raises his eyes from his book to say he does not see that ' "that has anything to do with it ... Why should not a clergyman turn thief as well as anybody else? You girls always seem to forget that clergymen are only men after all." '

What is it, then, that pretty Mary Walker, in common with half of Silverbridge and most of the county, refuses to believe? It is the accusation that the Reverend Josiah Crawley has stolen a cheque signed by Ludovic, Lord Lufton, for twenty pounds sterling. Mr Crawley, who first made his bow to the reading public in the *Cornhill* serialization of *Framley Parsonage* in January 1860, is still, a full six years later, Perpetual Curate of the poverty-stricken parish of Hogglestock in the northern ex-tremities of East Barsetshire, a parish which includes the brutish community of brickmakers at Hogglestock End, and brings with it the paltry income of £130 a year. On this sum Mr and Mrs Crawley, their son and their two daughters have tried to de-pend, budgeting £40 a year for meat, at least £25 a year for bread, a minimal clothes allowance of £10 per head annually, leaving £15 'for tea, sugar, beer, wages, education, amusements, and the like'. The living-room of their little house in Hoggle-stock is mean and wretched, with a carpet which diminishes annually through wear and tear, an old broken-down sofa, an aged armchair and an eighteenth-century desk heaped with de-crepit copies of Greek and Latin classics, all of them dog-eared and most of them stripped of their bindings. Noble-minded and religious yet arrogant, Mr Crawley revels in his poverty in a demented way. He rebukes his wife for lack of pride whenever he discovers that she has been secretly accepting the gifts of well-wishers to help to keep her children alive. In a heartfelt disquisition on the hardships and despair of people in the position of the Crawleys—'poor gentry—gentry so poor as not to know how to raise a shilling'—Anthony lists the charity of friends as being the most unbearable burden of all : 'the alms and doles of half-generous friends, the waning pride, the pride that will not wane.' In this book he etches the most delicate distinctions between degrees of generosity. Of the wealthy Archdeacon Grantley he tells us that he 'was a generous man in money matters—having a dislike for poverty which was not generous'.

For material for his terrible evocation of the poverty of the Crawleys Anthony Trollope had only to rummage through his own early memories. He had seen as Mrs Crawley does, 'the angry eyes of unpaid tradesmen, savage with an anger which one knows to be justifiable; the taunt of the poor servant who wants her wages', the almost insuperable difficulty, yet at the same time the absolute necessity, of dressing like gentlefolk. For the character of Mr Crawley he likewise had not far to look, for in his own father he had seen, as he makes us see in Josiah Crawley 'the darkness of his mind' and the 'poor racked imperfect memory'. Like Fanny Trollope, Mrs Crawley realizes that in certain moods her husband is half-insane. At Hogglestock there are days 'in which even his wife had found it impossible to treat him otherwise than as with an acknowledged lunatic', while the local farmers spoke of their pastor amongst themselves as a madman. All these symptoms had terrified Anthony and his brothers and sisters when their father's mind 'would not act at all times as do the minds of other men'. Crawley's passion for the classics and for teaching his children to construe and then to compose iambics, his touchiness, his unworldliness, his feverish obsessions—all these tally only too well with what we know of Anthony's father's state of mind for months, perhaps for years, before he was released by death in the tranquil little city of Bruges in the year 1835. How often must his mother have had to apologize to strangers for one of her husband's outbursts. He now put Fanny Trollope's words into the mouth of Mary Crawley : 'The truth is, sir, that my husband often knows not what he says ... There are times when in his misery he knowns not what he says—when he forgets everything.' Mrs Crawley, who had at the time of her marriage been an attractive, charming, well-educated girl, had soon lost her health and her looks but had kept intact a courage as high as that of the irrepressible Fanny Trollope herself. Mary Crawley strove to maintain in her children a certain respect for their dilapidated father : treating him at once 'with respect due to an honoured father of a family, and with the careful measured indulgence fit for a sick or wayward child'.

After many a twist and turn of fate, Mr Crawley is entirely exonerated of theft, since it is proved that the cheque had indeed been given to him, as in his muddle-headed way he had asserted, by his friend the Dean—or rather had been placed in an envelope which contained bank-notes given to him by the Dean. The great case is over, and those who heartily believed in Mr Crawley's honesty can crow over those who did not. Quaint though it may seem, one person who did not really believe in Mr Crawley's mental confusion about the cheque was his own creator, Anthony Trollope. Writing of *The Last Chronicle* as, in his own opinion, the best of all his novels, he admits in his autobiography that he does not find Mr Crawley's amnesia over the cheque credible: 'I cannot quite make myself believe that even such a man as Mr Crawley could have forgotten how he got it; nor would the generous friend who was anxious to supply his wants have supplied them by tendering the cheque of a third person.' He blames this failure on his own inability to construct a really mysterious plot, adding with most excusable complacency that 'while confessing so much, I claim to have portrayed the mind of the unfortunate man with great accuracy and great delicacy'. 'There is a true savour of English life all through the book,' he writes of *The Last Chronicle*; and this is marvellous and indeed true.

For his grand finale of Barsetshire, Trollope summoned back all the characters whom he loved best. Some, like old Lord de Guest, had died in the natural course of time before Anthony started on this sixth and last of his Barsetshire books. Another, the famous and redoubtable Mrs Proudie, wife of the Bishop of Barchester, dies, to the reader's eternal regret, two-thirds of the way through the book. Anthony was most unwilling to condemn Mrs Proudie to death. It was the result of a hasty impulse compounded of wounded sensibility and chagrin. One morning in the year 1866 Anthony Trollope was peacefully writing his novel at a desk in the long, light, book-lined drawing-room of the Athenaeum Club in Waterloo Place. This was his morning habit whenever he was obliged to spend the night in London. As he scribbled away he could not avoid eavesdropping on a lively discussion between two clergymen, who had seated themselves opposite to each other at the fireplace, and consequently close by the bearded, busy stranger at his desk. Each held a magazine in his hand, and they soon fell to discussing what they were reading—in both cases a serial part of one of the Barsetshire novels. They both condemned the recurrence of Trollope's favourite characters. 'Here,' said one, 'is that archdeacon whom we have had in every novel he has ever written.' 'And here,' said the other 'is the old duke whom he has talked about till everyone is tired of him. If *I* could not invent new characters, I would not write novels at all.' They then turned their guns on Mrs Proudie, and this was simply more than Anthony could bear. Getting up to his full height he towered in front of the fire between them as he told them who he was. 'As to Mrs Proudie,' he declared, 'I will go home and kill her before the week is over.' The clergymen were 'utterly confounded' and one of them mumbled an apology; but the deed was done—Mrs Proudie had received sentence of death.

Anthony much regretted having undertaken to kill off the Bishop's lady—'so great was my delight in writing about Mrs Proudie; so thorough was my knowledge of all the little shades of her character'. He says that since her death he had become equally fond of the Palliser couple, but even they did not fill the blank: 'I have never dissevered myself from Mrs Proudie, and still live much in company with her ghost.' In her lifetime Mrs Proudie had been awe-inspiring and alarming; in her death she became a figure of nightmare. She had, we learn for the first time in the chapter of *The Last Chronicle* entitled 'Requiescat in Pace', for some years suffered from a heart complaint, a secret known only to Mrs Draper, her lady's maid. She kept a medical stimulant in a locked closet in her bedroom, and when in pain she would privily swallow a draught behind bolted doors. After a final scene with the Bishop over the Sunday services at Hogglestock, she had gone upstairs to her room, apparently to take some of the medicine and to read the Bible. At about seven o'clock her corpse was found by Draper, who summoned Mrs Proudie's mild, fawning little clerical protégé Mr Thumble, who happened to be in the Palace. Just as Anthony Trollope had startled his readers on the first page of *The Last Chronicle* by the assumption that a clergyman might as easily become a thief as any other man, so in Mrs Proudie's death-bed scene he deliberately produced a realist's antithesis to the sentimental deaths beloved of Dickens's public. In this travesty of sudden death Mrs Proudie was not lying on her bed with her eyes devoutly closed, looking as though she had fallen asleep. She was not, in fact, on her bed at all, but at it, standing bulky and upright, her all-seeing eyes wide open. Her body, we are told, 'was resting on its legs, leaning against the side of the bed while one of the arms was close clasped round the bed-post. The mouth was rigidly closed, but the eyes were open as though staring at [Mr Thumble]. Nevertheless there could be no doubt from the first glance that the woman was dead. He went up close to it, but did not dare to touch it.'

Imperious Mrs Proudie, the tyrant, the bully, the 'would-be priestess' who had for nearly a decade domineered over the clergy of Barsetshire, can now only be referred to as 'it'.

The Last Chronicle of Barset was acclaimed by the critics of the periodical press; all lamented the adjective in the novel's title. 'What are we to do,—what *are* we to do, without the Archdeacon?' ran a laudatory notice in the *Spectator*. 'Mr Trollope *dare* not bereave us of the Archdeacon.' In *Blackwood's Magazine,* that prolific and popular lady novelist, Mrs Laurence Oliphant, accused Trollope of recklessly murdering Mrs Proudie: '... there are certain things which he had done without consulting us against which we greatly demur. To kill Mrs Proudie was murder, or manslaughter at the least. We do not believe that she had any disease of the heart; she died not by natural causes, but by his hand in a fit of weariness or passion'. In *Blackwood's,* Margaret Oliphant, who herself produced a number of now long-forgotten novels bracketed together as *Chronicles of Carlingford,* really let herself go in praise of Anthony Trollope and his last Barsetshire book: 'Honour to the writer who, amid so much that is false and vile and meretricious in current literature, beautifies our world and our imagination with such creations as these!'

Just why, in 1866, Anthony decided to ring down the curtain upon the teeming stage of Barsetshire we cannot know. The decision, however, was probably concurrent with a switch of his interests from country life to that of political London—although in even the most political of his novels he did not forgo fox-hunting scenes, nor eschew the spacious use of rich landowners' estates and country houses. During 1866 to 1867, while he was writing *Phineas Finn,* he was moreover contemplating a step which might or might not prove rash: he was making up his mind to resign from the Post Office, thus liberating himself from the habits of a lifetime, so as to devote himself to literature and later, as he hoped, to politics.

At the age of fifty-two Anthony Trollope had the sense and the courage to begin a new life.

Before he finally resigned from the Post Office, and thus from the Civil Service, Anthony Trollope had fortified his immediate financial future by accepting the editorship of yet another new periodical, the *St Paul's Magazine*. This enterprise was initiated by James Vertue, a prosperous printer who was yielding to the printer's immemorial temptation to become a publisher as well. Trollope himself did not think there was room for another literary magazine upon the London market, and did his best to dissuade Mr Vertue, who bearded him at Waltham Cross in an insistent mood. It was eventually agreed that the magazine should begin publication in October 1867, just one month after Anthony's departure from the Postal Service. He was to become a reluctant editor on his own autocratic terms, at a salary of £1,000 a year. Vertue also paid him £3,500 for the new novel, *Phineas Finn*, which formed the staple serial attraction of the first months of the *St Paul's Magazine*. His stipend as editor was guaranteed for two years; he stuck it out for three and a half and then resigned, concluding that his editorial standards were too high: 'I was too anxious to be good, and did not think enough of what might be lucrative.' From its commencement the *St Paul's Magazine* lost money steadily. It staggered on into the middle 'seventies and then folded.

No longer a Civil Servant, Anthony Trollope was now free to fulfil his old ambition of standing for Parliament. After describing George Vavasor's election for the Chelsea Hamlets in *Can You Forgive Her?* Trollope writes reflectively of the enviable privileged lives of the Members of Parliament at Westminster:

'There is on the left-hand side of our great national hall ... a pair of gilded lamps with a door between them ... Between those lamps is the entrance to the House of Commons, and none but Members may go that way! It is the only gate before which I have ever stood filled with envy,—sorrowing to think that my steps might never pass under it ... I have told myself, in anger and in grief, that to die and not to have won that right of way, though but for a session,—not to have passed by the narrow entrance through those lamps,—is to die and not to have done that which it most becomes an Englishman to have achieved.'

Charles Dickens, who had in his youth been a hard-worked Parliamentary newspaper reporter, did not take this rosy view of

British legislators and their work. Thackeray, on the other hand, had stood as a Liberal for Oxford in 1857 and was defeated by fifty-three votes. In his monograph on his old friend, Trollope roundly declares that Thackeray 'would not have shone' in the House of Commons owing to his 'intolerance of tedium', and his vague, desultory attitude to work of any kind. 'But he had his moment of political ambition, like others,—and paid a thousand pounds for his attempt.'

Before his own moment of ambition in November 1868, when he, like Thackeray, was defeated by a Tory candidate, Trollope had begun to find himself spellbound by British politics, and was often to be seen in the Strangers' Gallery. These frequent visits provided him with material for the House of Commons scenes in *Phineas Finn*. That distinguished Trollope scholar, the late Professor Bradford A. Booth, has pointed out that, although *Phineas Finn* is habitually classified as a political novel, politics in fact play as small a part in it as does religious belief in *Barchester Towers*: 'He had to content himself with allowing the House to serve as an alternating backdrop (with the country estates) for some very human actions and emotions. Of political philosophy there is virtually none. Of a social philosophy, including the complicated ethics of Victorian marriages, there is a great deal.'

Trollope apparently realized that he 'could not make a tale pleasing chiefly, or perhaps in any part, by politics'. He felt that if he put politics into a novel for his own pleasure, he 'must put in love and intrigue, social incidents, with perhaps a dash of sport, for the sake of my readers'. 'In this way,' he confidently adds, 'I think that I made my political hero interesting.' For his hero's origins Trollope went back to his own former life in Ireland, making Phineas the impoverished son of Dr Malachi Finn of Killaloe on the lovely southern shore of Lough Derg in County Clare. Anthony strangely thought that the fact of creating Phineas Finn as an Irishman had been 'certainly a blunder, —because Irish politics were not respected in England'. He even says that he chose Ireland only because he had invented the scheme of the novel while on a visit there. This statement would seem to be but partially accurate, for the fact that Phineas is the son of a small-town Irish doctor gives him in London political society the role of a born outsider whose charm and handsome looks can overcome prejudices as to his poverty and his indistinguished birth. The son of a small-town doctor from Tiverton or Devizes would never have been welcomed to the inner circles of London society—unless, like Miss Martha Dunstable's father, that English doctor had by some means amassed an acceptable fortune.

I have earlier explained how threadbare at this distance of time are the possibilities of identifying real-life prototypes for the characters in Trollope's novels. We know that a Bishop in *The Way We Live Now* was based on Trollope's memories of 'old Longdon', his headmaster at Harrow; that Sir Roger Scatcherd in *Doctor Thorne* is believed to have been a portrait of the bibulous Sir Joseph Paxton; that the red-headed Lord Chiltern in *Phineas Finn* and *Phineas Redux* has been supposed to be the eighth Duke of Devonshire. Thomas Sweet Escott, who wrote the first biography of Trollope at a date at which both Mrs Anthony Trollope and other relations as well as a few old friends of the novelist's were still alive, makes the tantalizing suggestion that everyone in London society had recognized Madame Max Goesler; he also writes that the politician Mr Daubeny was known to be a portrait of Disraeli. Escott identifies Phineas Finn himself with a magnetic Roman Catholic Conservative Irishman, a member for the Kings County at the early age of twenty-five. This was John Pope Hennessy, a young and brilliant Cork man who had come from much the same sort of dim, unpromising middle-class family background as Phineas himself, and had much the same early, meteoric success in London society as Phineas is shown to have achieved. Escott writes:

'As regards good looks, Phineas may have had something in common with Colonel King-Harman, whom the novelist occasionally met at the Arts Club, but at all other points Trollope's Irish Member, by his fine presence, winning manners and return to St Stephens after an interval of absence, suggests Sir John Pope Hennessy rather than any other representative of the Emerald Isle.'

This identification of Phineas Finn with the present writer's grandfather is also reported in a note by the Irish journalist T. P. O'Connor, who edited *T.P.'s Weekly* for many years.

On the publication of *Phineas Finn* in book form in March 1869, the *Daily Telegraph* accused its author of ungentlemanly conduct in drawing pen-portraits of living politicians such as Disraeli, Gladstone, Lord Derby, Lord John Russell and John Bright. To this charge he pugnaciously replied that none of his political characters was in any way related or intended to be related to any actual statesman of the day. In a letter to a woman friend about his novel *The Prime Minister*, which forms part of the Palliser series and was published in 1876, he tried to define the rather tenuous links between personality and political creed; all that he had taken from such men as Gladstone and Disraeli had been their political tenets. 'There are,' he wrote, 'nothing of personal characteristics here. When that has been attempted by me—as in all the Paliser people—the old Duke, the new Duke and Lady Glencora, there has been no distant idea in my mind of any living person. They are pure creations; and (as I think) the best I ever made.' Trollope's novels and tales swarm with more than two thousand different persons. All the inhabitants of this great hive were surely 'pure creations' but all owed their births to Anthony Trollope's observant eye and his attentive ear. He would no doubt have said, if asked, that he could have written his books shut up alone in a prison cell; and he was, perhaps, quite honestly unconscious of how many aspects of physical appearance, how many traits of character and of colloquial usage he derived from living people whom he knew, had seen, or had heard tell of in country-house drawing-rooms and in London clubs. In any case it is now too late to establish who was who. The personal descriptions in his novels are now far harder to decipher than the more sophisticated and self-conscious travesties of friends, relations and acquaintances in the novels of Marcel Proust.

(ii)

Anthony Trollope's vibrant and massive conception of the world of the Pallisers was not, at first, much appreciated by his readers and his critics. He was now being criticized in some quarters for creating characters who were '*too like* real life for literature' and it was said (one reviewer 'reminded the public) 'that Mr Trollope's sketches are so like to those whom one actually meets in society that one learns no more from them than we should learn from those whom we actually meet in society'. His 'multiplication of figures' went under attack in the *Saturday Review*, where it was suggested that 'if *Phineas Finn* is remembered a few years hence ... it will owe its vitality to its political sketches'. A more temperate critic in the *Spectator* wrote that Phineas Finn and the throng of his friends and enemies, the ladies who are in love with him and those who are not, never seem to indulge in self-analysis. This may perhaps be true of Phineas himself, whom the *Spectator* critic dismissed as 'terribly tame—if we may be allowed the bull' and whom Hugh

Walpole in his study of Anthony Trollope (in the *English Men of Letters* series, 1929) has called 'a hollow drum'. In reality Phineas Finn is neither tame nor hollow; he belongs to that gigantic category of passive persons with little volition to whom things merely happen. He gets his seat in Parliament by luck and owing to his father's lifelong friendship with one of his patients, Lord Tulla, who is patron of the pocket borough of Loughshane in County Galway. The dreary prospect of becoming a Dublin barrister and his years of reading with one in the Middle Temple had held no charm for Phineas Finn.

While still studying the law he had, through an Irish friend and M.P., been introduced into the circle of Lady Laura Standish, on whom his handsome face and Irish ways made such an impression that she fell in love with him but married a rich man instead. All of his flirtations seem quite sincere to Phineas himself, who does not pause to wonder why he should have fallen suddenly out of love with Lady Laura and, just as suddenly, into love with Miss Violet Effingham. Although engaged at home to a little Irish girl, Mary Flood Jones of Floodborough, he next dallies with the widowed millionairess, Madame Max Goesler, to such a tune that she offers him her hand and her fortune. In the same way he does not really expect to have to fight a duel with Lady Laura's brother, the wild Lord Chiltern of the scarlet hair, who has been aptly described as a fine example of Trollope's race of gentlemen-savages. Although astonished by his own swift success in London political society, Phineas remains an idealist at heart while at the same time conforming to certain upper-class British conventions. When he first gets promoted to a Junior Lord of the Treasury, for instance, he buys a horse so that he may ride with the rest of the fashion in Hyde Park. He also recognizes that the time has come to vacate his cosy rooms at Mrs Bunce's boarding-house in Great Marlborough Street and move to a smarter neighbourhood nearer to the Houses of Parliament. Passive as his general role is, Phineas Finn does harbour violent political views, especially about the wrongs of his native Ireland; because the Government of which he is a junior member has views on Ireland diametrically different from his own, he resigns and ends up at Killaloe marrying Mary Flood Jones. As we have already observed, Anthony himself thought Mary Flood Jones a very great mistake because he had to kill her off so that his hero could return to London and the scenes of his political and social truimphs in *Phineas Redux*, which, though finished in 1871, was not published until 1874, when it was serialized in the *Graphic*. *Redux* was generally considered a better book than *Finn*, the *Spectator* critic on this occasion calling it a 'charming chronicle'.

It is needless to say that the five-year gap between the publication of these two novels was not, for Anthony Trollope, a period of waste. During them he wrote *He Knew He Was Right*, *The Vicar of Bullhampton*, *Sir Harry Hotspur of Humblethwaite*, *Ralph the Heir*, *The Eustace Diamonds*, *An Eye for an Eye* and edited *The Commentaries of Caesar*. He also paid a visit to the United States, this time on official Post Office business, and was defeated as a Liberal candidate for Beverley. On his return to the States he went to a dinner at which Oliver Wendell Holmes, Ralph Waldo Emerson and James Russell Lowell were present. Lowell has left us a record of this meeting, which comprises our best, indeed our only, account of what an attempt to converse with Anthony Trollope was like. It is therefore worth reproducing here:

'Dined the other day with Anthony Trollope; a big, red-faced, rather underbred Englishman of the bald-with-spectacles type. A good roaring positive fellow who deafened me (sitting on his right) till I thought of Dante's Cerberus. He says he goes to work on a novel "just like a shoemaker on a shoe, only taking care to make honest stitches". Gets up at five every day, does all his writing before breakfast, and always writes just so many pages a day. He and Dr Holmes were very entertaining. The Autocrat started one or two hobbies, and charged, paradox in rest—but it was pelting a rhinoceros with seed-pearl.

DR. You don't know what Madeira is in England?

T. I'm not so sure it's worth knowing.

DR. Connoisseurship with us is a fine art. There are men who will tell a dozen kinds, as Dr Waagen would know a Carlo Dolci from a Guido.

T. They might be better employed!

DR. Whatever is worth doing is worth doing well.

T. Ay, but that's begging the whole question. I don't admit it's *worse* doing at all. If they earn their bread by it, it may be *worse* doing (roaring).

DR. But you may be assured——

T. No, but I mayn't be asshorred. I don't intend to be asshorred (roaring louder)!

And so they went it. It was very funny. Trollope wouldn't give him any chance. Meanwhile, Emerson and I, who sat between them, crouched down out of range, and had some very good talk, with the shot hurtling overhead ... I rather liked Trollope.'

At this 'dinner-party', which took place at the early hour of 3 p.m., and was given by the Boston publisher Fields, Anthony Trollope also met Nathaniel Hawthorne for the first time. 'Let me know on receipt of this if you will come,' Fields wrote to Hawthorne, who lived in Salem. 'I really hope you can, for Trollope is a fine boy and wishes to meet you very much.' To judge by a further note from Fields to Hawthorne, this particular aspect of the dinner-party had been a success: 'Trollope fell in love with you at first sight and went off moaning that he could not see you again. He swears you are the handsomest Yankee that ever walked this planet.'

On the loose in Washington and Boston, Anthony continued to exacerbate his friends with thin skins. One day he was asked about his writing by the mother of Madame Clara Louise Kellogg Strakosch, the memorialist. This was a question which only people who did not know Trollope would have been foolhardy enough to ask. To Mrs Kellogg he replied that he always chose words that would fill up the pages quickest. Recording this reply, her daughter Clara Louise remarked: 'English people when they are not thoroughbred can be very common.'

(iii)

Rose Trollope did not accompany her husband on this second trip to the United States. She remained behind, holding the fort at Waltham House, supervising the gardeners and the servants and dealing with proofs and publishers as was customary when Anthony was abroad. In 1865 the household had been depleted by the departure of Fred Trollope, their younger son, to sheepfarm in Australia at the age of just eighteen. Whether this youthful pioneer did not enjoy living with his parents we do not know. His father writes that it was due to Fred's own conviction that he was growing too fast to remain a schoolboy: 'My son Frederic had very early in life gone out to Australia, having resolved on a colonial career when he found that boys who did not grow so fast as he did got above him at school. This departure was a great pang to his mother and myself.' Frederic had promised his parents that he would return to England when he was twenty-one, so that he might have a chance to change his mind. Another year in Hertfordshire, however, failed to defeat the lure of the bush. The overgrown youth went out again, and this time finally, to Australia.

The Trollopes' elder son, Harry, had studied law and was actually called to the Bar in 1869. No sooner had this occurred than the prospect of a partnership in the very successful publishing house of Chapman and Hall floated on the horizon. His parents, and Harry himself, were well aware of what his father in this connection called 'the terrible uncertainty of the Bar'. Moreover in Harry Trollope's case the terror 'was not lessened by any peculiar forensic aptitudes'; these considerations induced the family 'to sacrifice dignity in quest of success'. As openhanded as always, Anthony Trollope bought the partnership for a large sum down, and Harry began to work at the publishers' offices at 193 Piccadilly. He only stayed in the firm for three and a half years, for he did not care for the work nor did he make a very good publisher. He did not exactly lose his father's money, but he had decided that he would betake 'himself to literature as a profession'. 'Whether he will work at it so hard as his father, and write as many books, may be doubted'—it is on this grim note that Anthony concludes his account of what can only have seemed to him to be his elder son's devastating lack of tenacity.

Both boys were now grown-up, one in London lodgings and the other in the wooden house he had built on his property, Mortray Station, near the township of Forbes in New South Wales. All the same, Waltham House was not altogether deprived of the enervating presence of the young. In 1863 Florence Bland, a niece of Rose Trollope's, that is to say a daughter of her sister, was enlisted into the Anthony Trollopes' household, and, a few years later, 'Flo' became her uncle's treasured amanuensis. Another child niece, whose name has not survived, would also stay at Waltham House from time to time. Immediately after the death of Tom Trollope's first wife, Theodosia, in April 1865, Anthony had sped down to Florence to comfort his brother and to bring back home Tom and Theodosia's only child, a beautiful, Italianate, precocious girl of twelve, named Beatrice but called Bice. The kindly thought of Uncle Anthony was not appreciated by this niece, who, however unhappy about the loss of her mother, would have preferred to stay at their house in Florence, where she was the pet of all her parents' friends, went out to evening parties, and treated grown-up persons on a basis of equality. 'I doubt whether you quite understand the antecedents of Bice's life,' Anthony Trollope wrote some years later to his friend Lady Pollock. 'The fault was that she had been too much spoilt in everything,—allowed to have her own way ... Everything was done for her that could be done ... the fault was my brother's in allowing her to have her own way, till her own way ceased to please her.' At Waltham Cross Bice had a pony to ride, and the company of two of her aunt's nieces during the spring and early summer of the year of her mother's death. She would have seen little of her uncle, who was always at work, either at Waltham or in London, but when she did see him she proved recalcitrant. One day he offered a five-pound note to each of the three girls if they could learn his favourite poem, *Lycidas*, by heart, and, although the others each won this stimulating prize, Bice made no attempt to learn *Lycidas* at all. She was, on the other hand, profoundly musical; Jenny Lind had once predicted, after hearing Bice sing at the Villino Trollope that, if properly trained and taught, the girl, in future years, would be able to mount the vertiginous ladder of international fame to become as celebrated as was Miss Jenny Lind herself.

In the summer of 1865 Tom Trollope came over to England to fetch Bice back to his newly acquired house in the Tuscan hills. The question of her further education now arose. At first a young Frenchwoman from a school in Brighton was engaged, but she found Florence too cold in winter and resigned her post. Her resignation gave Anthony and Rose their opportunity for, with their views on designing Italians, they were very nervous that Tom Trollope, then fifty-five, relatively rich and very, very deaf, might be snapped up in Florence without their being able to prevent it. Already rumours that the widower had opportunities to remarry ran through Florence: 'Lord love us,' wrote Robert Browning to his confidante, Miss Isa Blagden, 'how little flattering is woman's love—that is, the collective woman's love —the *particular* is another matter. It seems he [Tom Trollope] may throw his handkerchief to anybody in Florence.' So soon as they learned of the French governess's desertion in the spring of 1866, the Trollopes dispatched an English 'governess' of their own choice, a young lady of twenty-three, Frances Eleanor Ternan, an energetic and rather serious person with a large nose. Miss Ternan had a married sister living in Florence, so she soon felt at home. The then popular poet Alfred Austin and his wife were living in Tom's farmhouse, at Ricorboli, in the heights above Florence, and they could act as chaperones. The scheme of the plotters at Waltham Cross worked perfectly. In October 1866, the marriage took place in Paris and was attended by Anthony and his wife, by the child Bice, and by Fanny Ternan's sister from Florence, Mrs Taylor. Another sister, the notorious Ellen, who was Charles Dickens's youthful mistress, was presumably not invited to the ceremony.

This new marriage, almost eighteen months after Theodosia Trollope's death, aroused much speculation in Florence. Theodosia, with her Indian, Jewish and English blood, had always seemed a romantic, ethereal figure in Florence, where the English had admired her for her beauty and the Italians both for that and for her zeal as propagandist for a United Italy. Beatrice, her daughter, had been born after five years of sterile union with Tom Trollope. 'We have heard a rumour (someone told John Tilley in Kensington Gardens!) that Theodosia is about to make Tom a father', Anthony had written to his mother back in the summer of 1852. 'If so, why has Tom not told us what we should have been so glad to hear from him?' The birth of Beatrice, after Theodosia's prolonged childlessness, amused the cynical Italians and formed a topic for sly innuendo within the British community. Even Anthony and Rose had seemingly heard of these suspicions, and only Tom Trollope (and, while she lived, his mother) was unaware of what was being said, and of the guessing-game about Bice's paternity which was soon in full swing. Theodosia's death had once more brought these rumours to the surface. In August 1867, Browning told Miss Blagden in a letter from London that he had encountered Tom Trollope in the street and had naturally asked after his wife, an inquiry to which Tom made no reply. Repairing to the Athenaeum Club, Browning learned that, during the course of a row with her husband, the new Mrs Trollope had taunted him with the doubts on Bice's paternity and that they had agreed to separate. The story was repeated to Browning by another Athenaeum member whom he met on the Club steps as he was leaving. This individual asserted that he 'had heard of it from Anthony T.—I think in Paris'. Miss Blagden seems to have replied brusquely to Browning's letter, for she was prepared to defend her beloved Theo to the last; the whole tale, she wrote, was a calumny to which no one should give any credence. Robert Browning was prepared to accept this, but he evidently resented the way in which Isa Blagden must have reproached him for believing the story; 'Observe,' he wrote in reply, 'I never believed it ... and I at once applied to *you* for corroboration of it.' All he had done, he pleaded, was to repeat to her

'the deliberate statement of as veracious a man as I know that he had been told what I told you by Anthony T. himself ... I should be delighted also to think, if I possibly could, that the falsity of this report is 'good ground for disbelieving in all those old stories', as you suggest: that seemes to me not unlike the lady who would not credit the execution of Maximilian, seeing that John Brown was not married to the Queen after all.'

Tom Trollope's second marriage was childless. Beatrice grew to be a much-admired young lady, who married a Stuart Wortley in 1880, and died after the birth of her child in July 1881. Her contacts with her Uncle Anthony and her Aunt Rose were affectionate. When they had left Waltham Cross, Bice sometimes lived at their London house, 39 Montagu Square, where her virtuosity would captivate her rather unmusical uncle. 'I wish you could hear our Bice play & sing—(sing especially),' he wrote to a woman friend. "I do not suppose you have heard of her. She is my brother's daughter—was born in Italy, but is here now. Blumenthal and Arthur Sullivan tell me that they know nothing in private life like her voice. She affects me, as nothing else that I know in music.' It may well have been some memory of Bice's singing which led Anthony Trollope into making the subsidiary heroine of the last, unfinished novel of his old age, *The Landleaguers*, an aspiring operatic star.

(iv)

Anthony Trollope's mission to the United States in 1868 was a graceful valedictory compliment to his proven efficiency as a first-class negotiator—for, having resigned from the Civil Service in the previous year, he was none the less asked to represent the Postmaster-General abroad for the last time. His noisy diplomacy was successful, and a satisfactory Anglo-American Postal Treaty was the result. Anthony suffered hideously, stewing in the torrid heat of a Washington summer. His other, simultaneous mission, as a special representative of the Foreign Office, was to try to establish an international copyright agreement between Great Britain and the States. This proved, as he foresaw that it would, fruitless. Harpers' and the three or four other big American publishing houses which pirated English books wholesale, had formed a powerful lobby against such a copyright law. They were even specious enough to plead in a sanctimonious way that by pirating books they were serving to educate the great American public who could only afford English books that were cheap and that only by piracy could cheap books be distributed. Pirate publishing, they implied, was a patriotic means of providing a democratic service to American readers. Anthony's one consolation during what he described to his brother as 'a most disagreeable trip to America' had been to see Kate Field once more, to write to her when he could not see her, to advise her on her poetry and prose and to deride her sympathy with Women's Rights. To Anthony the position of women in the world of the mid-nineteenth century was ideal and should not be tampered with—just as the Irish should never, in his opinion, be granted Home Rule.

While he was in Washington neither the heat, the mosquitoes nor the intricate postal negotiations were allowed to interrupt the smooth and regular flow of novel-writing. *He Knew He Was Right* had been begun at Waltham House in November 1867, continued on board the Cunarder as it rolled and pitched its way across the Atlantic, and completed in the soggy summer of Washington on June 12th, 1868. On June 15th, he started a new novel, *The Vicar of Bullhampton*, which shows every sign of having been written under strain and is a lifeless, dull production save for the vivid portrait of the little prostitute Carry Brattle, who usurps the part of heroine from Miss Mary Lowther, another of Trollope's young ladies who dithers over whether to marry the man to whom she has engaged herself, or the man she loves. We may recall that, nervous of what effect a book concerning a prostitute would have upon his public, Anthony had relaxed his steadfast rule of never writing prefaces by providing one for *The Vicar*. This was a sincere apology for the Carry Brattles of Great Britain, more sinned against than sinning. Carry was, however, accepted by the critics with an unruffled calm, though one of the notices of the book thought the fallen girl heartless because she does not give a straw whether her London lover is hanged or not. *The Times* was totally unperturbed by the book's side-theme: 'It is a nice, easy, safe reading book for old ladies and young ladies, though we can fancy some of the latter class may be terribly provoked at Mary Lowther's high principle ... the general safeness of the story will make Bullhampton Vicarage welcome in all well-regulated families.' Far from seeming to be a bold, unconventional attack on contemporary hypocrisy, *The Vicar of Bullhampton* was treated as a damp squib, a book *The Times* could recommend to old or young ladies alike. For all his banging about the world there still clung to Anthony a certain aura of innocence that is endearing. Some of his typically Victorian terminology sounds odd today—his constant use of the word 'lover' to denote an engaged man is at first confusing, particularly when we find the most correct and virginal girls asking if they can bring back their lovers home to rectory tea. It is rather in his unguarded choice of names that his innocence, or his ignorance, shows most. Charles Dickens would never have sent Lily Dale (up in London with her uncle) to ride in Rotten Row accompanied by a gentleman whose *petit nom* was Syph. Nor is the Honourable Charles Glasscock a noticeably happy choice as the name for Lord Peterborough's son and heir.

He Knew He Was Right, which preceded *The Vicar of Bullhampton*, is one of Trollope's best but least-known novels. In the Bodleian Library at Oxford, amongst Anthony Trollope's business papers, are some examples of the methodical way in which he recorded the daily progress of his current novel. These working-tables are in columns, on the left the day of the month, on the right the amount written on each day. At the head of the working-table for *The Claverings* he has estimated that it will take '35 a week for 22 weeks=770 pages. Pages at 260.' It would be interesting, had all the working-tables survived, to analyse them in an effort to estimate when and why he was writing drearily in one novel, brilliantly in another. Was his work better in the summer when there was no hunting? Did the short-lived *St Paul's Magazine* cause him so much anxiety as to alter the quality (but not, of course, the quantity) of his fictional output? We cannot tell. Some of the tables, that for *The Claverings* for instance in 1867–8, are more human than they sound—four days in August with Henry in Paris, another four with Rose in the Isle of Wight, still writing every morning. In December 1864, however, something happened to snarl up Anthony's effortless routine. From December 30th, 1864 until January 5th, 1865, and again from January 10th to 13th, there are blank days marked simply 'Alas!'—when he has not been able to work. Since a few days in bracing Ramsgate are sandwiched between the 'alas' or wasted days, it is probable that Anthony could not write because he was ill.

Whatever may have been the reason for the blatant contrast in quality between *The Vicar of Bullhampton* and *He Knew He Was Right*, it is there for all to see. The latter is a sombre study in jealousy and obstinacy leading up to actual madness. At the close of its ninety-nine chapters it achieves what Henry James, who admired the book, has called 'an impressive completeness of misery ... Touch is added to touch, one small, stupid, fatal aggravation to another; and as we gaze into the widening breach we wonder at the vulgar materials of which tragedy sometimes composes itself.' The black and basic theme of this novel is decked out with a number of sub-plots, but these do not impinge upon the main story, for they are skilfully woven into it, whereas the two plots of *The Vicar of Bullhampton* veer away from one another and could easily have been dismantled and published as two totally separate books. In *He Knew He Was Right* Anthony was working once again upon a broad canvas such as that of *Phineas Finn, The Last Chronicle of Barset* or *Can You Forgive Her?* The scene shifts backwards and forwards smoothly—from one region of London to another, from London to Exeter, from Exeter to Florence and Siena. In Louis Trevelyan the anti-hero, the jealous, mule-headed young husband of the equally stubborn Emily, eldest daughter of Sir Marmaduke Rowley, Governor of the Mandarin Islands, Trollope has produced an adroit investigation into the course of mental disorder, first brought on by a silly obsession, but constantly increased by the smallest, simplest, most everyday misunderstandings. With his wide knowledge of human conduct, Trollope handles the gradual onset of Louis Trevelyan's insanity with as much ease and confidence as he does any other psychological phenomena which he had observed and then used for fodder for his novels. He excels at describing the troubling stages of senility, and also at portraying men, young or old, whose lives are solitary and whose minds are twisted. This latter group is chiefly confined to Trollope's old bugbear, the landed aristocracy. The Marquess of Brotherton is prone to attacks of diabolical anger in *Is He Popenjoy?*; in *The Bertrams*, the eccentric Marquess of Stapledean, a misanthrope resident in Westmorland, never listens to anyone but simply shrieks in fury when addressed (in one case by a clergyman's widow), and then lunges across his study and wrenches at the bell-rope to summon a footman to eject any unwelcome visitor to Broome Lodge; in *The Claverings* the embittered Earl of Ongar, while not technically mad, is a rotting carcase from past debauches who treats his bride in a manner which is most disagreeable and scarcely sane.

As in the novels of Balzac, jealousy in all its varied forms plays a great part in Trollope's works. There seems to have been nothing about jealousy that Trollope did not know, or could not imagine. He was vividly aware of this corrosive emotion's paramount place in daily life, although only a few, rare people have the courage to admit to such infection. In *Phineas Finn* and *Phineas Redux* there is a positive cat's-cradle of jealousies.

There is the jealousy of Phineas when he learns that Lady Laura Standish, whom he loves, is going to marry Mr Robert Kennedy of Loughlinter. There is the justified jealousy, leading to insanity and death, of Mr Robert Kennedy over Phineas Finn, whom his wife secretly adores and regards as her personal Phoebus Apollo. Then there is the wild jealousy of Lady Laura Kennedy when Phineas in his candid, carefree Irish way tells her that he has switched his love from herself to Violet Effingham, one of the prettiest heiresses in London; Phineas even asks Lady Laura's aid in winning Violet as his bride. The lovelorn and obtuse young man comes to see Lady Laura in Grosvenor Place at an hour when he knows that he will find her alone:

' "What is it, Mr Finn?"

' "I suppose I may as well tell you at once,—in plain language, I do not know how to put my story into words that shall fit it. I love Violet Effingham. Will you help me to win her to be my wife?"

' "You love Violet Effingham!" said Lady Laura. And as she spoke the look of her countenance towards him was so changed that he became at once aware that from her no assistance might be expected.

' "Mr Finn, I can hardly believe this of you, even when you tell me yourself."

' "Listen to me, Lady Laura, for a moment."

' "Certainly, I will listen. But that you should come to me for assistance! I cannot understand it. Men sometimes become harder than stones ... Do you speak of loving a woman as if it were an affair of fate, over which you have no control? I doubt whether your passions are so strong as that. You had better put aside your love for Miss Effingham. I feel assured that it will never hurt you ... Believe me," she said with a smile, "this little wound in your heart will soon be cured."

'He stood silent before her, looking away from her, thinking over it all. He certainly had believed himself to be violently in love with Lady Laura, and yet when he had just now entered her drawing-room, he had almost forgotten that there had been such a passage in his life.'

Two or three years later, living in exile with her father Lord Brentford in Dresden, after she has left Mr Kennedy's house for good, Lady Laura walks with Phineas upon the ramparts at Königstein. Here she admits to him her love and her suffering, how she had not been able to drive the demon of jealousy out of her heart, and how Phineas' love for Violet Effingham had cut her 'to the very bone'. Then there is the jealousy of Lady Laura's brother, the gentleman-savage Lord Chiltern, when he realizes that his friend Finn is trying to marry Violet Effingham, whom Chiltern himself loves. This particular episode ends inauspiciously with a duel in the sand-dunes near the fishing hamlet of Blankenberghe on the Belgian coast, twelve miles from Bruges. Other forms of jealousy inspire Phineas Finn's political enemies—enemies within his own Liberal Party such as Mr Bonteen—who feel that he is a raw Irish puppy going altogether too far too fast. Mr Low, in whose chambers Phineas read law for three years, and Mrs Low, who once had a weakness for her husband's pupil, are both jealous because Phineas has ignored their advice, chucked up his law career and suddenly won a seat in the House—a position to which Low himself has for long, plodding years aspired. Their jealousy is much increased by Phineas' social virtuosity and by his Nijinsky-like leap into the embattled world of high-powered Liberal party deliberations and intrigues. A further example of jealousy is that of Madame Max Goesler. Phineas, once again, does not realize that the lady is in love with him, and makes her a confidante of his love for Violet Effingham. Subtler than Lady Laura, Madame Max comforts Phineas when he comes to her in a very low state after learning that Violet Effingham has at last accepted Lord Chiltern:

' "In this country it is so much to be a lord," said Madame Goesler. Phineas thought a moment of that matter before he replied...

' "I do not in my heart believe that that has had anything to do with it," he said.

'But it has, my friend,—always. I do not know your Violet Effingham."

' "She is not mine."

' "Well;—I do not know this Violet that is not yours. I have met her, and did not specially admire her. But then the tastes of men and women about beauty are never the same..." '

In the *Finn* novels there is yet another form of jealousy or envy—that of Quintus Slide, the editor of the radical *People's Banner* who would like to have obtained a seat in the House with the ease with which Phineas got his; a good deal of Mr Slide's official time is spent in delving around for any spiteful piece of information with which he can pillory Phineas Finn in his newspaper.

These examples of jealousy come from the two *Finn* novels

only, but in most of Trollope's other novels—except for *The Warden*, *Miss Mackenzie*, *The Belton Estate*, *Cousin Henry* and *Dr Wortle's School*—jealousy plays a role almost, but not quite, as potent as that of money. It is an especially strong motive power in the sixth and last of the Palliser novels, *The Duke's Children*, published in 1880.

(v)

The strong-willed, pertinacious troop of characters in the Palliser novels pursued their creator down the arches of almost twenty years. The first one of all, *Can You Forgive Her?*, written in 1863 and issued in part numbers throughout 1864, coincided with the publication of Charles Dickens's *Our Mutual Friend*. In that year also Mrs Gaskell was at work on her last novel, *Wives and Daughters*. The final volume of the Palliser series, *The Duke's Children*, emerged in 1880 into a transformed literary atmosphere: at Oxford the undergraduate Oscar Wilde was founding his aesthetic movement and proclaiming its amoral aspirations; the young Henry James was writing *The Portrait of a Lady*. There was moreover by now a generation gap amongst English novel-readers—the young ladies to whom in their schoolrooms, Trollope as mentor had crept so close were now matronly mothers with daughters of their own. The reading tastes of these up-to-date girls would have been formed less by the works of old Anthony Trollope, with his tousled white beard and baggy trousers, than by Ouida's *Moths* or by the later novels of Rhoda Broughton, who had made her name with *Cometh Up as a Flower*, *Dr Cupid* and *Not Wisely but Too Well*. Should any of these modern young ladies have abstracted *The Duke's Children* from the weekly book-box from Mudie's, she would have found an absorbing, topical novel about the vagaries and rebellions of her own generation.

What a newcomer to the Palliser novels would not have realized in the 1880s was that this tale of splintering social barriers by rebellious youth in the high reaches of the British aristocracy forms but the sixth and final instalment of kaleidoscopic social history, which includes over the years the old Duke of Omnium, his nephew the future duke, Plantagenet Palliser, Palliser's outspoken wife, Lady Glencora, Phineas Finn and Marie Max Goesler, Lord and Lady Chiltern, the Duke and Duchess of St Bungay, Cantrips and several score of other characters. The reading young ladies of the 'eighties, with tight skirts and bustles and waists laced in for the hour-glass look, frizzled hair over the foreheads (a fashion which Queen Victoria thought made them look like 'little poodles'), would have found the old illustrations of, say, *Can You Forgive Her?* comically outmoded —Alice Vavasor, for example, languishing in her huge crinoline on the hotel balcony above the Rhine at Basle. But with *The Duke's Children* they would have been too late to meet the most dashing and delightful of all Trollope's women—Lady Glencora Palliser, later Duchess of Omnium. By the third page of the first volume Lady Glencora is dead. She lies in her grave in the parish burying-ground amidst the priory ruins at Matching, the ducal house in Yorkshire, 'almost within sight of her own bedroom window'. Unlike the death of Mrs Proudie, which was forced on him by the discussion he had heard at the Athenaeum Club, Lady Glencora's death is essential to the development of this great novel's central theme—the inability of the undemonstrative and widowed Duke to cope adequately with the daily problems which his two sons and his daughter present to him. The death of Mrs Proudie has no visible effect on the steady course of *The Last Chronicle of Barset*; the Duchess of Omnium's death in her early forties leaves her husband, her sons and her daughter adrift in a sea of misunderstanding, wealth and grandeur. The Duke, who had never reflected upon how important his wife had been to him, is left utterly prostrated by his bereavement:

'It was as though a man should be suddenly called to live without hands or even arms. Hitherto he had never specially acknowledged to himself that his wife was necessary to him as a component part of his life. Though he had loved her dearly ... he had sometimes been inclined to think that in the exuberance of her spirits she had been a trouble rather than a support to him. But it was as though all outside appliances were taken away from him. There was no one of whom he could ask a question.'

In Mrs Proudie's case Trollope had to dream up a long-standing heart condition which left his readers sceptical and angry. The death of Glencora Omnium is, on the contrary, characteristic and convincing. The whole family—'with a large accompaniment of tutors, ladies'-maids, couriers and sometimes friends'—had spent months amongst the Italian lakes and then moved to Rome. Here Lady Glencora had begun to connive at the mutual passion of her daughter and a twenty-two-year old boy from Cornwall; her interference in this without the Duke's knowledge was the worst of her legacies and led, as her actions so often before had led, into a sea of troubles. Her legacies to her only daughter had been beauty and the most stubborn obstinacy. Her elder son, Lord Silverbridge, had inherited her irresistible charm of manner, her egotism and a recklessness which enabled him to lose £70,000 in one go to swindlers at the Derby. Although high-spirited and gay, the Duchess had always been delicate and prone to catch cold, particularly when wandering as was her wont in the ruins of Matching Priory beneath a cold December moon and a frosty starlit sky. She does not die from a death-wish, she is eagerly planning a coming-out campaign for her daughter Mary in the near London season, for it is already early spring. The family stay a few days at their house in Carlton Gardens, and then head north for Matching, which had been handed over to his nephew and his wife on their marriage by the sybaritic, aloof old Duke of Omnium with the words: 'It's the most comfortable house I know.' Lady Glencora had made the rooms at Matching pretty as well as comfortable and she must now have been relieved to find herself at home again in all the ease of Matching Priory after a solid year of continental hotels, which no amount of ladies'-maids or couriers could have rendered domestic. But—'when she left town the Duchess was complaining of cold, sore throat, and debility. A week after their arrival at Matching she was dead.'

There is no doubt that Anthony Trollope himself saw this and the other five Palliser novels as forming one single unit, and regretted to think that each of the six books contributory to this unit would 'be forgotten by the most zealous reader almost as soon as read'. An eminent Trollopian authority, Dr Smalley of the University of Illinois, has suggested that a paragraph in the pages of the *Autobiography* dealing with *The Prime Minister* (a novel at that time criticized for its 'vulgarity') contains a hint that Anthony would like his readers to be in a position to recall the antecedent actions of the main characters, perhaps even to remember them as he himself has done 'for many years past . . . manufacturing within my own mind the characters of [Palliser] and his wife'. In another passage of the *Autobiography* he admits how much he has enjoyed writing his novels—a confession which runs counter to his official shoe-maker or craftsman–novelist pronouncements and is surely much nearer the truth. He describes periods when he has been able to imbue himself thoroughly with the characters he has on hand:

'. . . I have wandered alone among the woods and rocks, crying at their grief, laughing at their absurdities, and thoroughly enjoying their joy. I have been impregnated with my own creations till it has been my only excitement to sit with the pen in my hand, and drive my team before me at as quick a pace as I could make them travel.'

He could, it would seem, remember everything that Lady Glencora and her husband had said to one another over the years. This total recall of dialogue is not, in my own experience, usual amongst authors; in Anthony Trollope's case it is supporting evidence—if such be needed—that he was for ever listening to what his characters were saying in 'that world outside the world' within his head, a world which he had been exploring since early childhood. In December 1881, writing to Arthur Tilley, a son of Trollope's brother-in-law Sir John Tilley by his second wife, he raises a corner of the curtain which he customarily liked to draw over his natural and personal liking for praise:

'*Barchester Towers* was written before you were born. Of course I forget every word of it! But I don't. There is not a passage in it I do not remember. I always have to pretend to forget when people talk to me about my own old books. It looks modest;—and to do the other thing looks the reverse. But the writer never forgets. And when after thirty years he is told by some one that he has been pathetic, or witty, or even funny, he always feels like lending a five-pound note to that fellow.'

Do not these disarming words chime with the ring of truth?

(vi)

'This is Sunday Night: 10 p.m. [Edward FitzGerald wrote to a friend in the year 1873], and what is the Evening Service which I have been listening to? The "Eustace Diamonds"; which interest me almost as much as Tichborne [the Tichborne Claimant trial] I really give the best proof I can of the Interest I take in Trollope's Novels, by constantly breaking out into Argument with the Reader (who never replies) about what is said or done by the People in the several novels. I say "No, no! She must have known she was lying!"—"He couldn't have been such a fool!" etc.'

Edward FitzGerald, a minor poet and translator and unquestionably one of the letter-writers of genius in Victorian England, kept himself amused in his Suffolk hermitage by having a selected local boy read aloud to him the latest novels which arrived at Woodbridge in Mudie's boxes. FitzGerald was not alone in enjoying *The Eustace Diamonds*, for when published in

1872, the book achieved a wild popularity, which Anthony himself felt repaired 'the injury' which he fancied that his recent novels had done his reputation. While writing this swift and irresistible book he had had secret qualms that Lizzie Eustace might be turning out to be a mere mirror-reflection of Becky Sharp. He afterwards admitted that these fears were groundless—for, indeed, the whole fascination of Lady Eustace is that she is not, like Rebecca, a poised adventuress, but a malicious, wavering and surprisingly ignorant young woman who always manages to do things by halves and so to be found out. The plot, in which Trollope excels himself (for, as we know, he thought plots his weakest point), was not cut and dried beforehand. Even the 'robbery' at the hotel in Carlisle, when thieves carry off the empty iron coffer which usually contains the heirloom diamond necklace with which the widowed Lady Eustace refuses to part, was, Anthony tells us, quite unforeseen by himself: 'I had no idea of setting thieves after the bauble till I had got my heroine to bed in the inn at Carlisle; nor of the disappointment of the thieves, till Lizzie had been wakened in the morning with the news that her door had been broken open.' The picture of Lizzie Eustace's dilemma when faced by her friends, the hotel manager and the Carlisle police, is a perfect example of Anthony Trollope's insight—for the diamonds, which had spent the night under Lady Eustace's pillow, are still in her possession. What shall she do with them? Throw them into the sea?—but they are worth £10,000. Take them back to her Scottish Castle and bury them in the grounds? No. After perjuring herself over the presumed theft to the Carlisle police, Lizzie 'almost enjoyed it. As her mind went on making fresh schemes on the subject, a morbid desire of increasing the mystery took possession of her ... There was great danger, but there might be delight and even profit if she could safely dispose of the jewels before suspicion against herself should be aroused.' She continues the train journey to London with the friends who have been staying with her at Portray Castle, the diamonds locked in her travelling desk, and its key hung round her neck.

The Eustace Diamonds is a novel with an opening sentence devised to thrust the reader into what Anthony Trollope (who at times affected Latin) would have called *medias res*: 'It was admitted by all her friends, and also by her enemies—who were in truth the more numerous and active body of the two—that Lizzie Greystock had done very well for herself.' All that she had had to help her to entrap Sir Florian Eustace, a young bachelor baronet of great wealth, had been her looks and a useful gift for acting and for assuming tones and expressions which suited particular circumstances. A great beauty, with a perfect oval face, dark hair worn in a wreath round her head, and one curling love-lock hanging down to her shoulder, Lizzie had a single defect—her blue eyes which 'were too expressive, too loud in their demands for attention, and they lacked tenderness'. Trollope himself enunciates, in a further development of his description of Lady Eustace's eyes, his own conviction that the most soft and sweet and tender and true colour for a woman's eyes is green. As in many other instances, he tells us of his heroine's manner and carriage—Lady Eustace has a sinuous, snake-like grace which goes well with her character.

When the book opens Lizzie Greystock's campaign to captivate Sir Florian Eustace, a handsome and gallant young soldier of twenty-eight, is over and done with; she has married him and he is dead within a year. But in order to explain her character Trollope gives us a *resumé* of her past strategy and tactics. Sir Florian's humble admiration for the intellect that she possesses and he does not, puts a dangerous weapon in her hands. She reads poetry aloud to him by lamplight and explains to him the pleasures of the mind: 'And then she told him of such wondrous thoughts,—such wondrous joys in the world which would come from thinking.' At nineteen, Lizzie herself speaks perfect French, reads German and can understand a certain amount of Italian. The orphan daughter of a spendthrift Admiral, the only thing she really knows about money is how to buy jewellery on credit, and how then to pawn that to pay essential expenses:

'Certain things must be paid for,—one's own maid for instance; and one must have some money in one's pocket for railway-trains and little nick-nacks which cannot be had on credit. Lizzie when she was nineteen knew how to do without money as well as most girls; but there were calls which she could not withstand, debts which even she must pay.'

She knows that Sir Florian Eustace is a man of immense wealth and many estates 'quite unencumbered'. She also knows, before he tells her, that the doctors have condemned him to an early death from consumption: 'The fear of death never cast a cloud over that grandly beautiful brow ... Consumption had swept a hecatomb of victims from the family. But still they were grand people, and never were afraid of death.' Lizzie Greystock dreads that the ensuing English winter might kill Sir Florian off before they were safely married: 'Oh, heavens! if all these golden hopes should fall to the ground, and she should come to be known only as the girl who had been engaged to the late Sir Florian!' Both bride and groom are haunted by this fear of his death—but in Sir Florian's case because he loves Lizzie and does not want to die without possessing her. They are married in September and in the following month go south to Italy where Sir Florian, completely disillusioned as to his wife's hard, unloving, mercenary character, dies. Lady Eustace, who is pregnant, returns to England, an astoundingly beautiful and rich young widow. After her son's birth she sets up in a rented house in Mount Street and begins to turn her attention to her inheritance, which she is too ignorant to understand, to her Scottish estate in which she has only a life interest, and to retaining the family diamonds to which she has no vestige of right.

As a novel, *The Eustace Diamonds* swings briskly along like a well-sprung brougham and without trailing off into what Edward FitzGerald called Trollope's *longueurs*. The pace of the book is much aided by frequent flashes of irony, by intensely awkward situations, and, above all, by Trollope's lucid, lenient judgments on his characters' motives and behaviour. Many times we are brought to feel pity for Lady Eustace, who is one of those 'people who can be wise within a certain margin, but beyond that commit great imprudences'. He goes so far as to suppose that she must have felt a few regrets and even a little remorse after her husband's terrible death: 'There must have been qualms as she looked at his dying face, soured with the disappointment she had brought upon him, and listened to the harsh querulous voice that was no longer eager in the expressions of love.' Trollope's theory here is that 'as man is never strong enough to take unmixed delight in good, so may we presume also that he cannot be quite so weak as to find perfect satisfaction in evil'. That tolerance which the impatient Anthony seldom displayed in his own life he extended with a beautiful, a balanced generosity even to the most reprehensible inhabitants of his world outside the world. Moreover, in the case of Lady Eustace, he cherished a sneaking admiration for her—and most of his readers then or since have surely felt the same. It is significant of his attitude to the nervous and bemused Lizzie that he permits his favourite female character, Lady Glencora Palliser, to make a rash stand in her favour. Early on, before the diamonds have seemed to have disappeared, but when the legal right of Lizzie Eustace to keep them is a topic of the London season, the young widow arrives at an evening party at the

Pallisers wearing the famous diamonds. 'I like her for wearing them,' Lady Glencora typically remarks to Violet Chiltern—for Lady Glencora has far more respect for courage and spirit than for legal niceties or social conventions.

The old Duke of Omnium, growing weaker and gradually becoming childish, now spends most of his time at Matching, being looked after by Madame Max Goesler and by his nephew's wife. As aged people will, he develops an obsession, his predilection being the mystery of the Eustace diamonds; Lady Glencora goes so far as to have the latest gossip about the diamonds telegraphed to her from London to amuse the Duke. The Liberal politician, Mr Bonteen, is staying with a number of other guests at Matching Priory. Talk on one evening—and probably on every other evening too—centres round Lady Eustace's perjury. Mr Bonteen is, characteristically, very much against Lizzie Eustace and 'triumphantly' asks the company :

' "And as for that woman, does anybody mean to say that she should not have been indicted for perjury?"

' "That woman, as you are pleased to call her, is my particular friend," said Lady Glencora. When Lady Glencora made any such statement as this,—and she often did make such statements,—no one dared to answer her ... She had attained this position for herself by a mixture of beauty, rank, wealth and courage;—but the courage had of the four, been her greatest mainstay.

'Lord Chiltern, who was playing billiards with Barrington Earl, rapt his cue on the floor and made a speech. "I never was so sick of anything in my life as I am of Lady Eustace. People have talked about her for the last six months."

' "Only three months, Lord Chiltern," said Lady Glencora in a tone of rebuke.

' "And all that I can hear of her is, that she had told a lot of lies and lost a necklace ...

' "When Lady Chiltern loses a necklace worth ten thousand pounds there will be talk of her," said Lady Glencora.'

At this moment Madame Max Goesler, who has been sitting with the infirm old duke, comes into the billiard-room and whispers to Lady Glencora that he wants to be taken to bed.

' "Wants to go to bed, does he? Very well, I'll go to him."

' " He seems to be quite fatigued with his fascination about Lady Eustace."

' "I call that woman a perfect God-send. What should we have done without her?" This Lady Glencora said almost to herself as she prepared to join the duke. The duke had only one more observation to make before he retired for the night. "I'm afraid, you know, that your friend hasn't what I call a good time before her, Glencora."'

With this opinion of the Duke of Omnium's the readers of the story will perhaps agree.

It is on this note the Trollope ended *The Eustace Diamonds*. Just as he began the book with an admirable briskness, so he completes it in the same energetic mood. We are, for once, spared the lych-gate and the orange blossom and the departure for a honeymoon amidst the Swiss lakes. We are earlier told that Lizzie Eustace has made an unwise second marriage in the Episcopal church at Ayr 'far from the eyes of curious Londoners'. Her bridegroom is the Reverend Joseph Emilius, a preacher fashionable on the outskirts of Mayfair, but of Bohemian Jewish extraction. In *Phineas Redux* we learn without surprise that this marriage had not been a success; but in that novel it is proved that Mr Emilius already has a wife in Prague. He is also known to have committed the murder of Mr Bonteen but cannot be tried as there is insufficient evidence. He is, however, sentenced for bigamy, and Lady Eustace is once more fancy-free. It is with a genuine surge of pleasure that we greet her again in the pages of *The Prime Minister*, even though she has by then, alas, a rather tarnished reputation and a second-rate circle of pinchbeck friends.

(vii)

The Eustace Diamonds was serialized in the *Fortnightly Review* from July 1871 to February 1873, and was published as a book in December of the latter year. Trollope had taken the unusually long period of nine months to write his tale of Lizzie Eustace's misadventures. *Phineas Finn* had absorbed him for six months; its four major chronological successors, *He Knew He Was Right*, *The Vicar of Bullhampton*, *Sir Harry Hotspur of Humblethwaite* and *Ralph the Heir* had taken him seven months, five months, two months and four months respectively. During this same highly fertile period, 1867 to 1870, he also published *The Golden Lion of Grandpère*, *Linda Tressel*, and a batch of short and miscellaneous stories headed by *Lotta Schmidt*, Lotta being a pretty Viennese shopgirl who suffers from the standard complaint of most of Trollope's English heroines—an inability to make up her mind between two suitors for her hand.

While he was writing *The Eustace Diamonds* Trollope was also at work on an Enlish version of Caesar's *Commentaries*, which had been commissioned by John Blackwood for his new series *Ancient Classics for English Readers*. Freed for ever from his postal duties, he could, after his early morning rendezvous with Lady Eustace, spend the later morning and the afternoon on research for this potted classic: 'It has been a tough bit of work,' he wrote to Blackwood, 'but I have enjoyed it amazingly. It has been a change to the spinning of novels and has enabled me to surround myself with books and almost to think myself a scholar.' He began by going through the twelve Latin commentaries twice without a crib, and thus incidentally formed a new and enviable habit of reading Latin authors in the original for an hour or two every day. When his *Caesar* was finished he made the elegant gesture of giving the copyright to his friend John Blackwood as a birthday present. Anthony called it 'a dear little book' and 'a good little book'. Even when translating and condensing Julius Caesar, he had kept his favourite group of hypothetical readers in mind—English girls in English schoolrooms: 'A well-educated girl who had read it and remembered it would perhaps know as much about Caesar and his writings as she need know.' The little book was received by the critics with either faint praise or a deathly silence: 'Nobody praised it. One very old and very learned friend to whom I sent it thanked me for my "comic Caesar", but said no more. I do not suppose he intended to run a dagger into me. Of any sufferings from such wounds, I think, while living, I never shewed a sign; but still I have suffered occasionally.'

Sir Harry Hotspur of Humblethwaite and *Ralph the Heir* are, both of them, better books than *The Vicar of Bullhampton* but far and away less gripping than *The Eustace Diamonds*. *Hotspur* is set in Cumberland at Sir Harry's ancestral seat, Humblethwaite. Sir Harry and Lady Hotspur have lost their only son, and the whole estate, which is not entailed, will go to their daughter Emily, a fair, short girl: 'Her complexion was as fair as the finest porcelain; but there were ever roses in her cheeks, for she was strong by nature and her health was perfect. She was somewhat short of stature ... and her feet and hands and ears were small and delicate.' Emily Hotspur's rude health does not, however, save her from disaster. She falls irretrievably in love with her handsome cousin, George Hotspur, a complete scapegrace and a counterpart of George Vavasor, Alice Vavasor's cousin in *Can You Forgive Her?* In Trollope's novels cousins are seldom good news, the worst but most pathetic of the lot being Henry Jones in the novel *Cousin Henry*. Henry gets his uncle's estate, Llanfeare in South Wales, by a very curious form of fraudulent inactivity. The best Trollope cousin is Owen FitzGerald, the devil-may-care scamp of Hap House in County Cork, who, we may remember, when refused by the pale and delicate Lady Clara Desmond, elopes abroad with her pretty young brother instead.

In *Sir Harry Hotspur*, Emily's cousin George, beautiful and worthless, is heir to the baronetcy only; he concocts a scheme by which, married to Emily, he would join the title to the land once more for his own benefit. Kept by a London actress, whom he finally marries, George Hotspur is a weak deceiver; even when, for Emily's sake, Sir Harry Hotspur most reluctantly agrees to the engagement on condition that George gives up drinking, gambling and all other metropolitan pleasures, he finds he cannot stomach Emily's innocent efforts at his rehabilitation. When he escapes to London and his mistress once more, the roses in Emily Hotspur's porcelain cheeks begin to fade. Hoping to arrest her decline, Sir Harry and his wife take her to the Swiss and Italian Lakes, where she ends up in the Anglican cemetery at Lugano. After her death Sir Harry adopts as his heir a rich young peer to whom he is distantly related but who may never live at Humblethwaite Hall or be in the least interested in the old family estate. It is the breaking of the proud old man's heart, rather than the betrayal of Emily's, that gives this book a certain poignancy of despair. The Cumberland landscape —which Anthony had known when his mother and Tom were building a house there in his youth—like that of Westmorland in *Can You Forgive Her?* is so well evoked as to put out of court the theory that Trollope was oblivious to the beauties of the English countryside. Even his friend and admirer Frederick Harrison in his essay on Anthony Trollope, published in 1895, held this conviction, writing that Trollope cared little for the poetic aspect of nature. 'His books, like Thackeray's, hardly contain a single fine picture of the country, of the sea, of mountains, or of rivers.' He believed that, 'like other sporting men', Anthony's only appreciation of the countryside was formed by whether it was 'good or bad as it promised or did not promise a good "run"'.

Ralph the Heir, with its needlessly teasing brace of young cousins both of whom are named Ralph Newton, is the book in which Trollope worked off all the irritations he had personally experienced when standing as a Liberal candidate for Beverley in November 1868. Trollope himself considered *Ralph the Heir* to be one of the worst novels he had ever written: 'Ralph the heir has not much life about him; while Ralph who is not the heir, but is intended to be the real hero, has none. The same may be said of the young ladies,—of whom she who was meant to be the chief has passed utterly out of my mind without leaving a trace of remembrance behind.'

The year 1870, in which the translation of Caesar's *Commentaries* was completed, *The Eustace Diamonds* finished, and *An Eye for an Eye* and *Phineas Redux* written and put away for later publication, was also the year in which Anthony Trollope relinquished the editorship of the *St Paul's Magazine*. Two further big decisions were now made by Anthony and his wife:— to get rid of Waltham House and live for the future in London, and to sail the next year to Australia, to be present at their son Fred's marriage to a Miss Susan Farrand. This was to take place in December 1871. The move from Waltham House, with its happy, hospitable associations, was unpleasant enough but it seemed financially a necessity. Anthony also had a theory that he would give up hunting and so there was no reason for them to live in the country. Waltham had been a convenient headquarters for work in his large postal district; but now he had abandoned the Post Office, he was dependent upon his writings for a living, and he no longer had to harbour his clerks in an empty wing of Waltham House.

Resigning from the Post Office had filled him with regret, for he had long been proud of the radical changes he had made in the British postal system, often by forcing the hand of his superior, Sir Rowland Hill. During his thirty-three years in the service, he would have us believe that he had 'thought very much more about the Post Office than I had of my literary work'. He had set certain ideals before himself when he became a Postal Surveyor: that people in small villages should be able to buy stamps; that their letters should be delivered free and early in the day; that letter-carriers and sorters should not be overworked; that they should be properly paid and have adequate time off; that they should be made to earn their wages; and that 'pillar letter-boxes' which were considered by Trollope to be his own invention should be erected 'in the streets and ways of England', the first one being installed in Jersey. Over some of these aims he had had to fight: 'How I loved, when I was contradicted,—as I was very often and no doubt properly,

—to do instantly as I was bid, and then prove that what I was doing was fatuous, dishonest, expensive and impracticable! And then there were feuds,—such delicious feuds!' All this agitation was now over and done with. Anthony had given in his resignation in a fit of anger at the promotion of a much younger man over his head to the important position of Under-Secretary which had then fallen vacant. By leaving so suddenly, he forfeited his claim to any pension, which was never paid until a man was sixty. Of this step Anthony writes that it 'was not unattended with peril, what many would call rash, and which, when taken, I should be sure at some period to regret'. On the other hand he also describes himself at this time as sighing for liberty. So seriously had he taken his official duties at Waltham Cross that he was often driven into writing his novels at night as his mother used to do, as well as writing in his customary way at dawn. In the London season the Anthony Trollopes would come up to town (as the phrase went) two or three days in the week, and the official work had proved a hindrance to this. On balance, his retirement made him happy, but by the mid-'seventies his popularity was on the wane. To make a comfortable living he was forced to write more and more and more novels, as well as to contribute articles to the periodical magazines and to give paid lectures. There was no visible diminution of the agreeable style in which Anthony Trollope and his wife liked to live. On their return from Australia after twenty months' absence they set about looking for a London house, and finally chose one north of the Park, 39 Montagu Square, which they inhabited for eight years. The premium on the house, £1,250, was paid out of the advance Anthony had obtained for *The Eustace Diamonds*.

After a tedious eighteen-day delay, the liner *The Great Britain* sailed from Liverpool on May 24th, 1871. As well as Mr and Mrs Anthony Trollope, the cook from Waltham House was aboard, a wise addition to the little party taken with them most probably as a result of Fred Trollope's lurid reports of Australian bush *cuisine*. On the first morning out of Liverpool, Anthony was at work in his cabin on a new novel, *Lady Anna*. He left some manuscripts with his elder son, Harry, who was still holding down his job at Chapman and Hall's. *Ralph the Heir* was already being serialized in the *St Paul's Magazine*, while arrangements had been made for the sale of *The Eustace Diamonds* and for its serialization in the *Fortnightly Review*, beginning on the first of July. A strong-box guarded by Harry in his office at 193 Piccadilly contained the complete manuscript of *Phineas Redux*, which was later sold to the *Graphic* to appear in serial form. Also in the strong-box was the holograph of *An Eye for an Eye*, the very effective story of seduction and murder on the cliffs of Mohir in County Clare which had, according to the *Autobiography*, been 'some time written' and was not published until 1879. It amused Anthony Trollope to think that had *The Great Britain* been wrecked as her sister ship *The Queen of the Thames* had been off Africa that very March, there would have been quite a number of works of his which could have been posthumously published. He writes that he was uncertain how many hitherto unpublished books by a dead writer the public would stand: 'I fear that the numbers appearing month after month, and year after year, with persistent regularity—when the man who wrote them was all but forgotten,—would weary the British public. From the shade of Dickens they would have been accepted, but not, I fear, from mine.'

Before leaving London, Trollope had, of course, got a commission from Chapman and Hall for a solid, informative book on Australia and New Zealand, conceived as an aid to young men and women wishing to emigrate to the Antipodes. He had also arranged to write regular articles on these colonies for the *Daily Telegraph*. His book *Australia and New Zealand* came out in two volumes in February 1873, and ran to more than a thousand pages.* He himself describes the book as 'dull and long'; it was written on the spot, from day to day, with what he calls 'unflagging labour for a period of fifteen months'. Its interest today consists of the glimpses it gives of Australian life both in the bush and in the cities—for, like his book on the United States, the political and constitutional arguments, the statistics and the economics are no more of interest save to historians, and it is the social historian who will get most out of it in any case. It will, however, be worth our while to see how Anthony Trollope and his wife fared down under.

* An admirable small anthology from Trollope's book has been published by Nelson of Melbourne and Sydney, the work of Professor Hume Dow of Melbourne University (1966).

15 : Mutton for Tea

While kicking his heels in London waiting for the delayed departure of the boat from Liverpool, Anthony had been paying calls on friends to bid them farewell. He had luncheon at The Priory with George Eliot and Lewes to meet Turgenev, but he has left no comment on that Russian genius—and, indeed, most probably had never read anything which Turgenev wrote. One evening he dined with the Irish novelist Charles Lever, who called this meal 'a feast of Lucullus, capital talking'. Lever was an old friend from Dublin days, and was now an unhappy widower living as British Consul in Trieste. Anthony was apparently fonder of Lever than Lever was of him:

'I don't think Trollope pleasant, though he has a certain hard common-sense about him and coarse shrewdness that prevents him from being dull or tiresome. His books are not of a high order, but I am still always surprised that he could write them. He is a good fellow, I believe, *au fond*, and has few jealousies, and no rancours; and, for a writer, is not that saying much?'

This was the last occasion on which the two novelists met, for by the time that the Trollopes came back from Australia, Charles Lever was dead.

Lady Anna, the novel which he began to write on the first day out from Liverpool, was completed in the two months it took *The Great Britain* to reach the Trollopes' port of disembarkation, Melbourne, the capital of the colony of Victoria. Anthony is very specific about the rate at which he worked on *Lady Anna*: for eight weeks he wrote sixty-six pages of manuscript every day, save for one solitary day when he was ill. Each page of the manuscript contained two hundred and fifty words, and every word, he assures us, was counted. The scenes of the book are set in Bloomsbury, in the Lake District, in the Yorkshire rectory of Yoxham, and in the ruins of Bolton Abbey. The period Trollope selected is, for some obscure reason, the reign of William IV—that is to say in the old coaching days before the steam-engine; the coach from York to London by which Lady Anna travels took almost twenty-four hours to traverse the distance:

'The girl sat confounded, astounded, without power of utterance. She had travelled from York to London, inside one of those awful vehicles of which we used to be so proud when we talked of our stage coaches. She was thoroughly weary and worn out. She had not breakfasted that morning, and was sick and ill at ease, not only in heart, but in body also. Of course it was so. Her mother knew that it was so. But this was no time for fond compassion.'

In every way *Lady Anna* is, and was surely intended to be, an iconoclastic book. The *Saturday Review* critic called it 'the sort of thing the reading public will never stand except in a period of political storm and ferment', and felt constrained to reveal the plot of the novel so that Trollope's public 'may not be betrayed unawares into reading what will probably leave a disagreeable impression'. In extenuation the only thing which this reviewer could say for the novel and its author was that he had heard it suggested 'that the plot of this story is the carrying out of a bet'. Why did *Lady Anna* arouse so violent a revulsion? Is it a novel of adultery, atheism or sexual perversion? No; it is an admirable and moving novel about a dead earl's heiress daughter who chooses to marry a young journeyman-tailor from Keswick, an idealist who holds radical views, and has been her childhood sweetheart. Apart from its own excellence as a tale, *Lady Anna's* reception by the public casts a clear beam on to Victorian prejudices and is thus of socio-historical interest to us today. We have seen that the story of the little country prostitute, Carry Brattle, in *The Vicar of Bullhampton* provoked none of the shocked objections which Trollope had anticipated that it would. The tale of Carry Brattle's downfall was even recommended by reviewers as suitable for young ladies and for family reading; the story of Lady Anna Lovel and her journeyman lover, Daniel Thwaite, on the other hand, seemed an evil, dangerous attack not on morals or religion but on the social structure of English society itself. Why?

Lady Anna, although it deals with a pair of high-minded but socially unequal lovers, is not so much a love-story as yet another description of a monomania quite as extreme as that of Louis Trevelyan in *He Knew He was Right*, or of Mr Robert Kennedy in the Phineas Finn novels. The story, which involves us in intricate legal details, is never for a moment dull. The central figure is Lady Anna's mother, Countess Lovel, who would have preferred her daughter to die than to be happily married to Daniel Thwaite whom, towards the close of the book, the ferocious Countess tries to shoot with an old-fashioned pistol. Lady Lovel, born a Murray and very poor, had married a debauched old earl from social ambition. Before her one child, Anna, was born, he taunted Josephine Lovel with the fact that he already had a wife living in Italy and that thus she was his mistress, not his wife. He then disappeared on his yacht, and came back many years later to die at Lovel Grange. Meanwhile Lady Lovel begins a lawsuit to prove him bigamous, which his lawyers win for him. Hopelessly impoverished and having no settled alimony, she goes to live with her daughter in the house of a radical old Keswick tailor, Thomas Thwaite, who advances her money to the tune of £9,000. Anna is persecuted by other children in Keswick, but one boy always protects her—the tailor's son Daniel. They become secretly engaged as they grow up. Because of litigation over the Earl's will, in which half a million pounds are at stake, the Thwaites and Lady Lovel and her daughter go to London, taking cheap rooms in Wyndham Street. Since Lady Lovel has borrowed all his father's money, Daniel Thwaite has to work as a paid foreman, not as an independent master tailor. He and Lady Anna continue to regard themselves as engaged, but they still do not tell Lady Lovel. The heir to the earldom is a distant cousin, a fine-looking, well-bred boy who tries to marry Lady Anna, proposing to her amid the ruins of Bolton Abbey. When she tells him of her engagement to Thwaite, he is so horror-struck he can hardly speak. Later, through his lawyers, Lady Lovel hears of it and begins a silent persecution of her daughter by not speaking to her, and using separate rooms in the house. It transpires at last that Anna is legitimate after all, and so heiress to a capital which brings in £30,000 a year. Eventually, when she is twenty-one, she flouts her mother's wishes, marries Daniel Thwaite and gives half her fortune to her young cousin the Earl. It will be seen that it is not, as Henry James remarked of another Trollope novel, 'a very tangled skein'.

Trollope writes that his intention in letting her marry her tailor was to justify Anna and to carry his readers along with him in his sympathy for the faithful girl; but, he writes,

'everybody found fault with me for marrying her to the tailor. What would they have said if I had allowed her to jilt the tailor and marry the good-looking young lord? How much louder, then, would have been the censure! ... The horror which was expressed to me at the evil thing I had done, in giving the girl to the tailor, was the strongest testimony I could conceive of the merits of the story.'

Far from sympathizing with Lady Anna's plight, Trollope's readers thought her little better than an anarchist, and probably sacrilegious as well. During one of her tantrums over Anna's refusal to jilt Thwaite and accept the young Earl, Lady Lovel accuses her daughter of ingratitude and of committing a sin against God. The introduction of the Deity in this context is, I believe, unique even in Trollope's studies of snobs:

'"Foolish, ungrateful girl! It is not for Lord Lovel that I am pleading to you. It is for the name, and for your own honour. Do you not constantly pray to God to keep you in that state of life to which it has pleased him to call you;—and are you not departing from it wilfully and sinfully by such an act as this?" But still Lady Anna continued to say that she was bound by the obligation which was upon her.'

A friend of Lady Anna, a girl called Alice Bluestone, sums up for her the most usual Victorian concept of class distinctions as a safety-barrier. She is speaking to Lady Anna who is staying in the Bluestone parents' house in Bedford Square:

'"I think that a girl who is a lady should never marry a man who is not a gentleman ... That is how it should be;—just as there is with royal people as to marrying royalty. Otherwise everything would get mingled, and there would soon be no difference. If there are to be differences there should be differences. That is the meaning of being a gentleman,—or a lady." '

'"I believe that what I had better do would be to die," said Lady Anna. "Everything would come right then." '

Women friends of the Trollopes sent letters of protest, to which, in his punctilious way, he always replied. A Lady Wood was amongst those who objected to Lady Anna's fate. Trollope replied:

'Of course the girl has to marry the tailor ... To make the discrepancy as great as possible I made the girl an Earl's daughter, and the betrothed a tailor. All the horrors had to be invented to bring about a condition in which an Earl's daughter could become engaged to a tailor without glaring fault on her side.'

One of his persistent admirers, Miss Mary Holmes, had likewise written in resentment at Lady Anna's choice. Miss Holmes, a Roman Catholic spinster with whom he corresponded for fourteen years, was at times critical of his work. In July 1874 he wrote to her from Montagu Square to say:

'... You've trodden on ever so many of my most favourite corns. Lady Anna is the best novel I ever wrote! Very much! Quite far away above all others ! ! !—A lady ought to marry a tailor—if she chanced to fall in love with such a creature, and to promise him, & take his goodness, when she was not a bad lady. That is all! Will you deny it?'

After a honeymoon in Devonshire Lady Anna Thwaite and her husband sail, just as their creator was actually doing, 'for the new colony founded at the Antipodes', in which egalitarian land the marriage of a journeyman tailor and the colossally rich daughter of an earl would probably cause no comment. 'They would at any rate learn something of the new world that was springing up, and [Daniel Thwaite] would then be able to judge whether he would best serve the purpose that he had at heart by remaining there or by returning to England.' In the final, short paragraph of this novel, Anthony Trollope more or less promises a new book on the 'further doings' of the Thwaites in Australia—'of how they travelled and saw many things; and how he became perhaps a wiser man,—the present writer may, he hopes, live to tell'. Most unfortunately a second instalment about the Thwaites was never written. Anthony's only book with an entirely Australian setting is *Harry Heathcote of Gangoil*, a short novel based on young Fred Trollope's life as a sheep-farmer at Mortray Station in New South Wales. *John Caldigate* is sometimes classified as another Australian novel, although only one-third of it deals with gold-mining near the imaginary Australian town of Nobble. But what there is of the gold-miner's life is as good as anything that Trollope ever wrote.

(ii)

John Caldigate, like *Lady Anna* and *Dr Wortle's School*, has alleged bigamy as its primary theme. Its young hero has got into debt at Cambridge, persuades his father to buy him out of his inheritance, a house and estate called Folking, and sets off with a Cambridge friend to try his hand in the gold-mines of an Australian colony. On the eight-week voyage out he and his companion travel second-class—not because they need to do so, but because they think it a good first lesson in the art of roughing it, which they know to be in store for them in the bush. Also in the second-class is a mysterious and graceful woman, some twenty-three years old. Against the advice of more experienced passengers, and even of the Captain of the ship himself, Caldigate becomes entangled in a flirtation with this lady, Mrs Euphemia Smith, widow of a drunken actor; as the ship enters Hobson's Bay to dock at Melbourne, he finds himself inveigled into making her the proposal that they should regard themselves as engaged. Euphemia Smith is so clever that she even warns John Caldigate against herself: 'Women are prehensile things,' she remarks, 'which have to cling to something for nourishment and support. When I come across such a one as you I naturally put out my feelers.' After working successfully in the goldfields at Ahalala near Nobble, Caldigate goes up to Sydney, where Mrs Smith is engaged as a dancer at a music-hall; she follows him back to Ahalala, lives with him as his wife, but becomes so obsessive about making money that they quarrel and separate. When, as a rich young man, he returns to England and lives in his father's house, Folking, in Cambridgeshire, he marries a banker's daughter, with whom he had fallen in love before leaving England for the Antipodes. Just before the christening of his first son, he gets a letter from Mrs Smith, signed 'Euphemia Caldigate', and addressing him as her husband. She and three other goldfield acquaintances come over to England to blackmail him and, by dint of perjury, get Caldigate convicted and sent to prison. The solution of his predicament is worked out with great skill and ingenuity, turning on a forged Sydney postmark on a letter.

In *John Caldigate* Trollope's intimate knowledge of the technicalities of stamps and postmarks comes into use in a novel for the only time—although the writing of long or terse letters had always been a feature of his books. Henry James fancied that it was Anthony Trollope's Post Office career that inspired him to concoct so freely the private correspondence of his characters: 'It is possibly from this source that he derives his fondness for transcribing the letters of his lovelorn maidens and other embarrassed persons. No contemporary story-teller deals so much in letters; the modern English epistle (very happily imitated, for the most part), is his unfailing resource.'

John Caldigate was not written until after Anthony Trollope's second voyage to Australia in 1875 and was neither serialized nor published until 1877. The scenes in the gold-mines were most accurately based on personal experience in the mines at Gympie and Gulgong. He could not avoid being shown the workings at the base of 150-foot shafts, down which he was slowly lowered, with his foot in the noose of a rope. In his travel-book, which he was daily writing while in Australia and later in New Zealand, he praises the civility of the miners; but he remained convinced that gold sold at £3. 10s. or £4. 2s. the ounce had cost the miner £5 an ounce to bring to the surface, sift and sell to the mint or to one of the banks which had sprouted up in the new gold-rush shanty towns. On a goldfield at Gympie in Queensland, Trollope came across a schoolfriend of his own boys, a well-educated handsome youth, who may well have been the prototype for John Caldigate himself. When Anthony found him, he was standing in front of the little tent which he shared with an older working miner, and was occupied in eating a beefsteak out of his frying-pan with a clasp-knife. He and his colleagues had so far found no gold, and it did not seem to Trollope that they seriously expected to do so. The boy had 'no friend near him but his mining friend—or mate as he called him ... He had been softly nurtured and there he was eating a nauseous lump of beef out of a greasy frying-pan with his pocket-knife, just in front of the contiguous blankets stretched on the ground, which constituted the beds of himself and his companion.'

In his lengthy travel-book on the Antipodes, Trollope follows up his account of the old Harrovian gobbling meat out of a frying-pan with a strong warning, or as he puts it, his 'strong and repeated advice to all young English gentlemen' not to take up gold-mining in Australia as a career. *John Caldigate* implicitly provides the same warning. With his habitual and photographic powers of observation, he had watched miners sifting in their pannikins the clay or grit from their shafts which might or might not contain a few specks of gold. The goldfields were dotted with tents in which the men, rolled up in their blankets, slept two or three to a tent. When they had struck gold, a red pennon was run up on a crude flagstaff. Trollope was also shown the more expensive and ambitious method of getting gold—the mechanical crushing of blocks of quartz in the hope of coming across a vein of gold. He even investigated the miners' drinking habits, for, as we have seen, the dangers of alcoholism were never far from his mind. He learned at Gympie and Gulgong that as a general rule miners did not drink while at work, but that, after they had sold enough gold to the banks, they would go off on a wild drinking spree during which they might most probably spend all that they had made. There were exceptions to this rule—the experienced miner, Maggot, who is working in partnership with Caldigate and Shand, is quite unable to resist alcohol after only a few weeks. Caldigate tries to encourage him to lay off alcohol, but Dick Shand accompanies the man to the grog-shop and there they get drunk together. Shand soon becomes a drop-out through drink, and has to take a job as shepherd on the vast and lonely sheep-runs up in Queensland; after that he superintends Polynesian labourers on a sugar plantation. When at length he gets to England, he manages to give vital testimony which helps to get John Caldigate out of jail. To his family Dick Shand looks fifteen years older than when he went away; he now has hollow cheeks and sunken mouth and eyes. He has, however, become a teetotaller which is a source of great interest to his parents and to all Caldigate's friends. A clergyman with the unlikely name of Smirkie, who is married to one of Caldigate's cousins, is particularly vehement:

' "The man is a notorious drunkard. And he has that look of wildness which bad characters always bring with them from the colonies."

' "He didn't drink anything but water at lunch," said one of the younger girls.

' "They never do when they're eating," said Mr Smirkie, for the great teetotal triumph had not as yet been made known to the family at Babington. "These regular drunkards take it at all times by themselves, in their own rooms. He has *delirium tremens* in his face. I don't believe a word that he says."

' "He certainly does wear the oddest trousers I ever saw," said Aunt Polly.'

Euphemia Smith, who has falsely sworn that John Caldigate was her husband, has also fallen victim to alcohol and to the greed for gold. When she and her confederates come to England to blackmail Caldigate, he unwisely gives them £20,000 at the Jericho Coffee House in Levant Court in the City of London. He has not met Euphemia for several years and, when she raises her veil, he sees that she has lost her beauty and looks old and coarse and 'as though she had taken to drinking. But there was still about her something of that look of intellect which had captivated him more, perhaps, than her beauty.' Trollope is always compassionate to his alcoholics, nor, in this case, does he remotely condemn John Caldigate for living with Mrs Euphemia Smith; in writing about this liaison he is considerably bolder than when writing about Carry Brattle, the young prostitute in *The Vicar of Bullhampton*.

In *John Caldigate* there is a fresh study in monomania in the person of Hester Caldigate's mother Mrs Bolton. She is, in her own prim way, just as mad as Lady Anna Lovel's mother with her obsession about rank, or as Louis Trevelyan with his jealousy. Mrs Bolton's particular bent is a religious one, which involves making herself as uncomfortable as she can, seated upright on a hard chair with a Bible, from which she quotes ceaselessly, and some needlework on a small table at her side. She is, at the same time, odiously possessive with her daughter, disapproves of the marriage with Caldigate, who seems to her to have made his Australian fortune in an 'unholy' manner. When it transpires that Caldigate has certainly lived with, and may even have married, Euphemia Smith at Ahalala she is of course the first to believe her son-in-law a bigamist. Mrs Bolton remains implacable to the end of the book, and will never enter Caldigate's house, Folking, in the small parish of Utterden, ten miles from Cambridge. Mad or not, Mrs Bolton acts with great consistency. For her daughter's wedding she sits alone at the back of the church, wearing mourning and a thick black veil.

(iii)

The original intention of Anthony Trollope and his wife when they first planned to go out to the Australian colonies had been (we may remember) to attend Fred Trollope's marriage to Miss Susan Farrand. In the course of time this fruitful union produced six sons and two daughters. By a series of chances, the Trollope baronetcy, which dated from the reign of Charles I, descended to Fred's family—his third son becoming the fourteenth baronet. It would have gratified Anthony, and even more so his mother, to have known the future history of the baronetcy which in their lifetimes had been held by a distant cousin, Sir John Trollope, a connection of which they had both been exceedingly proud. The Anthony Trollopes' opinion of their daughter-in-law goes unrecorded; and the many, many letters which his parents must have written to Fred have all, according to Professor Bradford Booth, vanished. Fred was not making much money at Mortray Station, but his father was proud of him all the same: 'I am sure you will be glad to hear that I find my son all that I can wish—steady, hardworking, skilful and determined,' Anthony wrote to a new Australian friend. Rose Trollope stayed at Mortray Station for an extra six weeks, while Anthony was exploring Brisbane. "I have been up here alone, hammering away at the Colony,' he wrote to Frederic Chapman of Chapman & Hall, in September 1871. 'On the whole I have enjoyed it very much ... I have seen some good kangaroo hunting; but it does not amount after all to very much.'

At this early period of Australian colonization, each state—New South Wales, Queensland, Victoria, Western Australia and so on—was a separate colony, with its own Governor and legislature, and its own customs dues. Fred Trollope's station was in New South Wales, and Mortray itself was two hundred and fifty miles from Sydney. It was considered a small station in comparison with the large estates Anthony Trollope had visited in the Darling Downs; Fred had only 10,000 sheep, one enclosed sheep-paddock of 12,000 acres, two more of 7,000 acres each, a horse-paddock near the house of about 250 acres, and the 'home-paddock' round the house of fifty acres. The wooden house had been built by Frederic on a small creek which went almost dry in hot weather. The whole station was surrounded by what Anthony called 'interminable forest'. It took him, his wife and the Waltham House cook—who soon got herself a nearby squatter as a husband—three days by buggy to get from the nearest railway to Mortray, at the rate of forty miles a day. The wool-shearers lived in their own hut, with their own Chinese cook, a quarter of a mile from the wool-shed. By good luck the postman passed by Mortray on the public road twice a week. Apart from a publican's grog-shop three miles away, and a goldfield town twelve miles from Mortray Station, Fred and his shearers and shepherds lived in total isolation in the bush. There was no vestige of social life, no visiting except from travellers demanding a bed for the night. Fred and his three shearers got up at five o'clock in the morning, and worked till sundown or later. It seemed to Anthony that his son had 'more on hand than a British prime minister in June'. He protested at the cruelty with which Fred's sheep were slung about during the washing process, and wounded in the shearing.

There were four or five meals a day at Mortray, and the Waltham House cook, before she married to become what Anthony called 'quite the lady', had her hands full. On this first visit to Fred's station mutton was eaten day after day. When Anthony returned there a second time, the price of sheep had risen, so that the diet then offered by Fred and his wife consisted of beef. Potatoes were purchased as an ordinary part of the station stores; they were supplemented by what the opossums had left of the lettuces, tomatoes and cabbages in the garden. Under Rose's auspices dinner at eight 'was always dignified with soup and salad', but this was not normal at other stations. 'In other respects the meals were all alike,' wrote Anthony ruefully. 'There was mutton in every shape and there was always tea.' Fred had got in a stock of Australian wines and some bottles of brandy for his father. It was customary for the young shearers and for Fred himself to come in at about dinner-time completely fagged out. They would gulp a glass of weak brandy and water, drunk standing 'as a working man with us takes his glass of beer at a bar. But when they sat down with their dinner before them, the tea-cup did for them what the wine-glass does for us.' In subsequent jaunts to other bush stations the fare was not appetizing; Anthony absolutely jibbed at stewed wallaby, although it had been marinated and boiled in spiced wine. 'I am reduced to the vilest tobacco out of the vilest pipe, and drink the vilest brandy and water—very often in very vile company,' he wrote from Melbourne to George Eliot and G. H. Lewes, complaining that mentally he could no longer 'be at ease with all the new people and new things ... I am struggling to make a good book but I feel that it will not be good. It will be desultory and inaccurate:—perhaps dull, & where shall I be then?'

It is clear from his account of Mortray Station that the Trollope parents must have been quite terribly bored. The deep verandah, which was really used as a drawing-room, was where the men of the family smoked after dinner. Anthony tried to get up a whist table, but soon saw that the young men could not take it seriously and could not even remember the pips on the cards: 'Whist is a jealous mistress,' he reflected, 'and so is a sheep station'. The only refuge for the squatter on so distant a bush station as Fred's was to have recourse to books. 'He has no club, no billiard tables, no public house which he can frequent. Balls and festivities are very rare.' Squatters usually married early, as it was the only way they could get female company or at least get meals cooked and buttons sewn back on to shirts. Every squatter's station Trollope visited had a copy of Shakespeare's plays, and very often Macaulay's Essays and the novels of Dickens as well. In any case the evenings would, in the washing and shearing season, end early, for the men would be tired out and were required to get up at first light. 'As a rule,' Anthony noted, 'gentlemen in the colonies do not sit long over wine; and, as a rule also—and rules of course have their exceptions—the wine is not worth a long sitting.'

To eke out what may well have been a trying visit to Fred's wooden bungaloid home his father would go for long rides in the forest, ordinarily alone. It was a silent world inside the forest, broken only by the magpie's melancholy note or the bull-frog's roar. Kangaroos could be seen staring at you as though uncertain whether they should run away or stand still. Quite soon Anthony began to get that claustrophobia which tropical or virgin forests so frequently inspire. They are at once eerie and meaningless; Anthony complained that

'there arose at last a feeling that go where one might through the forest, one was never going anywhere. It was all picturesque, for ... the trees were not too close for the making of pretty vistas through them—but it was all the same. One might ride on, to the right or the left, or might turn back, and there was ever the same view, and there were no objects to reach unless it was the paddock fence.'

He wrote to Frederick Chapman of his nostalgia for the English hunting-field and for all the hunting he would miss while in the Australian colonies. 'I am living in the middle of the bush, as the primeval forest is here called, in most unsophisticated simplicity, eating mutton and drinking tea,' he told another friend. By May 1872, he wrote to George Smith that he had become 'heartily homesick ... I have interested myself with these colonial people,—as to habits, wages, ways of life & the like; but in regard to social delights I cannot cotton to them thoroughly'.

Since his projected book was to be political as well as merely descriptive, Trollope felt himself obliged to see and to give a verdict on the Australian aborigines, which he did with the same curious lack of sensibility with which he had written about the Negro slaves in Cuba, or the convicts in Bermuda. 'Their doom,' he writes of the original owners of Australia, 'is to be exterminated; and the sooner their doom is accomplished—so that there be no cruelty—the better will it be for civilization'. On another topic of the day, the three-year contracts for Polynesian labourers for the Australian sugar estates, he writes that he never saw one ill-used, nor ever heard of ill-usage. In fact he says that he believes that they 'were fostered too closely—wrapped up too warmly in the lambswool of government protection', and that their diet might be envied by the English rural labourer. Although he cannot exactly be said to have enjoyed all of his eighteen long months in the Australian colonies, Anthony Trollope was fair-minded enough to recognize that working conditions over there offered a completely new form of life, and a very much better one than that of the British working class at home. Any man meaning to work in Australia and New Zealand could earn enough for all his wants. 'The horror of this country,' he wrote to an English friend when back in London, 'is that let men work as they will there is not and cannot be enough for them all.'

Among the rich Australians, a form of hunting based on that

of England was practised. Anthony went to a meet of the stag-hounds on a heath outside Melbourne, and within view of the sea. Here a sumptuous hunt breakfast was served to some two hundred and fifty fox-hunting men and women. They ran a drag, and Anthony later learned that 'a turned down dingo' had been captured alive. On this occasion, Trollope had been mounted on a horse which he thought too small to carry his sixteen stone. He was proved to be right. He thought of his weight, of his near-sightedness and of the timber palings four and a half feet high which he was expected to jump. He hesi-tated between being scorned by his hosts as a coward, or risking his neck. He settled for the latter, and came a cropper over the first fence, which was made of wire as well as wood: 'The horse was quicker on his feet than I was and, liking the sport, joined it at once single-handed, while I was left alone and disconsolate. Men and horses—even the sound of men and horses—disap-peared from me, and I found myself in solitude in a forest of gum-trees.' In Queensland and New South Wales Anthony was taken out kangaroo-hunting, with three other men and four kangaroo-dogs. The pace of fleeing kangaroos was extremely fast, so the runs took only ten or fifteen minutes. An old kan-garoo will sometimes turn and fight the dogs, or the man who is hunting it; such kangaroos are powerful fighters and can inflict terrible wounds with their forepaws. In New South Wales Anthony was amazed to see a hunted kangaroo catch up a terrier in his arms 'and carry the little animal in his embrace through-out the run'. The terrier was unhurt.

Having toured New Zealand, the Anthony Trollopes made their leisurely way home via Hawaii and San Francisco to catch a Cunarder, after some days at the Brevoort House in New York. They were back in London, but homeless, in time for Christmas 1872. For nearly nineteen months they had been at the other side of the world. 'I am beginning to find myself too old to be eighteen months away from home,' Anthony wrote to G. H. Lewes and George Eliot. It had been an absorbing if sometimes testing and often uncomfortable journey through the Antipodes.

Waltham House, for all its spacious charm and romantic aspect, did not sell quickly, and when at last it did so Anthony found that he had lost £800 on the deal. 'As I continually hear that other men make money by selling and buying houses, I presume that I am not well adapted for transactions of that sort,' Anthony writes in *An Autobiography*. The Trollopes had, in fact, spent a good deal of money on improving the house, adding on the ground floor a 'very fine' drawing-room designed to harmonize with the mellow old brick of which the house was built. Waltham House was finally bought by Mr William Paul, known as the Rose King, who owned the Royal Waltham Cross Nurseries and specialized in old-fashioned roses—moss roses, the roses of Provence, damask and tea-scented roses. When Mr Paul purchased Waltham House he consulted two distinguished landscape-gardeners, both of whom advised him to make no alterations in the garden's layout: 'Leave it alone; as an old garden it is inimitable.'

Back from Australia the Trollopes rented a furnished house for the rest of the winter in Holles Street, Cavendish Square. At the beginning of February 1873, they purchased 39 Montagu Square, which, like its twin Bryanston Square, lies to the north of Oxford Street. It was not, Anthony wrote to a woman friend, 'a gorgeous neighbourhood, but one that will suit my declining years and modest resources'. In his autobiography he calls it 'the house in which I hope to live and hope to die'. To an Australian acquaintance he complained that he and his wife were 'going to enter into the ruinous pleasures and necessary agonies of furnishing it'. He wrote of rising prices: 'I remember I used to hear that a modest man might supply himself with beds, tables and a chair to sit on for £200. Now I am told that £1,500 for the rough big things is absolutely indispensable, and that pretti-nesses may be supplied afterwards for a further £500.'

Trollope's library, accumulated over the years, consisted by this time of some five thousand volumes. Bookshelves were thus the prerequisite, and these were immediately built along the walls of his future study at the back of the house and in the alcoves of the first-floor drawing-room. Florence Bland set her-self to tag and catalogue all these volumes, and was, in Montagu Square, more and more frequently employed as her Uncle

Anthony's amanuensis, although her Aunt Rose still sometimes made fair copies of the novels for the printers as she had been used to do ever since the distant Irish days. Anthony would dictate to his niece each morning. This habit may partly explain the enormous length of such later novels as *The Way We Live Now*, for there is all the difference in the world between one's own laborious longhand and carefree dictated sentences. Escott recalls that Trollope had once told him that 'however early the hour, however dull and depressing the dawn, we soon warm to our work and get so excited with those we are writing about, that I don't know whether she or I are most surprised when the time comes to leave off for breakfast'. At 39 Montagu Square, breakfast had been pushed forward until half past eleven. All this sounds like a convivial and co-operative morning effort—but indeed it was not altogether that, for 'Flo' was only allowed to work as a lowly mechanic on the novels; she was forbidden to make the very slightest comment. On one occasion she did timidly venture to suggest some trifling alteration—perhaps in grammar or perhaps in plot-consistency. Her uncle, no doubt bellowing in his wrath, tore up the complete chapter and flung it into the wastepaper-basket. The family breakfast-table was often uproarious when Harry or a guest would twit Flo about her bondage, asking her whether her celebrated uncle ever beat her with a stick. Flo, we must suppose, would smile, while Uncle Anthony, guffawing, is reported to have kept shouting out that some such punishment was sadly overdue.

When he bought 39 Montagu Square, Anthony Trollope was in his fifty-eighth year, but, according to a younger friend, 'bodily signs of advancing years multiplied on him after his first half-century'. Just ten days before his fifty-eighth birthday, in April 1873, that highly entertaining publication, *Vanity Fair: A Weekly Show of Political, Social and Literary Wares* came out with a cartoon of Anthony Trollope by 'Spy' (whose real name was Leslie Ward). Each week for more than thirty years Ward produced a coloured cartoon which was published under the general title *Men of the Day*.* This most unflattering portrait of Anthony, like all Ward's cartoons full-length, shows facing us an old gentleman, a cigar in his right hand, his left hand behind his back. The general impression this vivid cartoon gives one is that of an affronted Santa Claus who has just lost his reindeer, or found a nursery chimney blocked.

To have one's personal appearance distorted by a Spy cartoon

* See frontispiece of this book.

was a public honour no eminent man could well refuse. The text which accompanied the weekly *Man of the Day* was usually sharp, for *Vanity Fair* tried hard to live up to its proclaimed motto taken from John Bunyan: 'We buy the Truth.' On the whole Trollope got away with this comparatively unscathed, though he cannot have been altogether pleased:

'He is a student and delineator of costume rather than of humanity. He does not, as does George Eliot, pry into the great problems of life or attempt to show the mournful irony of fate ... He is a correct painter of the small things of our small modern English life ... His manners are a little rough, as is his voice, but he is nevertheless extremely popular among his personal friends ...'

Seven months after this cartoon was published, Anthony, on a ten days' jaunt to Killarney, was horrified to find that he had lost his hearing in one ear. This fretted and confused him dreadfully:

'I fancy I am going to be run over, and everybody seems to talk to me on the wrong side [he wrote to his friend Lady Wood, a neighbour in Montagu Square]. I am told that a bone has grown up inside the orifice. Oh dear! One does not understand at all. Why should any bones grow, except useful, working bones? Why should anything go wrong in our bodies? Why should not we be all beautiful? Why should there be dread?—why death?—and, oh why, damnation?'

Anthony's brother Tom, who was still living in Italy, had been totally deaf for many, many years. Socially, the deaf get very short shrift from those forced to repeat some trivial remark three or four times over before it registers; whereas the blind are forever being helped across a busy street or piloted around the furniture in some unfamiliar room. Anthony described this incipient deafness as 'a rumbling noise' in one ear. It was presumably this deafness which made him now yell louder than ever. On one evening at the Garrick Club, he and the Irish journalist William Russell were both bawling at such a pitch that fellow members threatened to send for the police if the two friends did not pipe down. Anthony's eyesight, always weak, does not seem to have been affected by the premature onset of old age. Although he had intended to give up hunting he could not yet bring himself to do so, and endured dreary train journeys from London to Leighton Buzzard for the meets. Even when he had finally decided to give it up, he kept three horses in London as well as a private brougham. 'The systematic way in which Mr

Trollope grinds out his work is very funny,' wrote Mrs Oliphant, the lady-novelist, in May 1876. 'It must have answered, for he seems extremely comfortable; keeps a homely brougham, rides in the Park, etc.' Anthony not only rode in the Park, but rode in the streets of London too. Members of the Garrick Club would watch through the windows as the burly old gentleman dismounted; a groom was in attendance to take the horse home. Thomas Sweet Escott would remark how much younger Anthony Trollope always looked when in the saddle.

As he aged, Trollope became more blustering than ever. On the title-page of a copy of the *Autobiography* George Augustus Sala summed up his old friend's characteristics thus: 'Crusty, quarrelsome, wrong-headed, prejudiced, obstinate, kind-hearted and thoroughly honest old Tony Trollope.' The only other individual on record as calling him 'Tony' was his own mother when he was a small boy. It does not, somehow, seem to be in the least suited to the Anthony Trollope we know.

Once his household was settled into 39 Montagu Square Anthony began, on May 1st, 1873, to plan out a colossus of a new novel. When it was completed he chose its title—which he had always done after and not before writing a new novel. The book, which came out as *The Way We Live Now*, was instigated by its author's belief that contemporary England, and most of all contemporary London, was stained purple by financial profligacy, large-scale fraud and a total lack of the most elementary principles of honesty. There are in fact only four out of its evil cast of characters who are actuated by motives other than greed, snobbery, flattery and barefaced cynicism. It is a very long book and on the whole a very fine one; the opening chapters are slow, and in the first of these, when we are introduced to Lady Carbury, a fashionable widow trying to make money by her pen, we are asked to read right through the letters which she has just written in her sanctum, the back drawing-room of her prettily furnished house in Welbeck Street. Trollope himself later judged the satire in *The Way We Live Now* as being exaggerated: 'The vices implied are coloured so as to make effect rather than to represent truth,' he tells us. '...Upon the whole, I by no means look upon the book as one of my failures;—nor was it taken as a failure by the public or the press.' The critics who reviewed the book were either shocked or angered, but the critic of *The Times* newspaper expressed gratitude for Trollope's candour. The *Spectator* disliked the book intensely and resented the 'atmosphere of sordid baseness which prevents enjoyment like an effluvium ... Mr Trollope is so rarely inaccurate that we suppose there is somewhere a world like that he describes; and so somewhere among the marshes there is a sewage-farm, and we would as soon go there for a breath of fresh air as to *The Way We Live Now* for entertainment.'

The Times man wrote of the novel as 'only too faithful a portraiture of the manners and customs of the English at the latter part of this 19th century. For all its exactitude, however, it is neither a caricature nor a photograph; it is a likeness of the face which society wears.' *The Times* also declared that 'Mr Trollope's hand has not lost its cunning, nor his mind its habit of just observation'. This latter comment did not at all tally with the verdicts of other reviewers of the book. One of these even suggested that Anthony himself closely resembled his own hack authoress Lady Carbury in *The Way We Live Now*:

'... he, too, has written all sorts of books, a hack translation of Caesar, a scratch volume of hunting sketches, a boys' Christmas book of Australian adventure, all of them with no higher aim than Lady Carbury's ... We will merely say that Mr Trollope, like Lady Carbury, writes up to what may be called the paying point.'

The damaging reviews, like the favourable one in *The Times*, came out as soon as the book was published, that is to say in October 1875; and, though he only grew to realize it later, Anthony Trollope's popularity was already on the wane. This was proved not only by unpleasant critical articles, but by a marked diminution of the sums that publishers now offered him for his work. From the forty-eight pounds he had earned as a young man in Ireland by writing *The Macdermots of Ballycloran* his earnings began, after *The Warden*, to climb; for *Framley Parsonage*, published in 1860, he was for the first time paid £1,000. For *Orley Farm* he got over £3,000. *The Way We Live Now* was the last novel which earned him a similarly large sum. After that only *The Prime Minister* brought him £2,500; and later his sales value began to dip. In the *Autobiography* he tots up for our benefit his total earnings to date—that is to say to the year 1876 when he was writing the memoir. The sum, drawn up with his usual exactitude, worked out at £68,959. 17s. 5d. His fifteen last novels, his little life of Cicero, his memoir of Thackeray and his short biography of Lord Palmerston were published after the *Autobiography* had been completed, parcelled up and put carefully away in his desk, with a note to his elder son Harry about its posthumous publication.

Very possibly because of the mixed reception of his angry onslaught on society in *The Way We Live Now*, Anthony for his next book retreated once again into what must have seemed the safe and beckoning world of the Pallisers. *The Prime Minister*, written in 1874 and released in monthly parts in 1876, is an altogether less unwieldy book than its immediate predecessor —for *The Way We Live Now* contains no less than 400,000 words. If the critics had been out gunning for Anthony Trollope in their notices of *The Way We Live Now*, their reception of *The Prime Minister*, with its inept and unconvincing pair of lovers, must have seemed to be a premeditated massacre of his own favourite characters. Only *The Times* wrote pleasingly of it. In an addendum to a page of his autobiography Anthony wrote: 'I am obliged to say that, as regards the public, *The Prime Minister* was a failure. It was worse spoken of by the press than any novel I had written. I was specially hurt by a criticism of it in the *Spectator*.' This *Spectator* article consistently accused Trollope of vulgarity. Plantagenet Palliser, now Duke of Omnium and Prime Minister, is called by this reviewer both vulgar and a pretentious snob. His wife the Duchess has turned into another woman 'actuated by a thoroughly ill-bred ambition ... that is not the woman whom so many of Mr Trollope's readers have admired'. The reviewer went on to say that readers would be 'half-inclined to believe that Mr Trollope's power itself had declined, that he was positively unable to give us the sketches in which we have taken such delight'. Only the scenes between the venerable statesman, the Duke of St Bungay, and Plantagenet, Duke of Omnium, are praised for their 'exquisite delicacy and skill'. The *Saturday Review* critic roundly declared that the book 'represents a decadence in Mr Trollope's powers. Such a decadence, however, was in the nature of things inevitable.' He also complained of the 'all-pervading sense of artistic vulgarity', and cruelly quoted Wordsworth's maxim. 'Minds that have nothing to confer, find little to perceive.'

The lacerating reception of *The Prime Minister* by the press made its author wonder whether his 'work as a novelist should be brought to a close'. It was not just the *Spectator* review which cut him to the quick, for there seemed to be a general consensus of critical opinion marshalled against the book. The reviewer in the *Illustrated London News*, for example, said he had finished reading the novel 'with a sigh of relief'; the *Athenaeum* felt only 'a languid interest' in Trollope's politicians; in New York an

313

article in the *Nation* found the new novel was as monotonous as the bricks in a series of nondescript city houses, while *Harper's Magazine* considered that *The Prime Minister* was both 'commonplace and sombre'.

I do not think that there can be much doubt that *The Prime Minister* is a pretty dull book, with a quantity of political scenes that are no longer stirring, and a heroine who, for once, fails to enchant the reader. Emily Wharton is tall and fair with grey eyes. She conquered men less by her beauty than by her voice: '. . . by those gifts and by a clearness of intellect joined with that feminine sweetness, which has its most frequent foundation in self-denial.' The last of these attributes is baffling, but it may have been meant to explain Emily's masochistic marriage, against all good advice, to Ferdinand Lopez, a stockbroker adventurer who tries to use his bride as a means of extorting money from her father. Lopez is unquestionably handsome, 'his beauty being of a sort which men are apt to deny and women to admit lavishly. He was nearly six feet tall, very dark and very thin, with regular well-cut features . . . his teeth were perfect in form and whiteness.' In very many of his physical descriptions of boys and girls, of men and women, Anthony often takes care to give us his considered opinion upon their teeth. Lady Eustace's teeth 'were without flaw or blemish, even, small, white and delicate'. In *The Small House at Allington* 'Bell's teeth were more even than her sister's; but then she shewed her teeth more'. Of Lucy Robarts in *Framley Parsonage* we learn that her 'small teeth, which one so seldom saw, were white as pearls'. Way back in Trollope's first novel, *The Macdermots of Ballycloran*, Pheemy Macdermot, despite her rustic appearance, has teeth which are 'white and good'. Arabella Trefoil in *The American Senator* has a small mouth but 'her teeth were excellent'. Madeline Staveley, the heroine of an under-plot in *Orley Farm*, was at her best when she smiled, 'just showing, but hardly showing, the beauty of the pearls within'; while Mary Lawrie, in *An Old Man's Love*, had lips 'too thin for true female beauty', but through these 'her white teeth would occasionally be seen, and then her face was at its best, as for instance when she was smiling; but that was seldom'. It is hard to assess whether this interest in human teeth was a personal fetish or foible of Anthony's own or, somewhat more likely, whether it is a sign that mid-Victorian teeth went rotten early and that dental hygiene was not so widespread as it is today. We do know that false teeth were already in much demand in those days, a trend which was probably itself due to early dental decay. We also know that Victorian false teeth fitted badly and might fall out at a moment's notice. There is, for instance, an authentic anecdote about old Lord Houghton (the former Richard Monckton Milnes) at an evening party at Buckingham Palace. Lord Houghton, who in old age took somewhat to drink, was happily dozing on a crimson velvet banquette in the Picture Gallery. The top row of his false teeth had dropped out, and become entangled in the cord of his pince-nez, so that to a passer-by the old gentleman seemed to be wearing some new, and probably Turkish or in any case exotic decoration.

Be that as it may, it can hardly have been Ferdinand Lopez's teeth alone that had fascinated Emily Wharton. In her choice of husband she displays not the remotest sign of that clearness of intellect which Trollope assures us was hers. She has simply allied herself with one of the most blatant rogues in the whole of London. Lopez was doubtless one of the causes of the use of the adjective 'vulgar' by critics of *The Prime Minister*. He seems like a displaced person in the world of the Pallisers, and his success with the Duchess of Omnium is too unlikely to be true. Lopez would, in fact, have been far more at home in *The Way We Live Now* where he would have encountered a thousand sympathetic beings hell-bent on making money by fraud, mis-representation, ambitious marriages or by kow-towing to that new element in London society, the rich and powerful money moguls of semitic blood. Ferdinand Lopez himself is even ass enough to try to get Lady Eustace to run away with him to Guatemala after asking her to buy shares in a patent preparation called Bios; but Lizzie Eustace is far too fly for that. She listens to his proposition of letting her buy a half share in Bios; would she object to that?

'"No," said Lizzie slowly, "I don't suppose I should object to that."

'"I should be doubly eager about the affair if I were in part-nership with you."

'"It's such a venture."

'"Nothing venture, nothing have."

'"But I've got something as it is, Mr Lopez, and I don't want to lose it all."'

Some days later, Lopez returns to Lady Eustace's little May-fair house. He addresses her as Lizzie for the first time:

'"Lizzie Eustace will you go with me, to that land of the sun,

' "Where the rage of the vulture, the love of the turtle,
     Now melt into sorrow, now madden to crime?"
Will you dare to escape with me from the cold conventionalities, from the miserable thraldom of this country bound in swaddling clothes? Lizzie Eustace, if you will say the word I will take you to that land of glorious happiness."
But Lizzie Eustace had £4,000 a year and a balance at her banker's. "Mr Lopez," she said.
' "What answer have you to make me?"
' "Mr Lopez, I think you must be a fool."
He did at last succeed in getting himself into the street, and at any rate she had not eaten him.'

Whatever her faults, you can always rely on Lady Eustace to hit the nail most dexterously upon the head.

It is, I believe, quite untrue to say, as we have seen that contemporary critics did say, that the Duke and Duchess of Omnium—Plantagenet Palliser and Lady Glencora—are in the least 'vulgarized' in *The Prime Minister*. They are both as authentically themselves as is Lizzie Eustace who lives 'in a very small house in a very small street bordering upon May Fair; but the street though very small and having disagreeable relations with a mews, still had an air of fashion about it'. Lizzie's circle of friends is almost more second-rate than ever before, but she remains as mercenary, as quick, and, above all, as beguiling as ever she had been in her very young days, at the time of the scandal about the family diamonds.

Ferdinand Lopez is an ambitious fool and Emily Wharton a stubborn one. Perhaps the finest passage in the whole book is that in which Lopez commits suicide by flinging himself in the path of a train at Tenby Junction, a great spider's web of steel rails which in some way seems to represent the complex horror of the commercial world that had killed him. It has recently been discovered that Tolstoy read *The Prime Minister* while he was writing *Anna Karenina*. He called it 'a beautiful book'. Lopez's suicide under a railway train at Tenby Junction may indeed have sealed Anna Karenina's fate, suggesting to Tolstoy a new and horrifying form of sudden death.

Ferdinand Lopez is a singularly obvious and ungifted adventurer: and it is likely that this slick young man has managed to snatch more of the limelight in *The Prime Minister* than the author had originally intended. We have, from time to time, observed how a number of Trollope's fictional characters seem to have taken charge of their creator's hand and pen, insisting successfully on playing a more important role than was at first allotted to them. A curious instance of such hogging of the stage occurs in *The Way We Live Now*. A layout for this novel, as methodically drawn up as all the other examples of how Trollope planned his books before he began writing them, has survived. This shows, as we have seen, that the dominant personality in *The Way We Live Now* was in no wise to be Auguste Melmotte, the upstart financial magnate who goes bankrupt and commits suicide. It was Lady Carbury, the heroic and industrious authoress of such pot-boilers as *Criminal Queens*, who had been selected by Trollope as 'The chief character—a position which he underscored after sketching out her life in the layout; yet once Melmotte comes on the scene he dominates it, and Trollope seems as eager as anyone in the book to relish the splendours of Melmotte's hospitality in Grosvenor Square. All that the supplanted Lady Carbury can now do is to give advice from the wings to her baronet son Sir Felix Carbury, another of Trollope's handsome and heedless young ne'er-do-wells. Like every other impecunious but extravagant youth in this novel, Sir Felix is after Marie Melmotte and her money. He proves, however, rather half-hearted as he listens politely to his mother's advice. 'Have you been at the Melmottes' today?' Lady Carbury asks her son, as he strides into her study demanding twenty pounds:

'It was now five o'clock on a winter afternoon, the hour at which ladies are drinking tea, and idle men playing whist at the clubs,—at which young idle men are sometimes allowed to flirt, and at which, as Lady Carbury thought, her son might have been paying his court to Marie Melmotte, the great heiress.

' "I have just come away."

' "And what do you think of her?"

' "To tell you the truth, mother, I have thought very little about her. She is not pretty, she is not plain; she is not clever, she is not stupid; she is neither saint nor sinner."

' "The more likely to make a good wife."

' "Perhaps so. I am at any rate quite willing to believe that as a wife she would be 'good enough for me'."

' "What does the mother say?"

' "The mother is a caution. I cannot help speculating whether, if I marry her daughter, I shall ever find out where the mother came from. Dolly Longestaffe says that somebody says that she was a Bohemian Jewess; but I think she's too fat for that."

' "What does it matter, Felix?"

' "Not in the least."

' "Is he civil to you?"

' "Yes, civil enough . . ."

' "Well, he does not turn me out or anything of that sort . . . He's thinking more of getting dukes to dine with him than of his daughter's lovers. Any fellow might pick her up who happened to hit her fancy."

' "And why not you?"

' "Why not, mother? I am doing my best, and it's no good flogging a willing horse. Can you let me have the money?"

' "Oh, Felix, I think you hardly know how poor we are. You have still got your hunters down at that place ! " '

Wayward Sir Felix was not the only cause of his mother's anxiety. Her daughter Hetta, whom their landed cousin Roger Carbury is courting, refuses to marry him and continues to love a weak character named Paul Montague. Hetta is as obstinate as many another Trollope heroine in this dilemma; but her case is aggravated by her discovery that Paul's American mistress, Mrs Hurtle, has come to town and is indeed living at a boarding-house in Islington. This revelation produces a nasty scene—but at the end of the book Hetta and Paul Montague marry with the double blessing of Roger Carbury and Lady Carbury. Before leaving the slimy world of *The Way We Live Now*, it may prove valuable to question the real motives for the critics' condemnation of the book. These motives can most justly be attributed to fear—the fear, for instance, that this brilliant novel contained more of the truth than was, at that moment in time, palatable to fashionable Londoners. This is only a theory, but it is in some ways supported by the fact that *The Times* alone praised—and indeed most warmly praised—the new book. Now *The Times* was still edited by the famous Delane, who ran the newspaper for thirty-six years. He was a champion of the oppressed, and at the same time a fierce crusader against moral evil. Delane had recently published in *The Times* a signed denunciation of a Californian swindler who had robbed and ruined a wretched English peer. He was a good friend of Anthony Trollope's, and certainly shared his views on the moral disintegration of London's society. John Delane is a reliable and highly intelligent witness for the defence of *The Way We Live Now*. So, by implication, is Henry Adams, who had returned to London from Boston in 1879 to find London society more or less deformed or disorganized by the breathless cult of money and by the vulgarity of the eagerly accepted *nouveaux riches*.

Moreover, the bitterness of Trollope's verdict on his upper-class compatriots may well, I think, have been influenced by his recent travels through the Australian bush, where he had met healthy men and assiduous women, people who were honest and open and hard-working. One of the rare straightforward characters in *The Way We Live Now* is the distant cousin of Sir Felix—a Suffolk squire named Roger Carbury, the man who wants to marry Hetta. He has a conversation about the Melmottes with Lady Carbury, who of course defends her son's rich friends and her own presence at a grand ball at their house in Grosvenor Square. Roger Carbury simply declares his mind: 'A social connection with the first crossing-sweeper would be less objectionable.' Here speaks the authentic voice of the old and honourable English squirearchy. It could be the voice of Mr Dale of Allington, of Lady Lufton at Framley Court, of the Thornes of Ullathorne, of Lord de Guest at Guestwick Manor —the very voice, in fact, of that Barsetshire which Anthony Trollope loved. After more than one hundred years his devoted, unflagging skill has made these vibrant voices re-echo to us yet.

(ii)

Anthony's formidable 250,000-word compilation on *Australia and New Zealand* was published early in 1873. On May 1st that year he began to write *The Way We Live Now*, but interrupted work on it to toss off the brisk adventure story, *Harry Heathcote of Gangoil*. The *Graphic* had asked him to supply them with a 'Christmas Story', the kind of story that he really most abhorred. However, as they were willing to pay him £450, he went at it with his customary zeal. He detested the whole concept of the Christmas Story, a form first popularized by Charles Dickens, and which the reading public now expected their favourite magazines annually to produce. Anthony thought the whole idea a humbug—he asserted that these stories had by then become 'fixed to Christmas like children's toys to a Christmas tree' and had 'no real savour of Christmas about them'. In expressing these feelings in his autobiography he takes the opportunity to parade once again as a journeyman-author:

"I feel, with regard to literature, somewhat as I suppose an upholsterer and undertaker feels when he is called upon to supply a funeral. He has to supply it, however distasteful it may be. It is his business and he will starve if he neglect it. So have I felt that, when anything in the shape of a novel was required, I was bound to produce it.'

The central idea of the little book—to portray the Australian Christmas which falls in the torrid heat of the summer—was at any rate an original one, and the risks of sheep-farming in the dry season keep the tale at a certain tension.

In the winter of 1874–5 Anthony Trollope, for the second time in his life, was really ill with some unspecified but severe form of liver complaint. Before this illness he had already decided to pay Fred Trollope a second visit in New South Wales, going this time alone, and spending two or three weeks in Ceylon on the way. There seems to have been no particular reason, save a natural curiosity, for his stop over in Ceylon, unless it were to visit Sir William Gregory who was Governor there from 1871 to 1877. Gregory was an Harrovian of Anthony's vintage, with whom he had hunted in old days in Galway; Anthony had also stayed at Gregory's country house, Coole Park near Gort. Although the stop over in Ceylon seems a little mysterious, the purpose of the journey to Australia was not. In a letter to his Edinburgh friend, John Blackwood, Anthony explained that he was not exactly worried about Fred's prospects. Fred now had two small sons at Mortray Station, with another one on the way: 'If he don't succeed in the long run I can no longer believe in honesty, industry, and conduct,' Anthony told Blackwood. 'But I believe I can give him a helping hand by going out. I can see what money I can advance him out of my small means and settle certain things with him.' For an ageing man of sixteen stone to go back to an Australian bush-station in the heat was a sign of generosity and of fatherly affection indeed. As usual, he succeeded in getting a commission from a London publisher, this time Nicholas Trübner, for a series of twenty letters on all he would see on his travels. These letters or articles appeared in the *Liverpool Mercury* and perhaps in other provincial newspapers as well.

He left England on the last day of February 1875, travelling overland to Brindisi, where he caught the P. & O. liner *Nigani*, for Ceylon. He had picked up his brother Tom in Rome and they had gone down together to Naples, Anthony seeing the ruins of Pompeii for the first time. The *Nigani*'s passengers did not go through the new Suez Canal, but went overland to Suez in jolting, dusty carriages; there they joined a better ship, the *Peshawar*. 'I never like the P. & O. Captains,' he wrote to his wife while still on board the *Nigani*. 'They always give themselves airs as fine gentlemen,—a fault from which the Cunarders are free.' Before leaving England he had bought, seemingly on Trübner's advice, a duplicating contraption, known as the Manifold Writer. This sounds like an early form of carbon paper, and would, seemingly, enable him to send several copies to Trübner, while presumably keeping one for himself. 'I find the working with that multiplying apparatus is a bore,' he wrote to his wife, 'not but that it is easy enough while you are doing it, but that it is so long & troublesome to arrange, and then it dirties your fingers in a disgusting manner.' Anthony Trollope was always an untidy traveller and tended to lose his luggage— or, almost as bad, to fear that he might have lost it. On boarding the *Peshawar* at Suez he found to his concern that a big bottle of ink in his travelling-desk had been smashed to pieces: 'There were three shirts on top to keep things steady. I wish you could see those three shirts, and there were 100 loose cigars ... Some wretch had pitched the desk down like a ball, and all my beautiful white paper! However that is now simply black-edged.' After staying at the Mortray Station with the Fred Trollopes and his grandsons, Anthony reached home, via Fiji, San Francisco and Boston in October 1875, having been away for eight months.

Aside from the newspaper letters for Trübner, Anthony Trollope had, of course, been writing two long novels overseas. The first, *Is He Popenjoy?*, which he was working on when he was taken ill before he left England for Ceylon, was finished at sea between Ceylon and Melbourne. The second, *The American Senator*, was begun in one of his son's cottages at the Mortray Station—it is easy to imagine that burly figure hunched over his desk on the verandah, which was covered in by striped blinds, giving it, with its sewing-machine and casual furnishings, the illusion of a room. Flowering creepers clambered all up the posts of the verandah; from the front of the house the ground fell away to the creek and to a gay attempt at a flower-garden. Further down was the vegetable-garden which opossums raided by night. Fred Trollope had inherited all his father's obstinacy, to which the autocracy he had imposed on his sheep-station gave free play. When he left the Mortray Station for Sydney and the long voyage home Anthony Trollope probably realized that it was most unlikely that he would ever see his younger son again. Nor did he do so. He had been a generous but possibly a detached parent; of his real relationship with either of his sons we know nothing of substance at all.

When, in the autumn of 1875, Anthony Trollope got back home from Australia after eight months away, he had two new, completed novels in his baggage—*Is He Popenjoy?* and *The American Senator*. The first of these books has always, in my opinion, been underrated—owing, perhaps, to its almost criminally idiotic title. We have noticed before Trollope's deliberate selection, from time to time, of what Henry James deplored as 'fantastic names'. It has in the past been suggested that such fatal choices came from an attempt on Trollope's part to emulate Thackeray, although it seems to me far more likely that he was influenced by the Tudor and Jacobean playwrights, the reading of whose works had for some years provided his chief form of mental recreation. Even as late as Sheridan writers for the English stage often used a surname to indicate trade or psychology—we have only to think of Lady Sneerwell in *The School for Scandal*. Trollope, however, dealt out some of his titles and his surnames with a hand of lead: Lord Grassangrains 'that well-known breeder of bullocks', or Lord Gossling of Gosling Castle, whose family name is de Geese and whose eldest son bears the courtesy title of Lord Giblet. Both these noble families figure in *Is He Popenjoy?* but hitherto Anthony had refrained from using one of his lamer jokes as the actual title of a novel. In an earlier generation Thomas Love Peacock had got away with fantasy book-titles; Anthony Trollope could not. The main plot of *Is He Popenjoy?* centres round the dubious legitimacy of a puny, half-Italian child, the only son of the ill-natured Marquess of Brotherton, and called, by courtesy, Viscount Popenjoy. What caused Trollope to select this particular name we cannot know. A popinjay means firstly, a parrot, and secondly, a fop or coxcomb. The dictionaries tell us that there is even a rather charming intransitive verb 'to popjoy'—meaning to amuse oneself. What is so specially irritating about the name of this child is that this novel is yet another serious, deadly onslaught on the contemporary values of English society in the 1870s.

An American scholar, Professor Polhemus, has lately pointed out that 'the world of *The Way We Live Now* and *The Prime Minister*, and of the lesser novels *Is He Popenjoy?* and *The American Senator*, runs out of control, like the dynamo world of Henry Adams'. He also draws a thoughtful parallel between the world of these four novels and the world that Marx and Engels described in the *Communist Manifesto*:—a world where 'there is no other bond between man and man but crude self-interest and callous cash-payment', a world that 'has degraded personal dignity to the level of exchange value', creating 'exploitation that is open, unashamed, direct and brutal'. Professor Polhemus does point out, however, that while Karl Marx was an optimist, Trollope's later years were years of pessimism and gloom.

The action of *Is He Popenjoy?* broadly takes place in three settings: the Deanery of Brotherton; Manor Cross, the Marquess of Brotherton's country house nine miles from this county town; and great houses in the fashionable quarter of London. Once again, the critics were made uneasy. One of them complained that although (in *Popenjoy*) 'we are among people who recall *Barchester Towers*, and pleasant Barchester circles' the author was not as fond of his new characters as he had been of his former ones; he was now creating people some of whom were malignant, some good-natured, and almost all of them lacking in any moral sense whatsoever. Another reviewer regretted that Trollope no longer represented 'his men and women with low, worldly aims or vicious propensities' as living at least beneath a blue sky amid 'the sweet breezes of heaven'. For Anthony Trollope in this last decade of his life the blue skies even of Barsetshire were clouded and threatening. Everywhere he looked he found moral pollution blanketing his world.

So increasingly intent was Trollope on plot and dialogue that he now hardly bothered to describe places. In *Popenjoy* the little city of Brotherton is dismissed as 'full of architectural excellencies, given to literature, and fond of hospitality'. It is only by a chance conversation in the third volume of the book that we discover that Brotherton is in Barsetshire—but it is in quite another part of the county to Barchester or Greshamsbury or any of the other places in which we love to tarry. Brotherton has its own cathedral, its own somewhat etiolated bishop and, naturally enough, its own dean, a worldly man brought up in his father's livery stables, who had gone into the Church, married the heiress of a tallow-chandler and ended up a rich and popular cleric. Dean Lovelace had 'preached his way to fame', but he was a snob:

'He who should have been proud of the lowliness of his birth, and have known that the brightest feather in his cap was the fact that having been humbly born he had made himself what he was—he had never ceased to be ashamed of the stable-yard ... [and believed] that the only whitewash for such dirt was to be found in the aggrandisement of his daughter and the nobility of her children.'

Dean Lovelace, a widower, lives with his adored only child, Mary, in the Deanery at Brotherton. While still not twenty, Mary inherits a fortune from her maternal grandfather, and thus becomes a figure of interest to the old Marchioness of Brotherton and her four daughters in the great house at Manor Cross amidst a park of fine oaks. The Marchioness's eldest son, Lord Brotherton, has lived in Italy for the last ten years, and her second son, Lord George Germain, stays penuriously at home managing the estate for his absentee brother. Lord George is a tall, dark man of thirty-three with a handsome head upon his shoulders, little sense of humour and a stern but affectionate nature: 'Birth and culture had given him a look of intellect greater than he possessed ... He was one who could bear reproach from no-one else, but who never praised himself even to himself.' Before the story begins, Lord George had thought himself heart-broken because his cousin Adelaide de Baron had refused to marry him, judging him too poor. Miss de Baron ended up marrying Mr Houghton, a very rich man of her father's generation, who has a large house in Berkeley Square. She had given much thought to the proposal of Lord George Germain, who, since his brother in Italy was supposed to be childless, would inevitably become a marquess in the course of time. Adelaide is one of the heartless group of Trollope girls who coolly assess their own attractions in money terms, using their beauty to captivate a wealthy young peer, or failing that a very rich old 'sinner'. Adelaide 'consulted her glass, and told herself that, without self-praise, she must regard herself as the most beautiful woman of her own acquaintance'—yet she would not risk poverty with a mere younger son.

Lord George's mother and sisters had been dreadfully put out by his blind passion for Adelaide de Baron, for he, like the girl herself, must marry money. It is just at this point that Mary Lovelace inherits her thirty thousand pounds. As a result of the intrigues of the ladies at Manor Cross and the determination of the Dean, Lord George proposes to Mary Lovelace, who accepts him. Mary Lovelace is a particularly well-conceived heroine; she loves gaiety and pleasure, is already a great beauty, but innocent of the world: 'Of her own money she knew almost nothing. Nor as yet had her fortune become a carcass to the birds.' Mary has, however, always cherished the secret dream of a fair-haired lover 'with laughing eyes, quick in repartee, always riding well to hounds'. Unfortunately, once she and her dour and swarthy husband move into their little London house for the season, they meet Jack de Baron at a dinner-party. Mary immediately recognizes her dream come true, for she finds in this young Guards officer 'that pleasure-loving look, that appearance of taking things jauntily, and of enjoying life, which she in her young girlhood had regarded as being absolutely essential to a pleasant lover'. Jack de Baron and Lady George form a close but innocent friendship playing bagatelle in Mrs Houghton's back drawing-room. This, needless to say, makes Lord George angry, for he suffers, as we have seen so many other Trollopian personages suffer, from jealousy; but with Lord George the disease is of a peculiar, rarified form, called by Trollope 'Caesarian jealousy'—that is to say that he trusts his young wife entirely but is haunted by the fear that she may seem to others to be fast, or indiscreetly pleasure-loving.

The Marquess of Brotherton, Lord George and the Germain family all get the thorough drubbing which Anthony metes out to his feckless aristocrats. To George Germain a cold demeanour matters more than the realities of happiness or love; but when, by dint of a couple of deaths, Lord George ultimately does become the Marquess of Brotherton, he ceases to badger Mary, for he finds that he is 'now never called upon to remind his wife of her dignity'. Dancing, which had previously been a gleaming white bone of contention between Mary and her husband, is now abandoned. The young Marchioness, we are assured, 'has never danced, except when, on grand occasions, she had walked through a quadrille with some selected partner of special rank; and this she does simply as a duty ... No man in London is better satisfied with his wife than the Marquis, and perhaps no man in London has better cause to be satisfied.'

Such is the reassuring tone which Anthony adopts in a final, tidying-up chapter of *Is He Popenjoy?*: 'It is now only necessary that we should collect together the few loose threads of our story which require to be tied lest the pieces should become unravelled in the wear.' Yet these anodyne endings of the sunless satirical novels simply serve as cheery curtain calls for the cast and do nothing to impair the dark mood that pervades this group of books. Even more than jealousy and spite—and both of these are present in *Popenjoy*—the naked thirst for money dominates this novel. The debonair, flirtatious Guardee, Jack de Baron, keeps trying to escape his fate in the person of an unmarried beauty, Augusta Mildmay, who is passionately in love with him. Guss Mildmay is a worldly girl who has not yet succeeded in catching a husband: 'She was certainly handsome, but she carried with her that wearied air of being nearly worn out by the toil of searching for a husband which comes upon some women after the fourth or fifth year of their labours.'

Guss Mildmay persists in sending Jack hysterical love-notes. When he is soft-hearted enough to reply by going to see her in Green Street she rewards him by weeping and with pleas to him to marry her. Except for Lady George Germain, young de Baron is almost the only character in *Popenjoy* who has not tried to marry money—but he has, of course, set his mind against marrying poverty. He gives Guss Mildmay a vivid word-picture of what their married life would be like, 'beginning life in lodgings, somewhere down at Chelsea': 'Have you no imagination? Can't you see what it would be? Can't you fancy the stuffy sitting-room with the horsehair chairs, and the hashed mutton, and the cradle in the corner before long?'

Jack is quite intelligent enough to realize that they have both been wrongly brought up, since they share all the tastes but none of the money of their friends and relations in the upper reaches of London Society:

' "You and I, Guss, have made a mistake from the beginning. Being poor people we have lived as though we were rich."

' "I have never done so."

' "Oh yes, you have. Instead of dining out in Fitzroy Square and drinking tea in Tavistock Place, you have gone to balls in Grosvenor Square and been presented at Court."

' "It wasn't my fault." '

With all the frenzy of unrequited love, Miss Mildmay even contemplates the contingency of her own father's death with eyes of hope. 'There will be something—when papa dies.' 'The most healthy middle-aged gentleman in London,' Jack de Baron retorts.

The light-hearted, unsullied friendship of Jack de Baron with what he terms his 'pet-friend' Lady George Germain is the only really happy and carefree relationship in this whole book—for I do not think that we can count that of the ambitious Dean and his adoring daughter. Towards the end of *Popenjoy*, when the spurious Italianate child of the book's title is dead, and Mary's brother-in-law, Brotherton, is known to be dying in Naples, Mary for a moment rebels. She had tried exceedingly hard to fall in love with her husband and to jog along with her senile mother-in-law and humdrum sisters-in-law; but now that she is about to have a child and will surely be Marchioness of

326

Brotherton in a matter of days, she can no longer stand the toadying to which she is subjected even within her husband's immediate family circle. The Dean gives her, as usual, worldly advice.

' "I don't mean you, papa; but at Manor Cross they all flatter me now because that poor man is dying. If you were me you wouldn't like that."

' "You've got to bear it, dear. It's the way of the world. People at the top of the tree are always flattered. You can't expect that Mary Lovelace and the Marchioness of Brotherton will be treated in the same way."

' "Of course it made a difference when I was married."

' "But suppose you had married a curate in the neighbourhood?"

' "I wish I had," said Mary wildly, "and that someone had given him the living of Pugsty." '

To her father her actual destiny is, however, one of infinite glory. Not only is she now a Marchioness, but her husband has, by his brother's death, become a man of great wealth. 'I suppose it's over forty thousand pounds a year since they took to working the coal at Popenjoy,' that cosy old matchmaker, Mrs Montecute Jones, writes to Mary, now her 'dearest Marchioness'. Mrs Jones is the only person who gives us any information on the course of the Marquess's princely income. As in *Mr Scarborough's Family*, the wealth of the Marquess of Brotherton is a direct result of the later stages of the Industrial Revolution. Mr Scarborough's income has jumped to £20,000 a year in his own lifetime, and is derived from the thriving potteries on his estate, as well as from exploitation of his land for the expansion of the pottery town of Tretton. It is in a way odd that, even in these most bitingly satirical novels of his later years, Anthony Trollope neither moralizes over, nor investigates, the working-class conditions which enabled persons such as Lord and Lady Brotherton to reopen and redecorate the old family house in St James's Square:

' "You don't mean St James's Square?" [Mary asked her husband]. But that was just what he did mean. "I hope we shan't have to live in that prison."

' "It's one of the best houses in London," said Lord George, with a certain amount of family pride. "It used to be, at least, before the rich tradesmen had built all those palaces at South Kensington." '

Mary, naturally enough, soon gets to like St James's Square:

'But then the family mansion had been so changed that no Germain of a former generation would know it. The old dowager, who still lives at Manor Cross, has never seen the change; but Lady Sarah, who always spends a month or two in town, pretends to disbelieve that it is the same house.' For two whole months of every year the Dean of Brotherton comes up to London to be cosseted by the Marchioness in St James's Square. As a boy in the livery stables in Bath he had been used to seeing his father touch his hat to clients as they came into the yard. Now, as a courteous and distinguished-looking old cleric, he is the father of a Marchioness and the grandfather of a future Marquess. Of all the people in *Is He Popenjoy?* it is Dean Lovelace alone who has satisfied a lifelong ambition and achieved his aims, though Anthony Trollope nowhere suggests that the Dean's ambition is admirable or his aims worthy. All he presents to us is the convoluted tale of one determined man's success in the jungle of Victorian society. A reviewer, who found the book to be an exercise in Trollope's 'least pleasant manner', also wrote that *Is He Popenjoy?* demonstrated 'how very slight are the barriers which part modern civilization from ancient savagery'.

(iv)

For unwonted reasons of verbal economy, and because so very little of the action takes place there, Trollope refrains from any detailed description of the town of Brotherton in *Is He Popenjoy?* He more than makes up for this deficiency by telling us a very great deal about Dillsborough, the market-town of the county of Rufford, in *Popenjoy's* successor, *The American Senator*. In the first sentence of Chapter One he confidentially informs us that he himself 'never could understand why anybody should ever have begun to live at Dillsborough'. This benighted town with its soothing name lies in a countryside too ordinary to attract 'tourists or holiday travellers'. It has no cathedral, and therefore no bishop, no dean and no dull or diverting clerical society in a close. Even the Saturday market is meagre and somnolent. There are no coal-mines in the vicinity. Dillsborough water is unfit for brewing beer or for dyeing cloth, and there is likewise no reason for a spa. Taken every ten years, the Dillsborough census always shows that the town's population is gradually dwindling. Dillsborough's best features are the Bush Inn and the old parish church 'which has not as yet received any of those modern improvements which have of late become common throughout England'. There is also a large brick house, dating from the reign of Queen Anne, and known as Hoppet Hall. The Hall's front door opens on to a side-street, but at the back of the house there are three acres of walled garden. In a busier town than Dillsborough this large property in the middle of the shopping area would have become valuable building land. Hoppet Hall belongs to Reginald Morton, a cousin of John Morton, the young squire of Bragton, the most consequential country house and largest estate near Dillsborough.

Having absorbed a good deal of local information about Dillsborough we are next faced with the taxing ramification of the Mortons' pedigree. It is thus no exaggeration to say that in its initial chapters *The American Senator* is hard work to read, for it creeps and crawls along; yet, once airborne, this book contains some of the sharpest and subtlest sequences of Trollope dialogue and, in Arabella Trefoil, the finest, the most fearless and the most tragic of all his doomed and desperate anti-heroines. Beside Miss Trefoil, Lady Eustace herself seems but a feather-brained and ingenuous little schemer, Lady Ongar uninventive and Lady Laura Kennedy sadly muddleheaded. Unlike Trollope's good girls, who are small and dark, and whose regular reward is marriage to the man they love, Arabella Trefoil is physically as well as morally constructed on a large scale —'a big fair girl, whose copious hair was managed after such a fashion that no one could guess what was her own and what was purchased'. Arabella has large, beautiful blue eyes that are never bright, a delicate but partly artificial complexion and movements of exquisite grace: 'No young woman could walk across an archery ground with a finer step, or manage a train with more perfect ease, or sit upon her horse with a more complete look of being at home there. No doubt she was slow, but though slow she never seemed to drag.'

Miss Trefoil is always magnificently dressed and never goes to stay anywhere without her own lady's maid, whose constant aid is as essential to her as food. Arabella is the only child of Lord and Lady Augustus Loftus, who live apart. She is thus niece to the Duke of Mayfair who owns a great ancestral house in Piccadilly and, when in Lincolnshire, lives at his seat Mistletoe, an ugly but luxurious palace 'with a frontage nearly a quarter of a mile long'. The Duchess of Mayfair detests her sister-in-law Lady Augustus, a banker's daughter ruined by her own husband: she is a mean, small-minded, vulgar elderly lady whose efforts to help Arabella marry richly have hitherto done the girl much more harm than good. Miss Trefoil has by now been in the marriage market for twelve long years; still unwed and still poor, at thirty her prospects fill her with despair. During a recent visit with her mother to Washington Arabella had met, and then become engaged to, John Morton of Bragton, a somewhat stiff young man who is Secretary at the British Legation, and is known in the Foreign Office as 'the Paragon'. Morton has the misfortune to fall seriously in love with her. Back on four months' leave, Morton has brought with him the American senator of the novel's title and, as part of an effort to show him the English way of life, he has invited him down to Bragton, a house which has been closed for decades. He has also invited his betrothed and her mother to Bragton, the sorry state of which horrifies Lady Augustus, who has already discovered that Morton has no more than £7,000 a year. He meets these ladies at Dillsborough railway station. They proceed to Bragton in hired carriages with torn and stained upholstery.

'Miss Trefoil had migrated to her mother's room, and there, over the fire, was holding a little domestic conversation.

' "I never saw such a barrack in my life," said Lady Augustus.

' "Of course, mamma, we knew that we should find the house such as it was left a hundred years ago. He told us that himself."

' "He should have put something in it to make it, at any rate, decent before we came in . . . I think it is a piece of impudence to bring one to such a place as this . . . The more I see of it all, Arabella, the more sure I am it won't do."

' "It must do, mamma."

' " . . . Is this the sort of place you'd like?"

' "I don't think it makes any difference where one is," said Arabella, disgusted.

' " . . . You're very fond of him, it seems."

' "Mamma, how you do delight to torture me; as if my life weren't bad enough without making it worse."

' "I tell you, my dear, what I'm bound to tell you—as your mother. I have my duty to do whether it's painful or not."

' " . . . I'll tell you what it is, mamma. I've been at it till I'm nearly broken down. I must settle somewhere;—or else die;—or else run away. I can't stand this any longer and I won't. Talk of work—men's work! What man ever has to work as I do? . . . I can't do it any more, and I won't. As for Mr Morton, I don't care that for him. You know I don't. I never cared much for anybody, and shall never again care at all." '

Arabella Trefoil is far more frank with herself than most of the Trollope girls angling for rich husbands. She does not even expect, and indeed from exhaustion would scarcely want, any man to fall seriously in love with her. She uses her looks, her smile 'as cold as though it had come from a figure on a glass window', her clothes, her style and her noble connections in order to secure a husband rich enough to give her the life of thorough-going luxury for which she yearns. Possibly the most purely worldly woman in all the works of Trollope, Arabella Trefoil pursues money, which she earnestly believes to be the secret of happiness. She is, in fact, a pseudo-realist in that she has no proper grasp on real values at all. As a duke's niece, she is accepted everywhere but she is now after twelve years and several aborted engagements, without friends. Her situation indeed resembles that of Hans Christian Andersen's little match girl peering into the window from the wintry street outside.

There is a fairly simple love-story in *The American Senator*, involving the book's official heroine, Mary Masters, and Reginald Morton, the owner of Hoppet Hall, and ultimately, after the early death of John Morton, of Bragton as well. It is, however, Miss Trefoil who gives the book pace. Her ruthless decision to pursue the landed bachelor, Lord Rufford, at whom she makes what seems about to be a very successful set while staying in his house and in the very presence of her fiancé, John Morton, so nearly succeeds that the reader feels as distraught as she herself does when, despite all her traps and lies, Rufford wriggles out of the noose at the last moment. Immediately after this, the faithful John Morton dies, leaving Arabella his watch and rings and a legacy of £5,000. Miss Trefoil is not intellectually clever, but she is brilliantly adroit. Like some belligerent Germanic potentate she has no interest at all in people except as enemies or allies. Her appreciation of rich living has an instinctive, animal quality: light and warmth and a shimmering form of security are her goals. When she, her mother, John Morton and the American senator are asked to go to a ball at Rufford's neighbouring house and to stay two nights, Arabella arranges to get to Rufford Hall with her mother in the Bragton phaeton, which goes faster than the Bragton carriage containing the senator and John Morton. She thus makes her entry unencumbered into this house to which she has never been before: 'Arabella was certainly very handsome at this moment. Never did she look better than when she got up with care for travelling, especially when seen by an evening light. Her slow motions were adapted to heavy wraps.' After the damp and empty Bragton, the scene at Rufford Hall enchants her soul:

'The sight of the hangings of the room, so different to the old-fashioned dingy curtains at Bragton, the brilliancy of the mirrors, all the decorations of the place, the very blaze from the big grate, forced upon the girl's feelings a conviction that this was her proper sphere. Here she was, being made much of as a newcomer, and here if possible she must remain. Everything smiled on her with gilded dimples, and these were the smiles she valued. As the softness of the cushions sank into her heart, and mellow nothingness from well-trained voices greeted her ears, and the air of wealth and idleness floated about her cheeks, her imagination rose within her and assured her that she could secure something better than Bragton. The cautions with which she had armed herself faded away. This,—this was the kind of thing for which she had been striving. As a girl of spirit was it not worth while to make another effort even though there might be danger?'

Arabella Trefoil's courage is, indeed, of a very high order for she goes it quite alone. The whole world is against her—not only Lord Rufford's family and friends, but even her aunt the Duchess of Mayfair who detests her, and almost her own mother whose aid in this new campaign she insultingly rejects. Defeated by them all, she ends by marrying another young diplomat who is going out as British Minister to Patagonia. By dint of persuading her uncle to let her be married from Mistle-toe—a suggestion of her future husband, the worldly-wise Mounser Green—Arabella manages to give her sudden wedding a certain aristocratic sheen, so that it is reported in the social columns of the newspapers. She airily surmounts the discredit of having been engaged to three different young men in one hunting winter, but inwardly she feels a bleak and incurable sense of boredom:

' "I wonder what you will think of Patagonia?" said Mounser Green, as he took his bride away.

' "I don't suppose I shall think much. As far as I can see one place is always like another."

' "But then you will have duties."

' "Not very heavy, I hope."

'Then he preached her a sermon, expressing a hope, as he went on, that as she was leaving the pleasures of life behind her, she would learn to like the work of life.

' "I have found the pleasures very hard," she said.'

As must be apparent from its title, *The American Senator* is not exclusively dedicated to the febrile activities of Arabella Trefoil. In the Senator from Mikewa, the irritatingly designated Mr Elias Gotobed, Anthony Trollope has invented a perfect vehicle for propagating his own views on the state of England—such pet aversions, for instance, as the sale and purchase of Church livings. Anthony is always kindly to the American characters in his novels, and he is able to poke mild fun at the Senator's rapacious search for information, while at the same time making many British institutions seem, by the time they have been explained to Mr Gotobed, to be very absurd indeed. Even Anthony's private fox-hunting passion is made to look ludicrous by the time Mr Gotobed has dealt with it and has stopped asking why the huntsman is not the Master of Hounds, why 'the dogs can't be brought out without servants to mind them', who pays for the hunt servants, why and with what money, whether the M.F.H. himself is not, as Gotobed surmises, 'a sort of upper servant', and why the huntsmen have not 'got a fox with them'. The Senator's final and most sententious verdict on a morning meet at the Old Kennels of the Ufford and Rufford Hunt Club makes his forbearing host lose his temper at last :

' "Upon the whole, Mr Morton, I should say that it is one of the most incomprehensible things that I have ever seen in the course of a rather long and varied life . . ."

' "I suppose," said Mr Morton angrily, "the habits of one country are incomprehensible to another. When I see Americans loafing about in the bar-room of an hotel, I am lost in amazement."

' "There is not a man you see who couldn't give a reason for his being there. He has an object in view,—though perhaps it may be no better than to rob his neighbour. But here there seems to be no possible motive." '

Towards the very end of the book, Senator Gotobed delivers a lecture in St James's Hall on *The Irrationality of Englishmen*. This arouses his audience to such fury that the police are forced to intervene.

The American Senator contains some more than customarily violent hunting scenes, in one of which a guest at Rufford is kicked on the skull by his wild mare, and dies a few days later. The Ufford and Rufford Hunt Club reappears in *Ayala's Angel* (written in 1878 but not published until June 1881). With his usual exactitude, Trollope leaves the same old huntsman in charge; but the Master is now Ayala Dormer's host at Stalham Park, Sir Henry Albury. Lord Rufford comes to the meet but, after six years of marriage to Miss Caroline Penge, a coal heiress from Wales, he has deteriorated in looks, has grown fat and hardly ever takes a fence any more. Miss Penge had been chosen by Rufford's sister, Lady Penwether, as a permanent protection against any more designing girls; and Lord Rufford had, in truth, been so shaken by his narrow escape from Arabella Trefoil that he accepted marriage with resigned docility. In the few sentences he speaks to the old huntsman, Tony Tappett, he quotes his wife's opinion about the lack of foxes in the home woods, and it is made clear that the dashing, flirtatious bachelor peer has been totally cowed by his wife, who even has her say in hunting matters. Tappett and Lord Rufford are discussing the fatal accident six years ago. The huntsman says that he never 'wants 'em to jump over nothing I can't help;—I don't, my Lord'.

'That's just what her ladyship is always saying to me,' said Lord Rufford, 'and I do pretty much what her ladyship tells me.'

It is hard to decide which is more worthy of pity—Arabella Trefoil giving formal dinner-parties in the British Legation in the capital of Patagonia, or Lord Rufford shackled for life to the sensible Caroline Penge. Lord Rufford was not the only man to find Arabella Trefoil alarming; she had ended by thoroughly frightening her creator himself. 'I have been, and still am very much afraid of Arabella Trefoil,' Anthony Trollope confessed in a letter written to a friend who had congratulated him upon *The American Senator*.

'The critics have to come, and they will tell that she is unwomanly, unnatural, turgid, the creation of a morbid imagination ... But I swear I have known the woman ... all the traits, all the cleverness, all the patience, all the courage, all the self-abnegation,—and all the failure ... Will such a one as Arabella Trefoil be damned, and if so why? Think of her virtues; how she works, how true she is to her vocation, how little there is of self-indulgence, or idleness. I think that she will go to a third class heaven in which she will always be getting third class husbands.'

During the later autumn and winter of 1875, Anthony Trollope
was at work on a new and secret book of which he could never
hope himself to see a single review. This manuscript bore the
simple title *An Autobiography*, and he stipulated that it should
be brought out as swiftly as possible after his own death. He
finished the manuscript in the spring of 1876, writing it all out
in his own almost illegible hand. While he was writing it he had
told no one about this memoir, but in the summer of 1878 he
spoke of its existence to his son Harry, telling him where he
would ultimately find it together with a note giving instructions
about a speedy publication. 'My intention is that it shall be
published after my death, and be edited by you,' he wrote. 'But
I leave it altogether to your discretion whether to publish or to
suppress the work ... If you wish to say any word as from
yourself, let it be done in the shape of a preface or introductory
chapter.'

To anyone trying to write about Anthony Trollope his autobiography is, obviously, an essential source. It seems, when you
first read it, to be candid, artless, complacent and truthful—and
so indeed to some degree it is. Yet however many times you
reread it you become more and more exasperated not by what he
chooses to tell the world about himself, but by the enormous
amount of personal feelings and intimate events which he has
chosen to leave out. On the first page of these memoirs he tells us
that he believes it to be impossible for any man to write down
everything about himself. 'Who could endure to own to a mean
thing? Who is there that has done none?' At the end of *An
Autobiography* he reverts to this theme, asserting that no man
has ever written a truthful record of his 'inner life', and that no
man in the future will ever do so. Rousseau 'probably attempted
it', but Anthony judges that Rousseau's *Confessions* were inaccurate. In the irritating penultimate paragraph of his book he
declares that his own real inner life cannot matter to any
reader:

'If the rustle of a woman's petticoat has ever stirred my
blood; if a cup of wine has been a joy to me; if I have thought
tobacco at midnight in pleasant company to be one of the elements of an earthly paradise; if now and again I have somewhat
recklessly fluttered a £5 note over a card-table;—of what matter
is that to any reader? I have betrayed no woman. Wine has
brought me no sorrow ... To enjoy the excitement of pleasure,
but to be free from its vices and ill effects,—to have the sweet,

and leave the bitter untasted,—that has been my study. The preachers tell us that this is impossible. It seems to me that hitherto I have succeeded fairly well. I will not say that I have never scorched a finger,—but I carry no ugly wounds.'

This self-portrait of one of England's greatest novelists is, as a matter of fact, both smug and deceptive. Alive, Anthony Trollope had learned to conceal his quivering sensibility by adopting a loud, extroverted manner. He was uncertain whether he would be read by posterity, but if he were to be so he wished to represent himself as a dull, straightforward old party who wrote novels at a mechanical speed and with moralistic aims. We can only conclude that he wrote *An Autobiography* with this misleading aim in view.

Two days after completing his own memoir, on April 30th, 1876, Trollope began work on the last of the Palliser novels, *The Duke's Children* which, as we have seen earlier, opens with the death of Glencora Palliser, Duchess of Omnium. The theme of this excellent novel is what would now be called the generation gap, for it concerns the widower Duke's anxiety about the future of his daughter Lady Mary Palliser, and the present conduct of his two young sons, Lord Silverbridge and Lord Gerald Palliser. Mary Palliser is in love with a Cornish youth, Frank Tregear, who although a gentleman, has no prospects of inheriting any money, and whom the Duke thinks far too lowly for his only daughter. Lord Silverbridge, who is expected to marry Lady Mable Grex, falls in love with the latest American beauty, Isabel Boncassen. After a stiff determined rearguard action by the Duke of Omnium, he is finally induced to accept the American marriage for his eldest son and that of his daughter to Frank Tregear. Isabel Boncassen, the only American heroine in all Trollope's novels, is convincing without being particularly interesting. In Lady Mabel Grex we meet a far more complex and unhappy girl. Lady Mabel, who lives with a companion in her father's house in Belgrave Square, is no Arabella Trefoil, although like that young woman she is alive to the need to marry money. She and young Frank Tregear had been in love, but could not marry on financial grounds. Tregear next falls in love with Lady Mary Palliser, while Lady Mabel Grex, who is still in love with him, makes rather hopeless efforts to marry Lady Mary's brother Lord Silverbridge. To do it she has to pretend to be in love with him, but she does this in so languid a way that she can never get him to propose to her; when she perceives that he is falling in love with the American

Miss Boncassen she is stirred into wily activity, but by this time it is altogether too late. Her dissipated father dies, the house in Belgrave Square is closed, and Lady Mabel Grex and her companion, Miss Casseway, retire to Grex, a great down-at-heel family house in a most beautiful part of Westmorland, where, Trollope indicates, the lonely girl will spend the rest of her life.

Mabel Grex is a good example of Trollope's aristocratic women who are victims both of their own emotions and of cruel social and financial circumstances. There is no moral to be drawn from Lady Mabel's plight, since she had done nothing to deserve it; when she tries to struggle out of it she is too truthful and too sincere to succeed. There is, indeed, no moral to be drawn from *The Duke's Children* at all. It is a much more mellow—even much more benign—book than the four harsh satires we have just been considering.

Trollope's grasp of the Duke's psychology throughout the political novels is masterly. In this last of the Palliser novels he has aged exactly as such a man would have aged, still unable to express the affection for his family which he wholeheartedly feels, and even more austere and less spontaneous than before. The pride which Anthony Trollope took in Plantagenet Palliser was justified:

'I think that Plantagenet Palliser, Duke of Omnium, is a perfect gentleman [he writes in the last chapter of *An Autobiography*]. If he be not, then am I unable to describe a gentleman ... I do not think it probable that my name will remain among those who in the next century will be known as writers of English prose fiction;—but if it does, that permanence of success will probably rest on the character of Plantagenet Palliser, Lady Glencora, and the Rev. Mr Crawley.'

(vi)

The novel which, chronologically speaking, followed *The Duke's Children* was *John Caldigate*, partly set in the goldfields of Australia, and which we have already considered in an earlier chapter. The book was begun in London in February 1877, and finished at sea in July—for, ignoring the marked symptoms of age, Anthony Trollope set out once more upon his travels, South Africa and its diamond-mines being now his goal. Once again he had promised his publishers delivery of a travel book and once again he was commissioned by Nicholas Trübner to write a set of articles for the British provincial press. Once again he suffered from the hateful 'multiplying writer', which he jetti-soned before going up-country in the post cars, for the carmen charged the traveller on the weight of the baggage he was lug-ging about the dry and dusty plains: 'I own I look forward with dread to some of the journeys I shall have to make in post cars. Five hundred miles at a stretch,—with five or six hours allowed at night,' he wrote to Harry Trollope. This last of his world-wide travels was, to Anthony, by far the least enjoyable. His mood was anything but expansive: 'I don't like anyone on board, but I hate two persons,' he reported back to his son from the s.s. *Caldera*. '. . . I think from all I hear and the little I see that I shall find the Cape a most uninteresting place. The people who are going there on board this ship are just the people who would go to an uninteresting Colony.'

When he reached Cape Town it proved just as detestable as he had anticipated—'a poor, niggery, yellow-faced, half-bred sort of a place, with an ugly Dutch flavour about it'. The Afri-can continent, of which hitherto he had seen only the part bordering the Mediterranean, seemed somehow to unnerve him, and even to affect adversely his epistolary style: 'Africa is al-ways queerer than the other quarters, more niggery and uncom-fortable,' he complained, again to Harry. Pretty soon homesick-ness set in: 'I do so long to get home. South Africa is so dirty.' From the marine resort of Mossel Bay he wrote that he was off on an expedition with a total stranger 'in quest of grand scenery —The grandest scenery in the world to me would be Montagu Square.' Joining up with a young man named Farran, who was travelling, it would seem, for a firm of plough-makers back home, Anthony gamely decided to share with him the cost of four horses and a carriage, in which they travelled slowly but with freedom, being no longer tied to public transport. At the end of the journey they sold the horses and the vehicle by auc-tion, netting £100.

Precisely why Trollope chose the South African Colonies as a subject we do not know—unless it were simply that they were much discussed in London and had lately become a major prob-lem to Disraeli's government, which could not decide whether they should be federated or not. James Anthony Froude had also spent a good deal of time roaming about the Cape, and on his return had acted as unofficial counsellor to the Secretary of State for the Colonies, the enlightened Earl of Carnarvon. Froude felt that colonial subjects were almost his private prov-ince as a writer and, as we have seen resented 'old Trollope banging about the world', when Anthony had gone to the West Indies. For Trollope to go to South Africa was, in Froude's eyes, poaching, and he now added to his original dictum. Froude had a silken voice and a sharp tongue: 'Old Trollope,' he remarked, 'after banging about the world so long, now treading in my footsteps, and, like an intellectual bluebottle, buzzing about at Cape Town.' Anthony got his South African book completed and published two years before Froude's own book was ready.

The book, *South Africa*, was published by Chapman & Hall in 1878. The most valued return the two volumes brought Anthony Trollope was a new, close friendship with Lord Carnarvon, with whom he had previously not been intimate. Carnarvon now consulted Trollope rather than Froude about a South African confederation. The doors of Highclere, Lord Carnarvon's famous house in Hampshire, were now open to Anthony, who, in these last years of his life, stayed there frequently. In the days of the statesman Earl the company at Highclere was so intellectual and so distinguished that his hospitalities were compared with Cicero's house-parties at Tusculum. Statesmen, writers, scholars, historians of established merit would all be found staying at Highclere while, to keep in touch with the future generation, clever boys from Oxford and Cambridge were at times invited too. At Highclere Trollope liked to play the Wykehamist and quote classical Latin tags, which possibly bored the company and is known to have produced a retort from Robert Browning, who was also a frequent guest in the house: 'My dear Trollope, this display of classical lore really reminds one of Thackeray's scholar who had earned fame and the promise of a bishopric by his masterly translation of Cornelius Nepos.' One day at Highclere, Anthony was indulging in 'classical small talk' with his host and Lord Carnarvon's cousin Mr Robert Herbert, the astute and long-suffering Permanent Under-Secretary for the Colonies. Robert Browning was also present at this discussion, as was an Eton master, Mr Everard. It was believed by Escott that it was this conversation that led Trollope to decide to write his life of Cicero, which was greeted with derision when published in the summer of 1880. Like his political ambitions, these efforts to be known as an authority on Caesar or on Cicero are best regarded as harmless fads.

Another great country house to which Trollope used to go was Waddesdon, the spectacular mansion of Baron Ferdinand de Rothschild, which was filled with perfect examples of the work of the best French painters, ebonists and porcelain-makers of the eighteenth century. Baron Ferdinand kept a *Livre d'Or*, quite in that old fashion of friendship books which had begun to be kept in Europe at the time of the Renaissance. Eminent guests were asked to write or—in the case of Millais and other painters—to draw a sketch for the book. When staying at Waddesdon in the spring of 1873, Anthony submitted to the Baron's request:

> 'You want me to indite something elegant and terse,
> I never writ a poem and I seldom made a verse.
> A novel in three volumes you would think a little long—
> A sermon or an essay would be coming out too strong.
> An anagram or rebus is quite beyond my power;
> Or a satyre, short in twenty words, illnatured sharp and sour.
> Pretty little witty things have never been my game.
> So I'll just write, as I always write, my own ill written name—

> ANTHONY TROLLOPE,
> *March 10—1873—*

Anthony Trollope's *South Africa* was published in March 1878. The following April, a few days after his sixty-third birthday, he settled down to write *Ayala's Angel*. He now had less than five more years to live, but during this period he produced eight novels, excluding *The Landleaguers* left unfinished at his death. He began to suffer from shortness of breath and pains in the chest, but he still bravely battled on in the literary and social worlds of London. Seeing him for the first time in 1879, Nathaniel Hawthorne's son Julian was much impressed by Anthony's vigour. It was at a publisher's party that young Hawthorne watched this strange, gesticulating old man 'with a ruddy countenance and snow-white tempestuous beard and hair ... He seemed to be in a state of some excitement; he spoke volubly and almost boisterously ... He turned himself as he spoke with a burly briskness, from one side to another ... his words bursting forth from beneath his white moustache with such an impetus of hearty breath that it seemed as if all opposing arguments must be blown away. Meanwhile he flourished in the air an ebony walking-stick ... He was clad in evening dress, though the rest of the company was, for the most part, in mufti; and he was an exceedingly fine-looking old gentleman.'

Until some fifteen years ago it was customary for anyone writing about Trollope's novels to treat the last eight of these with either condescension or disdain. Following in the footsteps of the critics of his own century they have felt that *Dr Wortle's School, Kept in the Dark, Cousin Henry, Ayala's Angel, Marion Fay, The Fixed Period, An Old Man's Love* and *Mr Scarborough's Family* all exhibit failing powers. Since 1955, however, three scholarly works have helped to resurrect these novels,* and to make it clear that at least four of them must be recognized as powerful and even inevitable developments of Anthony Trollope's later thought and style. Only one of these later novels can safely be discarded: this is *The Fixed Period*, which deals with euthanasia on a mythical Pacific island in the twentieth century, and is uninventive, silly and dull.

Cousin Henry and *Mr Scarborough's Family* are two further, deeper investigations of monomania and morbid psychology—subjects which Trollope first presented to his resistant public in *He Knew He Was Right* and which had also inspired *Lady Anna. Ayala's Angel* is calmer in mood, being the tale of the two Dormer sisters, one of whom, Ayala, lives in a gossamer world of fantasy seeking but never finding 'an angel of light' who would be worthy of her love. Her illusions gradually evaporate, and she ends up by loving and marrying an ugly, witty, authoritarian colonel with red hair, after refusing the proposal of her rich cousin Tom Tringle. Her sister Lucy, likewise a romantic, loves a penniless young sculptor, Isadore Hamel. These unworldly sisters stay, alternately, one with their rich relatives the Tringles, in a house at the top of Queen's Gate, the other with their impoverished aunt and uncle in Kingsbury Crescent. Both, therefore, experience life in a household of brainless luxury and life in a small, dark house run on cheese-paring lines in which darning old sheets is the order of the day. For Ayala neither of these ways of living is tolerable; she finds the Tringle households in London and up in Scotland heavy and vulgar, and the Dossets' home in Kingsbury Crescent mean and trammelling. When she is invited to stay at Stalham Park by the Alburys she discovers civilized country-house life for the first time. Like Arabella Trefoil, Ayala at once recognizes that this is where she

* I refer to A. O. J. Cockshut's *Anthony Trollope, A Critical Study* (Collins, 1955), to Professor Bradford A. Booth's *Anthony Trollope: Aspects of His Life and Art*, and finally to *The Changing World of Anthony Trollope*, by Professor Robert M. Polhemus.

belongs, but she does so without envy and without the remotest hope of marrying into such a sphere.

'Oh, what a world of joy was this;—how infinitely superior even to Queen's Gate and Glenbogie! The gaudy magnificence of the Tringles had been altogether unlike the luxurious comfort of Stalham, where everybody was at his ease, where everybody was good-natured, where everybody seemed to acknowledge that pleasure was the one object of life!'

Ayala Dormer, although vague and idealistic, does learn a lesson from all she sees. Amongst Trollope's young women, the ones who learn most, and adapt quickest, are only too often the Lizzie Eustaces of his world, stepping upon the weaknesses of others to reach the peaks of their own ambition. Ayala can at times be fanciful and irritating, but at least her motives are singularly pure and unstained.

If we count in the unfinished *Landleaguers*, we now have another eight novels by Anthony Trollope to be considered in the present book.

All the last novels save *Ayala's Angel* were copied out by Anthony's wife, presumably from the dictation taken down by her niece Flo. One of the many unanswered questions which I briefly mentioned far earlier in this book remains, as I then pointed out, unanswerable: to what degree did Rose Trollope influence, censor or appreciate her husband's successive novels? Writing on his way to Cape Town to their son Harry about whether to put 'Edited by Henry Trollope' on the title-page of a book which he was editing, Anthony suggested that Harry had better take his mother's advice on the quality of the book (which was a life of Bianconi, the Italian car-man at Clonmel, by his daughter): 'I should take Mamma's advice as to the goodness for she is never mistaken about a book being good or bad.' In *An Autobiography* he writes that his wife had always guided him in matters of taste in his novels—a task of extreme delicacy with someone as opinionated and hot-tempered as he. Her husband's health had by now become a great anxiety to Rose Trollope. For six weeks in 1878, while he was writing *Ayala's Angel*, Anthony went on a Scottish friend's yacht *Mastiff* for a relaxing trip to Iceland; he wrote a gay little booklet *How the Mastiffs went to Iceland*, which was, it seems, privately printed in 1878 by Vertue, with sketches by Mrs Hugh Blackburn.

This comfortable month on board the future Lord Inverclyde's yacht must certainly have been novel and pleasant. Trollope was not, however, in a very cheerful mood in the summer of 1878, for in March of that year he had given up hunting once and for all: 'Alas, alas, my hunting is over,' he wrote to William Blackwood. 'I have given away my breeches, boots and horses. The abnegations forced upon us by life should be accepted gracefully. I have not therefore waited to drain the cup to the last drop.' Only men and women themselves dedicated to some favourite sport will be able to understand how heart-rending this dispersal of his horses and his saddlery must have been. The only relic of his hunting days which he retained was a fox's brush, souvenir of 'a glorious run from Lubber Hedges Wood one frosty afternoon, when only John Ridley, James Stallibrass, and himself were in at the death'. When Waltham House was sold, and much of its contents auctioned off, Anthony had brought this Essex brush to his London house, and then to

Harting Grange. Not long before his death he summoned Stalli-brass and gave it to him, saying: 'When you are going to die pass it on to Ridley.' In 1897 the brush was still in the posses-sion of Mr Ridley's son.

Old Anthony was now finding he needed much more sleep than ever before. He wrote to George Eliot from Felsinegg in Switzerland where he and his wife were staying: 'Here we are on top of a mountain, where I write for four hours a day, eat for two, and sleep out the balance satisfactorily. I am beginning to think that the more a man can sleep the better for him. I can take a nap of nine hours each night without moving in these latitudes.' To his Hertfordshire connection, Cecilia Meetkerke, he confessed that he was at last beginning to procrastinate from fatigue:

'... in truth, I am growing so old that, though I still do my daily work, I am forced to put off the lighter tasks from day to day: To-morrow will do—and to-morrow! ... when I have been cudgelling my overwrought brain for some three or four hours in quest of words, then I fade down, and begin to think that it will be nice to go to the club, and have tea, and play whist, and put off my letters till the evening.'

In 1880 the Anthony Trollopes took a major decision—to get rid of 39 Montagu Square, and find a small country house in a region which might alleviate Anthony's attacks of asthma. The old man now frankly admitted that he was tired of London: 'I hate the dinner parties and all going out,' he wrote to his son Harry in June 1880. The house they chose, and took on a seven-teen-year lease, was called North End, and later renamed The Grange; it was at Harting, close to Petersfield in West Sussex, twelve miles from Chichester. The building had been con-structed from two former farmhouses, which had been joined together. It was rated as 'among the best and prettiest buildings in the district'. A long line of windows and doors opened on the lawn, which had as background a copse of fir trees and larches. There were seventy acres of land. A long shaded walk wound through the trees to a gate which gave direct access to fields running up on to the South Downs. Anthony wrote in reply to a question by Alfred Austin:

'Yes, we have changed our mode of life altogether. We have got a little cottage here, just big enough (or nearly so) to hold my books, with five acres and a cow and a dog and a cock and a hen ... I am as busy as would be one thirty years younger, in cutting out dead boughs, and putting up a paling here and a little gate there. We go to church and mean to be very good, and have maids to wait on us.'

Some months after the move to Harting, the local doctor, Cross, thought that he had detected symptoms of *angina pectoris* in Anthony Trollope. A second opinion was obtained from a young Dr Murrell, a heart-specialist with a consulting room in Portland Place. Dr Murrell reassured his patient: 'He says that I have not a symptom of A.P. and that Cross is an old idiot,' Anthony reported to his son. He told Harry that he himself did not believe that he was suffering from *angina pectoris*: 'But I have got to be old,' he wrote, 'and nearly worn out with another disease.' This secondary ailment was a severe hernia, for which he had to wear 'a huge truss'. At some time in these last years he would also seem to have suffered a minor stroke, since his right arm became half-paralysed: 'But I still am very good to look at,' he wrote to a new friend, the historian E. A. Freeman, 'and as I am not afraid to die I am as happy as other people.'

(ii)

From the sad state of his health in the last four or five years of his life, some deterioration in the rate of Anthony Trollope's writing and in the quality of his style would not surprise us: but, as a matter of fact, he was as hard-working as ever, and at least four of the group of novels which he wrote in this period are well up to his best standard. *Cousin Henry*, which he completed in London before the move to Harting, is with no shadow of doubt one of the best, as well as one of the most compact, books which Anthony Trollope ever wrote. This novel is as taut as an excellent play. It has only a handful of characters, but the young man of the title, whose full name is Henry Jones, is given priority all through. Trollope has boldly manipulated the hackneyed theme of a lost will and a mistaken inheritance to produce an agonizing portrait of a man whose very presence in a room never fails to arouse hatred and contempt. Henry Jones cannot look anyone in the eyes. Ever since his sly, untruthful boyhood, Henry has never inspired love, affection or loyalty. The servants at his Uncle Indefer's house, Llanfeare, detest him. His old uncle cannot bear him. His cousin Isabel, whom the old man would like him to marry, rejects his proposal out of hand, and when Henry asks her why she will not marry him she makes the charming rejoinder: 'Because,—because,—because you are odious to me!'

Cousin Henry is one of Trollope's novels with a really promising opening. There are no prosy explanations about genealogy, and when we do go back into the past it is in the most cursory fashion. Chapter One of *Cousin Henry* begins with a conversation between Indefer Jones, the old squire of Llanfeare, and his niece Isabel Broderick, a proud, plain-spoken girl who lives in his house:

' "I have a conscience, my dear, on this matter," said an old gentleman to a young lady as the two were sitting in the breakfast parlour of a country house which looked down from the cliffs over the sea on the coast of Carmarthenshire.

' "And so have I, Uncle Indefer; as my conscience is backed by my inclination, whereas yours is not——"

' "You think that I shall give way?"

' "I did not mean that."

' "What then?"

' "If I could only make you understand how very strong is my inclination, or disinclination—how impossible to be conquered, then——"

' "What next?"

' "Then you would know that I could never give way, as you call it, and you would go to work with your own conscience to see whether it be imperative with you or not." '

Another conversation a month later reveals that the old squire's conscience is driving him distracted. The cause of his anguish is indecision over his own will. Llanfeare is no longer entailed—he can leave it to whom he wishes. His nephew Henry Jones, who works in a London office, is the obvious heir, if only for the sake of the family name. But Mr Indefer Jones despises his cringing nephew and would prefer to leave the place to Isabel, whose mother was a Jones but whose father is a Broderick, living in Hereford with his second wife. Old Indefer loves his niece as much as he loathes his nephew; yet, from sheer sense of tradition he is prepared to sacrifice Isabel if he can force her to marry Henry Jones. In his eyes this is the only way he can be satisfied—knowing that, after his own imminent death, Isabel will be mistress of Llanfeare but will be called Mrs Jones. Trollope's later novels contain some terrifying examples of selfish old men—it has even been suggested that one or two of these are mocking self-portraits.

' "You do not care a straw for the family" [the petulant old man snaps out at Isabel].

' "You should not say that, Uncle Indefer. It is not true. I care enough for the family to sympathize with you altogether in what you are doing, but not enough for the property to sacrifice myself in order that I might have a share in it."

'"I do not know why you should think so much evil of Henry."

'"Do you know any reason why I should think well enough of him to become his wife? I do not. In marrying a man a woman should be able to love every little trick belonging to him. The parings of his nails should be dear to her. Every little wish of his should be a care to her. It should be pleasant to her to serve him in things most menial."

'"You are always full of poetry and books" [the squire of Llanfeare inexplicably answers].'

With her swaddling views on marriage, it is clear to us that Isabel could never be a real wife to cousin Henry Jones who, though unattractive in character, is

'not evil to the eye, a somewhat good-looking man, tall with well-formed features, with light hair and blue-grey eyes, not subject to being spoken of as being unlike a gentleman, if not noticeable as being like one. That inability of his to look one in the face when he was speaking had not struck the Squire forcibly as it had done Isabel.'

Isabel is, as a matter of fact, in love with a young clergyman, a minor canon attached to Hereford Cathedral. When, after her uncle's death, Henry Jones is named heir in his will, Isabel leaves Llanfeare to live in Hereford, but she obstinately refuses to marry her minor canon, William Owen, because they would not have enough to live on. In this not uninteresting scene Miss Broderick amplifies for the young man's benefit her attitude towards marriage and towards himself. In reply to a direct question she confesses that she does indeed love him:

'"You must know it all," she said, "though it may be unwomanly to tell so much."

'"Know what?"

'"There has never been a man whose touch has been pleasant to me;—but I could revel in yours. Kiss you? I could kiss your feet at this moment and embrace your knees. Everything belonging to you is dear to me. The Prayer-Book tells the young wife that she should love her husband till death shall part them. I think my love will go further than that."

'"Isabel! Isabel!"'

Mr Owen not unnaturally concludes from Isabel Broderick's sensuous declaration that she will marry him. Mr Owen, however, knows far, far less than we about Trollope's stubborn heroines. He has never heard tell of Alice Vavasor or Emily Wharton.

'"Keep away from me' [Isabel commands]. "I will not even give you my hand to shake till you have promised to be of one mind with me. I will not become your wife."

'"You shall become my wife!"

'"Never! Never! I have thought it out and I know that I am right..."'

While being a bit unusual, Isabel Broderick's ideas on love and marriage are merely tributary to the main stream of events in *Cousin Henry*. This 'craven' (as his cousin Isabel calls him) has quite by chance come across old Mr Indefer Jones's final will and testament in a volume of Jeremy Taylor's sermons. This will, which no one but two farmer witnesses and Isabel herself knew to exist, bequeathes everything at Llanfeare to the niece. For many years now Mr Indefer Jones has played that game of will-brandishing so popular with idle, crotchety old persons; he has made various wills leaving everything to Isabel, others leaving it all to Henry. When Isabel had absolutely refused to marry her cousin at her uncle's bidding, the old squire had made what was supposed to be a final will in Henry's favour, and had even quarrelled over it with his lawyer, who disapproved and protested. But a month's visit from young Henry Jones proved more than he could bear, and so, during Isabel's absence in Hereford, he had made another will in his own handwriting and had it duly witnessed. The psychological reactions of Henry when he finds this other will in the library are beautifully explored: he will not tell anyone that he has found a document depriving him of Llanfeare (in which he is now living) but, though greatly tempted, he lacks the courage to burn the will and so commit a criminal act rather than a sin of omission. He knows that sooner or later the new will must be discovered. He takes to sitting in the library, staring at the shelf of Taylor's sermons until the servants, thinking him mad, all give notice. In the end the will is found by Apjohn, the family attorney, who becomes suspicious on observing Henry's pallid, sweaty face and trembling hands. Mr Apjohn realizes that there must be some very good reason for the young man's constant presence in the library, where he sits all day and with a single candle through half the night. Cousin Henry goes back to his London office, and Isabel returns home in state, to the pealing bells of Carmarthen and the neighbouring villages: 'She was taken somewhat out of her way round by the creek and Coed, so that the little tinkling of her own parish church might not be lost on her.' Now a rich landowner, she arranges to give cousin Henry (who had not, after all, burnt the will) the rather niggardly sum of £4,000.

(iii)

While he was writing *Cousin Henry* Trollope had arranged for the serialization, in the *Whitehall Review*, of his short Irish novel, *An Eye for an Eye*. This stark and haunting tale had been written in three weeks in the autumn of the long-ago year of 1870. He had then put it by in his desk and did not allow it to appear for eight years. We cannot know the reason for this long delay. Published in book form in 1879, it had, with one single exception, poor reviews. It is yet another of the later Trollope novels which made contemporary readers uncomfortable and ill at ease. Were it not that he had written his first study of insanity in *He Knew He Was Right* in 1867, we might claim, as one student of Trollope has already claimed, that *An Eye for an Eye* initiated the series of Trollope's *romans noirs*.

By a skilful use of one of his favourite devices, the letter, Anthony tells us about the tragic heroine of this novel long before we see her. For the first four chapters, Kate O'Hara is merely a distant murky threat to the Earl and Countess of Scroope in their vast and gloomy country house, Scroope Manor, in a flat and unattractive region of Dorsetshire. It is not until the fifth chapter that we are at last transported to the coast of County Clare—to a cottage at the summit of the great, dark, striped cliffs of Mohir, which stand frowning at the Atlantic Ocean. One of the finest, yet most forbidding, sights in all Ireland, the cliffs of Mohir are far more impressive and more terrible than that tourist-trap the Giant's Causeway up in the Six Counties. These cliffs are six hundred feet high, and drop sheer down into the deep blue sea: '... below them rolls the brightest, bluest, clearest water in the world', writes Trollope in a bleak descriptive passage. South of the cliffs of Mohir lies broad Liscannor Bay, with a little fishing village on each side of it—the villages of Liscannor and Lahinch. Some two miles up from the village of Liscannor lies a rambling, one-storeyed little house, less than half a mile from the cliff head—Ardkill Cottage, in which a mysterious lady lives with her equally mysterious but beautiful daughter, Kate. Mrs O'Hara, still a handsome woman, is a recluse, who cannot even have the solace of gardening since the salt spray in the wind precludes the thriving of any flowers or shrubs. She takes lonely walks along Liscannor Bay, and in stormy weather may be seen seated on the top of the cliff, holding her hat in her hand as she lets the sea-wind drench her hair, while she watches the gulls screeching and circling below. From these details of her habits we learn, as we so often do in other Trollope case-histories, the wild tempestuous character of Mrs O'Hara.

A hackneyed but none the less perfectly valid moral is to be gleaned from the tale of Kate O'Hara's seduction by the nephew and heir of Lord Scroope, Frank Neville, who is stationed at Ennis with a detachment of the 20th Hussars. This moral is that boredom becomes automatically a very great danger. Kate O'Hara, who was brought up in Paris, has now lived all alone with her mother in their isolated cottage for a year. She has read every book in the house over and over again, and she has played every piece of music she knows on the piano, which twangs out of tune and is rusty from sea-spray. Their only visitor is Father Marty, the local priest. Mrs O'Hara herself is hardly an invigorating companion:

' "Mother," [Kate] would say, "is it always to be like this?"

' "Not always, Kate," the mother once answered.

' "And when will it be changed?"

' "In a few days—in a few hours, Kate."

' "What do you mean, mother?"

' "That eternity is coming, with all its glory and happiness. If it were not so, it would indeed be very bad." '

Kate O'Hara, though by nature a lively girl, becomes dull and deadened because her life is dull and deadly; but one day Father Marty deliberately brings Fred Neville, who is himself bored in the garrison-town of Ennis, and has hired a boat to go shooting seals. Fred Neville appears to Kate as 'an Apollo, dressed in sailor's jacket and trousers, with a sailor's cap upon his head, with a loose handkerchief round his neck and his hair blowing in the wind'. Fred quickly ingratiates himself with the ladies of Ardkill cottage, for he has an authentic and irresistible charm: 'It might be that the young man was a ravenous wolf, but his manners were not wolfish.' He sincerely promises to marry Kate, but once he has seduced her she loses her value in his eyes by giving him all that he had asked for; moreover he learns that her father is an alcoholic and a former convict. During his visits to Scroope Manor, the last of which comes after his uncle's death when he himself becomes Earl of Scroope, Fred is more and more beguiled by his sense of heredity, position and prospective wealth. Fred's change of heart is slow and comprehensible. His Irish love affair begins to seem to him 'squalid and mean': 'By a few soft words spoken to a poor girl he had chanced to find among the rocks he had so bound himself with vile manacles, had so crippled, hampered and fettered himself, that he was forced to renounce all the glories of his station.' Kate is already pregnant, but Fred Neville is too cowardly to go to Ardkill and tell them that now he cannot marry her. He is finally lured thither by Mrs O'Hara, who shows herself as fierce and obsessive a mother as Lady Lovel in *Lady Anna* or the Countess of Desmond in *Castle Richmond*. She manoeuvres Neville with his back towards the edge of the cliffs to Mohir, gives him a sudden kick, and he goes spinning down to be smashed to pieces on the jagged rocks below.

This is but the barest sketch of an extremely readable book. The role of the parish priest in *An Eye for an Eye* is a questionable one, for Trollope hints that Father Marty may have had designs in introducing the O'Haras to Fred Neville.

The figure of Father Marty is one of Trollope's best portraits of Roman Catholic priests. When he was posted to Belfast in 1853 he told someone that he preferred Irish Papists to Irish Presbyterians; and it is noticeable that, while he presented most of the Anglican clergy of Barchester as devious and worldly, he has, with one exception, nothing but good to say of Roman Catholic priests. This exception is Father John Barham, the priest from Beccles, who makes himself unendurable during a dinner-party at Carbury Manor for the Anglican Bishop of the diocese in *The Way We Live Now*. One of Anthony's most fervent yet most critical admirers, Miss Mary Holmes, was herself a Catholic and wrote to protest about Father Barham. In his reply Anthony very honestly explains his views regarding Catholic priests:

'I must say a word touching my priest in "W.W. Live Now". In the first place he is a thoroughly good man, anxiously doing his duty according to his lights, at any cost of personal suffering, one of whom one might confidently say that he was on the road to heaven. Then, let me,—if I may do so without arrogance—refer to a novel of my own which you yourself name in your letter, "The Macdermots", and say that in the character of Father John there I have drawn as thoroughly good and fine a man as I know how to depict. Then going back to the priest in the later novel, let me say that, when at Waltham, I became acquainted with the R.C. priest there, & opened my house to him in full friendship. He was a thoroughly conscientious man, an Oxford man ... so poor that he had not bread to eat. I & my wife were as good to him as we knew how to be;—but he would never desist for a moment in casting ridicule and opprobrium on my religion ... I was obliged to drop him. He made himself absolutely unbearable.

I have lived much with clergymen of your church, & have endeavoured to draw them in their colours as I saw them. But, because they were the priests of a church not my church, I have never drawn one as bad, or hypocritical or unfaithful.'

(iv)

In his lifetime, Anthony Trollope was most admired for his famous delineations of the worldly, cosy clerics of Barsetshire—Mr Harding, in *The Warden*, and Mr Crawley in *Framley Parsonage*, being the sole high-minded, spiritual clergymen in the whole extensive gallery. His bishops and his clergymen had always been portrayed with a light and lenient touch; but now, in *Cousin Henry*'s successor, *Marion Fay*, he startles us with a domestic chaplain who is as positively evil as he is self-indulgent; teetering on the verge of madness, he meditates upon the murder of his patron's son and heir. In this further example of the *roman noir*, Anthony does not spare the Anglican clergy any more than he spares the laity. The Reverend Thomas Greenwood is nominally domestic chaplain and private secretary to the Marquess of Kingsbury, but he is in fact the familiar—we can use no other word—of the Marchioness, Lord Kingsbury's second wife, a woman contorted by ambition for her three small sons and by a diabolical hatred for the Marquess's heir by his first marriage, young Lord Hampstead. The second Marchioness of Kingsbury, whose Christian name is Clara, is described with the same hostile irreverence which colours so many of Trollope's pictures of aristocratic circles, as against those of the country gentry. Lady Kingsbury is yet another obsessional woman, driven virtually insane by pride in her own rank as the wife of a Marquess:

'If words would not serve her occasion at the moment, her countenance would do so,—and if not that, her absence. She could be very eloquent with silence, and strike an adversary dumb by the way in which she would leave a room. She was a tall, handsome woman, with a sublime gait. To be every inch an aristocrat ... was the object of her life.'

Marion Fay, perhaps deservedly, has never been republished since its original appearance in book form in May 1882, only six months before its author's death. A sharpish attack on snobbery and the English caste system, it is, all the same, a weak and at times a very foolish book. Lord Hampstead is an earnest radical youth ashamed of bearing a title. He has selected for his closest friend a contemporary, George Roden, whose father is dead. Aside from his affection for George Roden, Hampstead feels that by this intimacy he is performing an egalitarian duty, since George, like Trollope in his own young days, is merely a clerk in the General Post Office in St Martins-le-Grand. Hampstead's choice of a plebeian friend infuriates his haughty stepmother. Yet even Lord Hampstead's liberal feelings are jolted when he finds that George has dared to fall in love with his sister, Lady Frances Trafford, that his love is returned, and that they regard themselves as engaged.

Roden's widowed mother lives in a tiny house in a side-street named Paradise Row. Calling on Mrs Roden, Lord Hampstead there encounters Marion Fay, a Quaker girl. He has never before seen a puritan maid wearing a white bonnet and a simple dress of Quaker grey. The novelty of Marion's appearance so startles him that he falls in love with her and determines to make her the future Marchioness of Kingsbury. Marion loves Hampstead, but she refuses to marry him, knowing that she is doomed to an early death from consumption, a disease that has ravaged her family. She dies before the end of the book, in circumstances recalling the death of Anthony Trollope's sister, little Emily, who lies in the quiet village churchyard at Hadley by Enfield Chase. Death has removed Marion's potential as a danger to the noble Kingsburys. Hampstead's sister Lady Frances is luckier in her love, for George Roden's mother suddenly reveals that her husband, now dead, was an Italian duke of ancient lineage. George wisely refuses to bear his comic title —Duca de Crinola—but the fact of his aristocratic background immediately changes the Kingsburys' attitude to him. He marries Lady Frances with her family's warmest approval, and is at once awarded by patronage, a distinguished position in the Foreign Office.

Feeble though it tends to be, *Marion Fay* rewards reading for the sake of the Reverend Thomas Greenwood and of the Marchioness. The moral of *Marion Fay* would seem to be that rank can, if you're not careful, send you mad. Further, I find it interesting that the very last of Trollope's full-length portraits of a Church of England clergyman is that of a demon who will stop at nothing to keep his comfortable berth in the Marquess's household, and who conspires with Lord Hampstead's step-mother to kill him so that her own eldest son shall inherit the title. This distressing presentation of the sleek, stout, pliant minion of a latter-day Lady Macbeth is a clerical vignette with a vengeance. It is as though Anthony Trollope had decided that the time for making the clergy likeable was now over, and that a black coat and a dog-collar were no longer guarantees of normally decent behaviour. It was thus, in his old age, that he called the Church of England's bluff. In England, *Marion Fay* won more critical praise than several of its predecessors. The *Saturday Review* said Trollope had 'reverted to his characteristic manner'; another reviewer thought it would be nice for readers to find themselves back in 'good society' and amidst hunting scenes. The New York *Critic* thought the book tiresome: 'It is a disappointment to find that Mr Trollope can be tiresome; but very, very tiresome and unnatural he is in the story of *Marion Fay*.'

(v)

In February 1879, Anthony Trollope suspended work on *Marion Fay* in order to spend a couple of months on his monograph on William Makepeace Thackeray for the *English Men of Letter* series, edited by John Morley. I have discussed this book in an earlier chapter, in the context of Trollope's short but adulatory friendship with Thackeray. This monograph completed, he wrote *Dr Wortle's School* in a vicarage at Lowick, in Northamptonshire, lent to himself and his family by the Reverend Lucas Collins, a classical scholar with whom he had made friends while writing his *Commentaries of Caesar* nine years before. *Dr Wortle's School* is a short novel, written quickly and completed some days before they all returned to London. After this book, he went back to *Marion Fay*, which was thus the last novel to be written in Montagu Square. His clerical surroundings at Lowick tickled his fancy:

'That I, who have belittled so many clergymen, should ever come to live in a parsonage! [he wrote to his host]. There will be a heaping of hot coals! You may be sure that I will endeavour to behave myself accordingly, so that no scandal shall fall upon the parish ... Shall I be required to preach, as belonging to the Rectory? I shall be quite disposed to give everyone my blessing ... Ought I to affect dark garments? Say the word and I will supply myself with a high waistcoat. Will it be right to be

354

quite genial with the curate, or ought I to patronize a little? If there be dissenters, shall I frown on them, or smile blandly? If a tithe pig be brought to me, shall I eat him? If they take to address me as 'The Rural Anthony' will it be alright?'

Lowick Parsonage was near Thrapston in Northamptonshire. At the end of April they were so snowed up there that they could scarcely cross the road to get to church. They returned to London, presumably for the Season, in May.

Dr Wortle's School is a study in social prejudice. Dr Wortle, who has been assumed by Michael Sadleir to be a self-portrait of Anthony Trollope, is an enlightened clergyman and Fellow of Exeter College, Oxford. Earlier in his career he was an assistant master at Eton and had married a Windsor clergyman's pretty daughter. Having obtained the living of Bowick, Dr Wortle had begun to take in boys destined for Eton; they lived in the parsonage, and were given excellent food. The fee, however, was two hundred pounds a year. He had soon found himself to have so many boarders that he was obliged to build a school on land adjacent to the glebe and purchased out of his own pocket. We are told that Dr Wortle refuses to take more than thirty aristocratic boys in the school-buildings. Because it is so expensive the establishment at Bowick has become famous in the county, and beyond it. The Doctor's friends suggest that by charging two hundred and fifty pounds he could double the number of boys, but he himself does not want to make more money or to lower the quality of the teaching. After failing for some time to find a married clergyman who must also be a scholar, with a wife who, although a lady, will act as matron, Dr Wortle has what he feels to be a real stroke of luck. He engages 'a small, wiry man' in Orders who had formerly been well known at Oxford 'as a Classic', had spent five years as vice-president of a classical college at St Louis, Missouri, and who has a beautiful American wife:

'Mr Peacocke's scholarship and power of teaching were acknowledged; he was already in orders; and it was declared that Mrs Peacocke was undoubtedly a lady. Many inquiries were made. Many meetings took place. Many difficulties arose. But at last Mr and Mrs Peacocke came to Bowick, and took up their abode in the school.'

The only thing wrong with this brace of paragons is that they are not man and wife, as Anthony, in the middle of the brusque third chapter, reveals. He addresses his readers, warning them that, as he ineptly calls it, he is going to 'put the horse of my romance before the cart'.

'It is my purpose to disclose the mystery at once, and to ask you to look for your interest—should you choose to go on with my chronicle—simply in the conduct of my persons, during this disclosure, to others. You are to know it all before the Doctor or the Bishop—before Mrs Wortle, or the Hon. Mrs Stantiloup, or Lady de Lawle. You are to know it all before the Peacockes become aware that it must necessarily be disclosed to anyone ... Our mystery is going to be revealed in the next paragraph—in the next half-dozen words. Mr and Mrs Peacocke were not man and wife.'

He suggests that it will annoy his readers to have the mystery solved so soon, but he was, of course, entirely justified in his schematic plan for the novel; it is the reactions of the Doctor and his wife, the boys' parents and the Bishop of Broughton to this anomalous situation which gives this book momentum. Dr Wortle shows compassion and generosity, even when aristocratic parents begin removing their boys from the school and he seems, by his quixotry, to have ruined its reputation and his own. I imagine that it is this trait in Dr Jeffrey Wortle's character which has led Sadleir and others to see in the Doctor a mirror of Anthony's own kindly self.

Dr Wortle's School, then, concerns a difficult moral situation and its effect upon everyone within its range. The facts of this situation are simple: when Peacocke first went to teach in St Louis he met two brothers, Colonel Ferdinand and Colonel Robert Lefroy. They were the sons of a Southern planter who had lost everything in the Civil War. The elder, Ferdinand, had married Ella Beaufort, the daughter of another ruined planter who had died when she was sixteen; Henry Peacocke fell in love with her. Although brought up as Southern gentlemen the Lefroy brothers 'had fallen by degrees into dishonour, dishonesty and brigandage'. They decided to head for the Mexican border, where a state of lawlessness notoriously prevailed. Ella Lefroy refused to go with them. Some two years later it was rumoured that a Colonel Lefroy had been killed fighting the forces of the United States government. To establish which Lefroy had been killed Peacocke went down to the Texas border, where he met Robert Lefroy, who assured him that his brother was dead. Ella Lefroy, supposing herself to be a widow, then married Henry Peacocke. In the course of time Ferdinand Lefroy, who had not been killed at all, came back to St Louis and suddenly confronted his bigamous wife. Next day he went off, and had never been heard of since. Unable to stay in St Louis, the Peacockes came to England and took employment at Dr Wortle's school. At this point the action of the book commences: Peacocke always means, in an indecisive way, to tell Dr Wortle the truth, but his hand is suddenly forced when Robert Lefroy, Mrs Peacocke's brother-in-law, turns up at Bowick. Dr Wortle, whom Lefroy first visits, pities the couple's plight, lets Peacocke go with Robert Lefroy to Chicago to establish the first husband's whereabouts, and allows Mrs Peacocke to stay on alone at the school, so long as she lives in purdah and does not eat lunch or dinner with the boys or look after their linen.

Sympathizing with Ella's loneliness, and not uninfluenced by her great beauty, Dr Wortle forms the cordial habit of calling on her in the evenings. The wholly innocent relationship of Dr Wortle and Mrs Peacocke becomes a scandal; highly-bred boys are removed from the school by their mothers and fathers, the Bishop chides the Doctor, the local *Gazette* and then a London weekly get hold of the story. Entirely owing to Dr Wortle's compassion, his school seems about to founder. On the way across the Atlantic, Lefroy tells Peacocke that in fact his brother had died a long while ago; on his return from the States Peacocke brings copies of death and burial certificates, and a photograph of Ferdinand Lefroy's tombstone in San Francisco. Like several other bad characters, Ferdinand Lefroy had died of *delirium tremens*. The Peacockes are married in London and go back to Dr Wortle's school, which fills up with grandees' sons once again.

The only peculiar aspect of this tale is Anthony's own attitude to the Peacockes. This is far less forgiving than that of Dr Wortle:

'Should they part? There is no one who reads this but will say that they should have parted. Every day passed together as man and wife must be a falsehood and a sin. There would be absolute misery for both in parting—but there is no law from God or man entitling a man to escape from misery at the expense of falsehood and sin. Though their hearts might have burst in doing it, they should have parted ... That he had lived a life of sin—that he and she had continued in one great falsehood—is manifest enough.'

In mid-Victorian eyes, and in Anthony's own, it was the fact of the Peacockes masquerading as man and wife which was so sinful. We have, in the other Trollope novels, quite a few men who have mistresses: in *Can You Forgive Her?* a whole chapter is devoted to an interview between George Vavasor and his cast-off mistress, now a pauper. The reader is intended to sympathize with Jane and not with Vavasor. In *The Way We Live Now* Paul Montague is followed to London by the dark, magnificent-looking American widow, Winifred Hurtle, whom he had loved in San Francisco and New York. Mrs Hurtle has a tempestuous nature, with 'a bit of the wild cat in her breeding'. She travels with a pistol and has shot at least one man through the head in the wilds of Oregon. Paul Montague has promised to marry her, but now reneges:

'"I know what lies they have crammed you with in San Francisco," [Mrs Hurtle tells him in the dining-room of a Lowestoft hotel]. "You have heard that up in Oregon—I shot a man. That is no lie, I did. I brought him down dead at my feet ... Do you suppose that the sight of that dying wretch does not haunt me? that I do not daily hear his drunken screech, and see him bound from the earth, and then fall in a heap just below my hand? ... My last word to you is, that you are—a liar. Now for the present you can go. Ten minutes since, had I had a weapon in my hand I should have shot another man."'

In *Sir Harry Hotspur of Humblethwaite*, George Hotspur, the villainous nephew of Sir Harry, is kept by an actress whom he ultimately marries. In none of these cases does Trollope bring a moral judgment to bear, because, I believe, these men and women were not pretending to be married and were not making a mockery of the sanctity of marriage. Ella Peacocke and her husband were in grave fault because they did distinctly proclaim to the world the untruth that they were man and wife. The fact that Henry Peacocke had taken Holy Orders, and could administer the sacrament or perform the ceremony of matrimony made his behaviour yet more heinous. It was this that shocked, for instance, Lady Margaret Momsen, a daughter of the Earl of Brigstock, married to a clergyman but 'quite as much the Earl's daughter as the parson's wife':

'... Lady Margaret was proud—especially at the present time.

'"What a romance this is, Mrs Wortle," she said: "that has gone all through the diocese!" ...

'"You mean—the Peacockes?"

'"Of course I do."

'"He has gone away."

'"We all know that, of course—to look for his wife's husband. Good gracious me! What a story!"

'"They think that he is dead—now."

' "I suppose they thought so before," said Lady Margaret.

' "Of course they did."

' "... Her brother came, didn't he?"

' "Her first husband's brother," said Mrs Wortle, blushing.

' "Her first husband!"

' "Well—you know what I mean, Lady Margaret."

' "Yes; I know what you mean. It is so very shocking, isn't it?
And so the two men have gone off together to look for a third.
Goodness me—what a party they will be if they meet! Do you
think they'll quarrel?"

' "I don't know, Lady Margaret."

' "And that he should be a clergyman of the Church of England! Isn't it dreadful? What does the Bishop say? Has he
heard all about it?"

' "The Bishop has nothing to do with it ..." '

Lady Margaret goes on to suggest that her nephew, 'dear
little Gus', may be harmed by the mere proximity of Mrs Peacocke. The doctor's enemy, the Honourable Mrs Stantiloup, is
circularizing all parents with boys at Dr Wortle's, urging them
to take their sons away. Gus Momsen is the son of Squire
Momsen of Buttercup.

' "I suppose Mr Momsen will allow you to send for Augustus
at once?" [said Mrs Stantiloup, turning to Mrs Momsen] ...

' "Mr Momsen thinks so much of the Doctor's scholarship,"
said the mother apologetically. "And we are so anxious that Gus
should do well when he goes to Eton."

' "What is Latin and Greek compared to his soul?" asked
Lady Margaret.

' "No, indeed," said Mrs Rolland. She had found herself
compelled, as wife to the Bishop, to assent to the self-evident
proposition which had been made.

' "... I do hope you'll be firm about Gus," said Mrs Stantiloup to Mrs Momsen. "If we're not to put down this kind of
thing, what is the good of having any morals in the country at
all? We might just as well live like pagans, and do without any
marriage services, as they do in so many parts of the United
States." '

(vi)

Anthony's next novel was *Kept in the Dark*. Once again, this
book has never been reprinted, but, unlike *Marion Fay*, it certainly should have been. It shows a man as morbidly jealous as
Louis Trevelyan in *He Knew He Was Right*, but Mr George

Western is not jealous of the present—he is jealous of the past. Cecilia Holt, one of the young blue-stockings of Devonshire, lives with her well-to-do mother in a house outside Exeter. Although she does not wear pre-Raphaelite robes, Cecilia and her bosom friend Francesca Altifiorla resemble the young ladies in Gilbert and Sullivan's *Princess Ida*. Cecilia's attitude to her mother is both exigent and patronizing:

'The mother seemed to be only there to obey the daughter's behests, and Cecilia was the most affectionate of masters. Nothing could have been less disturbed or more happy than their lives. No doubt there was present in Cecilia's manner a certain looking down upon her mother—of which all the world was aware, unless it was her mother and herself. The mother was not blessed by literary tastes, whereas Cecilia was great among French and German poets. And Cecilia was aesthetic whereas the mother thought more of the delicate providing of the table. Cecilia had two or three female friends, who were not her equals in literature but nearly so ... They formed the *élite* of Miss Holt's society, and were called by their Christian names ... Cecilia had no lovers till there came in an evil hour to Exeter one Sir Francis Geraldine.'

Sir Francis Geraldine is a forty-year-old Devonshire baronet with a small property, Castle Gerald, in that county. He and Cecilia fall in love, and she accepts his offer of marriage. Within a month, however, she finds him inattentive and unreliable. He scoffs at her intellectual interests and behaves as though by intending to make her Lady Geraldine he was doing her a great favour. Cecilia breaks off the engagement, but Sir Francis, in a rage, tells everyone in Exeter that it is he who has jilted her. Cecilia feels in a self-conscious way that everyone in the city is talking about her. She becomes ill, and her mother takes her abroad for a year. On their travels they fall in with an English bachelor of means and former Member of Parliament, George Western, who has a small estate near Ascot. He catches up with them in Rome, where he proposes to Cecilia Holt and is accepted.

Summarized like that, *Kept in the Dark* sounds boring and banal. It is neither. What Cecilia Holt keeps in the dark from her husband is the fact of her previous engagement. She does this from a most human and most awkward of motives—that Western, even before they were engaged, had told her bitterly that he had been jilted by an English beauty with the Cornish name of Mary Tremenhere. Cecilia feels that she cannot tell him her own story which is in a way so similar to his—for this would either sound a made-up tale or would seem to present her as a second Mary Tremenhere. Nor could she tell him the untruth which all her friends believed—that Sir Francis Geraldine had jilted her. Day after day goes by and she tells him nothing; on one occasion she writes him a long letter but does not finish it. John Millais, who drew the frontispiece for *Kept in the Dark*, chose this scene of desperate composition: Cecilia, with one elbow on a renaissance writing table, supports her head with one hand, the other holding reams of writing-paper. Above her a Venetian mirror hangs on the wall. Through the window a view of St Peter's emphasizes Cecilia's *locale*. After their honeymoon, and when they are settled at their house, Durton Lodge near Ascot, their happiness is wrecked by Sir Francis Geraldine, who, discovering that Cecilia has never mentioned him to her husband, writes Mr Western an odious letter revealing all. Sir Francis, a vindictive and unscrupulous man, is urged by a friend of his to refrain from disrupting the Western household. The baronet then propounds his own philosophy:

' "There is nothing recommends itself to my mind so much as even-handed justice ... I suffer as much as they do. But they shall suffer as well as I."

' "The most pernicious doctrine I ever heard in my life," said Dick Ross, as he filled his mouth with cold chicken pie.

' "When you say pernicious, have you any idea what you mean?"

' "Well, yes; awfully savage, and all that kind of thing. Just utter cruelty and a bad spirit."

' "Those are your ideas because you don't take the trouble to return evil for evil. But then you never take the trouble to return good for good. In fact, you have no idea of duty, only you don't like to burden your conscience with doing what seems to be ill-natured ... There is some idea of justice in my conduct, but there is none in yours." '

It so happens that Francis Geraldine is the only man in England whom Cecilia's husband, for personal reasons, cannot abide. On receiving the baronet's mischievous letter his whole esteem and respect for his young wife falls to the ground in dust. He leaves her, as he thinks, for ever, sending his lawyer to arrange with her about an allowance. Western then goes to live in a hotel in Dresden, while Cecilia, desolate but stubborn, refuses to beg his pardon. In the end their troubles are patched up by Western's widowed sister from Perthshire, Bertha, Lady

Grant. Cecilia Western becomes 'the happiest woman in all England', and prepares for the birth of her baby. Pride is the factor which is common to Sir Francis Geraldine, to George Western, and to Cecilia too. Western's behaviour on discovering the facts of the previous engagement is due to a form of hind-sighted jealousy: he cannot bear to think that a girl who has seemed to him so pure and noble-minded should ever have been in love before she met him—and in love with the brutal baronet at that. His mind clouded by this knowledge, he makes his neurotic flight abroad.

Just as Italy is, in Trollope's novels, chiefly a dangerous, conspiratorial land from which come nasty half-breed children like the hypothetical Lord Popenjoy or Julia Neroni in *Barchester Towers*, so is Germany a refuge for those of the English upper class whose marriages have collapsed. Mr Western goes to Dresden, the city in which Lady Laura Kennedy lived with her father once she had left her husband. Baden-Baden is the residence chosen by the Countess de Courcy when she leaves Courcy Castle never to return, and in her retinue travels her daughter Lady Alexandrina Crosbie, who has left her husband after six weeks of marriage. Lady Alexandrina dies in Baden-Baden and her family force her impoverished husband to pay two hundred and forty-five pounds for the transport of her coffin from Baden to the family vault in Barsetshire. Baden to Trollope's personages connotes gambling, drinking and every other form of self-indulgence. Paris, on the other hand, is merely a city passed through by English travellers heading south, a staging post for Florence or Venice or Rome. Having himself paid visits to Florence both before and after his old mother's death Anthony at times uses it as scenery for a chapter or two. On her European tour with her mother, Cecilia Holt's state of mind is expressed by her attitude to the Florentine Campanile. She is so possessed by the idea of being thought to be the girl Sir Francis Geraldine has jilted, that she scarcely sees the sights her mother so much enjoys:

'Mrs Holt had I think enjoyed her life. She had been made more of than at home, and had been happy amidst the excitement. But with Cecilia it had been for many months as though all things had been made of leather and prunello. She had not cared, or had not seemed to care, for scenery or for cities. Even when the mountains of Switzerland had been so fine before her eyes as in truth to console her by their beauty, she had not admitted that she was consoled. The Campanile at Florence had filled her with that satisfaction which comes from supreme beauty. But still when she went home to her hotel she thought more of Sir Francis Geraldine than of the Campanile ... it was the false accusation [that she had been jilted] rather than the loss of all her marriage had promised her which made her feel the Matterhorn and the Campanile to be equally ineffective.'

From this state of torpid melancholia Cecilia is salvaged by the presence in Rome of Mr Western. The only fault she can find in him is that he will go on praising the beauty of Mary Tremenhere, the jilt. Cecilia, like any other girl, would have preferred him to stop this, but does not know how to set about it:

'"You asked me once whether I loved her," he said one day: "I did; but I am astonished now that it should have been so. She was very lovely."

'"I suppose so."

'"The most perfect complexion that was ever seen on a lady's cheek."

Cecilia remembered that her complexion too had been praised before this blow had fallen upon her.

'"The colour would come and go so rapidly that I used to marvel what were the thoughts that drove the blood hither and thither. There were no thoughts,—unless of her prettiness and her own fortunes."'

Miss Tremenhere's callous conduct has wounded Western so severely that he looks older than he is: 'There was a tinge of grey through his hair, and there were settled lines about his face, and a look of steadied thought about his mouth, which robbed him of all youth.' Wherever he had travelled in Europe the memory of Miss Tremenhere had travelled with him, a beautiful spectre. Cecilia is quite aware of this, but she has so slight a knowledge of male psychology that she cannot understand why he talks so much about the girl; and, when the crisis comes, why he should be so disillusioned and outraged by the fact of her own engagement to Sir Francis Geraldine. For all her learning and linguistic abilities Cecilia Western is an innocent and a fool.

(vii)

Kept in the Dark was the first book which Anthony Trollope wrote in his new country house, Harting Grange. He next concocted that regrettable fantasia, *The Fixed Period*, which describes the euthanasia policy of the republican government of an imaginary Pacific island, Britannula. Neither an H. G. Wells nor a George Orwell, Anthony's forecasts of life in 1980 in this dreary novelette are mild and tame. There is a steam tricycle which conveys its users about their islet at the unheard-of speed of twenty-five miles an hour. These tricycles even have electric headlights. For cricket matches the inhabitants of Britannula use steam bowlers and catapults, and play with sixteen men a side. They also have a handy apparatus for the mechanical reporting of speeches, and they keep in touch with Australia by telephone. The *Times* reviewer denounced the book as 'essentially ghastly'; the *Nation* described it as 'an elaborate elephantine attempt at a joke by a person without any sense of humour'. The Britannulans' efforts towards legalized euthanasia are foiled by a British man-of-war training its guns on Gladstone, the island's capital. The theory, never put into practice, was that any person reaching the age of sixty-seven would be forcibly deposited in a kind of 'college', to be painlessly killed off after a period of one year. To us the only interest of *The Fixed Period* is that Anthony began to write it in December 1881, and completed it on the last day of February 1882—that is to say in his own sixty-seventh year, which, as it happened, was destined to be the year of his death. 'Men should arrange for their own departure,' he writes in *The Fixed Period*, 'so as to fall into no senile weakness, no slippered selfishness, no ugly whinings of undefined want, before they shall go hence and be no more thought of.' The friend who had lent him Lowick Parsonage, the Reverend William Lucas Collins, once suggested to him that this novel was 'a somewhat grim jest'. Anthony 'stopped suddenly in his walk, and grasping the speaker's arm in his energetic fashion, exclaimed "It's all true—I *mean* every word of it".' To someone else he stated that so soon as he could no longer write books, he would wish to die. This aspiration was, happily for himself, granted.

Having predicted life in the later years of the twentieth century, Anthony Trollope next sat down to write one of the greatest and the most organized of all his longer novels: *Mr Scarborough's Family*. Anthony was now virtually obsessed by the problems of old age. *Mr Scarborough's Family*, and its immediate successor *An Old Man's Love*, are each a study of the conduct of old gentlemen. Mr Scarborough, who, throughout the book, is on his death-bed, is a wealthy pagan landlord 'luxurious and self-indulgent and altogether indifferent to the opinion of those around him'. Mr Whittlestaff, in *An Old Man's Love*, is not to our modern eyes an old man at all, for he is nearly fifty years of age. He is a testy but generous man, and does what he believes to be right; so, in effect, does Mr Scarborough of Tretton Park in Hertfordshire—but what Mr Scarborough sees as right is, by all of those connected with him, regarded as unutterably wrong. He takes a fiendish glee in flouting every English custom and tradition, and in keeping both of his sons in suspense about his own will. He persecutes his sons, his lawyer and his doctor. Moribund though he knows himself to be, Mr Scarborough is still in full possession of his faculties, torments everyone in his vicinity, and is determined to satisfy his power complex to the last. Aware that he is dying, he seems to want to make other people suffer while there is still time.

Mr Scarborough's Family contains a mystery, but, unlike the mystery in *Dr Wortle's School*, it is not revealed at once. In the first chapter of the book, Mr Scarborough shocks the world by declaring his eldest son to be illegitimate, having been born before his marriage to his now defunct wife. This public statement not only defiles his wife's memory, but seems to wreck the prospects of that son, Captain Mountjoy Scarborough, an inveterate gambler who has hypothecated his expectations on Tretton Park to Jewish money-lenders. Captain Scarborough resembles the majority of Trollope's anti-heroes in being very dark: '. . . dark visaged, with coal-black whiskers and moustaches, with sparkling angry eyes, and every feature of his face well cut and finely formed'. Now the paradox of old Mr Scarborough's behaviour is that he appears to be acting as an individual bereft of conscience, yet his purpose in so doing is intelligent if unconventional. Mr John Scarborough is a landowner who loves his own estate at Tretton. Hating the British law of primogeniture, he had, as a young man, been married twice to the same woman—both marriages taking place on the continent, where, as all Trollope readers should know, any dishonest, underhand or sleazy legal act can be performed. Mr Scarborough's first marriage took place in a quiet, but legitimate way; the second marriage was solemnized after his eldest son was born. The purpose of this strange carry-on was known to no one but his wife and himself. It was the result of Mr Scarborough's own observation of human nature, for he was ever a suspicious man. When he disinherits his son Mountjoy, whom he loves, in favour of the priggish second son, Augustus, Mr Scarborough shockingly gives his lawyer the certificate of the second marriage only. Perfectly aware that Mountjoy has borrowed vast sums on postobits against his future inheritance, Mr Scarborough makes it plain to his son's Jewish creditors that they will not get one penny when he himself is dead. He next negotiates with the panicking Jews, who let him have all Mountjoy's notes-of-hand at a cut price, for they think it better to have money at present than nothing at all in the future. Having performed this ingenious ploy, and having treated the odious Augustus as his heir, Mr Scarborough drives his lawyer almost mad by producing the certificate of the first marriage, which, in British law, makes Mountjoy his heir once more. Mr Scarborough then signs a new will, leaving everything not entailed to Mountjoy, and cutting out Augustus altogether.

Not only is Mr Scarborough's behaviour, as I have suggested, intelligent, it is even inspired by a topsy-turvy wish to do good: 'In every phase of his life,' Anthony tells us 'he had been actuated by love for others.' After his death his friend and lawyer, Mr John Grey, speaks up for Mr John Scarborough:

' "One cannot make an apology for him without being ready to throw all truth and all morality to the dogs. But if you can imagine for yourself a state of things in which neither truth nor morality shall be thought essential, then old Mr Scarborough would be your hero. He was the bravest man I ever knew. And whatever he did, he did with the view of accomplishing what he thought to be right for other people." '

There is, inevitably, a love story in *Mr Scarborough's Family*. This concerns Florence Mountjoy, who refuses to marry her rascally cousin Mountjoy Scarborough. Her mother, admiring the dash and position in London society of young Captain Scarborough, tries to force her daughter to marry him, but the wayward girl is already in love with the penniless Harry Annesley. Florence is not a startling beauty:

'In figure, form and face she never demanded immediate homage by the sudden flash of her beauty. But when her spell had once fallen on a man's spirit it was not often that he could escape from it quickly ... Her voice was soft and low and sweet, and full at all times of harmonious words; but when she laughed it was like soft winds playing among countless silver bells. There was something in her touch which to men was almost divine. Of this she was all unconscious, but was as chary with her fingers as though it seemed that she could ill spare her divinity ... her eyes were more than ordinarily bright, and when she laughed there seemed to stream from them some heavenly delight ... her hair was soft and smooth, and ever well dressed, and never redolent of peculiar odours.'

In an effort to get this peerless daughter to cut loose from her passion for Harry Annesley, Mrs Mountjoy takes her to stay in the British Legation at Brussels with Florence's aunt and uncle, Sir Magnus and Lady Mountjoy. Sir Magnus 'was a tall, stout, portly old gentleman, sixty years of age ... whom it was a difficulty to place on horseback, but who, when there, looked remarkably well'. Florence quickly attracts fresh suitors in Brussels; the scenes in the British Legation are as animated as they are entertaining—but, of course, she marries Annesley in the end. This is, perhaps, the only agreeable episode in *Mr Scarborough's Family*, for the conclusion of the book is bleak indeed. Mr Scarborough's funeral in Tretton church is attended by the infuriated Jewish money-lenders whom he has tricked. To escape them, Mountjoy, now sole heir, has to make an ignominious sprint from the graveyard to bolt himself inside his own front door. Anthony suggests that all old Mrs Scarborough's schemes have been in vain, for his son will go on gambling and will allow the estate of Tretton Park to be devoured by money-lenders and other metropolitan sharks.

In his penultimate novel, *An Old Man's Love*, Anthony Trollope reverted to a favourite theme—the effect on a man of being jilted by the girl he loves. When we meet him, Mr William Whittlestaff, of Croker's Hall near Alresford in Hampshire, is an aged man of fifty. Twenty years before this, he had become engaged to a Miss Catherine Bailey, who had then backed out of the agreement. Whittlestaff is morbidly convinced that, because of the jilting, he is ridiculed by all his country neighbours. He has, in fact, a perilously thin skin. He has had certain advantages in his life—he had inherited enough money to purchase his country house, Croker's Hall. He is also hale: 'He had never had a headache, rarely a cold and never a touch of the gout.' His doctor had once recommended him to drink whisky, which Mr Whittlestaff likes because it is cheap. He has slightly old-maidish ways and has given his purposeless life a set pattern; one important element in this is to stroll along a wooded path while reading Horace. He had had one intimate friend in his life, a Captain Patrick Lawrie, who had died two years before the novel opens, and is followed to the grave by his widow. Their only child, Mary Lawrie, goes to live with Mr Whittlestaff, who in the course of time proposes to this ward. She accepts him out of gratitude, but tells him that she had once been in love with a man of about her own age, John Gordon. This young man unexpectedly turns up, having made himself a fortune in the diamond fields of South Africa. Mr Whittlestaff reluctantly decides to let Mary break her engagement and marry Gordon. He suffers, but tries to be philosophical: ' "It will all be the same a thousand years hence" he said to himself as he walked in at the club door.' The club is John Gordon's club, and Mr Whittlestaff has come up to London on a broiling summer's day to make his plan known to Gordon. He revels in an almost angelic sense of resignation, but he is, at the same time, pretty discourteous to Gordon. To avoid discussing Mary in the club, Mr Whittlestaff takes Gordon for a walk in Green Park:

' "Let us go into the Park. It is green and there is some shade among the trees." Then they went out of the club into Pall Mall, and Mr Whittlestaff walked on ahead without a word "No, we will not go down there," he said as he passed the entrance into St James's Park by Marlborough House. "We'll go on till we come to the trees; there are seats there unless the people have occupied them all. One can't talk here under the blazing sun;—at least I can't." Then he walked on at a rapid pace, wiping his brow as he did so. "Yes, there's a seat. I'll be hanged if that man isn't going to sit down upon it! What a beast he is! No, I can't sit down on a seat that another man is occupying ... There! Two women have gone a little farther on." Then he hurried to the vacant bench and took possession of it. It was placed among the thick trees which give a perfect shade on the north side of the Park, and had Mr Whittlestaff searched all London through he could not have found a more pleasant spot to make his communication. "This will do," said he.'

This little scene about a bench in a London Park seems to me to be a perfect example of the deft way in which Anthony Trollope can, at his best, delineate a character. It is also to be expected that Mr Whittlestaff cannot sit still when making his speech of renunciation: 'Here Mr Whittlestaff got up from the bench, and began walking rapidly backwards and forwards under the imperfect shade of the path.' Although he suffered neither from headaches nor from gout, Mr William Whittlestaff's nervous organization would, in a crisis, break down. This novel is written with a great economy of words; it closes with Mary Lawrie's marriage to the diamond speculator. This autumnal ceremony Mr Whittlestaff attends, but in no jocund mood:

'When October had come round, he was present at Mary's marriage, and certainly did not carry himself with any show of outward joy. He was moody and silent, and, as some said, almost uncourteous to John Gordon. But before Mary went down to the train, in preparation of her long wedding-tour, he took her up to his bedroom, and there said a final word to her. "Give him my love."

' "Oh, my darling! You have made me so happy."

' "You will find me better when you come back, though I shall never cease to regret all that I have lost." '

For his last novel, *The Landleaguers*, Anthony went back to the country in which he had first begun to write novels—Ireland.

One of Anthony Trollope's biographers has misleadingly asserted that the old novelist's last journeys to Ireland were a direct result of the shock which he and every other Englishman received from the assassination of Lord Frederick Cavendish and his secretary in Phoenix Park, Dublin, on May 6th, 1882. This was not so, for Anthony had already planned a visit to Ireland in February of that year: 'I am thinking of taking a run over to Ireland in reference to a book I am thinking of writing,' he wrote in a letter to his son Harry at this time. 'But as I should take Florence I could not go unless I could have you here with your mother.' He likewise wrote to George Bentley, editor of the periodical *Temple Bar*, to say that he was going to Ireland to write a novel about the 'lamentable' condition of that country. Accompanied by his niece, Florence Bland, he took the Irish mail-boat in May 1882. This initial tour did not suffice, however, for once he had begun work on *The Landleaguers* he found that he needed more material and set off once again for Ireland in August, returning home to Harting in September. Anthony and his niece stayed sometimes in hotels, sometimes in the country houses of Ascendancy families. Wherever he went Anthony was frequently breathless and in pain. He tried out new remedies, including an inhalation of saltpetre strongly recommended to him by Cardinal Newman. At night he found relief by sitting bolt upright in bed until the attack of what he still called 'asthma' had passed off. The only remedy he found effective was a nocturnal cup of hot tea, brewed on his primus stove; but it needed more than saltpetre and primus stoves to ward off the swift, sure feet of Death.

Anthony's handwriting, never noted for its legibility, had now deteriorated into a shaky scrawl; he recognized that he was suffering from what he called 'the disease of age'. To Alfred Austin, a young confidant of his later years, he wrote:

'I observe when people of my age are spoken of, they are described as effete and moribund, just burning down the last half-inch of the candle in the socket. I feel as though I should still like to make a "flare-up" with my half-inch. In spirit I could trundle a hoop about the streets, and could fall in love with a young woman just as readily as ever; as she doesn't want me, I don't—but I could!'

Possibly because he was staying at country houses and in the better-class hotels, Anthony found Ireland much quieter than the English newspapers had led him to believe—there were no riots or rows in any of the towns in which he stopped. His chief complaint was the one usual to all nineteenth-century tourists in Ireland—bad cooking. From Glendalough, County Wicklow, he wrote to his wife that the hotel was a 'beastly place', its single merit being that the tea and coffee were good: 'But the sauces! Everything is done with melted butter, and the melted butter is all varnish paste,—which you could paper a room with. However I am trying to get some work done.'

There is a certain symmetry and a species of fulfilment in the fact that Anthony Trollope's last novel was, like his first one, on a purely Irish theme. Forty years before, he and his friend Merivale had come upon the ruin outside Drumsna; back in Banagher he had begun to write *The Macdermots of Bally-cloran*. In between this first book and *The Landleaguers* on which he was now working he had written forty-five novels, most of them extremely long, and innumerable short stories and articles. He had been happily married and was the father of two sons. He had travelled the globe widely and with intelligence. He and his work had attained a height of fame which would have seemed incredible to the lubberly, touchy, shy young man who had wandered through the callows beside the Shannon at Banagher in the 1840s, and had discovered the joys of hunting with the Galway Blazers. He had enriched and entertained two generations of readers by introducing them to the inmost thoughts and motives of the myriad lively individuals with whom his books are peopled. He knew all about this, but he could not know that he had also put posterity in his debt.

These last nostalgic tours of Ireland had proved altogether too strenuous for Anthony Trollope's ageing heart. Back in England he found that his house near Petersfield made his ailments worse, and so he took two floors of Garlant's Hotel in Suffolk Street, and settled down to face as best he might the creeping damp and fogs of a London winter. On November 3rd, 1882, Anthony Trollope, as we have seen, suffered a fatal stroke after dining at his brother-in-law's house in Pimlico. In the nursing-home north of the Park he existed, speechless, for five weeks, until he 'joined the majority'—as his friend Lord Houghton used to call the act of dying. We cannot do better than to recall the final sentence of the autobiography. In this Anthony salutes us cheerfully across the deep, the grey waters of

Lethe: 'Now I stretch out my hand, and from the further shore I bid adieu to all who have cared to read any among the many words that I have written.' How could Anthony Trollope guess that his readers would number tens of thousands in the new century he did not live to see?

The Macdermots of Ballycloran, 3 vols. (Newby, London, 1847).

The Kellys and the O'Kellys: or Landlords and Tenants, 3 vols. (Colburn, London, 1848).

La Vendée: An Historical Romance, 3 vols. (Colburn, London, 1850).

The Warden, 1 vol. (Longman, London, 1855).

Barchester Towers, 3 vols. (Longman, London, 1857).

The Three Clerks: A Novel, 3 vols. (Bentley, London, 1858).

Doctor Thorne: A Novel, 3 vols. (Chapman & Hall, London, 1858).

The Bertrams: A Novel, 3 vols. (Chapman & Hall, London, 1859).

The West Indies and the Spanish Main, 1 vol. (Chapman & Hall, London, 1859).

Castle Richmond: A Novel, 3 vols. (Chapman & Hall, London, 1860).

Framley Parsonage, with illustrations by J. E. Millais, 3 vols. (Smith, Elder, London, 1861).

Tales of All Countries, 1 vol. (Chapman & Hall, London, 1861).

Orley Farm, with illustrations by J. E. Millais, 3 vols. (Chapman & Hall, London, 1862).

North America, 2 vols. (Chapman & Hall, London, 1862).

Tales of All Countries, Second Series, 1 vol. (Chapman & Hall, London, 1863).

Rachel Ray: A Novel, 2 vols. (Chapman & Hall, London, 1863).

The Small House at Allington, with illustrations by J. E. Millais, 2 vols. (Smith, Elder, London, 1864).

Can You Forgive Her? with illustrations by 'Phiz' and E. Taylor, 2 vols. (Chapman & Hall, London, 1864).

Miss Mackenzie, 2 vols. (Chapman & Hall, London, 1865).

Hunting Sketches, 1 vol. (Chapman & Hall, London, 1865).

The Belton Estate, 3 vols. (Chapman & Hall, London, 1866).

Travelling Sketches, 1 vol. (Chapman & Hall, London, 1866).

Clergymen of the Church of England, 1 vol. (Chapman & Hall, London, 1866).

Nina Balatka, 2 vols. (Blackwood, Edinburgh and London, 1867).

The Last Chronicle of Barset, with illustrations by George H. Thomas, 2 vols. (Smith, Elder, London, 1867).

The Claverings, with illustrations by M. Ellen Edwards, 2 vols.

(Smith, Elder, London, 1867).

Lotta Schmidt: and Other Stories, 1 vol. (Strahan, London, 1867).

Linda Tressel, 2 vols. (Blackwood, Edinburgh and London, 1868).

Phineas Finn, The Irish Member, with illustrations by J. E. Millais, 2 vols. (Vertue, London, 1869).

He Knew He Was Right, with illustrations by Marcus Stone, 2 vols. (Strahan, London, 1869).

The Vicar of Bullhampton, with illustrations by H. Woods, 1 vol. (Bradbury, Evans, London, 1870).

An Editor's Tales, 1 vol. (Strahan, London, 1870).

The Struggles of Brown, Jones and Robinson: by one of the Firm, with illustrations, 1 vol. (Smith, Elder, London, 1870).

The Commentaries of Caesar, 1 vol. (Blackwood, Edinburgh and London, 1870).

Sir Harry Hotspur of Humblethwaite, 1 vol. (Hurst & Blackett, London, 1871).

Ralph the Heir, 3 vols. (Hurst & Blackett, London, 1871), also 1 vol., with illustrations by F. A. Fraser (Strahan, London, 1871).

The Golden Lion of Granpère, 1 vol. (Tinsley, London, 1872).

Australia and New Zealand, 2 vols. (Chapman & Hall, London, 1873).

The Eustace Diamonds, 3 vols. (Chapman & Hall, London, 1873).

Phineas Redux, with illustrations by Frank Holl, 2 vols. (Chapman & Hall, London, 1874).

Lady Anna, 2 vols. (Chapman & Hall, London, 1874).

Harry Heathcote of Gangoil: A Tale of Australian Bush Life, 1 vol. (Sampson, Low, London, 1874).

The Way We Live Now, with illustrations by Luke Fildes, 2 vols. (Chapman & Hall, London, 1875).

The Prime Minister, 2 vols. (Chapman & Hall, London, 1876).

The American Senator, 3 vols. (Chapman & Hall, London, 1877).

South Africa, 2 vols. (Chapman & Hall, London, 1878).

Is He Popenjoy?: A Novel, 3 vols. (Chapman & Hall, London, 1878).

How the 'Mastiffs' Went to Iceland, with illustrations by Mrs Hugh Blackburn, 1 vol. (Vertue, London, 1878).

An Eye for an Eye, 2 vols. (Chapman & Hall, London, 1879).

Thackeray, 1 vol. (Macmillan, London, 1879).

John Caldigate, 3 vols. (Chapman & Hall, London, 1879).

Cousin Henry: A Novel, 2 vols. (Chapman & Hall, London, 1879).

The Duke's Children, 3 vols. (Chapman & Hall, London, 1880).

The Life of Cicero, 2 vols. (Chapman & Hall, London, 1880).

Doctor Wortle's School: A Novel, 2 vols. (Chapman & Hall, London, 1881).

Ayala's Angel, 3 vols. (Chapman & Hall, London 1881).

Why Frau Frohmann Raised Her Prices: And Other Stories, 1 vol. (Isbister, London, 1882).

Lord Palmerston ('English Political Leaders'), 1 vol. (Isbister, London, 1882).

Kept in the Dark: A Novel, with a frontispiece by J. E. Millais, 2 vols. (Chatto & Windus, London, 1882).

Marion Fay: A Novel, 3 vols. (Chapman & Hall, London, 1882).

The Fixed Period, 2 vols. (Blackwood, Edinburgh and London, 1882).

Mr Scarborough's Family, 3 vols. (Chatto & Windus, London, 1883).

The Landleaguers, 2 vols. (Chatto & Windus, London, 1883).

An Autobiography, 2 vols. (Blackwood, Edinburgh and London, 1883).

An Old Man's Love, 2 vols. (Blackwood, Edinburgh and London, 1884).

Letters, 1 vol., edited by Bradford Allen Booth (Oxford University Press, London, 1951).

Index

Characters and places from Trollope's novels are shown within quotation marks.